Off The Beaten Track
FRANCE

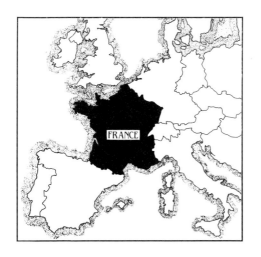

OFF
THE BEATEN TRACK
FRANCE

MPC

British Library Cataloguing in
Publication Data:
France. — (Off the beaten track)
1. France - Visitor's guides
I. Collins, Martin, *1941* - II. Series
914.4'04838

© Moorland Publishing Co Ltd 1988

Reprinted 1989, 1991

Published by:
Moorland Publishing Co Ltd,
Moor Farm Road,
Ashbourne,
Derbyshire
DE6 1HD
England

ISBN 0 86190 235 1 (paperback)
ISBN 0 86190 228 9 (hardback)

Colour origination by:
Quad Repro Ltd, Pinxton, Notts

Printed in the UK by:
Butler and Tanner Ltd, Frome,
Somerset

Cover photograph:
Aiguines (*Photobank International*)

Black and white illustrations have been
supplied as follows:

M. Collins: p61; French Government
Tourist Office: p127; M. Gray: pp15, 17,
20, 21, 25, 30, 31, 83, 85, 91, 94, 145, 147,
153, 162, 164; P. Guyot: p253; Hoseasons Holidays Abroad Ltd: pp47, 53,
66, 105, 107, 109, 267, 275, 289, 291, 294,
299; G. Irving: p265; R. W. Penn: pp171,
175, 177, 181, 182, 185, 197, 199, 201,
251, 254, 257; D. Philpott: pp301, 303; R.
Sale: pp43, 49, 59, 64; J. Thatcher:
pp225, 227, 231, 239.

Colour illustrations have been supplied
as follows:

M. Collins (River Orne, Crèvecoeur-en-
Auge, Carteret, Kaysersberg); Comité
du Tourisme-Finistère (Le Guilvinec);
M. Gray (Allouville-Bellefosse, Abbaye
de la Grande Trappe, Rouffach,
Colmar); Hoseasons Holidays Abroad
Ltd (Rennes, Rochefort-en-Terre,
Malicorne, Angers, Segré, Aigues-
Mortes, Carcassonne); G. Irving (Agay);
R. W. Penn (Valleraugue, Molines); R.
Sale (Le Mougau); P. Tavener
(Solesmes Abbey, Le Mans); J. Thatcher
(Aubenas)

Mrs J. Thatcher would like to thank the
Comité Départemental de Tourism,
Privas; the French Government Tourist
Office, London; her French friends in
the Ardèche and her husband for their
help in preparing chapter 9.

Note on Maps
The maps for each chapter, while comprehensive, are not designed to be used
as route maps, but to locate the main
towns, villages and places of interest.

Contents

	Introduction	7
1	Normandy (*Barbara Mandell*)	9
2	Brittany (*Richard Sale*)	37
3	Alsace et Lorraine (*Barbara Mandell*)	70
4	Pays de la Loire (*Michael Dean*)	101
5	Poitou-Charentes (*Michael Dean*)	124
6	Aquitaine (*Barbara Mandell*)	139
7	Beaujolais (*Roger Penn*)	168
8	The Cévennes (*Roger Penn*)	189
9	Ardèche (*Joy Thatcher*)	216
10	Le Queyras (*Roger Penn*)	243
11	Provence and the Côte d'Azur (*Don Philpott*)	260
12	The Midi (*Don Philpott*)	286
	Index	311

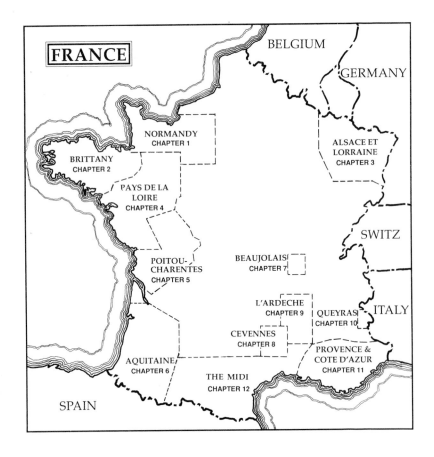

FRANCE

BELGIUM

GERMANY

NORMANDY
CHAPTER 1

ALSACE ET
LORRAINE
CHAPTER 3

BRITTANY
CHAPTER 2

PAYS DE LA
LOIRE
CHAPTER 4

SWITZ

POITOU-
CHARENTES
CHAPTER 5

BEAUJOLAIS
CHAPTER 7

L'ARDECHE
CHAPTER 9

QUEYRAS
CHAPTER 10

ITALY

CEVENNES
CHAPTER 8

AQUITAINE
CHAPTER 6

PROVENCE &
COTE D'AZUR
CHAPTER 11

THE MIDI
CHAPTER 12

SPAIN

Museums and Other Places of Interest

Wherever possible opening times have been checked, and are as accurate as possible. However, during the main holiday period they may be extended. Conversely, outside the main season, there may be additional restrictions, or shorter hours. Local tourist offices will always be able to advise you.

Generally all churches, and abbeys and monasteries still in use, are open every day from 9am-6pm, except during services. You should remember that these are places of worship as well as historical monuments, so dress and conduct should be appropriate.

Introduction

W estern Europe is a continent of great diversity, well visited not just by travellers from other parts of the globe but by the inhabitants of its own member countries. Within the year-round processes of trade and commerce, but more particularly during the holiday season, there is a great surging interchange of nationalities as one country's familiar attractions are left behind for those of another.

It is true that frontiers are blurred by ever quicker travel and communications, and that the sharing of cultures, made possible by an increasingly sophisticated media network, brings us closer in all senses to our neighbours. Yet essential differences do exist, differences which lure us abroad on our annual migrations in search of new horizons, fresh sights, sounds and smells, discovery of unknown landscapes and people.

Countless resorts have evolved for those among us who simply crave sun, sea and the reassuring press of humanity. There are, too, established tourist 'sights' with which a country or region has become associated and to which clings, all too often, a suffocating shroud — the manifestations of mass tourism in the form of crowds and entrance charges, the destruction of authentic atmosphere, cynical exploitation. Whilst this is by no means typical of all well known tourist attractions, it is familiar enough to act as a disincentive for those of more independent spirit who value personal discovery above prescribed experience and who would rather avoid the human conveyor belt of queues, traffic jams and packed accommodation.

It is for such travellers that this guidebook has been written. In its pages, no more than passing mention is made of the famous, the well documented, the already glowingly described — other guidebooks will satisfy the appetite for such orthodox tourist information. Instead, the reader is taken if not to unknown then to relatively unvisited places — literally 'off the beaten track'. Through the specialist knowledge of the authors, visitors using this guidebook are assured of gaining insights into the country's heartland whose heritage lies largely untouched by the tourist industry. Occasionally the reader is urged simply to take a sideways step from a site of renowned tourist interest to find one perhaps less sensational, certainly less frequented but often of equivalent fascination.

From wild, scantily populated countryside whose footpaths and byways are best navigated by careful map reading, to negotiating the side streets of towns and cities, travelling 'off the beaten track' can be rather more demanding than following in the footsteps of countless thousands before you. The way may be less clear, more adventurous and individualistic, but opportunities do emerge for real discovery in an age of increasing dissatisfaction with the passive predictability of conventional holidaymaking. With greater emphasis on exploring 'off the beaten track', the essence of France is more likely to be unearthed and its true flavours relished to the full.

Martin Collins
Series Editor

1 • Normandy

To a certain extent a visit to Normandy involves stepping back into history, either long past or well within living memory. On one hand there is William the Bastard, a complimentary title in those days, who was born in Falaise and died in Rouen but found time between to conquer and rule England while keeping a firm grip on his homeland as well. At the other end of the time scale there are long sandy beaches and rolling countryside over which the Allied forces swarmed in 1944, driving back the German army of occupation. Nearly everywhere you look there is evidence of these and other momentous events — magnificent churches and monasteries; fortified castles and elegant *châteaux*; museums filled with treasures; impressive monuments; ruined pillboxes and seemingly endless war graves, fields of white crosses set regimentally in grass as smooth and green as a billiard table.

But there is another, less militant side to Normandy where it is possible to wander through dense woodlands in splendid solitude, discover tiny villages and isolated farmsteads, rent a cottage or stay with a family in an atmosphere far removed from the popular tourist centres, often only a short drive away. Nor is there any prescribed method of travelling. Most of the lanes are wide enough for a car and, on the whole, the surfaces are good. Alternatively there is no difficulty in hiring horses and bicycles, or even a horse-drawn vehicle, be it a barouche or a caravan, while footpaths for the really energetic thread their way across the countryside, mostly signposted and covering literally hundreds of miles. Some are equipped with overnight hostels for hikers who plan their exploration on a long-term basis. The climate, by and large, is gentle, brisk but seldom freezing in winter and pleasantly hot and sunny during the summer months.

Whatever a visitor's inclinations may be, Normandy aims to satisfy them. The gourmet will discover a land not so much running with milk and honey as rich in butter, cream and cider. These ingredients find their way into a great many traditional dishes alongside such specialities as black sausages, braised tripe, salt-marsh mutton, grilled chitterlings sausages, chicken, duck and a variety of sea foods. The cheeses are famous for their flavour and variety and Calvados, the local cider-brandy, is the ideal complement to any meal. It scores over Cognac in the sense that it is drunk between courses as well as with coffee afterwards. Sports enthusiasts will find golf courses, tennis courts and swimming pools, rocks to climb, rivers and lakes for boating and fishing, beaches for bathing and windsurfing and facilities for other, less generally popular, activities such as gliding and parachute jumping. The spas cater for people who need medical treatment, are suffering from overwork or simply want to lose some extra weight while the casinos provide ample opportunities for gamblers to indulge in their favourite pastime. There are marinas for yachtsmen, often with sailing schools attached, camping sites for tents and caravans and information offices in most towns of any size which will provide details of these and other attractions available in their immediate areas.

Seine-Maritime and Eure

For visitors arriving from the north, bent on exploring the byways of Normandy, a logical place to cross the Seine, the border between the *départements* of Seine-Maritime and Eure, would be **Caudebec-en-Caux,** an attractive town overlooking the river. It is approximately 250km (156 miles) from Calais, an easy drive for motorists crossing the Channel, some 160km (100 miles) from Paris, 51km (32 miles) from Le Havre and a bare 36km (23 miles) from Rouen. Both Le Havre and Rouen are busy commercial ports, each has its own airport, good train services and facilities for hiring cars and bicycles as well as being worth visiting in their own right. Rouen, particularly, is a magical city which has been aptly described as a living museum, crammed with ancient buildings and recalling history on every side. It has a wide range of hotels, some excellent restaurants and has been a focal point for visitors since the Vikings took a liking to it more than a thousand years ago.

Caudebec-en-Caux is obviously not in the same category, nor has it a particularly historic atmosphere, especially since a disastrous fire in June 1940 destroyed many of the older buildings. A mere handful survived, including the thirteenth-century Maison des Templiers which has been skilfully restored and is now the home of a local history museum. Fortunately the fifteenth-century church of Notre-

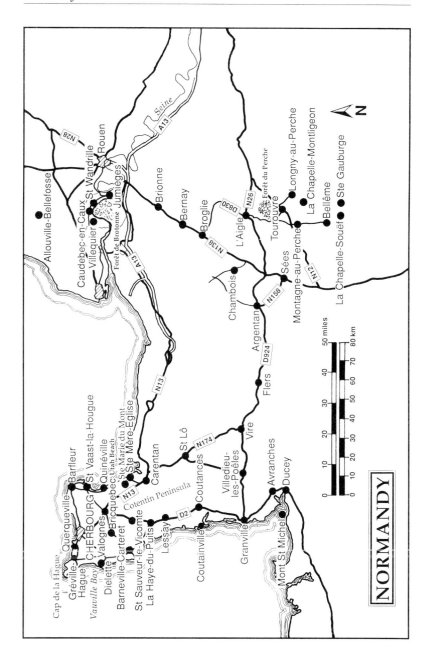

Dame, described by Henry IV as 'the most beautiful chapel in the kingdom', was virtually undamaged. It is rather austere inside with heavy pock-marked pillars from which little faces scowl down or grin impishly. The beautiful stained glass windows and the ancient organ with its hundreds of decorated pewter pipes are only slightly younger. Among the candle-lit chapels on either side is one of the Holy Sepulchre where an extremely detailed figure of Christ is watched over by seven large stone statues, the majority of them women. They came from Jumièges Abbey and have had their features restored, an operation that adds to the lifelike effect although the colour contrast in one or two cases is a trifle incongruous. When the whole church is filled with flowers the scent is almost tangible. The same applies to the Place du Marché outside where a market has been held since 1390 and where local tradesmen carry on the tradition every Saturday. The town also provides a number of up-to-date attractions like tennis, swimming and miniature golf. However it is as well to remember that a hotel room overlooking the Seine and the forest beyond can be something of a mixed blessing — it is a case of the view versus the noise from fairly constant road and river traffic.

A distinctly modern toll bridge, the Pont du Brotonne, opened in 1977, replaces the ferry which used to run from the centre of the town, a short *boules'* throw from the main waterfront hotels. But before paying up and driving across to the Brotonne Forest it would be a pity to miss some of the outstanding places of interest on the north bank in the department of Seine-Maritime. To the west is **Villequier** where the estuary and river pilots exchange places on ships making the Le Havre-Rouen run. However, it is much better known for its association with Victor Hugo, vividly recalled in the local museum which takes his name. The solidly built house overlooking the water belonged to the Valqueries whose son Charles married Hugo's daughter Léopoldine in 1843. The young couple died in a boating accident less than a year later and are buried with other members of the family in the little churchyard close by. Nobody claims that the house has been maintained exactly as it was in those days but it tends to give that impression. The beds are made, pictures and photographs hang on the walls and there are any number of personal items including letters and poems which add to the general atmosphere. The little sixteenth-century church with its original stained glass windows is also worth a visit.

The church at **Allouville-Bellefosse**, almost due north of Villequier, has quite a different claim to fame. It stands guard over the best-known tree in Normandy — a 1,300-year-old oak said to be one of the oldest in France. Two chapels, one above the other, have been built inside the hollow trunk, both of them roofed, floored and panelled in wood. Because it is getting on a bit, the tree and its main branches have been given extra support and a wooden staircase spiralling up round the outside provides access to the upper chapel. The trunk on either side of the entrance to the lower one, where the hole is not nearly so wide, has been worn to a satin finish by people edging their way in and out. For good measure there is a nature museum in an old farmhouse a short walk away. It is open to anyone with time on their hands and the good fortune to find somebody there.

Two abbeys which definitely should not be missed stand some 20km (12 miles) apart to the east and south of Caudebec-en-Caux. St Wandrille Abbey is the newer by less than half a century, having been founded by a young nobleman of that name in the Fontenelle valley in AD649. It soon became established as a seat of learning and produced the first history of a Western monastery before being sacked by the Vikings. However, once these marauding Northmen had settled down and become respectable Normans, they did as much as anyone to help the monks rebuild and re-establish themselves. The new abbey took the name of its founder and, with only a slight setback during the Wars of Religion, flourished until it came to grief during the Revolution. Among its subsequent owners was the English Marquis of Stacpoole who, to his credit, built the ornamental gateway. Eventually St Wandrille reverted to its original purpose with a compliment of Benedictine monks who conduct daily mass in Gregorian Chant and welcome visitors to the services. There are also guided tours past the massive columns which are all that remain of the fourteenth-century church, and into the splendid cloister, much of it still intact. The present monastery church is a fifteenth-century tithe barn, moved in piece by piece in 1969 and faithfully reconstructed, its porch converted into the Chapel of the Holy Sacrament with a shrine containing the head of St Wandrille added the following year.

A choice of roads, some of them delightfully rural, lead southwards through Le Trait, which has little apart from a small church to offer, and on to the remains of Jumièges Abbey, considered to be one of the most outstanding ruins in France. It started life in AD604 but, like St Wandrille, crumbled at the hands of the Vikings. In the tenth century William Longsword, who was Duke of Normandy at the time, set about rebuilding it, but the vast complex was largely completed under the watchful eye of Robert Champart, a Benedictine abbot who became Archbishop of Canterbury during the reign of Edward the Confessor. A year after the Battle of Hastings William the Conqueror, on one of his periodical visits to Normandy, attended the consecration of the abbey church. From that time onwards the monks had things pretty much their own way until they were thrown out during the Revolution. Jumièges was sold off at auction to become a stone quarry and the new owner, like others of his ilk in various parts of the country, proceeded to blow it up. Fortunately it changed hands again before being razed to the ground, since which time the ruins have been treasured and preserved. Today the twin towers of the façade, soaring above the surrounding trees and enclosing stone walls, can be seen clearly from across the river. Deprived of its roof, lantern and most of the chapels it is, nevertheless, a very impressive sight. A covered passageway leads to the smaller church of St Pierre beyond which there are ruins of the twelfth-century chapter house, the cloister and a large storeroom dating from approximately the same era.

Instead of driving back to Caudebec-en-Caux it is more fun to take the car ferry which operates across the river a short distance away. It appears to run more or less when required so quite a few people stop for something to eat and drink at the restaurants on either bank before taking their place in the queue. Once across, a small road climbs up into the **Forêt de Brotonne**. It is a delightful area filled with oak, beech and pine through which there are plenty of paths but very few roads for cars, especially as some of them have chains or bars across the entrance. However, there are adequate places to park before walking through the woods over deliciously soft carpets of fallen leaves. One interesting old oak, known as the Chêne à la Cuve, has four distinct trees growing out of a single trunk slightly above ground level. It seems to exert a special fascination for children whose shouts act like a radio beacon for anyone who finds the location difficult to detect. The road running north between the main forest and the river emerges into open country to give a totally different view of the Pont de Brotonne. From one vantage point it looks rather like a giant prehistoric lizard with transparent wings snaking its way into the hills opposite. Further on the road passes a series of extremely picturesque half-timbered houses, many of them expertly restored. Some have beautiful thatched roofs along the ridge of which an occasional owner has planted a row of flowers. The idea is sometimes repeated on the top of a thatched gateway and the thick stone walls on either side.

Once in and out of the forest again and heading south there are two more trees to inspect. They are gigantic yews, said to be getting on for a thousand years old, growing in front of the little church at **La Haye-de-Routot**. Both are hollow although one would not think it from the vast canopy of leaves and branches which cast deep shadows over the graveyard. A chapel has been built inside one and an oratory in the other but, unlike the oak at Allouville-Bellefosse, there is not enough space for anyone to walk inside. The village has also preserved an old communal oven, restored the *sabot*-maker's workshop and kept alive the festival of Ste Clare in mid-July. It is celebrated with fireworks and a bonfire which gives the participants a chance to pull out a flaming branch and so protect themselves from fire for the coming year.

Le Perche-Orne

Another area which can be surprisingly free of visitors, even at the height of the season, lies further to the south in what is known as Le Perche. It is a happy blending of forests, rivers and farmlands, dotted with ancient manor houses and an occasional abbey and is famous for its horses. Depending on time and inclination it is possible to weave one's way down through a labyrinth of country roads, discovering a host of tiny villages and interesting locations along the way, or follow one of the main routes and complete the journey in a matter of hours. The most obvious way is probably through **Brionne** with its ruined Norman castle and little fifteenth-century church and on to **Bernay**, associated with William the Conqueror through his

The market at Tourouvre

grandmother, the Duchess Judith, who founded the local abbey in 1013. There is an interesting museum in the old abbot's lodge, the much restored original church and two other small churches of note. One contains the statue of Notre-Dame-de-la-Couture, highly revered by pilgrims who gather there on Whit Monday. Some 8km (5 miles) beyond Broglie a road branches off to **L'Aigle** where there is a small museum concentrating on the Battle of Normandy. It includes wax figures of the Allied leaders and recordings of their voices made at the time. From here it is a short run to **Tourouvre**, a pleasant little town with some holiday attractions, which is a good base for exploring the country round about.

Tourouvre has its own special place in history. It was from there in the seventeenth century that many of the early settlers left to found Quebec, an event graphically recalled in stained glass in the local church. A companion window depicts the official reception given to one of their descendants, Monsieur Honoré Mercier, when, as Premier Ministre de Quebec, he paid a return visit in 1891. In addition the church still has its fifteenth-century stalls and a painting from the same date *The Adoration of the Magi* incorporated into the somewhat later altarpiece. Plans are under way for a small museum nearby but in the meantime Monsieur Feugueur at the hotel opposite is a fountain of information about the area. Incidentally, his wife produces a local speciality — chicken cooked in cider with apples — which is truly memorable.

Nudging the northern side of the town is the **Forêt du Perche** where, at the Carrefour de l'Etoile, there is a choice of eight roads, radiating out in all directions, a relic of the days when the woods were used extensively for hunting. One leads to **Bresolettes**, with eighteen inhabitants the smallest village in the *département*, and on past ponds filled with waterlilies to the Abbaye de la Grande Trappe. It was founded in 1140 and gives the impression of having been well maintained ever since. Visitors are asked to enquire at the porter's lodge, a small door near the main entrance, where the brother on duty will arrange a show lasting about 20 minutes covering the history of the abbey and something of the life of the monks. On occasions he will sell produce from the farm as well as the pamphlets and postcards displayed in the lodge. People arriving around midday, when most doors in France are firmly shut, may be invited to attend a brief service in the abbey church which the monks, having changed into white habits, conduct in Gregorian Chant. The nearby village of **Soligny-la-Trappe** will provide an hotel, somewhere to camp, a leisure park and opportunities for bathing and fishing in

The Abbaye de la Grande Trappe

addition to tennis and mini-golf. The Sentier de Grande Randonnée, designed for hikers who plan to take most of Normandy in their stride, passes the door.

Mortagne-au-Perche, the former capital of the region, is a good deal bigger but, apart from the church, comparatively little has survived from its earlier days. Beautifully manicured gardens in front of the town hall, dominated by a statue of a very small cherub on a very large horse, have a magnificent view over the undulating countryside. There are shops, hotels and restaurants, places to park a caravan and all the usual sports facilities. The whole place goes *en fête* in March with a lively Black Pudding Fair. A main road links Mortagne-au-Perche with Bellême which offers much the same in the way of attractions, some delightful old houses and a forest containing a large pool, a Roman fountain, a massive oak tree and several enticing walks.

Small, less frequented roads in the area have as much if not more to tempt the visitor than their busier counterparts. **La Chapelle-Montligeon**, although industrial, is a place of pilgrimage. Its enormous church, complete with modern stained glass windows, overshadows everything else and can be seen from top to terrace a good way off. However there is a slightly commercialised atmosphere about it, due no doubt to the fact that it is a popular holiday centre with a long list of sports and pastimes to attract the crowds.

Beyond the town, on the way to La Vove Manor, is the Moulin la Vove, a delightful old mill with turbulent water which can be admired from the grass verge and a bell to be rung by passers-by who would like to inspect it more closely. The Manor itself is open from May to September. It is a typical fortified *château* of the type that seems to pop up out of the trees nearly everywhere you look. They are austere and businesslike, sporting watch turrets with roofs like brimless witches' hats, grim stone walls and sometimes an ancient keep or a moat for additional protection. Courboyer Manor House is another case in point with a massive round tower and a reputation for being one of the finest in the district.

La Chapelle-Souëf, beyond Bellême, introduces a touch of variety. Les Feugerets is an elegant sixteenth-century *château*, unfortunately not open to the public but clearly visible from the road. Shallow stone steps with balustrades sweep up to the main entrance between two elderly detached buildings and it is easy to imagine Louis XIV's son, Le Grand Dauphin, riding up them with his friends on one of his many visits. On the other hand, L'Angenardière Manor allows people to wander through the grounds, past the walls and towers that were so essential to continued ownership in medieval times. It is not far from St Cyr-la-Rosière but is even closer to Ste Gauburge which is unusual in that the church has been deconsecrated and is used as an exhibition hall. This is attached to a manor house of comparable age, once part of a priory but now a private home. It has been said that after the monks were driven out during the Revolution local people got quite accustomed to seeing their ghosts returning in procession to their old stamping ground. If that is true they must be mildly surprised to see a much more up-to-date building on the far side of the lawn. It houses an interesting little museum specialising in the Perche of days gone by. There are sections devoted to a dozen different occupations, showing how hemp was spun and converted into cloth and clothes, how horses were shod and how *sabots* were made. Farm implements are much in evidence alongside the equipment needed for making cider and Calvados. In a building of its own there is a schoolroom complete with desks and a blackboard, everything necessary for lessons in history, geography, maths, science and biology and there are even hooks on which little coats of the period hang in an orderly line. The museum is open every afternoon from June to October but it is not always possible to see inside the church, although it does no harm to ask.

Another venue for exhibitions is La Lubinière, a sixteenth-century manor which was occupied until quite recently. The fireplaces still show traces of soot and the walls of the spiral staircase to the watch tower have been painted white which, at the moment, comes off on one's clothes.

Longny-au-Perche is much more accustomed to visitors, especially in September when there is a pilgrimage to the statue of Our Lady of Mercy in the chapel dedicated to her, one of two in the town. Designated a holiday centre, it has a leisure park, a caravan site, fishing, bathing, a swimming pool, tennis courts and bicycles for hire, not to mention opportunities for long, invigorating walks.

The old cathedral town of **Sées** would probably be more convenient than Tourouvre as a base for exploring the western side of the region. To begin with it is a delight in itself, full of religious institutions, far-from-modern houses and ancient buildings largely converted to present day use. The former abbey of St Martin is a children's home and it is only possible to examine the eighteenth-century Bishop's Palace from the outside. The same applies to the old market, a large round building, open to the world, with a quantity of pillars holding up a heavy wooden roof. The most impressive sight is the cathedral, an outstanding example of Norman Gothic architecture with some splendid stained glass, a decorated high altar and a folk museum tucked away in the chapter house.

Most people make for the Castle d' O which lays on conducted tours in the afternoons and will sometimes show visitors round in the morning, except on Tuesdays when it is closed all day. The whole place looks as though it could have escaped from Grimm's Fairy Tales — turrets, decorated windows, moat, parklands and all. Although the oldest part is 500 years old there is no sign of the heavy fortifications that most builders considered to be obligatory in those turbulent days. On the opposite side of the road, and slightly further on, the eighteenth-century Château de Sassy is a study in contrasts. Built in the classical style but very much at home in its rural surroundings, it is known especially for its tapestries and the superb formal gardens, laid out on immaculate terraces down the side of the hill. The *château* stands between a group of lakes and the small town of St Christophe-le-Jajolet where pilgrims congregate twice a year — in July and October — to take part in processions and attend the Blessing of Cars. Although, like St George, St Christopher was demoted some years ago he is still regarded as the patron saint of travellers, sportsmen, airmen and motorists. A statue of him, looking rather pensive and carrying a most attractive child, stands beside open fields near the church.

High on the list of nearby places to visit is the Haras du Pin, home

The fortified Manor of Argentelles

of the national stud. One look at this extremely impressive establishment is enough to explain why it is sometimes called the Versailles of Horses. Three roads, usually described as 'rides', converge on Colbert's Court, named after the statesman who founded the stud in 1665. It was planned and built some 50 years later and, although the *château* at the far end is not open to visitors, grooms are on duty to show people round the stables in the wings. During the season there are colourful processions of horses and horsedrawn vehicles which attract large crowds while punters are catered for on the adjacent racecourse in September and October of each year. The best time to visit the Haras du Pin is between July and February when the greatest number of stallions are in residence, although there is always a nucleus of horses to be exercised or put through their paces in the grounds. They range from thoroughbreds to hacks and from Norman cobs to Percherons, a massive breed which is native to Le Perche and famous all over the world.

The Percheron is said by some people to be descended from the Arab cavalry of Abd el Rahman, the Saracen leader who was defeated at Poitiers in AD732. Be that as it may, the Percherons soon became very French indeed with fresh Arab blood introduced at intervals, in fact the chevrons on the coat of arms of the Counts of the Perche are sometimes described as the hoofprints of war horses that

Chambois

took part in the Crusades. As time passed the breed developed along more domesticated lines, working in the fields, pulling carts and coaches and even appearing in trotting races over ploughed land in the mid-nineteenth century. At about this time trans-Atlantic breeders started to import Percherons and today they are to be found as far afield as North and South America, Scandinavia and Japan. Sadly the advent of the car and the tractor took its toll. It is only occasionally that one of these splendid horses can be seen grazing out in the open or communing with a herd of local cattle.

From Le Pin the usual conglomeration of small roads thread their way through farmlands which seem to be largely populated by horses, past Exmes with its archaeological connections, or Champobert where the *château* and chapel can be seen on request during the season, to the Manor of Argentelles. It is a fairly typical fifteenth-century fortified house, softened by a flower-filled courtyard and is open on Sundays and holidays in the afternoon from mid-April to late October. Almost as eyecatching is the extremely handsome farmhouse next door.

Chambois is one place where ancient history rubs shoulders with modern war. A large stone keep dating from the twelfth century dominates the centre of the village, cheek by jowl with a stele commemorating the American, Canadian and Polish troops who joined up there in August 1944 to cut off the German retreat. At **Mont-Ormel**, a bare 10km (6 miles) to the north-east, a large monument flanked by tanks and watched over by trees and flag poles, commands an extensive view over the western landscape. An announcement carved on stone in English, French and Polish marks the site where, on 19, 20, 21 and 22 August the 1st Polish Armoured Division sealed off the Falaise-Chambois gap, bringing about the defeat of the encircled German 7th Army. It was also the end of the Battle of Normandy.

Amongst the most rewarding *châteaux* from the point of view of decorations and furnishings is the one at **Le-Bourg-St-Léonard**, south of Chambois and on the direct route from L'Aigle to Argentan. It stands aloof from the surrounding village behind long stretches of lawn although there is space to park outside the gates. The building is almost entirely Louis XV and consequently has all the detached elegance of the eighteenth century. It is beautifully panelled inside and has some fine tapestries setting off its rather ornate furnishings to perfection. Guided tours are arranged each morning and afternoon but it is closed on Tuesdays.

The nearest town worthy of that description is **Argentan** which was badly damaged in the war but nevertheless managed to preserve its two main churches, although both have had to be restored considerably. The larger, St Germain, is fairly elaborate but St Martin steals its thunder somewhat with ancient stained glass windows which are still intact. There are the remains of a castle with a viewing table on the tower and a Benedictine abbey where the art of lacemaking is kept alive by the nuns. Apart from an exhibition of Point d'Argentan, which was invented by their predecessors some 200 years ago, there is usually someone on hand to explain the finer details and draw attention to the difference between original specimens and modern needlepoint lace. The town's other attractions and amenities include a racecourse, riding stables, a swimming pool and a clutch of small hotels and restaurants. It is also a convenient point from which to set out for Vire and the Cotentin Peninsula.

Manche

A choice of route on this occasion is not too easy to suggest. Some motorists will opt to follow the River Orne from the small town of Putanges-Pont-Ecrepin, past the Rabodanges Dam and along the Gorges-de-St-Aubert, stopping frequently on the way. Rabodanges, for example, has a seventeenth-century castle and anyone who is prepared to walk for up to an hour can inspect the ruins of the isolated Moulin de la Jalousie and all that is left of the ancient Devil's Bridge that keeps it company. The gorges have to be seen on foot but one outstanding view can be obtained from the Roche d'Oëtre which demands less effort and includes the services of an *auberge* as well. St Roch is a sixteenth-century pilgrim chapel where penitents in traditional dress attend a special *pardon* in the second half of August. It is also conveniently close to the Château de St Sauveur, a smallish house dating from the reign of Louis XIII, filled with delightful pictures, furniture and other items from the same period. It is open at weekends and on some weekday afternoons during the season but closes in February. From here it is an easy run to Vire. Other travellers will prefer the more direct route through **Flers** which does not seem to be particularly interested in tourists as such. They are allowed to walk in the grounds of the *château*, attend services in the twentieth-century church and study fossils, painting and weaving in the local museum but precious little else.

Vire, inspite of being badly mauled during the war, is much more welcoming. It is proud of the pitifully few remnants of its long history — a clock tower in the main square, a rebuilt church and a small part of the keep built by England's Henry I, son of William the Conqueror. However it makes up for its lack of obvious antiquity with a modern sports stadium, a number of tennis courts, covered and open-air swimming pools and one or two perfectly respectable hotels and restaurants for travellers who decide to linger a while. There is a large lake that meets the needs of water sports enthusiasts, trout are on hand for any fishermen who can catch them and the town is strategically placed for excursions to other places of interest thereabouts.

St Lô, only 39km (24 miles) to the north, had an even worse time in 1944. It too has been rebuilt, somewhat less attractively, supplying the old quarter with a flower garden where the ramparts used to be. The Musée des Beaux-Arts has some worthwhile tapestries, both old and new, and is housed in the Hôtel de Ville, a couple of blocks or so from the damaged church of Notre-Dame on the road leading out to the stud. Although not as regally housed as its opposite number at Le Pin the stud makes compulsive viewing for anyone interested in horses, particularly when the magnificent stallions are there in force from about the middle of July to the middle of February.

Inspite of being well inside the *département* of La Manche, St Lô is not on the Cotentin Peninsula which actually starts at Carentan. It is a town without a great deal of character although it has an imposing church which dwarfs everything else for miles around. There is a small yacht harbour, a racecourse across the marshland to the south and a national trotting school for jockeys. This probably explains why one tends to meet them in the most unlikely places, including Utah Beach.

Utah, with Omaha to the east, is where the Americans landed on D-Day. The site is marked by a former German blockhouse and a modern memorial crypt set about with a tank, an anti-aircraft gun and three landing craft all protected from onshore winds by a sand dune. The paratroops were dropped fractionally inland around the villages of **Ste Marie-du-Mont** and Ste Mère Eglise. The former possesses a delightful old church and a very informative landings museum while the latter has the distinction of being the first place in France to be liberated. The drop is commemorated in stained glass in the twelfth-century church of **Ste Mère Eglise** but the lifelike figure of a paratrooper caught up on the belfry has been removed and, at the moment, nobody appears to know if his absence is temporary or permanent. Across the road the Airborne Troops' Museum is filled with reminders of the first days of the invasion accompanied by an American commentary. A Douglas C 47 has a hanger to itself and a notice at the entrance to the grounds recalls Private William Tucker who joined the battle on 6 June 1944 and survived to become vice-president of one of the largest railroads in America. Other items of interest are a Roman milestone and, bridging the centuries, a symbolic milestone marked '0' — the first of hundreds which trace General Patton's lightning advance from Normandy to Metz in Alsace et Lorraine. On the outskirts of the village an ancient farmhouse has been transformed into a museum. There is all the appropriate furniture plus fittings with Madame Tussaud type figures occupied with their daily chores and a young child in a sturdy-looking playpen of the day. Everything necessary to keep the farm going is on display and it is open morning and afternoon, apart from Tuesdays, from April Fools Day to the end of September.

A road follows the coast northwards past small holiday resorts like Quinéville with its protected yacht harbour and Fontenay-sur-Mer, which is not really *'sur mer'* (by the sea) at all but has a golf course by way of compensation. Judging by the map, the road running along the coast has distinct scenic possibilities but, in reality, there are very few places where the dunes are low enough to see the water at all. For this reason it is not a bad idea to head for **Valognes** instead, if only to visit the cider museum. It is full of equipment from a less mechanised age, although some basic designs have changed

*Ste Mère Eglise with the first of the milestones which trace
General Patton's advance across France*

very little over the years, and traces the whole process from tree to bottle. For anyone not acquainted with cider-making it is interesting to discover how the rather sugary soft drink is transformed into a clear liquid with intoxicating possibilities. Local people maintain that it goes well with sea food, a theory which can be tested at **St Vaast-la-Hougue**, the centre of the oyster industry. The large oyster farms at Le Vauban are open to the public but for the uninitiated who shy away from these delicacies, either in their natural habitat or served up on a dish with lemon, there are plenty of other things to see and do.

The yacht marina at St Vaast-la-Hougue has about fifty berths for visitors with all the usual amenities and there is tennis, riding and fishing, a sandy beach and facilities for tents and caravans. Sightseers can inspect the mariners' minute chapel on the far side of the harbour, venture further afield to the seventeenth-century fort at the end of a long sandspit or walk the length of the jetty to the lighthouse to admire the views. The more adventurous can trudge across to the inshore Ile de Tatihou at low water where, if they are not careful, they will be marooned when the tide comes in. Hotel accommodation is available and idle hours can be whiled away very happily outside a quayside café watching the fishermen at work.

Barfleur is another picturesque little fishing port but has the disadvantage that it dries out completely. There are at least three pleasing, if modest, small hotels, a lifeboat station and a lighthouse which is one of the tallest in the country. Like a number of other places it was popular with Normans dashing backwards and forwards to England in the eleventh and twelfth centuries and displays the seal of the *Mora*, William the Conqueror's ship, rather ostentatiously on the quay. A footpath with some most impressive views passes close by on its way round the peninsula and down as far as Avranches. The coast road along the cliffs is also spectacular in places with plenty of opportunities to stop. However, quite a few motorists who want to stretch their legs leave their cars at Fermanville and walk along the Vallée des Moulins to the viaduct. A less frequented inland road through Le Vast, with its little waterfalls, follows the River Saire through fertile country with woods on either side before joining the seemingly endless heavy traffic, thundering resolutely along the dual carriageway into Cherbourg.

To be honest, **Cherbourg** is not everybody's idea of the perfect home from home. In other words, it is a typical Channel port, noisy and down to earth with functional buildings and a general air of putting business before pleasure and not having a great deal of time for the latter. Nor is it strictly off the beaten track although it sees fewer tourists than in the days of the great Atlantic liners which put in there. However it is worth a quick visit, if only for nostalgic reasons, when one is in the immediate vicinity. Predictably the most comfortable hotel is close to the railway station and the docks while the large marina is half the town away from the Yacht Club and the beach is nothing to get excited about. Conversely it has a casino, a skating rink, a golf course on the outskirts, an airport, regular ferry services to the south of England and Ireland and plenty of trains in and out. No foreigners are allowed into the naval base but they are welcome at the Fort de Roule with its wartime museum, at the Musée des Beaux-Arts and in the greenhouses and natural history museum of the Emmanuel-Lais Park.

From Cherbourg, travelling west towards the more rugged terrain of Cap de la Hague, there are plenty of opportunities to dally on the way. For instance, **Querqueville** is a good place to pause and visit the 1,000-year-old chapel of St Germain, the oldest religious building on the peninsula. Nacqueville Château, just outside the hamlet of La

Rivière, dates from the sixteenth century. Its walls and towers are half-covered in ivy, blending perfectly with the surrounding park filled with flowers, ornamental shrubs and trees. From Easter to the end of September there are guided tours on the hour every afternoon except on Tuesdays and Fridays unless it happens to be a public holiday. The Dur-Ecu Manor was built along rather more unconventional lines, due in part to the fact that it was restored 400 years ago on foundations that were laid in the ninth century.

The painter Jean Millet spent his early years in the area so the church at **Gréville-Hague** will look familiar to anyone who knows his work but no attempt has been made to restore his birthplace at Gruchy and turn it into a museum. At this point the road swings inland, making for open country that can be rather bleak when sea mists creep in over the moors, changes its mind to take a look at tiny Port Racine and carries on towards the lighthouse, isolated on its island facing Alderney across the Race. The scenery round the other side of Cap de la Hague is very similar although the twentieth century asserts itself with an all-too-obvious nuclear processing plant at Jobourg which has an information centre open in the afternoons for anyone who is interested. Those who prefer to turn their back on it have the option of a short drive to the Nez de Jobourg and a walk along the cliffs. The rewards are a small *auberge*, a lot of seabirds and exceptional views across Vauville Bay to the atomic power station at Flamanville. A few small villages along the edge of the bay have their own specialities to offer. **Biville** attracts pilgrims to the tomb of Blessed Thomas Hélye who died in 1257, about the same time as the church was built, and is a brisk 15 minutes' walk from the Calvaire des Dunes. The only port in the vicinity is **Diélette**, almost too small to be more than a bolt-hole in an emergency but it has a nice sandy beach at the entrance when the tide is out.

A gem among showpieces within easy reach is **Bricquebec**, clustered round its sixteenth-century castle with a tower that pre-dates it by some 200 years. A road runs through the heavily fortified archway into a courtyard where, surprisingly, there is a small *auberge*. By day guides shepherd their charges round a little museum in the clock tower and a restored thirteenth-century crypt, eventually pointing them in the direction of the keep. Its four storeys fell in a long time ago but there are steps, more than 150 of them, up to the viewing platform — a rewarding climb for anyone with the necessary stamina and determination. At twilight it is even more magical, silent except for the crickets and an occasional bird, filled with the atmosphere of bygone days if you ignore the promise of a good dinner wafting out through the windows of the hotel. The Abbaye de Notre-Dame-de-Grâce is a newcomer by comparison, founded in 1824 just outside the town. Women as well as men are allowed to visit the monastery, which makes a pleasant change for everyone, provided they time their visit for 3.30pm except on Sundays and holidays.

The next part of the journey still lies to the south but involves one of those 'do we head west or east?' decisions. Choose south-east and it is a short run to St Sauveur-le-Vicomte which is not as impressive as it sounds due mainly to wartime bombing. The castle is practically non-existent but there is an attractive little church with a statue of St James of Compostela and a museum dedicated to the life and works of Barbey d'Aurevilly who earned himself the title of Lord High Constable of Literature. Some 12km (7 miles) further on, beyond a strip of marshland, is **La Haye-du-Puits**, a perfectly ordinary little place on weekdays but quite amusing on Sunday mornings. The crowds are much in evidence, doing nothing particularly important as far as one can see, music blares out all down the main street from loudspeakers placed rather too close together for comfort and a young man roasts up to a dozen Sunday joints at the same time on a contraption, not unlike an abacus, set up on the edge of the pavement. Mont Castre makes a pleasant deviation at this point as long as time is no object. Not that there is a great deal about except ruins, which comprise a church and an old cemetery, but a pathway leads up to the remains of a Roman lookout post commanding a long distance view of the peninsula. It is so all-embracing that the site was returned to active service during the Battle of Normandy.

On the other hand, plan a trip south-west from Bricquebec and the sea is roughly 15km (9 miles) away with **Barneville-Carteret** dead ahead. This is actually three entities for the price of one. Barneville contributes an exceptionally well decorated church; the beach is popular with holidaymakers and caters for them accordingly while Carteret weighs in with a Customs Officers' Path along the headland and a colourful port with all the usual cafés and paraphernalia associated with fishermen. Visiting yachts are not encouraged, although space can usually be found for them, as it is for cars when their owners decide to catch the ferry for an excursion to the Channel Islands. Much the same can be said for **Port Bail**, further down the coast. It is not in the same league as far as water skiing and skin diving are concerned but it duplicates most of Carteret's other holiday attractions, has its own ferry to Jersey and any number of camping sites.

Whichever route is chòsen, be it south-east or south-west, it will almost certainly join its opposite number at **Lessay**, famous mainly for its abbey church founded in the eleventh century. It suffered so drastically in 1944 that it had to be almost entirely rebuilt, using all the original bits and pieces that were lying about. Although it is virtually devoid of decorations inside this adds to its tremendous dignity. The high altar is so heavy and plain that it could have graced a pagan temple, an impression carried through by the stained glass windows which owe a lot to Irish Celtic manuscripts. In contrast, there is nothing dignified about the Holy Cross Fair in September which has been held more or less regularly for the past thousand years. It is a boisterous mixture of sideshows, sales of dogs and horses, local crafts, traditional dancing, *al fresco* meals and modern amusements. In other words it is a typical example of celebrations of this kind in Normandy but is rather bigger than most of them. There is an aero club in the area and an interesting castle at Pirou, well fortified and surrounded by water, which has a tapestry on the lines of the one at Bayeux depicting the conquest of southern Italy instead of William's exploits in England in 1066.

Purists maintain that Lessay marks the end of the Cotentin Peninsula. They point out that the sea would only have to rise 10m (33ft) or so, flooding the marshes and grazing lands which separate the town from Carentan, and the whole northern section would revert to being one of the Channel Islands. But the *département* of La Manche does not write off one-third of its territory so easily and officially the Côtes du Cotentin continue merrily on their way round to the border with Brittany. The seaboard is well endowed with small coastal resorts, long sandy beaches and, apart from Coutainville and Granville, is blissfully lacking in organised entertainments.

Coutainville makes up for this apparent lapse in forward planning with everything from a casino, horse racing and golf to the whole gamut of popular sports, both by land and water. Nor does it forget to provide horses, boats and bicycles for hire. In some ways the resort could be described as a recreation centre for **Coutances** which is far more restrained. It has an outstanding cathedral, as befits the religious centre of the area, a couple of small churches, beautiful public gardens and an interesting local museum. It is the kind of town that needs to be enjoyed at leisure. Apart from one up-market establishment occupying an old *château* with a restaurant of equal quality the hotels are in no way out of the ordinary, but then they do not charge nearly so much!

Granville is made up of a bit of all worlds and in spite of being

Villedieu-les-Poêles is well-known for its copper wares

somewhat on the beaten track is well worth seeing, especially out of season. The ancient quarter, built largely of granite, stands above and beyond the modern town. It is a fascinating place to explore with its narrow streets and grim-faced houses, the austere church of Notre-Dame and traces of English occupation in the fifteenth century and of the Germans who followed in their footsteps after exactly 500 years. A stroll round the ramparts and out to the lighthouse on the Pointe de Roc takes in a sea-water aquarium complete with minerals and shells and a museum that includes both war and fashions. Another glimpse of old Granville can be found in the waxworks museum, there is a garden that once belonged to the Dior family, better known for haute couture, a casino, golf courses and a small beach with a swimming pool. From a busy port inside the promontory excursions leave for Jersey and the Chausey Islands, somewhat closer to the mainland. Fishing boats share the Port de Plaisance with a marina that keeps up to 200 berths for visitors, protected from tides that are reputed to be the strongest in Europe. A carnival is held in winter and a *pardon* of the sea in summer with an open-air mass, displays of banners and a torchlight procession.

Villedieu-les-Poêles, inland from Granville, holds a procession

The Patton Memorial, Avranches

every 4 years — 1987 was one of them — to honour the Knights of Jerusalem who have been associated with the town since the twelfth century. It is a custom dating back to 1655, roughly the time when local craftsmen became famous for their copper work. They are still in evidence today with a plethora of little shops spilling their wares out onto the pavements to tempt visitors in search of souvenirs. There is a bell foundry that is open on weekdays, a House of the Lacemaker and a copper museum showing the original processes and some of the results, while a visit to a copper workshop rounds things off nicely.

Travellers who feel that their supply of abbeys is running low will find at least two more tucked away in the woods. **Hambye**, to the north, has a magnificent ruined church open to the four winds with attendant buildings that have been restored. They include the chapter house, a spacious kitchen and an upstairs dormitory besides an old refectory which is furnished and has tapestries on the walls. At Lucerne Abbey, to the south-east, the decorated façade and the bell tower are original and, in spite of some lean years, the eighteenth-century organ has survived remarkably well. Visitors are welcome all day except at lunch time but the Abbot's Palace across the water is private and not on view.

A banner over the Villedieu-les-Poêles to Granville road announces the presence of a zoo, emphasised by a glass case containing a stuffed ostrich, a crane and a clutch of eggs. Some of the resident animals are very much alive while others have been dead for years.

Avranches is a town steeped in history but modern enough to close off whole areas for a cycle race. It was at the entrance to the cathedral, unfortunately destroyed during the Revolution, that England's Henry II did penance for the murder of Thomas à Becket at Canterbury. On the other side of the town a monument marks the place where General Patton paused before launching his famous offensive towards the Ardennes. The site is American territory with soil, trees and Stars and Stripes all brought over from the United States. The town museum is largely concerned with the early days of Mont-St-Michel. According to legend St Michael appeared twice to St Aubert, the Bishop of Avranches, instructing him to build a chapel on Mont Tombe. Eventually, tired of waiting, the archangel prodded the Bishop on the head with his finger, making a hole in his skull. The oratory was built in double quick time and the head of St Aubert found a resting place in the Basilica of St Gervais-St Protias surrounded by gold, silver and stone from the old cathedral.

Fishermen with a taste for salmon and solitude will doubtless make for **Ducey** on the banks of the River Sélune to the south. It is within easy reach of the Roche Qui Boit reservoirs and the Vezins lakes where any members of the family who get tired of waiting for a bite can take lessons at the local sailing school. Alternatively visitors in search of history will find a thirteenth-century *château* and an American cemetery and war memorial at St James before rejoining the main road at Pontorson, on the border with Brittany.

Further Information
— Normandy —

Museums and Other Places of Interest

SEINE-MARITIME AND EURE

Caudebec-en-Caux
Museum of Local History
Maison des Templiers
Open: 10am-12noon and 2.30-6pm,

mid-June to mid-September. Otherwise Saturday afternoons, Sunday and holidays only.

Jumièges
Jumièges Abbey
Open: 9am-6pm May to September. Otherwise 10am-12noon and 2.30-5pm. Closed Tuesday, 1 Janu-

1,300 year-old oak at Allouville-Bellefosse, Normandy

The River Orne, Normandy

ary, 1 May, 1 November, 25 December.

St Wandrille-Rançon
St Wandrille Abbey
Guided tours 10.30 and 11.15am, 3 and 4pm, Sundays 11.30am.

Villequier
Victor Hugo Museum
Open: 10am-12noon and 2-5pm. Extended to 7pm April to September. Closed Tuesdays, Mondays in winter and from November to end of January.

LE PERCHE-ORNE

L'Aigle
Museum
Open: Palm Sunday to mid-November 10am-12noon and 2-6.30pm. Closed Mondays.

Argentan
Benedictine Abbey — Display of Lace
2 Rue de l'Abbaye
Open: 2-4pm except Sundays and holidays.

Church of St Martin
Apply at the presbytery, 25 Rue de la Poterie.

Argentelles Manor
Open: Sundays and holidays 4-7pm, mid-April to third week in October.

Bernay
Museum
Open: mid-June to mid-September 10am-12noon and 3-7pm. Otherwise 3-5pm. Closed Tuesdays, January and 25 December.

Castle d'O
Guided tours 2.30-6pm. Closed

Tuesdays and 5pm out of season. Morning tours on request.

Haras du Pin
Guided tours of stables 9am-12 noon and 2-6pm. Apply at the lodge.

La Trappe Abbey
Enquire at porter's lodge.

La Vove Manor
Open: 10am-5pm, May to October.

Le Bourg-St-Léonard
Château-Le-Bourg-St-Léonard
Guided tours 9am-12noon and 2-6pm. Closed Tuesdays.

Longny-au-Perche
Notre-Dame-de-Pitié Chapel
Church of St Martin. Apply M. le Curé, 1 Rue de l'Eglise.

Mont-Ormel
War Memorial
Near Chambois

Mortagne-au-Perche
Church of Notre-Dame
On request at town hall.
☎ 33250422

Sassy Château
Open: Palm Sunday to All Saints' Day 3-6pm. Daily July and August. Saturdays and Sundays out of season.

Sées
St Latrium Cathedral
Son et Lumière in summer.

Ste Gauburge
Farm Museum
Open: 2-7pm daily June to mid-October.

MANCHE

Avranches
Avranchin Museum
Open: 9am-12noon and 2-6pm
Easter to end of September. Closed
Tuesdays.

Botanical Gardens
Open: until 8.30pm Easter to end
of September; July and August
until 11pm with illuminations to
mid-September.

St Gervais-St Protias Basilica
Treasure open 9am-12noon and 2-
6pm. Apply sacristan in the
church. Closed Sunday mornings
and Mondays.

Bricquebec
Castle and Museum
Guided tours 10am-12noon and 2-
6.30pm, July to mid-September.
Closed Tuesdays and last Saturday
and Sunday in July.

Champrepus Zoo
Open: 9am-7pm March to November.

Cherbourg
Emmanuel-Liais Park
Open: 8am-7.30pm during season
otherwise 8.30am-5pm. Greenhouses 2-5pm except Saturdays,
Sundays and holidays. Natural
history museum in Liais' former
home 10am-12noon and 2-5pm
May to September; 2-5pm September to April, closed Sunday mornings, Tuesdays and holidays.

Museum of Fine Arts
Open: 10am-12noon and 2-6pm.
Closed Tuesdays and holidays.

War Museum
Open: 9am-12noon and 2-5.30pm
October to March except Tues-
days.

Coutances
Cathedral, public gardens, local
museum.

Flers
Château grounds
Open: daily 7am-7pm.

Museum
Open: Easter to mid-October 2-
6pm. Closed Sunday and Monday.

Granville
Aquarium near lighthouse
Open: 9am-12noon and 2-7pm
Palm Sunday to mid-November.

Old Granville Museum
Next to entrance through ramparts
Open: 10am-12noon and 2-6pm,
April to first Sunday in October.
Otherwise Wednesday afternoons
and weekends. Closed holidays
out of season.

Waxworks Museum
Guided tours 9.30-11.30am and
2.30-6pm mid-July to mid-September.

Gratot
Remains of Argouges Manor
Open: 9am-1pm and 2-7.30pm,
closes 7pm out of season.

Hambye Abbey
Open: 10-11.30am and 2-6pm.
Closed Tuesdays out of season, 25
December and throughout Janu-
ary.

Lucerne Abbey
Open: 9am-12noon and 2-5.45pm.

Pirou Castle
Open: 10am-12noon and 2-6pm.
Closed Tuesdays September to
mid-June.

Ste Mère Eglise
Airborne Troops Museum
Open 9am-12noon and 2-7pm
Easter to mid-November. All day
July and August. The remainder of
the year weekdays on request.
10am-12noon and 2-6pm Sundays
and holidays.

Farm Museum
Open: 10am-12noon and 2-7pm
April to September. Closed Tues-
days.

St-Lô
Fine Arts Museum
Open: July and August 10.30am-
12noon and 2.30-5pm. Otherwise
2.30-5pm only. Closed Tuesdays
and holidays.

Stud
Open: mid-July to mid-February
10-11am and 2.30-4.30pm.

St-Sauveur-le-Vicomte
Barbey d'Aurevilly Museum
Open: 10am-12noon and 3-6.30pm,
September to June. Closed Tuesdays. (Apply to keeper in the rest
home, also in the
castle).

Valognes
Hôtel de Granval-Caligny
32 Rue des Religieuses
Open: 11am and 2.30-6pm
Wednesday to Saturday inclusive.

Cider Museum
Logis du Grand Quartier
Open: 10am-12noon and 2-6pm

mid-June to end September.
Closed Wednesdays and Sunday
mornings, also 14 July and 15
August.

Villedieu-les-Poêles
Copper Museum
Rue Général Huard
Guided tours 9am-12noon and 2-
6.30pm, June to mid-September.

Bell Foundry
Rue du Pont-Chignon
Open: 8am-12noon and 2-6pm except Sundays and Mondays out of
season.

Tourist Information Offices

L'Aigle
Place F. de Beina
☎ 33241240
Open: June to September.

Argentan
Place Marché
☎ 33671248

Avranches
Rue Général de Gaulle
☎ 33580022

Barneville-Carteret
Place Dr Auvret
☎ 33049058

Bernay
Town Hall
☎ 32433208

Caudebec-en-Caux
At the Mairie
☎ 35961112

Cherbourg
2 Quai Alexandre III
☎ 33530544 and at the railway station May-September ☎ 33443992

Coutainville
Place 28 Juillet 1944
☎ 33470146
Open: June to mid-September.

Flers
Place Général de Gaulle
☎ 33650675

Granville
15 Rue Georges Clemenceau
☎ 33500267

Mortagne-au-Perche
Place Général de Gaulle
☎ 33250422
Open: mid-June to mid-September.

St Lô
2 Rue Havin
☎ 33050209

Tourouvre
In church porch during season
☎ 33257455 *Gîtes* from Mairie de
Tourouvre, 61190 Tourouvre
☎ 33257455

Valognes
Place Château
☎ 33 401155
Open: mid-May to September.

2 • Brittany

When the Saxons, heading west across Britain and pushing the native, Celtic British before them, had isolated the Celtic bands from each other, creating what were to become Wales and Cornwall, some of the British fled, in fear and despair, across the sea. They landed in an area of north-west Europe not too dissimilar from the country they had left behind and, in consequence, they called it Little Britain, later dropping the 'Little' to give Bretagne, Brittany. Some of the settlers even went as far as to call their area Cornwall. Now Cornouaille is the name of the southern part of the *département* of Finistère. With them the settlers brought their legends, of King Arthur and his knights, of Merlin and other magicians, and these old tales sat easily in the deep, mysterious woodlands that then covered the area, and are now so sadly rare.

The Celtic settlers were not, however, the first to have populated the area. Thousands of years before, a race had erected huge stones, for purposes still not clear. Brothers to those who built Stonehenge and Avebury, these megalithic peoples have left perhaps the finest legacy of their existence anywhere in the world. The chief site is Carnac with its vast avenues of stones, but the whole province is covered with magnificent sites.

When, following the megalith builders and the Celtic settlers, the Romans had come, and had then retreated to the Alps, the Franks invaded the land that now bears their name, defeating the Breton Celts at the end of the eighth century. Within fifty years the province re-established its independence, defeating the Franks in battle, declaring Brittany an independent dukedom and settling down to 600 years of fiercely defended isolation, beating back all attempts at invasion by successive waves of French and English soldiers. Only in 1514 when the Breton duchess, Anne, married not one, but two French kings — one at a time rather than together! — did Brittany finally become part of France, a union sealed by the 1532 Treaty of Vannes.

The contorted rock strata is one of the many interesting features to be found in Brittany

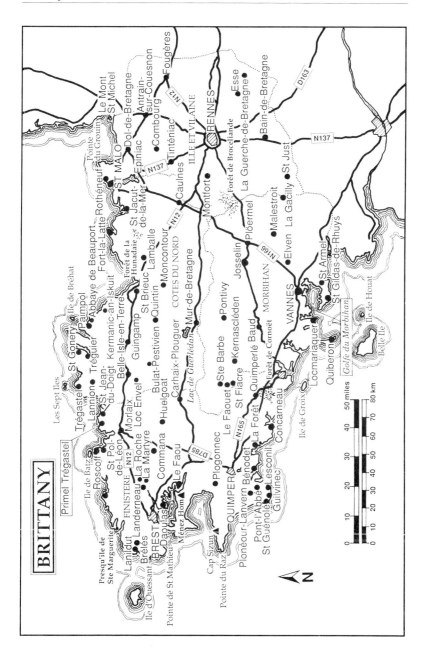

Thereafter Brittany, not surprisingly in view of the length of its coastline, became the centre of French sea power, in terms of exploration, wealth-bringing piracy and fishing, and in purely naval terms. Even today Brest is still of great importance to the French Navy.

Brittany is large, only a province of France and yet comparable in size with Denmark, Belgium or Wales. This should allow scope for considerable variation in scenery, though in fact the lack of any real highland means that inland Brittany has little diversity, large areas of agricultural land peppered with fine remnants of the ancient forest. But within this landscape there are nuggets of fine river scenery and many very pretty villages, frequently worth more than a passing interest. But Brittany also has around 1,250km (800 miles) of coastline, much of it offering magnificent seascapes.

Brittany has striven hard for its own identity. The line of castles along the eastern border of the *département* of Ille-et-Vilaine testify to this, as does the continuation of the distinctively Breton features, the *pardons*, the *crêperies*, the cider drinking — there is no genuinely Breton wine — and the language. Brittany's climate is not too dissimilar from that of south-western Britain, except, perhaps, in the *département* of Morbihan where it is both sunnier and warmer, and is not really for those who holiday purely for lazy days on hot beaches. Rather it is for the explorer, for those interested in country and village, and in history.

And just in case that sounds a little dull, where else in France do they have races for 2CVs and tractors not on land, but on the sea?

Finistère

Finistère is the first *département* of Brittany that many visitors see as they leave the Brittany Ferry at Roscoff. It is also the *département* which is the most Breton, the furthest from France. Even its name derives from its position at the extreme western end of Brittany, itself almost an island tacked onto the western end of France.This is *'Finis Terrae'*, the end of the world, and though that name is Roman, the Celts themselves had the same idea in mind when calling it *'Penn at Bed'*. Finistère has some marvellously 'soft' countryside but also has the harshest of Brittany's land, the most storm-lashed coasts, the only areas of remote, barren highland and as a rule it also has buildings to match, low and angular away from the wind and clinging to the land. The people cling too, but they to their Breton heritage, its language, folklore and costume.

It may seem a strange idea, but to most tourists using the Brittany Ferries route to **Roscoff**, the first off-the-beaten track spot is Roscoff itself. Since the ferry port is too far away from the town for a casual

stroll, and now boasts a terminal building that provides all a traveller's needs, most tourists bypass the town itself, thankful either to
have reached the port safely and content to wait for the boat, or
happy to be in France after several hours at sea, and anxious to be
away to their holiday headquarters.

Roscoff is a fine town, built around one of the fanciest church
towers in the whole of Brittany, and with an array of excellent
granite-built houses, dating chiefly from the sixteenth- to eighteenth-century period when the town prospered on the wealth of the
corsairs. The town's fortified walls near the seafront date from the
same period, a necessity in case those that were unwillingly providing the town's wealth decided to visit, to attempt to retrieve it. Near
the seafront a tower and plaque commemorate the landing, in 1548,
of Mary Stuart, later to become Mary, Queen of Scots. She arrived at
the tender age of 5 to be engaged to the Dauphin, the heir to the
French throne, who was then at the even tenderer age of 3! No plaque
commemorates the arrival of another Royal Scot nearly two centuries later. Here Bonny Prince Charlie came ashore after the disastrous
campaign of 1745, and the defeat at Culloden. While in the town be
sure to visit the marine aquarium which holds specimens of channel
fauna. It is fascinating to see what you have just, or are about to, sail
over.

Those with more time, and an enthusiasm for ferries, can visit the
Ile de Batz (pronounced 'Ba') a place almost never visited by the
English tourist, but with a marvellous, rugged, wave-dashed north
shore, and a more tranquil southern shore, quiet coves and a forgotten village. On the island a sixth-century Welsh saint, Paul (in Breton,
Pol), landed, forcing a dragon to jump into the sea at the aptly named
Trou du Serpent. St Pol's name is commemorated in the town, **St Pol-
de-Léon** just south of Roscoff, which is also normally sped past *en
route* inland or homewards. Here, be sure to visit the buildings under
the two huge landmarks — the twin towers of the cathedral of St Pol
and the spire of Notre-Dame-de-Kreisker. The towers are 50m (160ft)
tall and top a fine Gothic building which holds the skulls of thirty-
five notables from the past, as well as the skull, a finger and an arm
bone of St Pol who died on the Ile de Batz at 104 years of age. By
contrast the interior of the church below the 80m (260ft) spire seems
almost mundane. As an aside, the headquarters of SICA the organi-
sation that runs the famous local cauliflower and artichoke trade is
in St Pol-de-Léon, its presence here starting a shipping business that
at first took the vegetables to England, but grew into one whose chief
cargo is now tourists.

Westward, from Roscoff to the Pointe-de-St Mathieu, is the Côte des Abers. 'Aber' here is the same as the Welsh word that preceeds Aberystwyth, for example, and means a water junction. Normally this junction is river and sea — though not, as a quick visit will show, at Abergavenny — and here the name is usually translated as the Coast of Estuaries, a series of massively incut estuaries lying all around the coast as rivers drain down from high inland Finistère. The first part of the coast is pleasant, but dull, matters improving once **Brignogan-Plage** is reached. Here there is one of the best menhirs, standing stones, in Brittany although, sadly, it has been badly served by history. The stone stands beside the road that leads from village to sea; a house has been built beside it; and a cross has been cut into, or fixed on, its top. When first erected this stone, a huge granite block nearly $9^1/_2$m (30ft) high must have been marvellously impressive. The cross on top of it — you would need to climb the stone to see if it had been chiselled or glued — is proof of the immense power the menhir had on a population well removed from its erectors. So powerful a symbol was it — in local legend this is Men-Marz, the Stone of Miracles — that there was a need to Christianise or, more likely, to de-paganise, to neutralise, its power. The house and road are sad, such a stone needs space. One interesting note is that the house is 'Ty Menhir', the same name it would have been given in Wales.

Beyond the menhir the sea is reached near a beach of sand so white that it seems unreal, set between granite blocks which offer adventure to any beachgoer with a steady head.

The first part of the Côte des Abers, or Coast of Estuaries, is also known as the Coast of Legends (Côte de Légendes), the reason being not the Celtic mythology which is so strong in Finistère, but the number of shipwrecks that took place on the razor sharp backs of rock that edge in the fjord-like estuaries. Many stories tell of shipwrecks that were assisted by false lights hung out on the shore. Aber Wrac'h is the largest and, perhaps, the finest of the estuaries. Go to the **Presqu'Ile de Ste Marguerite**, the almost-island of St Margaret. 'Almost-island' — what a very fine expression for a peninsula thinned almost to causeway size on its landward side. Ste Marguerite is ringed offshore by a half-circle of real islands, or, in their case, islets, and offers some of the very best seascapes. Further along the coast are a series of villages that were once exclusively the homes of fishermen. **Lanildut** on the Aber-Ildut is a particular favourite and nearby **Brélés** has the added interest that it is positioned at the point where, technically, the Atlantic Ocean and the English Channel meet.

La Martyre

South, and inland, is another menhir, Kerloas, the tallest in Brittany at nearly 10m (32ft), elegant, almost aloof and beautifully sited to lend the maximum mystery to its form. South again is the **Pointe de St Mathieu**, with one of the most evocative sites in the whole of Brittany, the salt spray and wind-lashed remains of a Benedictine monastery, orignally founded in the sixth century and destroyed during the French Revolution. The founding monk was St Tanguy, but the point, and the monastery, took St Matthew's name when a boat, bringing the head of the Gospel writer here from Ethiopia, floundered in high seas and all on board were saved through a channel miraculously carved when the relic was held aloft. Offshore are several small islands, and the large Ile d'Ouessant, all of which form part of the French equivalent of a national park. The islands can be visited and while they are well and truly off the beaten track, the trip can only be recommended for those who like their seascapes not only wild and rugged but very, very remote.

South from Brignogan-Plage is a series of very fine small towns which should form part of anyone's itinerary. First is **Landerneau** where there is one of the last (*the* last?) bridges in Europe on which there are inhabited houses. It really is a most extraordinary slice of old history to walk over a bridge similar to those that are so often seen in old prints of London. The buildings look more modern (Pont de Rohan dates from around the start of the sixteenth century) but that cannot be helped. It is a pity that the shops and, especially, the shop fronts are not a little less intrusively modern. South from Landerneau are Daoulas and Le Faou, the former with the magnificent remains of a Romanesque abbey, the latter a pretty village with several sixteenth-century houses with slate frontages. South again be sure to visit Ménez Hom, a little way from Trégarvan, from where, the view over the River Châteaulin is quite breathtaking.

But do not hasten away from Landerneau.Further up the River Elorn which is spanned by the Pont de Rohan, be sure to visit La Roche to see the romantically overgrown remains of an old castle on a steep knoll right above the river itself.Then go inland, to visit **La Martyre.**

Since the parish close (*enclos paroissial*) is such an essentially Breton feature, it seems, at first sight, unwise to mention them in a book devoted to the more unusual aspects of the countryside. However the normal tour of closes usually takes in St Thegonnec, Guimiliau and Lampaul-Guimiliau — the Circuit de Trois Enclos — and there are others, the building of a close not being confined to the richer, merchant towns. At La Martyre the essentials of a close are all present, church, triumphal arch, ostuary and calvary, and while its constituent parts may not be as grand, as magnificent, as its better known neighbours, the village close does have both a simple dignity and a wholeness that are quite moving. Today, thankfully, the ossuary houses not the bones of the dead moved on from the graveyard when space became limited, but a small exhibition of drawings and articles on the close.

From La Martyre a very good country road leads through Sizun and past Commana to the Monts d'Arrée, the highest land in Brittany and part of the Parc Régional d'Armorique. As **Commana** is reached a road right allows a quick visit to the *allée couverte* of Le Mougau, a most beautiful megalithic burial site.

The highest point of the Monts d'Arrée is actually Ménez Kador, but what hold the eye and beg to be climbed are the rock-outcropped heights of Roc'h Trévézel. The walking here is excellent, barely beaten paths between the ferns and gorse, among granite castles. From one such granite castle, to the south of the main road, the view inland is expansive and compelling. What take the eye are the far off conical hill, just west of south, topped by a chapel to St Michael, the patron saint of mountain tops, and the white domes of the nuclear power plant of Brennilis beside the reservoir in the hollow below the high ridge. With what seems an irony of coincidence, the marshy land of this hollow, impenetrable and hostile area, was known by the Bretons as the 'Mouth of Hell'.

Off the ridge, but still within the Parc Régional d'Armorique is **Huelgoat**, a charming village — with a museum of clothes irons! — standing at the edge of one of the park's great joys, a remnant of the ancient forest which once covered much of the inland area hereabouts. Close to the town are some natural features which have been given fanciful names, the Devil's Grotto, and so on. But for all that the names are a bit out of place, the features themselves are impressive, even the steps and walkways being justifiable on the grounds that the less intrepid would also like to see the sights. Not so attractive however, is the sheer vandalism of inscribing the name 'La Roche Tremblante', on the side of a huge, 100 ton, logan rock in the forest. Logans are rare and deserve better treatment — they are delicately balanced rocks which, though huge, rock when pushed giving rise, as a result, to many legends, chief of which was that their trembling foretold the future to anyone who understood the beat.

Go beyond the obvious however, and you can be off the beaten track in an ancient forest landscape, the valley floor festooned with huge boulders, green-cased. This ancient forest is linked with the Celtic legend of Arthur. Here in this secret forest, he would apparently go to rest. The far reaches of the forest, hardly a walk from Huelgoat, more a drive to and, then just beyond, St Ambroise, envelope the early waters of the River Aulne, at this stage and for many a mile, one of the most beautiful of all Brittany's rivers. At nearby **Carhaix-Plouguer**, the church of St Trémuer has a statue of the saint holding his head in his hands, literally that is, not in despair. The story of the statue concerns Commorrus, a sixth-century count of Cornouaille who, having been warned that he would be killed by his son, murdered his first four wives as soon as they became pregnant. A fifth wife gave birth prematurely and successfully hid the child, Trémuer, but was killed when she became pregnant again. Many years later Trémuer met Commorrus, who was instantly struck by the youth's likeness to his fifth wife and cut his head off as a precaution. The saintly lad picked up his head, walked to Commorrus' castle and threw a handful of earth at it so that it collapsed and buried the murderous count.

Westward from Le Faou, over the River Châteaulin is the **Presqu'Île de Crozon**, a bent trident-shaped piece of land, the two northern tines forming parts of a national park and offering some very fine seascapes; the best being that from **Pointe de Dinan** to the huge rock formation known, with good reason, as the Castle of the Giants; the southern tine forming a rim of the almost totally enclosed Baie de Douarnenez. On this, its northern rim, is a fine series of marine caves, huge grottoes into which it is possible to sail. Approach by means other than water is not possible for the ordinary mortal and it is best to take one of the boat trips on offer to view the caves. On a fine afternoon this is a very pleasant way to acquire a tan. On the southern rim of the bay, no visitor with an interest in ornithology should miss the seabird reserve of Cap Sizun, a noted spot for both gulls and auks, cormorants and petrels. Beyond is the mysterious Baie des Trépassés, the Bay of the Souls of the Dead. Many believe this to be a reference to the numerous shipwrecks on its jagged, enclosing arms or to the legendary transporting of the bodies of dead Druids from here to the burial island of Sein, but it is more likely to be just a misinterpretation of the very unsinister Breton name, Boe an Aon — Bay of Streams — into Boe an Anaon — Bay of Souls. However since the Pointe du Raz is France's equivalent of Land's End or John o' Groats, the bay is rarely as quiet as the grave.

Offshore here is the reputed site of *Is*, legendary drowned capital of Cornouaille, a town that was so beautiful that the capital of France was built to be as beautiful — Par-Is.

Back inland the best Breton cooking for miles around is to be found at the Auberge de Leurbiriou, on the road going west from Plogonnec towards Le Juch. A couple of days' stay here, with the hospitality and cuisine on offer, and you may see less of the surrounding countryside than you had intended. But do not miss the fabulous sculpture in the church of Locronan.

South is **Quimper**, capital of Finistère and in many ways the complete Breton city. It is still small enough to explore comfortably

Quimper

on foot, however, and there is much that is of interest away from the main tourist highways. Perhaps the best idea is to go south of the River Odet and climb Mont Frugy, the tree-bedecked hill. From its flanks the view of the old town, dominated by the magnificent cathedral, is superb. For a really spectacular day and the best of all entries into Quimper, take the Odet boat from **Bénodet**. The trip passes trees and fields, old castles and houses, even crossing a lake — Kerogen, where the river widens amazingly — before the twin spires of the cathedral of St Corentin come into view.

Near Quimper, **Plonéour-Lanvern** and **Pont-l'Abbé**, are two excellent villages in which to see the traditional Breton lady's headpiece, the *coiffe*. They are worn on Sunday mornings and, in Pont-l'Abbé, on Thursday morning. Near Pont-l'Abbé, at **Combrit**, is an interesting museum of mechanical music — from fairground organs to music boxes.

As traditional as the *coiffe* is the return of the fishing boats to the ports around the Pointe de l'Enmarch'h. At **St Guénolé**, **Guilvinec** and **Lesconil**, for instance, the boats return at around 4.30pm each weekday and unload to the quayside markets. Close by La Forêt-Fouesnant, at the resort town of **Concarneau**, there is a museum to the history of local fishing.

Going east and fast approaching the *département* of Morbihan, one last ancient site is still to be visited, the Rochers du Diable, the

Devil's Rocks, north-east of **Quimperlé**, a strange jumble of huge boulders beside a beautiful river, the Ellé. The rocks are named from the legend of a Celtic saint who lived among them and chased the devil away from the area when he came to harass him. South of Quimperlé, the River Behan is one of Brittany's better spots for oysters. Also south is the beautiful oak and beech **Forêt de Carnoët**, a link with the legend of St Trémuer at Carhaix, because one version of the tale sites Commorrus' castle here.

Lastly in Finistère, travel north to the land lying east of Morlaix which, therefore, feels as though it should be in Côtes du Nord *département*. The village of **St Jean-du-Doigt** is named for a finger of St John the Baptist held in a reliquary in the church. It has been said many times that there are enough relics of some saints to build several bodies and so it is a claim that must be treated with caution, especially since this forgotten corner of Brittany seems such a strange repository for such a thing, and the dismemberment of the saint's body seems equally strange. Outside the church there is a fountain, itself said to be sacred,which fills a basin into which the finger is dipped at intervals. The water thus blessed is said to be a miracle cure for eyes bathed in it, the cure having given rise to an annual *pardon* of eye complaint sufferers. In addition to the finger, the church also holds some of the finest silverware of any of the province's churches.

Nearby another finger, here of hard rock, points out into the sea at **Primel-Trégastel**. This holiday village has the benefits of both a sandy beach and a rocky headland. Another fine coastal spot is the bay between the mainland and the Pointe de Barnenez. The point itself has, at its summit, perhaps the finest of all Brittany's megalithic remains, the Tumulus of Barnenez, an incredible structure of dry-stone walls, about 70m (225ft) long, 25m (80ft) wide and 8m (25ft) high covering eleven burial chambers each reached by a narrow, low passage. A site definitely not to be missed.

Morbihan

The *département* of Morbihan, or, more correctly, The Morbihan, is the only one of Brittany's *départements* to have a Breton name, that name deriving from the area's most obvious feature, the huge sea lagoon (the Gulf of Morbihan) lying to the south of Vannes, and known in Breton, as the 'Mor Bihan', the little sea. The gulf's enclosing arms almost touch, at the Pointe de Kerpenhir, south of Locmariaquer, being separated by little over half a mile of water from the headland of Port Navalo. This almost total enclosure brings

The Tumulus of Barnenez, the finest prehistoric site in Brittany

to the villages along the gulf's shore a calmness not often experienced on the wild coasts of Finistère, which in turn produces a mildness of climate that is quite surprising.

In Breton history the area around Vannes, the Vannetais as it was known, played an important role.The significant battle that ended the War of Succession and so decided who would rule Brittany, was fought at Auray, on the main river that feeds into the gulf. But many centuries before that battle the area was already important to man. Within the *département* are the finest of Brittany's megalithic sites, perhaps the finest, and certainly one of the most enigmatic, collections of prehistoric sites anywhere in the world. The megalithic alignments north of Carnac are so famous that they need no introduction, and there is little justification for their inclusion here — whatever their original purpose might have been, they are no longer off the beaten track. There is just time to mention that the stones are, not surprisingly, the source of numerous legends: that they are the soldiers of a Roman army, turned to stone for threatening a Christian saint; that they all leave their holes at midnight on Christmas Eve to drink at the River Crac'h, leaving exposed treasure that the very brave may try to retrieve; and many more. But some time should be spent exploring the area's prehistory. At Kercado is the oldest of all the monuments, and still one of the most impressive, and no visitor should miss the Grand Menhir Brisé and the Table des Marchands near **Locmariaquer**. The Grand Menhir now lies in five pieces, the victim, it is widely believed, of a lightning strike in the eighteenth century. When standing this 350 ton stone would have been 20m (65ft) tall. Just the accomplishment of its erection is astonishing, without considering why. The best current theory is that it formed a pointer for a huge observatory, erected to predict seasons and eclipses. Some say it was sighted from the Quiberon peninsula, which if true gives some idea of its size — there are 8 miles of water between here and there. The Table des Marchands is a huge dolmen, probably a burial chamber. The largest flat table stone is 6 x 4m (20 x 13ft) and is part supported by a stone that has been deliberately shaped to a cone and is covered with strange symbols. Some see crooks and a cooking pot, some see ears of corn and the sun.

But for a real treat, take the short boat trip from Larmor-Baden to the **Ile de Gavrinis** to see the decorated stones of the burial chamber there. The abstract swirls and spirals make this one of the wonders of the world. Finally, the visitor who dives might visit the next, tiny, island, **Er Iannic**, where two of the very few stone circles in Brittany are sited. One is now completely submerged, the other nearly so and diving — a snorkel will just about do if conditions are right — is fascinating.

The gulf is not all old stones however. There is fine boating here, good swimming and some beautiful views, especially from Pointe d'Arradon. For the bird watcher the area is amazing, the salt marsh margins, especially on the southern gulf shore, the **Presqu'Ile de Rhuys**, being especially renowned for summer feeding ducks, geese, spoonbills and egrets. Try the gulf reserve site of **St Armel** on the eastern shore. Alternatively go to the Rhuys pensinsula. It is rarely visited in comparison to the more famous Quiberon peninsula, yet it has seascapes that are its equal: rocky, wind-lashed coves, a sandy lee side and the marshy gulf side. Do not miss the little village of **St Gildas-de-Rhuys**, with a fine Romanesque abbey church on the site of a monastery founded by the British monk Gildas, famous as the source of many Arthurian legends.

The Quiberon peninsula cannot be recommended for the summer visitor as its single road is clogged with traffic for most weekend hours and frequently during the week as well. In winter it is a different story, and then the western edge, which takes the full brunt of Atlantic storms, is the place to experience nature in the raw. It is aptly named the Côte Sauvage, the Savage Coast. Off the peninsula is Belle-Ile, another well known spot, so go instead to the **Ile de Houat**, a smaller island to the east, a peaceful, little frequented fishing island served by boats from Port Navalo, and Quiberon. Or better, go to the **Ile de Groix**, to the west off of Lorient. The whole island, about 24sq km (some 10sq miles) is a museum to an ancient way of life, because in addition to an actual museum to the tunny fishing and sea-faring way of life of the islanders, there are two waymarked paths around the island which visit the most charming and most interesting sites.On its south-eastern tip there is also a fine seabird reserve.

Inland, Morbihan has some of the finest river scenery not only in Brittany, but also in Europe. Begin by going to the extreme west of the *département* to visit the town of **Le Faouët**, which stands besides the River Ellé, but also in the centre of a piece of quiet countryside, fields, woods and streams.The town derives its name from the Breton *faou*, a beech-tree, which is very appropriate. It is a fine place with a beautiful, huge, sixteenth-century covered market built with massive wooden legs and roof beams. Nearby are two tiny villages with excellent chapels. **Ste Barbe** has a Gothic building from the early sixteenth century, and a fountain where a floated hairpin told a girl she would be married within the year. If the hairpin sank she would not. **St Fiacre** has a fifteenth-century chapel holding what is probably the finest rood screen in Brittany, a marvellous late fifteenth-century work with fine carving including some excellent grotesques.

Eastward do not miss the equally beautiful chapel of **Kernascléden**, which has the best collection of fifteenth-century wall paintings in France. Legend has it that this chapel and that of St Fiacre were built by the same workmen, ferried by angels between the two sites so that the work was not held up. Sadly for the legend it is known that the Kernascléden chapel was completed 30 years before St Fiacre.

Just east of Kernascléden is the valley of the River Scorff, by common consent the most beautiful of all Morbihan's rivers, the stretch between Guémené-sur-Scorff and Plouay probably being the finest. It is almost impossible to choose a particular section of the river here as the best part, but a leisurely day would probably be best. Start at **Guéméne** with the remains of an old castle and a fine array of medieval buildings. **Persquen** has an interesting parish close, while **Lignol** lies in a deeply wooded section of the valley. Next is Kernascléden itself, and then comes the Forêt de Pontcallec, perhaps the most picturesque of all the wooded areas, with many views that would grace a postcard. There is a nineteenth-century *château*, viewed across a lake, and incomparable woodland views. From the tiny village of St Albaud to the Pont-Neuf, a distance of about 3km (2 miles), the forest is crossed by GR34, one of the very fine series of

Grandes Randonnées, long-distance footpaths, that criss-cross the French countryside. No special knowledge is required to follow a GR, the signing being excellent and obvious, and the following of this small section can be highly recommended.

Next east is the River Blavet with, on its banks at the northern end of the *département*, **Pontivy**, once the capital of Brittany and called Napoleonville. Neither name nor status lasted a great length of time, but just long enough for the town to acquire some prosperous buildings which it has, gratefully, maintained. Napoleon's name was given as a reward for loyalty. The present, and older name is from the founding Welsh monk who had the first bridge built over the Blavet. South of Pontivy the Blavet flows delightfully through quiet countryside, less wooded than that of the Scorff Valley, but not really the worse for that. The waters of other rivers, themselves worth exploring, the Sarre, the Brandifrout and the Tarun are collected as the Blavet grows towards Hennebont. On the Tarun just a couple of miles from its confluence with the Blavet is **Baud**, a pleasant village with, just outside on the southern side of the main road to Hennebont and Lorient, an odd statue with a chequered history. It is called the *Venus of Quinipily* and has been variously ascribed to the ancient Egyptians, the Celts, the Romans and as a worthless fake of no antiquity at all. How it came here is not known, but what is known is that it was the basis of a cult in the seventeenth century that came perilously close — or so said the local churchman — to pagan idolatry. Consequently the local bishop came and supervised as the statue was thrown into the river. The locals waited until the bishop had gone away, and retrieved it for posterity.

East again the river pattern is disturbed by the high **Landes de Lanvaux**. This was once barren moorland, but it has been increasingly 'reclaimed' for farmland and forestry. The ancient nature of the landscape still shows occasionally: a piece of wild heath, an ancient menhir. In 1944, after the landings at Normandy, a genuine battle took place here between the Breton resistance fighters and a unit of French paratroopers, and the occupying Germans. The battle site, near **St Marcel**, is marked by a (well hidden) memorial.

The Landes push the south-flowing rivers east towards Redon. First is the Claie that flows by St Marcel itself, and next is the Oust which flows through **Josselin**. Josselin is famous for its castle, a marvel of Renaissance architecture, but slightly off the beaten track is the Musée de Poupées, the Doll's Museum, now established in the castle stables. The museum is formed around the collection of the Rohan family and has over 500 examples.

The castle at Josselin

Downstream (the Oust is Brittany's longest river) is **Malestroit**, an old town with fine timber-framed houses, beyond which the river joins the Aff flowing from the *département* of Ille-et-Vilaine. Here is the Mortier, a river section enclosed by the Ile des Pies dam, a sanctuary for water birds of all kinds. The views, to chapels, rocks, wood and farmland, and the wonderful birdlife make this one of the finest spots in the whole of Brittany. The area is one of the chief centres for Breton folklore and culture, and over the marshes here the 'White Lady' floats, sometimes wreathed in mist. Those who follow her call are apparently drawn far away.

The Aff, which has joined the Oust, flows down from the Forêt de Broceliande, covered in the section on Ille-et-Vilaine, and that link with an ancient landscape has made it a centre for ancient crafts. There are numerous riverside paths through tiny hamlets of characteristic shale houses, the odd manor house or small castle. The valley is the least frequented of all, the genuine off the beaten track river, and should be savoured at length. But do go to **La Gacilly**, a fine town brimming with ancient crafts, a small industry of flower-based beauty products and, it seems, a flower-filled window box for every window.

The last valley is the Yuel that joins the Oust south of Ploërmel. **St Léry**, near the border with Ille-et-Vilaine, is a beautiful village with a fine array of old houses. Down river is the Etang au Duc, a fine lake-like expanse of the river that offers good sailing in beautiful surroundings. **Ploërmel** has near it, and appallingly badly preserved beside the dual carriageway coming in from Josselin, the Colonne des Trente. This is one of the most important of all Breton chivalric sites where, during the War of Succession, thirty knights from each side — English knights on one side — fought a duel to save greater bloodloss in their respective garrisons. The battle lasted all day despite which there was surprisingly little loss of life, the routed English losing nine men. Bad road planning means the site is little visited, though much sped past.

Throughout the Morbihan there are numerous castles, some very famous. Largoët Fortress, also known as the Towers of Elven, stands to the west of the road, the N166 from Vannes to Ploërmel and Malestroit. All that remains of the fourteenth- and fifteenth-century castle — knocked down in the late fifteenth century when the owner backed the wrong side in the fight between Brittany and France — are two huge, beautiful towers, and some low ruins. The huge, 60m (195ft), octagonal tower is a massive fourteenth-century construction, while the restored fifteenth-century round tower with pyramidal roof is more delicate. There is a real drawbridge and a fine view across a lake. It is enchanting.

Ille-et-Vilaine

This *département* is named from its principal rivers which meet at the town of Rennes, capital of both the *département* and Brittany. The Vilaine flows south to the Golfe du Morbihan while the Ille or, rather, the Ille-Rance Canal joins Rennes to the Channel near St Malo. Thus the two waters split the *département* from side to side, though the waterway does not form a barrier between Brittany and the rest of France, that barrier being further to the east. There, unlike in past centuries when Brittany strived to maintain a very real and fortified barrier with France, the boundary is fluid. France starts in a gradual way somewhere closer to Finistère, and by the time eastern Ille-et-Vilaine is reached the countryside and people are more French than Breton.

As a holiday centre Ille-et-Vilaine is blessed with few beaches, though Dinard is a very notable exception, nor is it blessed with the mild climate of Morbihan and its gulf. It makes up for this lack by an abundance of quiet countryside and pleasant, secluded villages and towns, and the marvellous line of castles along the old border between Brittany and France.

As with Roscoff in Finistère, many visitors who arrive or depart on a Brittany Ferry do not see **St Malo**, except as a hugely fortified port on the horizon. Again it is worth the time of exploration. Named after a founding Welsh monk, the present town was built on an island in the bay offshore of the original town, which had been greatly plundered by pirates. Only over the last three centuries has the island under St Malo been permanently connected to the mainland by a causeway over a widening sandbar.The town's insularity, well defended by still awesome defensive walls, built a fierce independence, the inhabitants considering themselves neither French, nor Breton, owing allegiance to no man. They were highly skilled sailors, skills they put to use in exploration — Jacques Cartier, a local man, discovered and named Canada — and in piracy, and later in legitimate trade, a trade that financed, in the seventeenth and eighteenth centuries, the array of fine granite buildings, and the excellent cathedral. There are several excellent museums in the town; the *donjon*, not the dungeon, but the keep, the English form being a misinterpretation of the French, has one to the town, while in Rue de Toulouse there is a fine Dolls' Museum.

From the town two boat trips are possible. A short trip across the bay leads to the island of Grand Bé, named from the Breton word for a tomb and, appropriately, holding the grave of the writer Châteaubriand. A longer trip follows the River Rance inland, a fine trip that can be combined with a visit to the tidal barrage power station, the world's only such station.

Near St Malo, on the road towards Rennes, is a museum of cider, a fascinating insight into that most Breton of drinks.

North-east from St Malo is a short section of the Emerald Coast, the *département*'s only piece of coastline, reaching its northern extreme at the **Pointe du Grouin,** north of Cancale, a real nose of land, poked into the English Channel. The views from it, including Mont St Michel, are excellent, and the incut cliffs of the headland are equally good for poking about in. A small offshore island is a bird sanctuary. **Cancale** itself is more popular, especially with the oyster fancier, being famous for their production.

At nearby **Rothéneuf** is a site that is not only off the beaten track but will soon be on no track at all. In the rocks above the sea here, in the early part of this century, an eccentric named Fouré spent a quarter of a century carving a group of sculptures of pirates and sea monsters. The sculptures are perhaps best described as grotesques, the work normally associated with church gargoyles, though on a grander scale.But the years have taken their toll, the endless battering by sea and wind gradually obliterating the work. Soon no trace of the sculptures will exist which, even if you would have preferred them not to have been carved in the first place, is sad.

Further south there is some fascinating country around **Dol-de-Bretagne**, not least the town itself whose cathedral is claimed by many to be the best in Brittany. It is certainly a very fine building, but some find its curiously asymmetric front less appealing than the symmetric cathedral of Quimper. Near the town is one of the few megalithic sites in this far corner of Brittany, but a very interesting one. The menhir, at **Champ-Dolent** about 1km (half a mile) south of the town, is 9m (about 30ft) high, and hugely impressive as well as huge. Legend has it that it fell to earth and is sinking slowly into the ground. When it has disappeared the world will come to an end. Strangely, the site — the Field of Grief — is named not as a consequence of this worldly egg-timer, but from a legendary battle between the armies of two brothers fought too long ago to be dated.

Also near Dol-de-Bretagne is Mont Dol — about 3km (2 miles) to the north — an odd table-topped mountain, that was a Celtic holy place and still has a summit chapel. The chapel started life as one in a chain of semaphore signalling stations from Brest to Paris, and the good visibility also offers stupendous views over the local country and, especially, over the Baie du Mont St Michel. A visit to this most magnificent site is certainly off the beaten track for Brittany — it's in Normandy! But a spectacularly different journey to it starts in Ille-de-Vilaine at **Le Vivier** on the coast north of Dol-de-Bretagne. From there a coach leaves across the sands and drives straight into the sea, where it folds up its wheel and becomes a boat for the last part of the journey.

Leaving Dol on the D795 towards Combourg the road soon passes a small village, **Epiniac**, that so typifies much of inland Brittany. It is not especially pretty or interesting, but it has a remarkable legend of women so lazy that they were forced to do their washing at night by candlelight. As a penance their ghosts do it still, so beware the small flickering lights, because if the women see you they will demand assistance with the wringing of their clothes, and anyone who wrings, rings also the bell of his own doom.

Alternatively, leave Dol on the D155 to Fougères and reach **An-train-sur-Couesnon**, a distinguished village close to the Normandy border at the meeting point of two rivers, the Couesnon and the Loisance. It is a pleasant town, with some good fifteenth- and sixteenth-century houses set in narrow, winding lanes, a very fine twelfth-century Romanesque church and, about 1$\frac{1}{2}$km (1 mile) to

the south, the Château de Bonne-Fontaine.This is an elegant combination of country mansion and castle, its round towers with their
conical roofs and high-set windows looking like crouched witches
peering through slit eyes. The illusion is hard to maintain once the
little stone chimneys breaking through the roofs have been spotted.
The park alone is open to the public, no real loss as the view to the
château is included in the park entrance fee, and the visitor can stroll
through the woodland where, it is said, Brittany's famed Duchess
Anne meted out justice whilst sat in the shade of an oak tree.

The *château* is more off the beaten track than the one at Fougères,
though, it has to be said, neither is it as splendid, as its more famous
neighbour. One of the problems with writing about the little visited
is that it can prevent the mention of the real gem. So visit **Fougères**
not for the *château*, but for a couple of other delights. But see the
château anyway!

There are two churches in Fougères, and neither should be
missed. From the outside the church of St Leonard, built over many
centuries from the twelfth century onwards, is a curious barn-like
building, with an equally curious pagoda-like tower, but is set in a
fine park in the town, close to the fourteenth-century half-timbered
houses of the Place du Marchix, and is certainly worth a look. The
second church, the fifteenth-century St Sulpice, is close to the castle,
a slim, elegant, soaring Gothic church which contains an apparently
miracle-working statue of the Virgin and Child. The statue is much
older than the church, probably twelfth century, and has been much
renovated since being rescued, in the fourteenth century, from the
castle moat into which it had been unceremoniously thrown by
heathen English soldiery. North-east of the town, around the D177
to St Hilaire du Harcouët, make time to visit the Forêt de Fougères,
a beautiful, chiefly beech, wood criss-crossed by paths, with dotted
menhirs and legends of Celtic Druids. An ideal spot for a picnic.

Combourg was the boyhood home of the writer Châteaubriand.
Not well known in English, in France, Châteaubriand is regarded as
a literary genius, though his sombre, melancholic style is not to all
tastes. His home, Château Combourg, is a centre for literary pilgrimage, but is worth a visit, especially to stand in the Cat's Tower — Tour
de Chat — and to contemplate what it must have been like as a
young, impressionable boy, to have spent each night alone in this
tower — the writer's father distributed his family all over the *château*
for reasons now obscure — when it was reputedly haunted by, of all
things, a previous owner's wooden leg that stamped about the cor-
ridors, pursued by a black cat.

Combourg itself is also worth a visit, if only for the view to it from across the reedy lake on its southern side, the chimneyed conical roofs of the castle rising, fairy-tale like, from the woods beside the grey-roofed houses.

South of Combourg, in **Tinténiac**, visit the Musée de l'Outil et de Métiers, the Museum of Tools and Crafts, in an old house called the Grain Store — Le Magasin à Grains — in the Quai de la Donac. This is a delightful collection of old crafts and agricultural implements, suggesting most strongly the similarities between the agricultural peasantries of Europe who wrestled with the same seasons and the same difficulties and probably little understood, or cared for, the reason their lords occasionally threw them into combat with each other. Tinténiac itself is a fine old town with a number of interesting buildings from the twelfth to the seventeenth centuries.

Rennes, Brittany's capital, tends to be off the beaten track to those, the majority, who find the prospect of driving into a town with a population of over 200,000 people, daunting. In practice if the visitor goes in August, when, it seems, France goes on holiday, the town is quiet, the parking easy, and the very fine, old town centre worth the effort. Start at the Palais de Justice, a fine seventeenth-century building, once the site of the Parliament of Brittany, that can be visited — worthwhile for the eighteenth-century Flemish tapestries — then go along Rue Brilhac, Rue Hermine and Rue du Gueslin to the Place St Sauveur. Here go left, then right in Place du Calvaire to Rue du Chapitre. Here is the very heart of the old town, and the only part of it to have escaped a huge fire in 1720 that virtually razed the town to the ground. Go right into Rue de La Psalette for the very best of the old town, an enchanting, narrow, large-cobbled street of timber-framed houses, each different enough from the next to give a modern town planner sleepless nights, yet in truth combining to a wonderful whole rarely achieved by modern, regulated building. About half way up the street open, cautiously, a large wooden door to the right. Inside is a truly delightful courtyard.

Following the road round brings the visitor to the cathedral, a recent, late eighteenth- early nineteenth-century, building that seems a little heavy for the area. By contrast the nearby Porte Mordelaise, the last remaining part of the fifteenth-century town wall, is beautifully proportioned, tall, but elegant, even delicate, with a fine arched doorway.

South of Rennes are some fine interesting sites. The Roche-aux-Fées, near Esse is, perhaps the most beautiful megalithic site in France, a wondrous construction of over forty huge rocks, some

Old Rennes

weighing 40 tons, whose name translates as 'Fairies' Rock', since there was a legend that it was built by fairies and that it was impossible to count the stones. By tradition a boy and girl who start out in opposite directions to walk around the monument, each counting the stones, will have a happy marriage if, when they meet, their tallies differ by less than two. Modern scholarship now believes that the monument was not a tomb, though its true purpose is not known.

Nearby, **La Guerche-de-Bretagne** is a fine medieval town, and an excellent centre for exploring the area of south-east Ille-et-Vilaine, much of which is quiet and little frequented. **Bain-de-Bretagne**, on the opposite side of the Roche-aux-Fées, can be used as a similar centre. It is less good as a town, though it is well sited by a lake, and just outside to the west, is the chapel of Le Coudroy containing a stone with a small hole, child's foot size, used as a healing stone for children with walking difficulties or foot ailments.

West again, at **St Just,** is the second biggest concentration of megalithic sites in Brittany — after Carnac — though the sites are not well signposted and not at all well documented. The casual visitor can just enjoy the exploration of this little visited area, while those keener to obtain information on the sites can ask the *curé* (priest) of the church of St Just, who is a mine of information.

Lastly go west of Rennes towards the border with Morbihan. At **Montfort,** visit the Ecomusée, the local history museum, if only to see a fiendish, and fiendishly clever, stone sling made from a split stick and called, for reasons obvious when you see it, '*le pied de cochon*', the 'pig's foot'.

South-west from Montfort is the Forêt de Broceliande, an area steeped in the Arthurian legends, a wild, mysterious woodland, worth every hour spent in it. It was to here not Glastonbury, so legend says, that Joseph of Arimathea brought the Holy Grail, and the forest is still haunted by the ghosts of Arthur, Guinevere and Lancelot. Each June the Arthurian legends form the basis of a local festival. Near the village of Tréhorenteuc is the Fountain of Barenton, a holy water fountain capable of curing mental disorders, and sacred to the Druids. Here too is the Val Sans Retour, the Valley of No Return, where Morgan le Fay held Merlin prisoner, and the Perron Merlin, a flat stone which summons thunder if water from the fountain is sprinkled on it. Mention of the Druids recalls that their presence here preceded the Arthurian legends — the forest has been a place of mystery for a long time. Periodically the modern French Druids — about as genuine as those that frequent Stonehenge on Midsummer's Day, ie, not very — pull out all the site marking signposts in an effort to keep the forest's secrets. If you arrive after such a raid, the forest really is off the beaten track.

Côtes-du-Nord

As the name implies, this *département* is dominated by its coastline which, though shorter than that of Finistère, seems to exert more of an influence over the area. At one time the *département* was divided in two by a language barrier, Breton-French, along a line running

A quiet inlet near Ploumanach on the north Brittany coast

almost straight, due south from St Brieuc. Today, with the pushing of the language westward, to its last stronghold in Finistère, this no longer applies. Instead there is another barrier, a north-south one dividing Armor, the land of the sea, from Argoat, the land of the forest. Even this barrier is artificial, though, the land of the forest having all but gone now, the pockets that remain being jealously, and rightly, guarded.

St Brieuc is the *département*'s capital and chief town, though it has no great merits for anyone seeking other than a modern city. There is an old quarter, though it is small, standing close to the cathedral, a building which resembles less a place of worship than a small village, all turrets and spires heaped, apparently haphazardly, on top of one another. The town is, however, a reasonable place from which to explore the fine coasts of the *département*. To the east are the Emerald Coast, shared with Ille-et-Vilaine, and the Penthièvre coast.

The Emerald Coast is beautifully named, and its delights are best sampled by choosing one of several excellent headlands which offer views to its incut bays. **Pointe du Chevet**, north of the pretty fishing village of **St Jacut-de-la-Mer** — famous not so much for its fish as a series of eleven excellent beaches in its immediate vicinity — has magnificent views, especially to the Ile des Hébihens, while Pointe de St Cast allows fine views eastward along the length of the coast itself. The village after which the headland is named, **St Cast**, is perhaps the most beautiful resort on the coast, with a backdrop of conifer forest and a foreground of sand. Less well known is the Baie de la Frênaye to the north, where sand gives way to a more rugged rock scenery, and views across to Fort-la-Latte.

Fort-la-Latte could not, in some senses, be claimed as being off the beaten track, and yet there are many who have seen pictures of it and have never visited it. It is not easy to reach, demanding a walk of around $1^1/_2$km (1 mile) but is well worth the effort. It was started in the ninth century, though what the visitor sees today is several centuries later, the archetypal castle set on a headland about 60m (200ft) above a savage sea, protected by a couple of impressive ravines.

The view from the castle is excellent and no less impressive is that from nearby **Cap Fréhel** where the cliff is higher, around 70m (230ft). On rare days the Cherbourg peninsula can be seen. The headland is a renowned seabird nesting site, but was once famous for an entirely different reason with St Malo's sailors. Once they had rounded the Cap, their wedding vows were suspended! Cap Fréhel is at one end of the Penthièvre Coast, the next fine headland of which is **Cap d'Erquy**, named after a delightful fishing village, famous for its scallops, known here as *coquilles St Jacques*. Inland a little, the Château Bien Assis is less well known than Fort-la-Latte, but is of interest for being one of the last castles built in France, sections dating from as late as the seventeenth century.

North of St Brieuc is the Côte du Goelo, with a seemingly never-ending line of very fine beaches, many with a little village attached. **Binic**, close to St Brieuc, is a busy little place, and **Brehec** is a little difficult to find down some minor roads, but is beautifully set between high cliffs. Legend has it that it was here that the first settlers or refugees from Britain landed in Brittany. Inland, go to **Kermanic-an-Iskuit** where the chapel has a tremendously vibrant fifteenth-century fresco of the *Dance of Death*, skeletons being shown dancing with all classes from kings to ploughmen, to emphasise death's levelling nature.

A little north of Brehec is the Abbaye de Beauport, one of the most romantically sited abbey ruins in the whole province. On the drive north you pass a large, pleasant lake to the left, studded with rich, elegant houses. To the right, the view opens out across a green valley to the sea and then, suddenly, there is the abbey ruin. What survives is thirteenth century.

Beyond the abbey is **Paimpol**, a pleasant fishing/holiday village to the north of which, beyond Pointe de l'Arcouest is the **Ile de Bréhat** reached in a 10-minute ferry ride from the point. The island is traffic-free, a haven for trees, shrubs, flowers and birdlife. The northern coast is a fine jumble of granite boulders tinged with the pink that gives this new section of the coast its name, the Côte de Granit Rose, the pink granite coast. There is a fine old fishing village and a very worthwhile air of calm.

Over the estuary to the west of Paimpol and then north, the **Sillon de Talbert** is worth seeing, a long (3km, 2 miles) and very narrow (only 30m, 100ft) spit of shingle, that extends in a long sweep out into the sea. The spit is covered in salt-tolerant plants and is used for the collection of seaweed on a commercial basis. To the south is **Tréguier**, the town famous for its soaring 'pink' granite cathedral. If it is sunny go inside to see the coloured patterns drawn by the stained glass on the stone slab floor. Look, too, for the statue of St Yves between a rich and a poor man. This most beloved of all Breton saints and the patron saint of lawyers was asked, or so it is said, by a rich man to adjudicate on a case he had brought against a poor man, claiming that his impoverished neighbour was living by inhaling the smells from his kitchen! St Yves found in the rich man's favour ordering, in payment, the sound of a coin rattling in a tin.

St Gonery chapel

North from Tréguier is one of the great delights of the area, indeed of Brittany, the little chapel with the corkscrew spire, at **St Gonery**. St Gonery, a Celtic monk, built the earliest part of the building in the eighth or ninth century. That part now contains a stone trough, not the monk's coffin, but a ballast trough from his ship, used on the voyage to hold the cooking fire. The monk's skull is also preserved in a glass case that sits on a sedan chair-like structure which is used to carry it in procession! But the real joy is the art work — the superb creatures carved on the roof beams so that the beams seen to come from their mouths and the equally good friezes with legendary animals carved with that great Celtic flare for savage mystery. Best of all is the frescoed ceiling of the main chapel. The paintings are of both the Old and New Testaments, the old following the Creation, Adam and Eve, and Cane and Abel. Originally the figures were nude, but at some stage this lack of propriety was catered for by the addition of robes. The New Testament scenes include an explicit Slaughter of the Innocents. The whole ceiling has a wonderful vibrancy and an uncompromising realism. It is well set off by a later, framed painting, a Deposition of moving sadness. All in all a most remarkable building.

Beyond the chapel, the shore is a chaos of fine granite boulders, at the **Pointe de Château**, but also has some good stretches of sand — a fine, unfrequented spot. Its more famous near neighbour, the Chaos Rocheaux, near Trégastel, is better, but more popular. North

Abbaye de la Grande Trappe, near Bresolettes, Normandy

Château de Crèvecoeur-en-Auge, Normandy

of it, the group of islands — Les Sept Iles — must be visited (by boat from Perros-Guirec) by all birdwatchers, being one of the most important bird sites in the whole of France. Here there are all members of the auk family, besides many gulls and petrels, and the mysterious cormorants, in undertaker's black, their wings held stiffly out as though to encircle the living. The reserve suffered badly in the wake of the *Torrey Canyon* and *Amoco Cadiz* tanker disasters, but is, thankfully, recovering.

Now go inland, south of Lannion, to the Argoat proper, where there is a small knot of castles. The ruins of Tonquédec are set in woodland in the valley of the Léguer, a beautifully evocative building, walls fully 4m (13ft) thick. A still passable circular stairway leads to the battlements and superb views. Coatfrec is even more hidden, half-lost among ivy and shrubs. It lies, almost never visited, in the same Léguer valley, but closer to Lannion. Last is Kergrist, not a medieval castle, but a later, fortified, manor. Between the castles of Coatfrec and Tonquédec is the chapel of Kerfons, a fine fifteenth-century building with a marvellously carved rood screen and some very good sixteenth-century stained glass.

Travelling south it is possible to follow the Léguer valley most of the way to **Belle-Isle-en-Terre**, a nicely situated, though curiously named town. From here almost any trip into the Argoat is worthwhile, but especially the one to **Loc-Envel**, a very pretty little village set between two fine woods, the Coat an Noz and the Coat an Hay, the Night Wood and the Day Wood. This oddity is probably Druidic in origin: twins of any kind held a special fascination for the Druids. The woods are excellent for walks and picnics, an interesting view back in time to when most of this area of Brittany really was the Argoat, the land of the forest.

An even better village, one less well known though less well sited, is **Bulat-Pestivien,** just beyond the high ridge which is a continuation of Finistère's mountain backbone. The village is a real gem, with, at its heart, a large church with a 66m (220ft) spire, the tallest in Brittany. In the vicinity there are three sacred fountains, a clear link with ancient times. Those holidaying late could attend the impressive *pardon* held here on the Sunday following 7 September.

South again, pick up the River Blavet , as picturesque here as it is in Ille-et-Vilaine. Near Kergrist it flows through the Chaos, or Gorge de Toul-Goulic, or, rather, it flows under it because for around 400m (440yd) the river is underground and can be heard thundering along below the boulder-strewn valley floor. Some of the boulders are huge, and may even have served as shelters for Stone Age man: they

Dinan

are also beautifully moss-covered. To the west, the Gorge du Coronc, about 3km (2 miles), north of Locarn is more off the beaten track, but not quite so spectacular. The Gorge de Toul-Goulic is passed by GR341, and this pathway now hugs the Blavet fairly close as it heads towards the Lac de Guerlédan, Brittany's largest lake, a man-made reservoir for a hydro-power station. Close to the lake, GR341 crosses to the River Daoulas and traverses the Gorges du Daoulas where the river has bitten deep into the rock, forming a narrow, steep gash which is alive with plant life even though it is shadowed. To the east, near **Mur-de-Bretagne**, a fine town, the Gorges de Poulancre are equally good. Also near the town there is an interesting, well signed route that hugs the water of Lac de Guerlédan around its 48km (30 mile) shoreline. That is a long way to walk with a similar — even though everchanging in aspect — view, but a section of it is very rewarding.

Northwards the two towns of **Quintin** and **Guingamp** are worth visting. The former is prettily set with remains of the old town walls, the lower part of a never completed seventeenth-century castle and some fine timber-framed houses from the sixteenth and seventeenth centuries. Guingamp is now bypassed by a good road, and so has become little frequented, but it too is a fine town, with the ruins of old fortifications and fine sixteenth-century half-timbered houses.

Eastward, **Moncontour** is another fine, but thankfully largely neglected town, and to the south Mont Bel-Air is Côtes-du-Nord's highest mountain — at 340m (1,105ft) — with a correspondingly expansive view. It is a good spot, a little spoiled by the transmitter masts, shared by a recently built chapel approached by eight beech tree-bordered walks. These, apparently, represent the rays of the sun, the site formerly being dedicated to the pagan Celtic sun-god.

North-east, beyond Lamballe, in the Forêt de la Hunaudaie, a fine spot enclosing the impressive ruins of the huge Château de la Hunaudaie. The ruins, overgrown by greenery in most romantic style, date from the fourteenth century, and prove the point that many English folly builders were trying to make, that a good, well sized ruin is a good deal more picturesque than a shiny new building.

Lastly, head south of Dinan to the area around **Caulnes**, itself a very pleasant country market town. To the east of the town is a string of very pretty villages, each well set and with its own interest. Several have the remains of old castles or fortified manor houses to add to their attractiveness. No one place stands out, so just motor quietly eastward from Caulnes, on the D25 to Guitté, passing the Châteaux de Couëlan and Beaumont. Then on across the Roplémol lake to Guenroc and St Maden, and along the D39 to Tréfumel and Le Quiou with the Château le Hac. Those interested in fossils should note that these last two villages lie close to limestone outcrops rich in fossils from the Tertiary Era.

Further Information
── Brittany ──

Museums and Other Places of Interest

FINISTERE

Plogonnec
Auberge de Leurbiriou
On the road from Plogonnec to Douar-

nenez, 2km (1¹/₄ miles) from Plogonnec.

Botforn en Combrit
Museum of Mechanical Music
On the road from Pont-l'Abbé to Bénodet
Open: daily 5-7pm.

MORBIHAN

Ile de Groix
Ecomuseum and Waymarked Trails
Museum Open: daily except Monday
mid-June to mid-September 10am-
12.30pm and 2-5pm.
Waymarked Trails Open: daily mid-
June to mid-September 9.30am-
12.30pm and 3-7pm.

Josselin
Doll's Museum at Josselin Castle
Open: daily except Monday May-Sep-
tember 10am-12noon, 1-6pm;
Wednesday, Saturday, Sunday and
holidays March, April, October, early
November 2-6pm.

Largoët
Fortress
(The Towers of Elven)
Open: daily March-mid-November
9am-6pm.

ILLE-ET-VILAINE

St Malo
Castle Museum
Open: daily Easter-mid-September
9am-12noon, 2-5.45pm.

Doll's Museum
Open: daily 10am-12noon, 2pm-7pm.

Antrain-sur-Couesnon
Château de Bonne-Fontaine
Park open in summer months 2pm-
6pm.

Combourg
Château de Combourg
Open: daily except Tuesday, Easter-
September 2-6pm.

Tintinéac
Museum of Tools and Crafts

Open: daily except Monday July-September 10am-12noon, 2.30-7pm.
Open on request October-June.

Montfort
Local History Museum,
Open: daily except Monday July-September 10am-12noon, 2-6pm Tuesday-Saturday 2-6pm Sunday; daily
except Monday and Saturday October-
June 2-6pm.

COTES DU NORD

Near **Matignon**
Fort-la-Latte
Open: daily June-September 10am-
12.30pm, 2.30-6.30pm.

Near **Paimpol**
Beauport Abbey
Open: all year round, 9am-12.15pm,
2-7pm. Daily.

Near **Lamballe**
Château de la Hunaudaie
Open: daily July-August 10am-1pm,
3-7pm. Easter-June, September
Sundays, holidays only 3-7pm.

Tourist Information Offices

Finistère
Comité Départemental du Tourisme
　　du Finistère
34 Rue de Douarnenez
BP 125
29104 Quimper
☎ (98) 537272

Morbihan
Comité Départemental du Tourisme
　　du Morbihan
Hôtel du Département
BP400

56009 Vannes
☎ (97) 540656

Ille-et-Vilaine
Comité Départemental du Tourisme
  d'Ille-et-Vilaine
1 Rue Martenot
35000 Rennes
☎ (99) 029743

Côtes-du-Nord
Comité Départemental du Tourisme
  du Côtes-du-Nord
1 Rue Châteaubriand
BP 620
22011 St-Brieuc
☎ (96) 616670

3 • Alsace et Lorraine

Despite anything the history books may say, one does not, these days, refer to Alsace-Lorraine — it is the quickest way to become thoroughly unpopular. Alsace et Lorraine or Alsace Vosges Lorraine are two acceptable alternatives. The reason is quite simple. In 1871 Alsace and a large part of Lorraine were acquired by Germany under the Treaty of Frankfurt and the new area, known as Alsace-Lorraine, was only restored to France in 1919. Both Alsace and Lorraine found themselves back in German hands in 1940, to be liberated for the second time 5 years later at the end of the war in Europe.

Even before they suffered these shared misfortunes the two had a great deal in common. They were each inhabited by the Celts, taken over by the Romans, devastated by the Huns and had their full share of war and pestilence during the Middle Ages before eventually being united with France. Their contributions to French history were many and varied. For instance, Joan of Arc was born in Lorraine, the *Battle Hymn of the Army of the Rhine*, composed in Strasbourg by Rouget de Lisle, is much better known as the *Marseillaise* and the famous Cross of Lorraine became the emblem of the Free French under General de Gaulle. Albert Schweitzer was a native of Alsace and in 1885 a small boy from the Villé area was the first person to be saved by Louis Pasteur with his newly-discovered anti-rabies vaccine.

Geographically, the regions also complement each other. They lie side by side in the north-eastern corner of France, stretching from Luxembourg to Switzerland with Alsace facing Germany across the Rhine. Rivers and canals abound in the area, ranging from the Meuse and the Moselle to the Grand Canal d'Alsace which marches with the Rhine and is wider than either the Suez Canal or the Panama Canal. The Vosges mountains, although not in the same league as the Alps, have some spectacular scenic routes snaking their way up through forests of variegated pines to wooded peaks and deep blue lakes gouged out by the glaciers of a bygone age. In summer this area offers

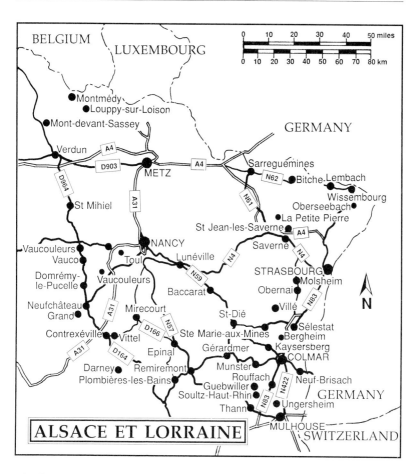

ideal conditions for walking, climbing, riding, fishing, boating and swimming, turning its attention to winter sports when the cold weather sets in. Warm springs, particularly in the south-west, have produced a number of fashionable spas, some with a whole range of tourist attractions thrown in for good measure.

Inspite of its extensive national parks Lorraine has rather more industrial areas then its neighbour, particularly round the northern plateau in the vicinity of Metz and Nancy, leaving Alsace to concentrate on wine. Vineyards cover the hillsides from Marlenheim, west of Strasbourg, to Thann 120km (75 miles) to the south, with a special Route du Vin, duly signposted, which calls in at picturesque villages and historic towns along the way. There is also a Flower Route across the plains and, for anyone with a tendency to get lost in unfamiliar country, plaques mark the many deviations along the Road of For-

tified Castles in the far north-east. Added to all this are a Green Road
with views across to the Black Forest, a mountain circuit known as
the Route des Crêtes, a Cheese Road liberally sprinkled with inns
specialising in local dishes and even a complex of little roads rejoic-
ing in the overall title of the Routes of the Fried Carp which is self-
explanatory.

There are many different ways of getting to Alsace et Lorraine.
Apart from the international airport at Strasbourg, several towns
such as Colmar, Metz, Mulhouse and Nancy are connected by air
with other parts of the country. Frequent train services run from
Paris and the Channel ports as well as from the Benelux countries,
Germany and Switzerland, with the added advantage of motorail
facilities that operate to and from Strasbourg, Nancy, Metz and
Mulhouse. France has very few long-distance buses but coach
companies organise tours in and around the main centres, comple-
menting the boats that take sightseers for jaunts up and down the
rivers and round the lake at Gérardmer. Local bus services are
excellent, cars can be hired in the major centres and bicycles are
available at quite a few of the larger railway stations.

Motorists have an even wider choice. Visitors whose time is
limited might well opt for the *autoroute* from Paris through Reims to
Metz and from there either southwards, northwards or on to Strasbourg. Other alternatives would be the main route from Brussels
through Metz and Nancy to the Vosges, from Germany through
Saarbrücken or from Switzerland across the border to Mulhouse.
Major roads link all the main towns such as Epinal, St Dié, Haguenau
and Verdun while a wealth of secondary roads wander peacefully
through the countryside, providing access to any number of interesting towns and villages. There are *châteaux* and ruined castles,
churches both impressive and otherwise, museums, battlefields
with trenches from World War I and a Nazi concentration camp of
much more recent vintage for anyone whose primary interest is
history. On the sporting side every second hamlet appears to have its
own individual pathways, usually covering about 25km(15 miles),
clearly marked through fields of flowers, along the banks of mountain streams, past waterfalls or into the shade of nearby forests. Some
of the larger places run excursions up into the mountains, others
offer hunting or fishing, riding or water sports but tennis and golf are
not so easy to find. Almost without exception there is a small *auberge*
or *logis*, possibly with a modest room or two in addition to its own
selection of local dishes.

Some Alsatians insist that the reason the Romans stayed so long was that they enjoyed the cooking. It seems a bit far-fetched but there is no doubt that Brillat-Savarin described it as the most mouth-watering region in Europe and that *brioche* with *foie gras* became a popular hors d'oeuvres at the Russian court. Amongst a whole host of dishes which should not be missed are *baeckaoffe*, a concoction of beef, lamb and pork marinated in Reisling and cooked with onions and potatoes; *matelote de poissons*, which contains several different fish in a Reisling sauce, pheasant with grapes and sauerkraut, fried carp, venison, perch with almonds and any of the many varieties of tart, usually filled with Munster cheese, onions or fruit. Local beer is very popular and so are wines like Tokay and Gewürtztraminer. Eaux-de-vie come in well over a dozen different flavours from the familiar raspberry, pear and black cherry to more surprising things like holly. Anyone in search of souvenirs should keep an eye open for *fois gras* in earthenware pots, Vosges honey, porcelain, glass, pewter, copperware and linen and cotton materials which have been selling like hot cakes for hundreds of years.

The people of Alsace et Lorraine are great ones for *fêtes* and festivals and hardly a week goes by without someone, somewhere, celebrating something. The main centres like Strasbourg do things in style with events of the calibre of the International Music Festival in June. Flowers and folklore predominate nearly everywhere. Gérard-mer is smothered in daffodils for the Fête des Jonquilles in April, Neuf-Brisach prefers lily-of-the-valley in May, followed by Saverne with its Festival of the Rose, while Sélestat, like a number of other places, gets August off to a colourful start with a Carnival of Flowers. Regional costumes are a feature of the Fête du Mariage de l'Ami Fritz in Marlenheim, strolling fiddlers have their own day at Ribeauvillé, firework displays are a midsummer attraction in the mountains and Thann is not nearly as bloodthirsty as its Cremation of the Three Fir Trees would suggest. Both wine and beer provide ample excuses for celebrations as do such items as *sauerkraut, paté-en-croûte* and *quiche Lorraine*. December is marked by dozens of Christmas festivities, many of them dedicated to St Nicolas, and by the Fête de Ste Odile, who is the patron saint of Alsace and has a special mountain named after her. Myths and legends are accepted as a matter of course, whether they are miracles with religious connections and therefore much venerated or diabolical manifestations brought about by the odd giant or by witches and sorcerers, some of whom have whole towers to themselves.

Exploring Alsace et Lorraine is both easy and very enjoyable, whether you follow one of the popular routes or branch off down any of the hundreds of side turnings that can, but very seldom do, degenerate into cart tracks. Finding a hotel is just as simple except in the main tourist resorts at the height of the season. Obviously Strasbourg, home of the Council of Europe and the Court of Human Rights, has a vast number of hotels and restaurants of every description while Metz, Nancy and Mulhouse can offer much the same variety but with fewer to choose from, especially in the upper income brackets. Even quite small towns with only a modest *auberge* or two can provide high quality food at reasonable prices and will often run to rooms with private bathrooms, although swimming pools and tennis courts are the exception rather than the rule. Camping sites are a different matter. Some are fairly basic but the more up-market ones include a whole range of attractions such as tennis and volley-ball, riding, swimming, boating, windsurfing, bowls and pedalos for hire, either on the premises or in the immediate vicinity. It is even possible to find a winter site if your caravan is designed for low temperatures. It is as well to remember that the winters here can be as cold as anywhere in France apart from the Alps but spring and autumn are pleasantly invigorating and summer, give or take a short spell in August, is seldom uncomfortably hot. Tourist offices in the larger towns and main holiday resorts will often help in finding furnished accommodation but this is somewhat thinner on the ground than one might expect.

Motorists heading for Lorraine along the Paris *autoroute* cross the Meuse just south of **Verdun**, a town whose martial history goes back to Roman times. It is a fairly war-orientated area altogether. The countryside around positively bristles with forts, cemeteries, memorials and monuments pinpointing the various battlefields. Students of World War I should find it extremely interesting, particularly as the Fort de Vaux, the Fort de Douaumont, the enormous and vaguely Egyptian-looking Ossuaire de Douaumont and the Memorial Museum full of documents, uniforms, arms and equipment, are all open to visitors.

The town itself looks back a good deal further with places like the citadel, built by Vauban on the site of an ancient monastery. A twelfth-century tower is all that remains of the Abbaye de St Vanne but to one side of it, below ground level, the seemingly endless rooms and passages that originally sheltered troops in the reign of Louis XV are carefully preserved. The cathedral of Notre-Dame was rebuilt after a fire in 1048, the cloister was added a touch later to be followed in the eighteenth century by the Palais Episcopal. The Hôtel de la Princerie was a private house in the Middle Ages but is now the home of a comprehensive museum with exhibits spanning more than two thousand years. The River Meuse and its attendant canals flow through the town past a leisure park and a couple of very comfortable hotels.

A day spent touring the valley of the Meuse presents a slightly different picture depending on which direction you decide to take. To the north are such places as **Mont-devant-Sassey** where there is a nice old church, **Montmédy** whose ancient hilltop village is isolated behind ramparts enclosed in trees, and **Louppy-sur-Loison**, known for its sixteenth-century *château* which lays on guided tours each afternoon throughout the season but puts up the shutters on Mondays and during the rest of the year. To the south, almost surrounded by the Meuse and the Moselle, is the National Park of Lorraine, a delightfully wooded area full of ponds, some of which are distinctly marshy, little villages of varying attraction and the Lac de Madine complete with a holiday atmosphere and a monument to the men of the American 1st Army who died there in September 1918. **St Mihiel**, on the Meuse to the west, has successfully preserved some outstanding sixteenth-century sculptures by Ligier Richier in its two ancient churches inspite of all the fighting that went on thereabouts. Opinions are divided as to which is the most emotive but the experts tend to give a slight edge to the sepulchre in the Eglise St Etienne as far as intricate workmanship is concerned.

Metz, on a direct line from Verdun, has been a city of considerable importance from the time it was founded to the present day. It has a busy airport, the main *autoroutes* go either through or round it, and commerce flourishes, as does the university established in 1972. Inspite of all this it also holds plenty of attractions for visitors as well as being a convenient centre from which to explore the surrounding area. In the first place there are something like fifty churches, starting with the impressive cathedral of St Etienne. It began life as two separate chapels back in the twelfth century, was added to every hundred years or so, given extra towers and some magnificent stained glass windows and even managed to preserve some of its treasures during the Revolution. These can be seen in the Grande Sacristie almost any afternoon except on religious holidays. Considerably smaller than the cathedral, but none the worse for that, are the church of St Pierre-aux-Nonnains, once part of a seventh-century monastery then incorporated into the fortifications and eventually returned to its original function, and the Chapelle des Templiers almost next door. They share the large, well shaded Esplanade with a much-decorated Palais de Justice and the Lac des Cygnes beyond which a footbridge crosses a narrow arm of the Moselle.

It is only a short walk from the Esplanade to the Place St-Louis, the centre of the old town with its historic houses and attractive arcades where money-changers used to carry on a thriving trade. About the same distance further on is the definitely warlike Porte des Allemands, a splendid mixture of battlements and towers guarding either end of a heavily-fortified bridge. Sorcery is the name of the game on one bank while the towers opposite look like matching pepperpots complete with witches' hats. The Museum of Art and History is another place worth visiting. The building itself is old enough to have the remains of some Roman baths in the basement from where it wends its way up through the Middle Ages to sections devoted to artisan workshops, Napoleonic uniforms, natural history and contemporary art. Opera lovers are catered for by the theatre in the Place de la Comédie, there are concerts of ancient music, the Trinitaires concentrates on jazz and there is a special centre looking into the kind of sounds we can expect to hear in years to come.

Sightseers who prefer to collect ruins by the dozen rather than one at a time should head straight on, due east, to **Sarreguemines** and the Parc Naturel Régional des Vosges du Nord. This can be done along the *autoroute*, branching off just before it makes a final spurt into Germany. A slower way is to select any of the minor roads across the countryside, avoiding industrial centres in favour of agricultural landscapes, clumps of trees, tiny lakes and ponds and villages that have no pretensions when it comes to a place in a tourist guide. Even Sarreguemines is a fairly uninteresting frontier town, or it would be but for the fact that it has a formidable reputation for producing ceramics and has set up a small museum full of pottery and china which is open daily except on Mondays and public holidays.

A reasonably fast road leads on to **Bitche** where the dour and extremely workmanlike citadel built by Vauban in 1679 overshadows everything else. It battled determinedly against invasion during the Franco-Prussian War but with no more success than the nearby Fort du Simserhof achieved 70 years later when it was one of the most important sections of the ill-fated Maginot Line. A limited number of tours of Simserhof are arranged every month, with the exception of July and August, but visitors who want to join one of them must apply in writing to the military authorities in Metz. Of course this takes time so it means planning the trip well in advance.

These days the Parc Naturel Régional des Vosges du Nord is not bothered by frontiers as such and is all of a piece with the Naturpark Pfalzerwald, its German counterpart across the border. But there is no need to venture quite so far in search of ruined *châteaux* and medieval fortifications which, more often than not, turn out to be much the same thing. The hills round about are peppered with the remains of a dozen or more, some of which have received a certain amount of attention while others consist of little apart from a few mouldering walls hidden from sight in the trees. Avid inspectors of ruins can almost castle-hop their way through, parking the car on each occasion (and remembering to lock them up — there are notices everywhere to remind visitors about this), and trudging along well-worn paths for up to half an hour or so to inspect these weathered piles of ancient stones. People who are more discerning, less energetic, or perhaps both, make their own selection beforehand and ignore all the other tempting signs along the roadside. Such a list might well include the Château de Falkenstein, founded on a hilltop in 1128. It was considerably battered during the next few centuries and eventually left to its own devices. However it is a good place to clamber about and anyone who dislikes heights can spend the time inspecting a variety of caves, both natural and man-made, in the rock below. The impressive thirteenth-century Château de Fleckenstein, hard by the German border, has been undergoing restoration work since 1968. As a result it has a small museum and a refreshment bar among its other attractions and is open from the beginning of March to the end of November. The Château de Hohenbourg, with the remains of a keep and some Renaissance sculptures, is not really in the same class but it is conveniently placed for anyone who wants to take the tiny twisting road down to Climbach and on through the Col de Pigeonnier to Wissembourg.

Wissembourg is an attractive little town that has been extremely warlike in its time, even giving its name to a battle fought near there in 1870. It has preserved some delightful old houses and a church, said to be the largest in Alsace apart from Strasbourg cathedral, whose statues had their heads cut off during the Revolution. It was built in the thirteenth century on the site of an old monastery and an even older pagan temple and, although dedicated to St Peter and St Paul, manages to find space for St Christopher as well. It is pleasant to wander round the old quarter and visit the Westercamp Museum which concerns itself with early history, furniture, traditional costumes and the Franco-Prussian War. There are a number of small hotels and restaurants in the town which are reasonably priced and the local sporting activities include hunting and fishing, a swimming pool and several country walks. During Whitsun everyone turns out for the annual festival, celebrated with songs and dances, horse shows, processions and plenty of food and wine.

An interesting route back, provided one enjoys taking the smaller, less frequented roads whenever feasible, would be through **Cleebourg**, a picturesque hamlet which owns both a vineyard and a wine cellar and **Lembach** with its almost-attendant lake and the doubtful distinction of being close to the Maginot Line. It lays on guided tours of part of the defences during July and August, even working through the lunch hour when it is necessary. Alternatively there is the Route des Villages Pittoresques linking such enchanting hamlets as **Oberseebach** and **Hunspach**. They are chock full of typical Alsation half-timbered houses some with great bridal bouquets of flowers cascading from every ledge and windowsill, gardens which are a riot of colour and even roundabouts that have been turned into floral masterpieces. Although the area is known for its traditional costumes they are rarely seen except at festivals, people going about their everyday business wear exactly the same sort of clothes as their counterparts anywhere else.

Niederbronn-les-Bains, to the south-west, is a spa, popular with local people and with historic connections. It was founded by the Romans, who made a point of installing themselves as closely as possible to any health-giving spring, but suffered badly at the hands of the Barbarians some 400 years later. After that nothing much happened until Count Philippe de Hanau took a liking to the place in the sixteenth century and set about putting the baths back into working order. They have prospered ever since, adding various attractions from time to time such as shooting, fishing, tennis, swimming, a casino and, more recently, naturism.

The Parc Naturel Régional des Vosges du Nord has something for everyone. It supports both agriculture and forestry, trains local craftsmen and tempts visitors to explore both on horseback and on foot. Numbered among its lakes is the Etang de Baerenthal, an especially good place for anyone interested in birdwatching. In addition, the local Poney [*sic*] Ranch du Dachsthal arranges riding trips into the forest, fishing is encouraged in the rivers and ponds thereabouts on payment of the usual fee and the Club Vosgien will assist hikers with all the information they need. Two municipal camping sites are provided along with bathing, picnic spots and pedalos for hire. By way of contrast one can visit the Château de Lichtenberg, considerably restored and open daily from April to October, or **Meisenthal** which has specialised in glass-making for around 200 years and has painstakingly gathered together sufficient examples to fill a small museum.

La Petite-Pierre, a fortified village further to the south-west, has a sixteenth-century castle and is very proud of its game park and hunting reserve. An added advantage is that it is only a short distance from **St Jean-les-Saverne**, known chiefly for its flowers and a round platform called L'Ecole des Sorcières where, according to legend, witches congregate at night. Apparently they move on later to a cave they have appropriated under the Chapelle St Michel which was originally intended as a sepulchre. **Saverne** itself, which straddles the Canal de la Marne au Rhin, has a splendid *château* all set about with columns, sculptures and balustrades. Its visitors have included kings and cardinals as well as army personnel who used it as a barracks for nearly 100 years. There is also an older *château* plus some attractive houses, a church and a small museum. However, for horticulturists the high spots must be the Rose Garden with its 1,300 different varieties and the Jardin Botanique just outside the town.

The usual choice between highways and byways confronts the motorist heading for Nancy. The quickest way is more or less straight and not very scenic whereas there are plenty of trees and streams, the odd lake and places to stop for an *al fresco* meal on the back roads to **Baccarat**. Here, visitors can look round the modern church and the attractive Musée du Cristal, displaying the types of glass made in the village since 1764. The next stop might well be **Lunéville** where the *château*, a modest replica of Versailles, puts on a Son et Lumière le Grand Carrousel on Friday, Saturday and Sunday evenings during the summer. Daytime attractions include a visit to the *château* where the museum has a charming collection of figurines and the Musée de la Moto et du Vélo with its fascinating display of bicycles and motorcycles built before 1939. A *château* just outside the town provides an excellent, if rather expensive, menu and may even have a room available if one thinks to book in advance. **St Nicolas-de-Port** has a very viewable church and, if you are in the market for another *château,* a guided tour through the semi-regal apartments of the Château de Fléville, on the outskirts of Nancy, takes rather less than an hour.

Of course it would be much quicker to drive straight from Metz to **Nancy**, a distance of 56km (35 miles) along the *autoroute*. Although definitely on the beaten track, especially for continental visitors, its attractions are so numerous and so varied that one would miss a great deal by simply driving past. It has just as much history as Metz but fewer churches, more museums, botanical gardens and a large park including a zoo and a sports stadium roughly 2 minutes' walk from the famous Place Stanislas. There are just as many shops, hotels and restaurants, the Ballet Theatre has a repertoire ranging from Diaghilev to Moses Pendleton, both rock and ancient music are popular as are the traditional performances at the Opera House. Other attractions include a handful of heated swimming pools, an 18-hole golf course a short distance from the town, a racecourse, riding stables and an extensive forest where people are made extremely welcome but vehicles, on the whole, are not. With so many things to see in Nancy it is fortunate that most of them are to be found in a relatively small area in the centre of the town. The obvious place to start is the Place Stanislas which is large, ornate and positively glistens with gold paint from one end to the other. The best idea is to park the car in the nearest available space and wander round on foot past highly ornamental gates, busy fountains, statues and the eighteenth-century Hôtel de Ville. The Arc de Triomphe, built at about the same time in honour of Louis XV, is very similar to the one in Rome. It faces the old residence of the Governors of Lorraine down a wide avenue known as the Place de la Carrière which has exactly the same atmosphere. A little to one side is the Ducal Palace, an elegant building spanning several centuries and flaunting most of them to good effect. Antoine of Lorraine, looking very purposeful on a splendid charger, occupies the niche of honour over the main door while inside is an exceptionally varied and interesting museum.

At this stage it saves a great deal of energy and shoe leather if one hires a horsedrawn vehicle for a tour of the old town. It takes in churches like the Eglise et Couvent des Cordeliers, so called inspite of the fact that the cloister is all that remains of the ancient monastery, and the Porte de la Craffe which has served as both a prison and a fort. Other museums worthy of note are the School Museum founded by Emile Gallé at the turn of the century, the Musée des Beaux Arts, the Zoological Museum with its tropical aquarium and, slightly further afield, a museum devoted to the history of iron. On the face of it this hardly sounds like an outstanding holiday attraction but once inside its fascination becomes apparent. Most men gravitate to the machine section where an early narrow-gauge steam engine attracts the biggest crowds. Anyone interested in glass should make a point of touring the Daum Crystal Works in the Rue des Cristalleries between the river and the Canal de la Marne au Rhin. It is interesting to watch the experts in action, which visitors can do each weekday morning and all day Saturday as well.

Anyone with an afternoon to spare and an interest in musical instruments would find a visit to Mirecourt very rewarding, especially if it includes a slight deviation to **Sion**, known not so much for its church and small museum as for the view. There is a hotel close to the summit where cars can be parked while their owners complete the journey on foot. From here a scenic route runs along the Corniche Gaston Canel, past the monument Barrès to Vaudémont, followed by an easy run to **Mirecourt**. The town is associated with lace and embroidery but its main claim to fame lies in the manufacture of musical instruments. The initiated will recognise names like Cognier and Terrier in connection with violas and violins, Pagès for guitars and Gérome for mandolins. The local museum traces the history of this highly specialised art and it is possible to visit factories where instruments are still being made. Any members of the party who are tone deaf or simply disinterested can wander through the arcades of the seventeenth-century market place, look round the church any time except on Sunday afternoons or visit the Chapelle de la Oultre by simply asking permission from the custodian who lives almost on the premises.

If neither glass nor musical instruments appeal to you an alternative would be to drive straight from Nancy to **Toul**, 23km (14 miles) away along the *autoroute*. The road bisects the forest, passing Parc de Haye with its two museums, one devoted to aircraft and the other specialising in cars. Their opening hours have not been synchronised particularly well. The former can be visited on Saturday and Sunday afternoons from January until August whereas the latter opens on Wednesday afternoons as well but is closed from the middle of November to the beginning of March. Toul is a town with considerable military connections in addition to the church of St Gengoult with its somewhat flamboyant cloister, an ancient cathedral and several delightful houses, the whole lot almost completely surrounded by walls and water. It has nothing very inviting in the way of hotels and restaurants but one can get a bed for the night and something to eat next door as well as swimming and skating in the town.

A major road of no particular interest connects Toul with **Vaucouleurs**, the starting point of Joan of Arc's mission to save France. A small church has been built over the thirteenth-century crypt, once part of the *château* which, itself, has all but disappeared. However, the old archway through which she led her troops is still standing. Much of the excavation work was done by Henri Bataille who makes a point of showing people round, explaining the layout which is largely below ground and inviting them to inspect his private, miniscule museum. He has a very soft spot for the English who, he says, donated enough money for him to buy and restore an ancient tower in the town. The somewhat larger museum further down the hill pays tribute to Joan of Arc and also makes mention of Madame du Barry, a local girl whose subsequent achievements, although less heroic, assured her of a place in French history. As Louis XV's mistress she exercised considerable political power while he was alive but paid for it on the guillotine in December 1793.

These days, when 20km (12 miles) or so is neither here nor there, Joan of Arc would probably be regarded as another local resident. She was born in 1412 at **Domrémy-la-Pucelle**, a village which would doubtless have remained completely unknown if she had stuck to her spinning and ignored the voices she heard in the Chenu Woods. As it was, she went off to identify the Dauphin, pit her wits against the English, stand trial for heresy and witchcraft and die in the market place at Rouen, all before she was 20 years old. It is no small wonder that the family home, a typical peasant's cottage with a sloping roof, bare walls and absolutely nothing inside, received the constant attention it needed to prevent it falling down ages ago. A small museum and the village church where she was baptised are the only other places of interest apart from the basilica, built on a hillside at the edge of the Chenu Woods, decorated in part with the story of her life and consecrated in 1926, less than a decade after she was canonised in Rome.

Neufchâteau, reached by road but bypassed along a winding footpath through the woods, had early Roman connections. Fortifications were added during the Middle Ages but all trace of them was eliminated on the orders of Richelieu who made a habit of destroying anything that got in his way. Nevertheless it still has two attractive old churches and a splendid staircase in the Hôtel de Ville. It is surrounded by small villages like **Grand** with its Roman ruins, the remains of an amphitheatre and a museum full of mosaics. **Contrexéville**, on the other hand, relies entirely on its thermal baths to attract visitors, providing them with some very comfortable hotels and tennis, swimming and riding as well.

Vittel, of bottled water fame, is no distance away. It adds two 18-hole golf courses to a similar list of amenities, plus a racecourse, a flying club, a large park where one can watch polo and attend concerts during the season and a great many flowers. Folklore and traditional costumes are paraded in August for the benefit of townspeople, visitors and anyone who happens to be camping nearby. An attractive and fairly scenic road connects the spa with **Darney** which played host to part of the Czech army during World War I and later installed a Czechoslovak Museum in the town hall. An equally pleasing road skirts Vioménil within easy walking distance of the

Joan of Arc's birthplace at Domrémy-la-Pucelle

source of the Saône, passes the Valley of the Druids, edges its way round the Bouzey reservoir and ends up in the suburbs of **Epinal**.

Although not very large, Epinal is an energetic sort of place with a positive mania for collecting things. For instance, the Musée des Vosges et de l'Imagerie, which stands at one end of an island in the middle of the Moselle, has found space for bits and pieces of ancient architecture, medals and coins of comparable vintage and a host of items relating to folklore and traditions. Its picture galleries display works by Rembrandt, Brueghel and Van Loo amongst others with the same aplomb as they show off modern artists like Picasso and a clutch of local painters who are not nearly so widely known. In addition it houses the Musée International de l'Imagerie with some of the original highly coloured and distinctive drawings that were inspired by the early illustrators. Methods and treatment differed according to the nationality of the artist concerned and one English contribution shows the wreck of the *Colville*, a West Indiaman driven ashore at Weymouth during a particularly ferocious nineteenth-century storm. The collection has a serious rival in the Imagerie Pellerin Gallery, a fair distance away on the main bank of the river, which was established 200 years ago to ensure that the art form survived. Meanwhile the Parc du Château, complete with ruins and a lake, collects animals for its mini-zoo and the Parc du Cours prides itself on having gathered together a splendid selection of exotic trees and plants. Two churches, one old and one new, more or less complete the picture and there is an American cemetery 7km (4 miles) to the south with a memorial to several thousand soldiers who were killed there in the closing stages of the battle for Europe.

The roads running south from Epinal can be very busy during the season because they provide immediate access to the high spots of the Vosges. The main road from Nancy bypasses the town and follows the Moselle to **Remiremont** with its picturesque houses, old churches, eleventh-century crypt and a brace of quite entertaining museums, after which it divides its destinations between Luxeuil-les-Bains in the south-west and Mulhouse, the gateway to both Switzerland and Germany across the Rhine. There is, however, no need to follow the crowds. A variety of minor roads wend their way through the foothills to **Plombières-les-Bains** where the Romans founded a spa which has been well patronised over the centuries. If anyone had had the foresight to keep a visitors' book it would have been worth its weight in gold by now with signatures like Montaigne, Voltaire, the Empress Josephine, Cavour and Napoleon III, the last two of whom spent their time together planning the unification of France and Italy. It would be interesting to know where they all stayed. There are no likely castles in the vicinity nor any recent ruins with imperial connections. The Maison des Arcades is quite eye-catching but nothing like large enough for someone accustomed to holding court at Versailles or Fontainebleau. The baths vary considerable in age and are easily identified by the features of their founders, namely the Emperor Augustus, Napoleon Bonaparte and Napoleon III. The town is equipped for tennis and swimming, has a casino, a selection of hotels and apartments and a limited number of camping sites. Nearby attractions include the Fontaine Stanislas with its own little hotel, the Musée Hippomobile at Aillevillers-et-Lyaumont and the glass factory at La Rochère, founded in 1475 and still producing some exquisite articles. It is open to visitors every weekday afternoon, excluding public holidays, from May to September but the glassblowers and engravers are on holiday during August so only the museum and the shop are on view. There are also some very inviting woods and waterfalls at Faymont and Géhard in the opposite direction along the valley of the Roches.

The biggest and most tourist-conscious of the dozen or so mountain lakes is **Gérardmer,** a sizeable expanse of water with a town at one end. There is nothing historic about it but this does not affect its popularity in the least. On the other hand it could not, for the moment anyway, be described as an international holiday playground. It is a

The main street at Remiremont

very good place from which to explore the Vosges mountains, there is something in the sporting line to occupy every member of the family and for most of the year it has plenty of space for everyone. However, during August, when the whole of France seems to be on holiday the shores are crowded with people swimming or lying on the grass while others dash about in motor boats, water ski or proceed in a more leisurely fashion under sail. Launches are on hand for organised excursions round the lake, small craft including ped-alos can be hired by visitors who prefer to do things their own way and fishermen can go off in search of solitude on payment of a daily fee. There are two covered swimming pools, tennis courts, a skating rink, bowls and a casino as well as trips up into the mountains to inspect waterfalls, valleys created by ancient glaciers and vantage points recommended for their views. Festivals are arranged at inter-vals throughout the year, celebrating spring with flowers, summer with fireworks and winter with the Fête of St Nicolas. Cross-country skiing takes over as soon as there is enough snow. The many ski-lifts start working full time, trails are clearly marked over a wide area and all the necessary equipment is available for hire.

Accommodation is plentiful at a predictable variety of hotels, both in the town itself and at half a dozen mini-resorts within a radius of 10km (6 miles) or less. On every side scenic drives wriggle their way round one mountain peak after another, revealing ever-more magnificent views and alternating with narrow tracks that appeal to hikers but are quite unsuitable for four wheels unless they happen to be attached to a tractor. However the main road to Colmar takes things easily as far as the Col de la Schlucht where it crosses the Route des Crêtes on its way through to Munster. The town of Munster itself is hardly worth a detour although it is a popular tourist centre and an ideal place from which to plan a walking holiday. It is also very close to Gunsbach where the house once owned by Albert Schweitzer has been turned into a museum. Anyone interested in the life of this famous doctor would find it highly illuminating because it emphasises so many different facets of his character through books and music, medicine, sermons and photographs. There are guided tours each morning and afternoon, lasting approximately half an hour. An alternative mountain road circles round, past the White Lake and the Black Lake and back to the Route des Crêtes at the Col de la Schlucht where most people stop to inspect the high altitude garden. It is open from June to the middle of October and contains hundreds of plants from all over the world that only feel at home with their heads in the clouds. Holneck, beyond it on the opposite side of the road, is one of the highest peaks with views over the Vosges, across the plain of Alsace to the Black Forest and, on a crystal clear day, even provides a glimpse of snow on the Alps. To the south Grand Ballon, the highest point in the range, boasts a hotel and a café complete with souvenirs and parking space for coaches and cars while the occupants climb up to the monument at the top.

Hereafter it is downhill most of the way with constantly changing views and, perhaps, a pause to look at the ruined Château de Freundstein or a detour to Vieil Armand with its large crypt, war cemetery and monuments to the men of both sides who died there in World War I. For all practical purposes the Route des Crêtes and its plethora of little farmhouse *auberges* ends at Uffholtz. It is virtually a suburb of Cernay, an industrial town with a history museum, a stork park and a steam train that puffs its way along the valley of the Doller to Sentheim, finds nothing much to do there and returns the way it came.

The town of **Thann**, 6km (4 miles) from Cernay, should definitely not be missed. According to legend the saintly Bishop Thiébaut, having given all his fortune to the poor, left his episcopal ring to his servant but when the unfortunate man tried to take it off the body the thumb came away as well. He hid this relic in the top of his pilgrim's staff and set off for his home in the Netherlands. One night the servant stopped to rest in a clump of fir trees, laying his staff aside and somehow damaging the home of a bumblebee. In the morning he could not get it out although the bee emerged without any trouble. At the same moment three bright lights appeared over three nearby trees. They were seen from the Château d'Engelbourg by the Countess de Ferrette who, having heard the whole story, decided to build a chapel on the site of the apparition. The news got round and a small village grew up to cater for the needs of the pilgrims who came flooding in, calling itself Thann after one of the trees. This is why three fir trees are burned at the end of June outside the church, leaving the crowds to squabble over the ashes afterwards. The *château* changed hands several times before it was eventually abandoned the resulting ruins being known, somewhat unkindly perhaps, as the Eye of the Sorceress.

The Collégiale St Thiébaut, described by some people as a church and by others as a cathedral, is generally agreed to be one of the most outstanding examples of Gothic art in Alsace. It dates from the fourteenth and fifteenth centuries and nearly everything about it is original. It possesses a whole regiment of sculptures and statues, both inside and out, including two of the saint and a beautiful Virgin of the Winegrowers whose mischievous-looking Child hides a bunch of grapes behind His back. The magnificent choir stalls have touches of humour in the form of tiny carved figures including the gossip, the bespectacled man, the scholar and the fiddler. When the doors are locked it only takes a moment to pop into the tourist office in the block opposite and explain one's predicament.

The Musée des Amis de Thann, in an old Corn Market overooking the river, is hardly 2 minutes' walk away. It not only traces the history of the town in some detail but also concerns itself with such diverse subjects as mineralogy, wine making, local art, folklore and aspects of World War I. The Witches' Tower, practically next door, is all that remains of the old fortifications but the town has a great fascination for storks which, in turn, have fascinated the people of Alsace for centuries. Riding stables and long-distance footpaths complete the list of attractions apart from a tennis court belonging to one of the *auberges*. There are very few places to stay and, apparently, no camping sites but visitors in search of a comfortable hotel have only to drive the 22km (13 miles) to Mulhouse which has plenty of accommodation and a great many things to see.

As one would expect **Mulhouse** is reasonably large and very busy. Apart from its industrial interests it has an international airport and a constant flow of road and rail traffic heading backwards and forwards between France and Germany, Switzerland, Austria and Italy. The sad fact is that so many people do pass through without ever realising how much they are missing. The town's museums attract specialists in several different fields while at the same time providing much of interest for the merely curious. Collectors and car enthusiasts spend hours in the Musée National de l'Automobile, described by one expert as the most outstanding he had ever seen. There are about ninety different makes of cars numbering some 500 vehicles in all. It was originally a private collection belonging to Hans and Fritz Schlumf, two brothers who were textile industrialists with a passion for vintage cars. They went bankrupt in 1976, and 2 years later the vehicles were scheduled as historic monuments, housed in a vast hall which was once a textile factory and opened to the public in 1982. Amongst the exhibits are 123 different Bugattis, the largest collection in the world, including the two Royales, a limousine and the incomparable Coupé Napoléon which belonged to Ettore Bugatti. Also on view are Fangio's Maserati, Charlie Chaplin's Rolls Royce and the Porsche 917 that won the Le Mans 24-hour race in 1971, along with so many others of the same calibre. Facilities are available for disabled visitors who find the walkways, covering more than a mile, rather too much of a good thing. There is also a restaurant and a playground for children which is open in the summer. When they get tired of following parents round the man-sized models they can try out one of eight little replicas, including a 1950 Ferrari F1, on a road circuit through a miniature village.

Like the Musée de l'Automobile, the Railway Museum claims to be unique and houses a collection going back about 150 years. Stephenson is represented in the foyer by the Aigle, a splendid engine that began its tour of duty in 1846. In the sheds behind are ornate carriages built for people like Napoleon III, his containing a travelling medicine chest with enough pills and potions to discourage even the most determined germ. The Fireman's Museum is just next door and there is a Musée des Beaux Arts, a Mineralogical Museum, a History Museum, a Museum of Printed Cloth with special demonstrations of the process involved and a Musée du Papier Peint crammed with machines and literally thousands of historic documents.

The town's additional attractions include stained glass windows in the church of St Etienne, the ancient chapel of the Chevaliers de St Jean-de-Jérusalem, a view from the top of the tower in the Place de l'Europe and extensive botanical gardens across the Canal du Rhône au Rhin where most children head straight for the zoo. As if all this were not enough an Ecomusée has been established at **Ungersheim**, a few kilometres north-west of Mulhouse. Some thirty-five buildings, anything up to 800 years old, have been reconstructed on a large site with space for many more. The complex is open all year round and in December St Nicolas arrives with his donkey and hot chocolate and gingerbread for the children.

This is a good place from which to join the Wine Route at **Soultz-Haut-Rhin** for the journey north. The village is practically a suburb of Guebwiller which earns its living from textiles and wine. Guebwiller has been in existence for hundreds of years during which time it has accumulated a good deal in the way of local history and folklore, now on display in the Musée de Florival opposite the church of Notre-Dame. It is also well blessed with nearby small hotels and restaurants complete with rooms and is conveniently close to the Lac de la Lauch where the fishing is said to be excellent and to woods that blanket the valley and the slopes of the Grand Ballon.

Admittedly the Route du Vin twists and turns a bit through the vineyards, sometimes joining the main roads and sometimes wandering off in search of an attractive little hamlet, but on the whole it is fairly flat. **Rouffach** is a good place to stop, partly on account of its old houses, the Witches' Tower inhabited by storks and the thirteenth-century church of Notre-Dame, the first Gothic building in the Haut-Alsace. Its favourite anecdotes recall more than a nodding acquaintance with Henry V and the fact that it once had a gallows of its very own. It was also in the direct firing line during the Allied advance in 1945. Another good reason for pausing is that there is a first rate hotel with tennis, swimming and delicious food and wine in the immediate vicinity.

Practically every village in the neighbourhood has something of interest to offer like an ancient church or a ruined *château* while **Neuf-Brisach**, to the east, rubs shoulders with the Grand Canal d'Alsace. It is worth seeing for the giant locks, hydro-electric plant and sleek bridges that carry the road onto the island, with its own camping site, and across the Rhine into Germany. The town is small and perfectly octagonal, contained in massive double ramparts built by Vauban who is the subject of a small museum at the Porte de Belfort, open every morning and afternoon except on Mondays. There are two or three modest hotels, an 18-hole golf course and a steam train that runs up to **Marckolsheim**, known chiefly for its Museum of the Maginot Line. It is open every morning and afternoon from mid-June to mid-September, thereafter only on Sundays and public holidays until it closes completely in November.

Colmar, a short distance away, is considered by many people to be the most beautiful town in Alsace. It is historic, brimming over with extremely eye-catching houses festooned with flowers, ancient buildings and enchanting little streets and alleyways. A good way to get your bearings is to join one of the guided tours arranged, sometimes on request, by the Syndicat d'Initiative. After that there is nothing to beat wandering about at a more leisurely pace, revisiting places of particular interest and discovering little gems that were missed the first time round. Fortunately most of them are to be found in a comparatively small area of the old town between the Unterlinden Museum and Little Venice on the banks of the canal.

The Musée d'Unterlinden occupies an ancient monastery and contains amongst its treasures the famous Issenheim Altarpiece painted by Mathias Grunewald in the early sixteenth century. A block or so away is an elaborate seventeenth-century house with so many sculptured heads that it really could not be called anything other than the Maison des Têtes. By way of a bonus it has a restaurant as well. Next comes the Eglise des Dominicains, built around 1500 but planned much earlier than that. It has some fine stained glass windows and Martin Schongauer's *Virgin of the Rose Bush* depicting a pensive figure dressed in scarlet against a background of matching flowers, green foliage and tiny birds with angels in attendance. St Martin's church, which is even older, is the next logical port of call to be followed by a cluster of elderly houses including the Maison Adolph dated 1350 and the Musée Bartholdi, birthplace of the sculptor whose most widely-known work is undoubtedly the Statue of Liberty.

Once in the Grand Rue historic buildings come thick and fast, everything from the Old Hospital to the ancient Customs House overlooking one of Bartholdi's fountains. Spare enough time to see the Eglise St Matthieu, the Maison Pfister, the tiny Maison au Cygne and the Ancien Corps de Garde before going on to the Tanners' Quarter. Beyond it is Little Venice where typical old houses rise from the water with more trees and flowers than can be seen in the original and, blissfully, quite free of motor boats and launches. Finally, when all these possibilities have been exhausted, there is a Natural History Museum in the Parc du Château d'Eau.

Several small hotels and some good restaurants are dotted about the old quarter with a couple of larger establishments close to the airport and to the railway station. A motel, unfortunately without a restaurant, can be found on the road to Strasbourg. Colmar believes in entertaining its guests and to this end provides swimming and

A street in the old quarter of Colmar

riding, conducted tours and excursions, paths for hikers across the plains and up into the mountains and places to pitch a tent or park a caravan.

There are two obvious points of re-entry to the Wine Route — **Turckheim** which has three ancient gates and a night watchman who does his rounds during the season and **Ammerschwir**, a once-fortified village with a Rogues' Tower. The latter is on the main road to **Kaysersberg** where there is another Albert Schweitzer museum, this time in the house where he was born. The village has changed hands several times since the Romans used it on their repeated forays up and down the Rhine but inspite of its turbulent history some antiquated buildings and much of the old world atmosphere have survived. The fifteenth-century bridge is still operational but the castle with its solid round tower is considerably the worse for wear. An interesting old church adjoins a cemetery of comparable vintage and the chapel of St Michel built in 1463. It is a delightful place to wander about, visit the little museums and possibly stay at a local hotel, which can be either up-market or on the basic side. **Kientzheim,** next door, has a lot in common in the way of buildings and atmosphere but scores an extra point for its Wine Museum.

The next place of interest is **Riquewihr** with its sixteenth-century buildings and a decorative tower-gateway called the Dolder that goes back to 1291 but has been reinforced at regular intervals since then. It is the home of the Archaeological Society Museum and vies for attention with the Musée d'Histoire des PTT d'Alsace which traces the progress of the local postal service from the days when runners set out with their version of the cleft stick. Stamp collectors and anyone with a soft spot for postcards can call in any time from April to November, leaving the rest of the party to inspect the Robbers' Tower which stays open throughout the year and has its own torture chamber.

Ribeauvillé, a little further up the Route du Vin in the foothills of the Vosges, boasts a thirteenth-century Slaughterers' Tower but is equally proud of its resident storks. It was a great place for itinerant musicians in the Middle Ages and celebrates the fact with a Festival of Strolling Fiddlers, overlaid with folklore and traditions, on the first Sunday in September. A variety of hotels and an ample supply of country walks make it a popular centre for exploring in the vicinity. The Château of St Ulrich would be a good place to start as it is only a few kilometres away so it is possible to walk there, inspect the fairly extensive ruins on their tree-covered hilltop and be back in 2 or 3 hours. Alternatively, anyone interested in mining might prefer **Ste Marie-aux-Mines** with its old silver and lead workings and a chapel used by miners in the fifteenth century. An added incentive is that the silver mine is open daily during July and August. There is a prehistoric Celtic camp outside **St Dié** which, in turn, has a cathedral and the church of Notre-Dame-de-Galilée linked by a medieval cloister, a museum and an extensive library. German tourists often head in the opposite direction to visit their war cemetery outside **Bergheim**, a village which contributes some fortifications, a fourteenth-century church and a linden tree said to be 1,000 years old.

Haut-Koenigsbourg, dominating the countryside from its perch on a mountaintop, 10km (6 miles) north of Ribeauvillé, was once a vast medieval fortress. However it was destroyed by enemy action in 1633 and left to decay for more than 250 years before being completely rebuilt. Parts of the building are still closed and the whole place is out of bounds to tourists on public holidays and all through January. A small winding road crosses the Route du Vin, tempting the motorist to visit Sélestat with its full complement of elderly buildings, a liberal sprinkling of wrought-iron work, a fine Humanistic Library and a reputation for taking more than a passing interest in flowers. It is usually crowded for the Floral Carnival in August, particularly with holidaymakers intent on spending their time out of doors. There is a large sports centre with an open-air swimming pool and motor boats on the River Ill. Facilities are available for hunting and fishing, well clear of the marked paths that cover enough terri-tory to satisfy all but the most determined long-distance walker. Other amenities include a holiday village and plenty of space for campers. In addition, nearby **Kintzheim** has an animal park, an Eagle Reserve with demonstrations of falconry when the weather is good and one of the best-preserved castles in the area.

Further off the wine track, with its vineyards at refreshingly short intervals, **Villé** concentrates on local crafts and provides access to a scenic, if occasionally tortuous, series of little roads that blaze a trail to Struthof. It is here that guides are on hand to show people round the well maintained but infinitely depressing Nazi concentration camp with all its horrific reminders of death and deportation. The tour lasts for over an hour any morning or afternoon except at Christmas and on New Year's Day. On the other hand one can head up through the woods to Mont Ste Odile. The lady in question is the patron saint of Alsace and her mountain with its crowning monas-tery is a recognised place of pilgrimage. As so often happens the pagans were there first, leaving behind traces of a mysterious wall that twists about for several kilometres with no apparent rhyme or reason for its sudden changes in direction. A festival in honour of Ste Odile is held there on the 13 December every year with similar events taking place in towns and villages all over Alsace.

The Route du Vin can be rejoined at **Ottrott** and Obernai, the former having some not very outstanding buildings, a reputation for red wine and a busy little tourist train that runs up to Rosheim and back again. **Obernai** is very picturesque with its thirteenth-century fortifications, dignified old houses, typical cobbles at the street inter-sections, a corn market and an attractive market square. Apart from the considerably up-dated Hôtel de Ville and the church of St Peter and St Paul, there is a decorative six-bucket well dating from the sixteenth century. It is more like a folly than a functional piece of architecture with carved pillars holding up the roof and very new-looking buckets filled with flowers. Visitors can ride, fish, swim, find accommodation in the holiday villages or bring their own tents and caravans.

Molsheim falls into roughly the same category as Obernai except that it is slightly smaller and was once the home of Bugatti cars. Its most outstanding feature is the 300-year-old Slaughter House, a very respectable construction that belies its name with gables not unlike those of the Maison des Têtes in Colmar, a double stairway up to the main entrance on the first floor and long balconies full of plants. Its chief function these days is to provide space for a great many local

A four-bucket well at Rosheim

wines that can be sampled on the premises, leaving room for a little museum.

Marlenheim marks the end of the Route du Vin and is an easily forgettable town although it offers opportunities for hunting and fishing, has an extremely good restaurant with rooms attached and is only a short run from Strasbourg along a fast road which turns quite suddenly into an *autoroute*.

There is really nothing you cannot do in Strasbourg if you put your mind to it. It is a simple matter to fly to Paris, London, Rome or Brussels, catch a train with or without your car for company, drive across the frontier into Germany almost before you have left the suburbs behind and even board a mini-train for a sightseeing tour round the city. Air trips are laid on to give visitors a bird's eye view of the capital, motor launches ply up and down the rivers and canals and, when time is no object, there is really nothing to beat a cruise along the Rhine. Evening entertainments include theatre, opera, concerts of all descriptions and an International Music Festival in June. The city is by no stretch of the imagination off the beaten track, especially since the Council of Europe and the Court of Human Rights moved in. However only a very few people who decide to explore Alsace would leave without even glancing at the capital so a brief summary of its many attractions may not come amiss. There are a great many hotels of all types and at all price levels, masses of shops and restaurants, churches, art galleries and museums. Holidaymakers can play golf and tennis, skate, ride, fish and indulge in all the usual water sports. Flying lessons are available at the local aero clubs and the Official Information Office is extremely helpful when it comes to excursions and accommodation.

The most noteworthy places of interest include the cathedral of Notre-Dame where it takes over an hour to see everything properly, the Musée du Château des Rohan with its grand apartments and a whole host of other museums. The Musée des Beaux Arts has some memorable paintings, the Museum of Decorative Arts is especially proud of its collection of ceramics and the Musée Alsacien is the place to go for anything connected with Alsace whether sophisticated or frankly rural. Other museums are devoted to history, archaeology, modern art and zoology. After this it is time to take a brisk walk. La Petite France, overlooking the canal, is extremely neat and picturesque. The Barrage Vauban is close at hand which is more than can be said for the Cour du Corbeau and its antiquated bridge where certain types of criminals were once put in iron cages and left to die. The Place Kléber, the Place Broglie and the Rue de Dôme are amongst other sights to be seen before moving out of the old town to the tree-filled Place de la Republic, the Orangerie and the Palais de l'Europe where visitors are discouraged when Parliament is in session. Whatever your personal impressions of Strasbourg may be one thing is immediately apparent — it has come a long way since the days of Julius Caesar when the fishing village of *Argentoratum* began to prosper and changed its name to *Strateburgum*, the city at the crossroads of Europe.

Further Information
—Alsace et Lorraine —

Museums and Other Places of Interest

Baccarat
Crystal Museum
Open: morning and afternoon mid-July to mid-September except Tuesday and Sunday mornings. Otherwise afternoons but only Saturday and Sunday from May to mid-June. Closed October to April.

Cernay
Museum
Open: July and August, Wednesday and Friday afternoons only.

Colmar
Bartholdi Musée
Open: morning and afternoon throughout the season, Wednesday and Saturday only November to March.

Eglise des Dominicains
Open: daily April to mid-November

Musée d'Unterlinden
Open: April to October 9am-12noon and 2-6pm. November to March 9am-12noon and 2-5pm, closed Tuesdays. Closed 1 January, 1 May, 1 November and 25 December.

Natural History Museum
Open: July and August, 2-5pm. April, May, June, September, October and November, Wednesday, Saturday and Sunday only 2-5pm. Closed December to March.

Domrémy-la-Pucelle
Joan of Arc's Birthplace and Museum
Open: morning and afternoon, closed Tuesdays and mid-October to end of March.

Epinal
Imagerie Pellerin
Guided tours: morning and afternoon, afternoon only on Sunday and public holidays.

Musée des Vosges et de l'Imagerie
Open: morning and afternoon, closed Tuesday, 1 January, 1 May, 1 November and 25 December.

Gunsbach
Schweitzer Museum
Guided tours mornings and afternoons.

Haut-Koenigsbourg
Open: morning and afternoon, closed January and public holidays.

Kaysersberg
Albert Schweitzer Museum
Open: morning and afternoon at Easter and from May to October.

Kientzheim
Wine Museum
Open: July to September mornings and afternoons.

Eagle Reserve and Mountain of Monkeys
Open: afternoons from April to mid-September and on Wednes-

The quayside at Carteret, Normandy

Le Mougau, near Commana, Brittany

Fishing boats at Le Guilvinec, Brittany

day, Saturday, Sunday and public holiday afternoons until mid-November.

Louppy-sur-Loison
Château
Guided tours July to September afternoons. Closed Monday and the rest of the year.

Lunéville
Château and Museum
Open: morning and afternoon except Tuesday. Son et Lumière Friday, Saturday and Sunday evenings from July to mid-September.

Musée de la Moto et du Vélo
Open: mornings and afternoons except Monday.

Marckolsheim
Museum of the Maginot Line
Open: mid-June to mid-September mornings and afternoons.

Metz
Cathedral of St Etienne
The crypt is open morning and afternoon, Sunday afternoon only. Closed on religious festivals. Treasure open afternoons except religious festivals.

Museum of Art and History
Open: morning and afternoon except Tuesday.

Mirecourt
Museum of Stringed Instruments

Mulhouse
Automobile Museum
Open: daily 10am-6pm except Tuesdays 1 January and 25 December.

Fine Arts Museum
Open: mornings and afternoons, closed Tuesday, Whit Monday, 14 July, 1 and 11 November, 25 and 26 December.

Museum of Printed Cloth
Open: morning and afternoon except Tuesday and public holidays.

Museum of Printed Paper
Open: morning and afternoon except Tuesday and public holidays.

Railway Museum and Fireman's Museum
Open: daily except 1 January, 25 and 26 December.

St Jean-de-Jérusalem Museum
Open: morning and afternoon May to September except Tuesday, 1 May, Whit Monday and 14 July.

Nancy
Château de Fléville
Guided tours: afternoons July and August; Sunday and public holiday afternoons only from April to June and September and October.

Daum Crystal Works
Open: weekday mornings and all day Saturday.

Ducal Palace and Museum
Open morning and afternoon except Tuesday.

Eglise et Couvent des Cordeliers
Open: morning and afternoon, closed Monday, Easter, Christmas and 1 January.

Fine Arts Museum
Open: morning and afternoon except Monday morning, Tuesday and public holidays.

Porte de la Craffe
Open: morning and afternoon,
mid-June to August. Closed Tuesday.

School Museum
Open: morning and afternoon.
Closed Tuesday, Easter, 1 January,
1 May, 14 July and Christmas.

Zoological Museum
Open: afternoons only. Closed
Tuesday except during school
holidays.

Neuf-Brisach
Vauban Museum
Open: 9am-12noon and 2-5pm.
Closed Tuesday.

Obernai
Train from Ottrott to Rosheim
Sunday and public holiday afternoons leaving at 2.30pm and
4.30pm.

Parc de Haye
Aircraft Museum
Open: January to August Saturday
and Sunday afternoon.

Car Museum
Open: March to mid-November
Wednesday, Saturday and Sunday.

Plombières-les-Bains
Spa town with ancient baths.

Pont-à-Mousson
Prémontrés Abbey
Open: mornings and afternoons.

Riquewihr
Dolder Museum
Open: morning and afternoon at
Easter and July and August. Other-
wise Saturday afternoon and
Sunday. Closed November to June.

Postal Museum
Open: morning and afternoon
April to mid-November. Closed
Tuesdays except in July and Au-
gust.

La Rochère
Glass Factory and Museum
Open: May to July, September and
October 2.30-5.30pm. Factory
closed on Sundays and holidays;
museum only May to September
2.30-6pm.

St Dié
Museum
Open: mornings and afternoons.
Closed Mondays and holidays.

Ste Marie-aux-Mines
Museum and Silver Mine
Open: July and August morning
and afternoon.

Saverne
Château
Museum open morning and after-
noon except Tuesday during July
and August but Sundays and
public holidays only during May,
June and September.
Rose Garden morning and after-
noon from mid-June to the end of
September.
Jardin Botanique from June to
August in the afternoon.

Sélestat
Humanistic Library
Open: morning and afternoon,
closed Saturday afternoons, Sundays andpublic holidays.

Strasbourg
Archaeological Museum
Open: April to September 10am-

12noon and 2-6pm; October to March 2-8pm. Closed Tuesdays, Good Friday, Easter Sunday, Whit Sunday and 1 May.

Cathedral of Notre-Dame, including the museum
Open: daily.

Château des Rohan
Opening times as Archaeological Museum times.

Decorative Arts Museum
Opening times as above.

Fine Arts Museum
Opening times as above.

Folk Museum
Opening times as above.

Old Customs House
Open: daily 10am-12noon and 2-5pm.

Palais de l'Europe
Open: morning and afternoon except Saturday and Sunday, November to March, public holidays and when Parliament sits.

Zoological Museum
Open: Wednesday, Friday, Saturday, Sunday 2-5pm. Thursday 10am-12noon and 2-5pm.

Struthof
Nazi Concentration Camp
Guided tours: morning and afternoon. Closed 24 December and 1 January.

Thann
Collégiale St-Thiébaut
If closed enquire at the Tourist Office.

Ungersheim
Ecomusée
Open: May to August 10am-10pm. March, April, September, October 11am-6pm. January, February, November, December 11am-4pm.

Vaucouleurs
Municipal Museum
Open: mid-June to mid-September morning and afternoon. Closed Tuesday.

Verdun
Citadelle
Underground fortifications open: morning and afternoon, but closed from mid-December to mid-January.

Hotel de la Princerie Museum
Open: morning and afternoon from Easter to end of September. Closed on Tuesdays.

Fort de Vaux
Open: daily from mid-February to mid-December. Museum open mornings and afternoons except from mid-December to mid-January.

Vieil Armand
Museum
Open: morning and afternoon, April to October.

Vittel
Bottled water factory. Guided tours mid-April to mid-September: morning and afternoon. Closed Saturday, Sunday and holidays.

Wissembourg
Château de Fleckenstein
Open: daily March to November.

Westercamp Museum
Open: morning and afternoon,
closed Sunday morning, Wednesday and in January.

Woerth
History Museum
Open: morning and afternoon
from April to October, thereafter
Saturday and Sunday only.

Tourist Information Offices

Colmar
4 Rue Unterlinden
☎89-41-02-29

Epinal
13 Rue de la Comédie
☎29-82-53-32

Gérardmer
Place Déportés
☎29-63-08-74

Metz
Place d'Armes
☎87-75-65-21
Also at the station.

Mulhouse
9 Avenue Maréchal Foch
☎89-45-68-31

Nancy
14 Place Stanislas
☎83-35-22-41

Strasbourg
Palais des Congrès
Avenue Schultzenberger
☎88-35-03-00
Also at the station.

St Dié
31 Rue Thiers
☎29-55-17-62

Verdun
Place de Nation
☎29-84-18-85
Open: May-mid-September.

Vittel
Rue de Verdun
☎29-08-42-03

Wissembourg
At the town hall
☎88-94-10-11

4 • Pays de la Loire

Pays de la Loire is one of the French regions that is something of a mish-mash. It is not an historical grouping of *départements*, and in many respects the historical ties of the *départements* pull in different directions. Indeed, the area that most people think of as the 'Loire Valley' mainly lies outside the 'Pays de la Loire' area! The Loire enters Pays de la Loire just east of Saumur, working its way through Angers and Nantes to the Atlantic Ocean just beyond St Nazaire. The region, though, is one of rivers, and both Sarthe and Mayenne, the two northernmost *départements*, are named after their respective rivers. Both flow into the Loire eventually. The Loire itself is a wide and dominating river as it passes through the region, with the result that in the summer it is full of sandbanks and is distinctly uninspiring, whereas in winter it is dark and foreboding.

There is little river traffic on the Loire itself, and it is out of bounds to hired pleasure craft. However, the other rivers in the area, and especially those in the old Anjou area — the Sarthe and the Mayenne — are extremely well suited to boating. It is possible to hire cruisers from a number of places, and British boat operators have a presence here at Angers. The roads are generally very quiet, except a few of the major ones, where freight lorries speed eastwards to Paris.

Whichever way you come into the region (unless you are coming from the south), you come firstly into the influence of **Le Mans**. The A11 motorway from Paris to Rennes runs around the city outskirts, crossed by one of the main routes southwards from the Channel Ports. All too often people drive around Le Mans, and certainly avoid what looks like, on a map, a daunting city centre. However, it's not too bad, and even parking is relatively easy. The old quarter is worth devoting some time to, set alongside the huge cathedral (St Julien), and overlooking the Sarthe.

There has been quite a lot of good restoration work, and many of the old houses contain studios or trendy shops, with prices only the French could charge. The hill down to the river is quite steep, with the result that there are a number of bridges and tunnels, which add an extra dimension to the exploration. As one would expect, Le Mans has a good range of hotel accommodation, which makes it a good base for touring. If you want to visit the famous racing circuit, it is some 4.8km (3 miles) south of the city, between the N158 and D139. There is an interesting car museum there too.

Head, however, west towards Mayenne. Much of the countryside bears resemblances to Normandy, and this is inevitable as it is an area of overlap. The route passes into, in fact, a regional park — that of Normandy-Maine. This is an ideal area for walkers, especially in and around the Sillé Forest, through which the road D35 passes, at **Sillé-le-Guillaume**. Once a northern stronghold of Maine, the town now relies much on the attractions of the Sillé Forest. It has a reasonable level of basic accommodation, and good facilities for walking and riding. The GR36 and 37 long-distance footpaths pass through the town and forest, offering good opportunities for the serious walker. Unfortunately the castle is not open to the public.

It is possible to keep within the regional park boundaries after Sillé, and make a pleasant exploration north-eastwards on byroads, keeping south of Alençon. This takes you through the picturesque Alpes de Mancelle (Mancelle Alps) around St Léonard-des-Bois to the Perseigne Forest. This forest is bisected by several pretty valleys covered in forest. There are several minor roads to help exploration, but it is an area to explore on foot, following the GR22 footpath or any of many waymarked paths. From Perseigne Forest, it is possible to head back to Le Mans, or up into Normandy.

The D35 from Sillé crosses into the Mayenne *département*, and passes through some pleasant countryside before reaching Bolis. Here take the D241 through Hambers to Jublains, where there are the remains of the Roman fort of *Neodanus*. It is possible to visit some of the remains, surrounded by a thick wall with towers. The fort seems to have been as strategic an importance in Roman times as Mayenne has been since. Mayenne is only a short distance from Jublains.

Mayenne sits astride the Mayenne River, and so has been of importance throughout the ages, even in World War II, when the town was badly damaged. The castle dates originally from the eleventh century, but was rebuilt in the fifteenth. Unfortunately, it is not open to the public. The church (Notre Dame) is early Gothic, but with considerable alterations since. The river was once navigable as far as Mayenne, but lack of use and maintenance led to regular closures. Today the river is navigable only as far as Laval, further downstream, although a project is underway to restore navigation to

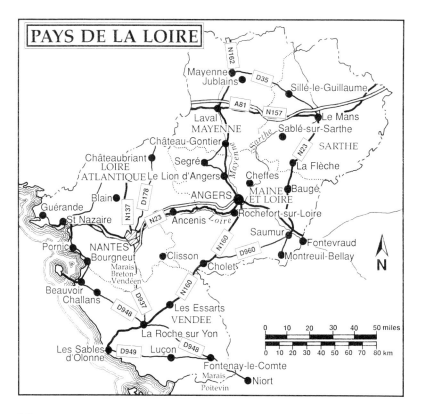

Mayenne.

Just north of Mayenne the countryside again falls within the bounds of the Normandy-Maine Regional Park, but the bulk lies within Normandy. To the west of Mayenne is a stretch of forest, and one can make a pleasant drive by taking the N12 from Mayenne towards Fougères, but turning left into the forest just after La Meltière towards Chaillard. If one takes the D165 from Chaillard to Andouillé then the D101 to Monflours, it is possible then to turn southwards and follow a pretty route (D250/D162) along the side of the Mayenne to Laval. Alternatively, the N162 runs straight from Mayenne to Laval.

Laval sits astride the Mayenne, and is the county town for the Mayenne *département*. Laval has two *châteaux*, called appropriately enough the New Château (which now houses the Law Courts) and the Old Château. The Old Château houses a museum about the painter Henri Rousseau, who was born in the town. The old quarter has some impressive town houses and retains a medieval feel. The modern part of the town is on the opposite bank, and lacks any atmosphere. There is an interesting museum housed on a *bateau-lavoir* (laundry boat) with various mementoes and artefacts. The quay also has a boat for trips along the river. A word of warning if you plan to stay overnight — the town is not far from the motorway, and so is popular with businessmen. It is worth booking ahead, or stopping to book something mid-afternoon, otherwise you may find everything full. And there is little else within easy striking distance.

Just south of Laval is the abbey of Port-du-Salut, founded in the thirteenth century, and renowned for its cheese. The licence was sold to a commercial company in 1959, but men (only) can visit the abbey. Following the Mayenne River downstream is possible by boat, car, or on foot, and almost the whole length to Château-Gontier is pretty. And even where the road moves away from the river, it is possible to drive down to riverside villages and hamlets, or to locks.

At Château-Gontier cross the river and take the D22 to Daon, a pretty road passing through fertile agricultural land. All the countryside around this area was home to a major Royalist uprising in 1793. Much of the west of France rose. The uprising in Maine became known as the Chouannerie, after the call signs the rebels made — that of an owl hoot (tawny owl = *chat-huant*). While the uprising in the Vendée — which we shall come to shortly — was organised, that of the Chouannerie was more along the lines of a guerrilla war with small disorganised groups. The type of countryside we are now in is known as *bocage* — small fields with plenty of hedges and woodland, and was ideal for this type of action.

After some initial success the Blancs (the 'whites' or Royalists) were relatively quickly put down by the Bleus (the 'blues' or Republicans), and thousands were shot or guillotined in the repression that followed. The Vendée held out somewhat longer. It is hard to imagine all that took place in this quiet countryside.

At Daon continue on the D22, but turn right into the heart of the countryside to Marigné, and then to **Chenillé-Changé**. This pretty village on the Mayenne has a water mill doing an impersonation of a small castle, but nice all the same. Continue to follow the river (D287) until you reach the D770. Before heading eastwards, a diversion is worthwhile into **Lion d'Angers**. This town is famous for its national horse stud (Haras Nationaux). Visits are possible by advance arrangement. Otherwise take the D770 towards Châteauneuf, but turn off onto the D74 through Sceaux and Ecuillé to the Château du Plessis Bourré. This is a typical 'fairy-tale' *château*, in a light, almost white, stone which is reflected in the still moat. Its relative isolation probably explains why it has survived relatively intact. The

Château du Plessis Bourré

interior matches the exterior. Guided visits are available.

From the *château* head to **Cheffes**. For those who enjoy *châteaux*, or a nice hotel with a difference, the Château de Teildras is highly recommended; a sixteenth-century *château* now a 'country-house' hotel. Not the sort of place for a quick lunch! From Cheffes follow the river northwards — on either bank — to **Châteauneuf-sur-Sarthe**. Châteauneuf is a busy riverside town with simple hotel accommodation, some good restaurants, and a selection of shops.

Again follow the river, the best route being the D108 to Chemiré, then switching banks, the D159 to **Sablé-sur-Sarthe**. Sablé has some small hotels and plenty of shops but little character. Perhaps you get that impression because where you reach next is so overwhelming. From Sablé take the D138 the short drive to **Solesmes**. There is only one thing that people come to Solesmes for, and that is the abbey. Although founded in the eleventh century, the present buildings largely date from the late nineteenth and are quite austere.

However, one visits Solesmes to hear the Gregorian chant and it is possible to attend Mass and Vespers services. Solesmes is one of the places where the art of plainchant was rediscovered and restored, and so set the 'style' for others. There is a shop where you can buy records of the monks' singing as well as other items (women are allowed here!). Opposite the abbey is a good hotel, the Grand.

For a good view of the abbey itself continue past the abbey, across the bridge and turn left into Port de Juigné. A left turn opposite a café takes you into a very small square beside the river. Alternatively, on crossing the bridge, bear right and continue as far as Juigné-sur-Sarthe, where you can park by an observation point. From Juigné take the D22, then a side road to Avoise. Follow the river through Parcé, which has some old houses overlooking the river and a riverside camp site. Cross banks here and follow the D8 to **Malicorne**. On entering the village, there is a pretty *château* with a moat (not open), and then a shady car park beside a mill on the river. A nice place to picnic, although there are a couple of restaurants in the village. There are several potters working here too. From Malicorne, one can head back to Le Mans, if required.

It is a short hop through the wooded countryside (D8/D12) to **La Flèche**, which is on the Loir (which, just to confuse you, is not the Loire). This important commercial town is dominated by the Prytanée Militaire. Founded as a Jesuit college by Henry IV, who spent his youth in the town, it is now a military college. The chapel (St Louis) looks relatively boring from the outside, but is dramatic inside with baroque decoration. There is limited hotel accommodation, but of a good standard. The town has a lot of woodland surrounding it, with waymarked paths, and the GR35 footpath runs just to the south, and through the town.

South of La Flèche, **Baugé**, now a small farming town surrounded by pleasant woodland, has several interesting buildings. The town hall is housed in what was the *château*; and the St Joseph *hôpital* contains its original panelled pharmacy, complete with a collection of various boxes and containers. The town's main claim to fame is housed in the Chapelle des Filles du Coeur de Marie (the Chapel of the Sisters of Mary's Heart). It is a cross, double armed, found in Constantinople in the thirteenth century and supposedly made with pieces of the True Cross. The double-armed cross became the emblem of the Dukes of Anjou (the Cross of Anjou), although the symbol is known today as the Cross of Lorraine. From Baugé it is possible to take a short drive along the Couasnon River, eastwards to Pontigné, where the church has some fine wall paintings. Slightly further east, at Noyant, walkers can pick up the GR36 footpath.

After Baugé the countryside begins to open up towards the Loire. The D938 goes to Longué, and then the N147 to Saumur. **Saumur**, of course, is a key town on the Loire, and so very much 'on' the beaten

The water mill at Malicorne

track for tourists. Its reputation — largely derived from its strategic position — is somewhat bigger than one would expect for the size of the town. There is a good level of hotel accommodation, which means that Saumur could be explored in the evening, after a day spent visiting the countryside. The castle, built of the local pale stone, looks most impressive.

Roads run along both sides of the Loire, although the south bank is by far the most attractive, and more interesting. From Saumur, one can also head south on the N147, into Poitou-Charentes, following more-or-less the valley of the Thouet. **Montreuil-Bellay**, about halfway between Saumur and Thouars, is a pleasant small town with two *châteaux* in one, and parts of the medieval town walls. Just east of Saumur is **Fontevraud**, reached on either the D145 through Fontevraud Forest or via the D947 along the Loire. The village is traditionally the meeting point of Poitou, Anjou, and Touraine. However, its main claim to fame is the great abbey, dating from the twelfth century, but partly rebuilt in the sixteenth. The Plantagenets were great patrons. The church (Notre Dame) is pure Romanesque and contains tombs of several Plantagenets, as well as monuments to Henry II (of England), Eleanor of Aquitaine, and Richard the Lionheart. The cloisters were rebuilt in the sixteenth century in a style reflecting the church, although one can see the influences of the period. The most surprising building is the kitchens, which looks like the top of a spire, with lots of chimneys sticking out. Return to Saumur either along the river or through the Forest. Alternatively, one can head eastwards along the Loire towards Chinon and Tours.

If one follows the Loire from Saumur, on the south bank, one quickly reaches **St Hilaire-St-Florent**, where much of the well-known Saumur wine is made and marketed. You can take your pick from the rows of shops all eager to sell their wares; or alternatively, see what the surrounding small farmers offer. Caves in the cliffs are known for storing wine, but they are also used for growing mushrooms, and the Mushroom Museum (Musée du Champignon) gives an insight into the industry. Before the caves were used for wine and mushrooms (and even afterwards), families made their homes in them. A detour across the countryside inland (D161 to Milly, then D69 and D177) to Rochemenier, offers the chance to visit a museum which shows what life was like for these peasant farmers. Quite different and highly recommended.

The road from St Hilaire continues through Chênehutte (which holds a Mushroom Fair in May) to **Cunault**. The church (Notre Dame) is very pretty, saved from total ruin in the nineteenth century. The carving is quite remarkable, especially inside on the capitals, which have all manner of scenes and monsters. At Gennes one can keep to the riverside road, through Le Thoureil and Juignes, to Ponts-de-Cé, or cut across country to Brissac-Quincé, which has a fine *château*, albeit a mixture of styles from medieval to seventeenth century. The *château* overlooks the large park. From Brissac it is only a short distance to Ponts-de-Cé and thence to **Angers**.

The pale stone that dominated building further back up the Loire, suddenly and dramatically gives way to a black shale in the *château* at Angers. Even when it is sunny it is difficult to drum up enthusiasm for Angers' *château*, overlooking the waters of the Maine, from which the old part of the town rises. Angers is a good touring base, with a reasonable selection of hotels. However, many of the town centre ones do not have parking facilities. The whole city can be explored on foot, with the main sights within easy reach of one another. Do not miss the quite outstanding tapestries in the *château*, dating from the fourteenth century, but almost lost in the Revolution. All good guidebooks cover the city well. A pleasant way to spend an evening is to take a trip on one of the restaurant boats, operating from opposite the *château*. These provide a meal (rather expensive) and a

The château *at Serrant*

guided trip along the river.

From Angers, it is possible to retrace one's steps to Saumur, but on the north bank of the Loire. Alternatively, one can head north to Le Lion d'Angers or Châteauneuf-sur-Sarthe. Angers was, of course, the capital of Anjou, and both west and south, the city is surrounded by the vineyards that produce the well-known Anjou *rosé* wines, although one does find sweeter wines to the south in Côteaux du Layon. It is westwards into the vineyards that the route now heads, taking the D111 to follow the Maine to its confluence with the Loire, and then crossing the Loire at Béhuard.

This arrives at **Rochefort-sur-Loire**, a pleasant village with old houses and a restored twelfth-century church. The D751 to Chalonnes is called the Corniche Angevine. It is cut into the cliffs overlooking the Loire flood plain, and commands some surprisingly dramatic views. Cross the Loire again at Chalonnes, and take the D961 northwards to **St Georges** (sur-Loire, it claims!) to visit the Château of Serrant, one of the finest in Anjou, which is just off the N23 towards Angers.

Whilst Serrant lacks the fairy-tale quality of other *châteaux* further up the Loire, it retains an elegant symmetry enhanced by the use of the dark shale and light tufa stone. It took over 100 years to build, so the style is all the more amazing in its consistency. It is possible to visit the interior (open daily, except Tuesday), which is well furnished, with some fine tapestries. From Serrant one can now return to Angers, or continue along the Loire towards Nantes.

As previously, it is possible to follow the river on the north or the south bank. The major towns and cities lie primarily on the north bank, so the main and consequently busier route (N23) follows the north side. The south bank retains a fair amount of character, and the roads are less busy and far prettier. One can cross the river at several places, so it is possible to swap sides regularly. Walkers can also follow the river, either by sticking to the roads, or by following the long distance footpath GR3 which switches from being close to the river to being further inland from time to time.

At **Ancenis** is the traditional border with Brittany, and the strategic importance of the town can be seen in its castle, although it has some sixteenth- and seventeenth-century additions. Return to, or cross to, the south bank of the Loire and continue along the D751 towards Nantes. The extent of the flood plain is quite extensive, and the river's rambling nature means that some of the area is quite marshy. After La Varenne cut inland to **Loroux-Bottereau**. The church has some superb frescoes, dating from the twelfth century, saved from a nearby chapel, including some of Charlemagne. It is now just a short hop to Nantes.

Nantes and Rennes have often been rivals as 'capital' of Brittany, although Nantes had more French influence in it than Breton, because of the Loire. Now Nantes, and its *département* of Loire-Atlantique, are in Pays de la Loire, Rennes is viewed as the 'capital', although many people in Nantes will still tell you they are Breton and proud of it. Nantes' prosperity was built on foreign trade, notably the golden triangle of slaves and sugar, and this prosperity, reflected in the private and public buildings, has to a large extent been preserved. The castle, the cathedral, and a fine selection of museums — especially the Fine Arts Museum — are well worth visiting. The city has a wide range of hotel accommodation, but as a touring base it is limited in scope, as the sights of Brittany and Vendée are just that little bit too far for comfort.

The D178 follows the Erdre River north-east out of the city, into some pleasant countryside, with evidence of ancient forest from time to time. At Corquefou it is possible to detour to Sucé, where the river broadens and there are lots of water-sports opportunities. Shortly before La Meilleraye is the Voireau Reservoir, which is a major feed for the Canal de Nantes à Brest, and the Voireau Forest. This is very much border country — between Brittany and Anjou — often fought over in late medieval times when Brittany, controlled by its dukes, sided with the English against Anjou, controlled by the French. As a result the style of building of *châteaux* in this area changes from *'château'* to castle, or at the least, fortified *châteaux* or manors. **Châteaubriant** is a good example, although the surrounding countryside can only hint at what it was like when places like the town controlled great areas of forest.

Châteaubriant is overlooked by its castle, and the changes in architectural style bear witness to its continued importance across the ages. The castle is open daily from mid-June to mid-September, except Tuesday. Of the older part all that remains are some of the ramparts, plus the huge keep. Opposite are the sixteenth-century Renaissance-style buildings built by Governor Laval which overlook some pretty gardens. East of the town are several large areas of woodland, ideal for picnicking. The D775 from Châteaubriant skirts across the northern part of the *département*, crossing the main road from Nantes to Rennes at Derval. At Guémené-Penfao, turn southwards to Blain on the D15. This goes through the Gâvre Forest — which offers many walking opportunities — to the Carrefour de la Belle Etoile. Here some ten roads and tracks meet up, so make sure you continue on the D15 down to Blain.

Blain town stands on one side of the Nantes to Brest canal, opposite the ruins of its castle (not open to the public). The canal towpath is ideal for serious walkers, and there are plenty of villages along the canal for provisions, as well as small inexpensive hotels and *gîtes d'étape*. From Blain skirt the bottom of Gâvre Forest on the D164, then turn on to the D2 across to **St Gildas**, a pretty village set in the woods with a twelfth-century church. Turn south here to Pontchâteau, which is just south of the main N165 dual carriageway that runs the length of southern Brittany. Take the D33 towards Herbignac.

A little way outside Pontchâteau is a fine calvary, called La Madeleine, with a Stations of the Cross stretching across parkland. The Calvary is the scene of regular pilgrimages, sometimes with people in traditional costume. Calvaries are relatively common in Brittany, with illustrations of the Passion either carved in the granite, or depicted with statues, beneath a crucifix. There is a good view of the surrounding countryside from a little further on. Continue along the D33 which now skirts the top of the Brière Regional Park, turning off the road to the Château de Ranrouët. This is quite an imposing castle dating from the late twelfth century and currently being restored. At Herbignac turn south to Guérande, either on the D774, or on the prettier D47 and D51 which run along the western edge of the Brière.

Guérande is a quite remarkable town, retaining the complete run of city walls. Its wealth was largely built on salt from the salt pans to the south-west, but the town retains a great deal of character, especially during the summer period when cars are banned from inside the city walls (and consequently it can be fiendishly difficult to park!). It is possible to walk around the walls, which have four gates and six further towers. Alongside the tourist office there is a small museum (open April to September) in the main — St Michael's — gate, which has some interesting exhibits of local life. Inside the walls a rough grid pattern remains, with the church (St Aubin) in the centre. The church is a mixture of styles, and there is some fine stained glass.

The salt pans are just outside the town, centred upon **Saillé.** The bay where the pans are was turned into marsh by a change in sea level, and the area has been exploited since. The pans are formed by banks of soil, and the water level is controlled through a system of canals, so that only a shallow depth is left in the individual pans, or *'oeillets'*. As a result the salt from the sea water crystallises as the water evaporates. The salt is collected and left to dry out completely, before being left in huge piles at the edge of the pan. Saillé has a small museum (Maison des Paludiers, open June to September) showing artefacts and elements of the life of the salt workers. Immediately south of Saillé is the large popular resort of **La Baule**, with its superb beach and excellent facilities for all sorts of sports, including golf. There is a full range of hotels from small pensions up to the famous Hermitage, as well as self-catering villas and apartments.

The D92 from Saillé actually takes us the opposite direction, through the salt pans and then, after the small port and resort of La Turballe, along the increasingly rocky coast. There are some super views right along here. Continue through Piriac, another seaside town, along the coast road. This turns inland to go around a bay, and at St Molf head back towards Guérande. Then take the D51 to St Lyphard, and the Grande Brière Regional Park.

The Brière is a great area of marsh and bog, some 6,600 hectares (16,500 acres). Once a low forested basin, the area was flooded by the sea to create a marsh, and then the dying vegetation created peat bogs. From the Middle Ages the drainage has been improved, but the area, through whose heart no roads run, remains a haven for wildlife and waterfowl. The whole area was common land for all the local people, who until recently continued their traditional crafts of thatching, wickerwork and cutting peat. It is possible to take boat trips through the Brière from a number of places.

At **St Lyphard** it is possible to climb the church tower in July and August for a view across the Brière, as well as back towards Guérande. Continue along the D51 to Mayun, which is known for its wickerwork and baskets, then after following the D33 for about half a mile back towards Pontchâteau, turn right onto the D50. This road links the small islands that lie in the Brière. The most attractive is the Ile de Fédrun, which is just off the D50 near St Joachim. The road runs around the edge of the island. One of the thatched cottages is open to the public (open June to September), and retains a typical interior. The village holds a boat race during the local festival on 15 August.

Rejoin the D50 at the Ile de Aignac. At **Rosé** the Maison de l'Eclusier (former lock-keeper's house) which controlled the water level of the marsh, is open (June to September) with a display about the Brière. At Montoir it is possible to pick up the N171 back towards Nantes, or around St Nazaire to La Baule. Alternatively head towards the spectacular toll bridge across the Loire to the southern part of the *département*.

This modern toll bridge cuts out the long drive back to Nantes, and subsequently back again. However, if you want to head due south either way is practical. The toll bridge is a superb piece of engineering, and leads quickly into the flat countryside known as the Pays de Retz. Traditionally this has been the extreme southern part of Brittany, and it bears a number of resemblances to the Presqu'ile de Guérande, just north of the Loire. The area is today perhaps best known for the production of 'Gros Plant' wine, a dry white similar to Muscadet.

The coast is dotted with small seaside towns, many of which retain their character and life throughout the year, unlike say, St Jean de Monts. **Pornic**, just off the dual carriageway, is a case in point. A pleasant town, with a small fleet of fishing boats, it is set on the hillsides of a narrow inlet. It is best explored on foot, and there are some very pleasant walks alongside the sea (Les Corniches) and in the old part of the town. There are plenty of reasonable small hotels along this part of the coast too.

A little further down the main road is **Bourgneuf-en-Retz**, lying on the edge of a huge marshland area known as the Marais Breton-Vendéen, which extends as far south as the Vie River at St Gilles-Croix de Vie. It was once a huge bay, now drained and laid over to pasture. Unlike the Marais Poitevin further south, the image it presents is rather flat and stark, yet it does have a certain charm about it. Bourgneuf has a small, but interesting, museum of local history (open daily, except Tuesday), with exhibits of *coiffes* (lace head-dresses) and local life. The road divides here to either hug the coast, or head inland towards Machecoul (or alternatively back towards Nantes).

Whichever way is taken you cross the Marais. The drainage dykes are dotted with little huts with cranes and fishing nets. The farm-houses — known as *bourrines* — are unique to this area. The very low, single storey houses with thatched roofs are often surrounded by brown and white cows. The Marais marks the end of Brittany's traditional boundary, and the start of the Vendée. There is a change too in the architecture, and many say, in the climate. The Vendée, although it faces the Atlantic, does have a form of micro-climate with sunshine hours as good as the Riviera, and often temperatures not too far behind. Consequently, the coastal strip has seen considerable development, largely due to second homes of residents of Nantes. The result is that places like St Jean de Monts look like ghost towns for most of the year, and are impossible to get around in the height of summer! Even so, a number of towns have retained their charac-ter, and certainly inland little has changed.

Taking the coast road from Bourgneuf one reaches Beauvoir, where it is possible to make a detour to visit the island of **Noirmoutier**. For a long time Noirmoutier was only accessible at low tide, across a causeway. Today the visitor has the option of a toll bridge, but the causeway is more fun. Drivers should take note of the advice signs (in English) at Beauvoir about the tides. In spring and autumn the island has a pleasant character, especially with the blossom that abounds. As in Guérande, there are still a few salt pans active, and one can see the salt piled up alongside the pans from time to time. Part of the little museum at La Guérinière is devoted to the production of salt. After Noirmoutier the actual coastal strip is planted with forest, largely as a measure to hold the sand and dunes together. A good point to turn back inland towards Machecoul.

Machecoul, the historical 'capital' of Retz, and Challans, on the edge of the Marais, are fairly ordinary towns, with some tourist accommodation. **Challans**, though, undergoes a transformation on market day. The market is on Tuesdays, and is especially famous for its trade in ducks — get there early in the morning to sample a really good French market, full of local produce, sights, smells, and char-acters. Heading eastwards again, leaving the marshland area, the countryside takes on a more wooded and green flavour, and we pick up the main road heading south from Nantes to La Roche-sur-Yon (D753 then D937). Not far off this road is the Château de la Chabotterie, in fact a typical fortified manor house. (Take D18 from Les Lucs.) It was here that the leader of the Royalist uprising, Charette, was captured and imprisoned. There is an interesting museum about the uprising with uniforms and other exhibits.

La Roche-sur-Yon is the 'county' town of the Vendée, and is perhaps only remarkable for the fact that Napoleon decided to build the town from scratch, calling it, appropriately, Napoléon-Vendée. His grand design remains today, even if his name does not, except on the main square. The regional tourist office is just off the square, and the staff here are especially helpful, with plenty of information available. The town was built for strategic reasons, to control the subdued Vendée after the Royalist uprising. La Roche has, at its southern edge, an important stud farm, which it is possible to visit.

Heading north and eastwards from La Roche, one enters the heart of what is called 'La Vendée Militaire' — Military Vendée, although the area does extend outside the *département* itself. This was the location of the great Royalist uprising after the Revolution. The uprising is little known outside France, but it was an important episode in French history, as it sealed the fate of the Royalist cause.

After the execution of Louis XVI in January 1793, insurrection broke out in the area, largely as a reaction to the persecution of the clergy in what was a fiercely Catholic area; but no doubt egged on by the intervention of other European nations against France. The uprising covered much of the north-western corner of France, including Anjou where the uprising was known as the Chouannerie, but where action was dispersed. In the Vendée many of those who had fled Paris had gathered, along with the Catholic Royalist Army, so an ideal opportunity was presented which was taken. At first all went well for the Royalists, with the Army doing well at the eastern edge, while in the marshes and woodlands — the *bocage* — the tactics were of a guerilla-warfare style. The rebels adopted the symbol of the double armed cross with a heart, ironically still the symbol of Vendée today.

Within a couple of months the Republican forces (nicknamed the Blues) hit back in force, and after a major defeat at Chemillé the Royalists were pushed back, eventually into Maine and Brittany, where they fell apart in disorder. The Republican reaction followed with thousands of Royalist supporters shot or guillotined, and much of the Vendée was devastated. Even so, the uprising continued in the Vendée during 1794 and, despite a ceasefire, into 1795. The Royalists found their support diminishing, and eventually the Republicans succeeded in pacifying the whole region, having captured and executed the main leaders, notably Charette.

The countryside remains similar to how it was then, with narrow lanes, woods, and thick hedgerows, so one can get a good idea of what it was like. From La Roche head north-east along the N160 towards Cholet. **Les Essarts** has the ruins of a castle originally built in the eleventh century, rebuilt in the fifteenth and destroyed in 1794. It is open daily. Just after Les Essarts, pick up the N137 towards Nantes, but turn right on the D763 or D54 to **Clisson**, which was one of the key bases during the uprising and consequently suffered as a result. It was so well ruined that most people left.

It was rebuilt by the sculptor Lemot and architects the Cacault brothers who had returned from Italy, greatly influenced by what they had seen. As a result the town has an unexpected Mediterranean feel about it, which makes a walking tour quite enjoyable. Clisson was a border town controlled for a time by the Dukes of Brittany, so its *château* was important. The ruined *château* overlooks the Sèvre Nantaise River and is very attractive, with a moat which you cross to get in. North and west of Clisson is the main area for the production of Muscadet, a fine dry white wine, and there are plenty of opportunities for tasting and buying, either at shops or from individual producers.

From Clisson the road follows the Sèvre Nantaise (so-called to distinguish it from the Sèvre Niortaise in Charente-Maritime), towards Mortagne-sur-Sèvre. About 16km (10 miles) after Clisson, on the south bank of the Sèvre (follow D755 or N149 then D753) are the ruins of the Château de Tiffauges, once the home of Gilles de Rais. He was a nobleman who fought alongside Joan of Arc against the English. After Joan of Arc's death his extravagances used up all his fortune, and he turned to alchemy and devil-worship, sacrificing young children. Eventually hanged and burned, Gilles de Rais was (ironically) immortalised as Bluebeard in Perrault's fairytales. The *château* ruins cover a wide area, although the keep and one tower are the best preserved.

Mortagne-sur-Sèvre is set in a pretty location on the Sèvre River, and offers some reasonable hotel accommodation. Uranium ore was discovered close to the town, and so there are a number of mines nearby. From Mortagne head south-west on the N160 back towards La Roche. The countryside has changed significantly and is now much hillier, climbing up to Mont des Alouettes, where three windmills stand. Originally there were seven, and they were used during the Royalist uprising to send messages, different positions of the sails representing different things. The view from the hill is quite spectacular, across the *bocage* countryside below, and the hills behind.

A little further on is Les Herbiers, and if one takes the D755 it is possible to explore the hills. At **St Michel-Mont Mercure** the church tower can be ascended for a tremendous view — as far as the sea on a good day. North of St Michel is the Château du Puy du Fou, which has regular *son-et-lumière* presentations through the summer. Just south of St Michel (about 4.8km, 3 miles, on the D26) is **Le Boupère**, which has an interesting fortified church, which includes a guardroom on top of the tower. From Le Boupère cut across country to **Pouzauges**, which is a pleasant old town, overlooked by the ruins of another of Gilles de Rais's (Bluebeard) castles. There is another fine view from the top of Puy Crapaud, a nearby hill, which encompasses the whole of the Vendée.

From Pouzauges head southwards on the D752 to **Mouilleron-en-Pareds**, birthplace of two great Frenchmen — George Clemenceau and Jean de Lattre de Tassigny. There are two museums covering their lives in the town. Clemenceau, nicknamed 'The Tiger', was the French Prime Minister who led them to victory in World War I. De Lattre de Tassigny had a very distinguished military career leading the French army, and receiving Germany's surrender for France at the end of World War II. The road continues south towards Fontenay-le-Comte, but turn off to Vouvant, whose church (Notre Dame) has an exceptionally well decorated façade, more closely allied with Poitou-Charentes.

Vouvant is at the edge of a large forest area — Le Forêt de Mervent-Vouvant — where the river valleys have enabled dams to be built for water reservoirs and to make electricity. It is possible to drive through the forest, alongside the resulting lake, and there are opportunities for boating and fishing, as well as lots of waymarked paths. Follow the lake until you pick up the D65 to **Fontenay-le-Comte.** Fontenay has a unique position, lying at the foot of the hills, astride the Vendée River, reaching into the coastal plain and *bocage* as well as the Poitevin Marshes (Marais Poitevin). The town is a good touring base, with various hotels, and can provide a good introduction to the Vendée at the Vendée Museum, which has some very interesting exhibits tracing the development of the region. Although in the Vendée, and therefore the Pays de la Loire, the town has close ties with Poitou, and was for a long time (and indeed is still regarded as) the capital of Lower Poitou. The town reached its peak during the

Renaissance, consequently there is a considerable amount of Renaissance architecture, including in the church the Virgin's Chapel (Chapelle de la Vierge), the Château de Terre-Neuve and many houses in the old quarter around the church. It is only a short hop into Poitou-Charentes from here, on the D745 to Parthenay, or the N148 to Niort. Immediately south of the town is the Poitevin Marsh (Marais Poitevin), divided into the 'dry' and the 'wet' marsh. It is possible to explore this area from Fontenay, but the 'wet' marsh is described in the details about Niort in the Poitou-Charentes chapter.

Now turn westwards and skirt the top of the marsh along the D949 to **Luçon**. It is, of course, possible to drive through the marsh area, as an alternative. Luçon now lies on the edge of the 'dry' marsh, but was once a sea port at the edge of the gulf that became the marsh. The city (for it has a cathedral) is best known for one of its bishops — Richelieu — who later became a cardinal and played an important role in the history of France. When he first became bishop in 1608 the city was recovering from the end of the Wars of Religion, and the cathedral and Bishop's Palace were in need of repair. Richelieu took all these problems in hand. The cathedral, dating from the twelfth century, has a mixture of styles, although the overwhelming one is Gothic. It is also possible to visit the cloisters of the Bishop's Palace, next to the cathedral.

Luçon is a good place from which to visit the 'dry', that is the chiefly drained, part of the Poitevin Marsh. The D746 southwards from Luçon quickly brings you into the marsh, which has very dark, almost black soil, and so is greatly used for growing cereal and similar crops, although there is some pasture. The D746 runs down to the sea at **L'Aiguillon-sur-Mer**. *En route* it passes the ruined Benedictine abbey of St Michel which was destroyed during the Wars of Religion. L'Aiguillon is actually set behind a line of dunes (now a bird reserve), but has everything one needs in a small seaside town. A little further along the coast is the pleasant seaside town of **La Tranche-sur-Mer**. Much of the hinterland here is used for horticulture, especially bulbs, and La Tranche has a huge flower festival, called the 'Floralies' during March and April, with a parade of floats and other celebrations. Returning along the edge of the marsh (D747), the road passes through **Angles**. Stop to look at the church, where one of the gables carries a huge bear reputedly turned into stone by a local hermit. Take time too to visit **Moricq**, on the River Lay, just outside Angles. The fishing port here retains a large fortified watchtower. The road then turns back north to join the D949 towards Les Sables d'Olonne.

Anyone who enjoys gardens should make a point of visiting La Court d'Aron, which is on the D949 — you can't miss it. The gardens of the *château* (which can also be visited) have been transformed into a series of displays, which vary according to the time of year. It is especially beautiful in spring, and also when the roses bloom. Continue on the D949 either back to Luçon, or on towards Les Sables d'Olonne.

The coast has a small number of towns, before reaching the popular town and resort of Les Sables d'Olonne. **Jard-sur-Mer** is very nice, with some hotel accommodation and a lot of villas. Next door, in **St Vincent-sur-Jard**, is the house to which Georges Clemenceau retired, and which is now a small museum. Just before Les Sables is **Talmont-St-Hilaire**, with its ruined *château* overlooking what was the port. **Les Sables d'Olonne** is a good stopping place, with a good range of hotel accommodation. The fishing port is always busy and bustling, and the area between the port and the beach, where most of the shops are, is being progressively pedestrianised. The town also has a large theatre, a casino, and all that one could need in a seaside town.

From Les Sables, one can return to La Roche-sur-Yon, and thence to Nantes, to continue into Brittany or Normandy, or eastwards up the Loire. Alternatively, one can retrace steps through Fontenay, and head into Poitou-Charentes.

Further Information
— Pays de la Loire —

Museums and Other Places of Interest

Angers
Château and Tapestries
Open: daily except holidays,
9.30am-12noon and 2-6pm.

St Maurice's Cathedral

Maison d'Adam
Rue St Aubin

Fine Arts Museum
Open: daily except Monday,
10am-12noon and 2-6pm.

Baugé
Croix d'Anjou
Chapelle des Filles du Coeur de Marie

Bourgneuf-en-Retz
Pays de Retz Museum
6 rue des Moines
Open: daily 10am-12noon, 2-5pm.

Brissac-Quincé
Château
Open: daily except Tuesday 9am-11.30am, 2-4.30pm.

Chabotterie
Château
Open: daily April-September,
10am-12noon, 2-6pm.

Châteaubriant
Château
Open: daily, except Tuesday, mid-
June-mid-September, 10am-
12noon, 2-7pm.

Court d'Aron
Gardens
Open: April-September, 10am-
7pm. Château interior open June-
September, 10am-12noon, 2-6pm.

Les Essarts
Château ruins
Open: daily 9am-12noon, 2-6pm.

Ile de Fédrun
Chaumière Briéronne (thatched
house)
Open: JuneSeptember, 10am-
12noon, 3-7pm.

La Flèche
Prytanée Militaire

Chapel of Notre Dame des Vertus

Tetre Rouge Zoo

Fontenay-le-Comte
Notre Dame Church and Belfry

Château de Terre-Neuve
Open: June-September 9am-
12noon, 1.30-7pm.

Vendée Museum
Opposite church
Open: Tuesday-Friday, 10am-
12noon, 2-6pm.

Fontevraud
Abbey and Buildings
Opem: daily 9am-12noon, 2-6pm;
afternoons only October-March.

Laval
Old Château
Open: daily except Monday 9am-
12noon, 2-6pm.

Henri Rousseau Museum
Open: daily except Monday 9am-
12noon, 2-6pm.

Bateau-Lavoir Museum
Open: daily except Monday 9am-
12noon, 2-6pm.

Lion d'Angers
National Stud (Haras Nationaux
de l'Ile Briand)
Advance permission is required to
visit.

Montreuil-Bellay
Château
Open: July and August, 9am-
12noon, 2-6pm.

Mouilleron-en-Pareds
Museum (Clemenceau)
Open: daily except Tuesdays and
public holidays.

Museum (de Lattre de Tassigny)
Open: daily except Tuesdays and
public holidays.

Nantes
Château
Open: daily except Tuesdays and
public holidays, 10am-12noon, 2-
6pm.

Museum of Fine Art
Open: daily except Tuesday, 9am-
12noon, 2-6pm.

Local Art Museum
Open: daily except Tuesday, 9am-
12noon, 2-6pm.

Maritime Museum
Open: daily except Tuesday, 9am-
12noon, 2-6pm.

Plessis-Bourré
Château
Open: April-September, 10am-12 noon, 2-7pm, except Wednesday.

Port-du-Salut
Abbey
Open: daily 9am-6pm.

Puy-du-Fou
Château
Open: July-September 10am-12 noon, 2-6pm except Mondays. Regular *son-et-lumière* presentations during the season. Details from local tourist offices, or at La Roche-sur-Yon.

La Roche-sur-Yon
The Stud (Haras)
Boulevard des Etas-Unis
Open: July-March 10am-12noon, 2-5pm.

Town Museum
Open: Tuesday-Friday 10am-12noon, 2-6pm.

Rosé
Maison de l'Eclusier
Exhibits about the Grande Brière
Open: daily June-September 10am-12noon, 3-7pm.

Saillé
Maison des Paludiers
Open: June-September 2-6pm.

St Hilaire-St Florent
Mushroom Museum
Open: March-October 10am-12noon, 2-6pm.

St Michel Abbey
Ruins
Open: July and August, Tuesday, Thursday, Friday, 10am-12noon, 3-5pm.

St Michel-Mont Mercure
Church Tower
Open: daily 8am-12noon, 2-5pm, except during services.

St Vincent-sur-Jard
Clemenceau's House
Open: daily except Tuesday 9am-12noon, 2-4pm.

Saumur
Château
Open: daily except Tuesday 9am-5pm.

Maison du Vin

Cavalry School Museum
Open: daily 9am-12noon, 2-6pm.

Tank Museum
Open: daily 9am-12noon, 2-6pm.

National Horse Riding School
Home of the famous Cadre Noir team.
Visits arranged by tourist office.

Serrant
Château
Open: daily April-October, except Tuesday, 9-11.30am, 2-6pm.

Solesmes Abbey
Church only open to the public. Gregorian Chant sung at Mass (9.45am) and Vespers (5pm).

Talmont-St-Hilaire
Château
Open: March-October, 9am-12noon, 2-7pm.

Tiffauges
Château
Open: May-September, except Tuesday, 9am-12noon, 2-6pm.

Tourist Information Offices

Ancenis
Place du Pont
☎ 40 83 07 44
Open: daily except Sunday, 10am-
12noon, 3-6pm.

Angers
Place Kennedy
☎ 41 88 69 93
Open: daily except Sunday
9.30am-12noon, 2-6pm.

Baugé
Hôtel de Ville
☎ 41 89 12 12
Open: daily except Tuesday 11am-
12noon, 3-6pm.

La Baule
Place de la Victoire
☎ 40 24 34 44
Open: daily except Sunday, 9am-
12noon, 2.15-6.30pm

Brissac-Quincé
Mairie
☎ 41 91 22 13
Open: daily except weekends,
10am-12noon, 3-6pm.

Challans
Rue de Lattre-de-Tassigny
☎ 51 93 19 75
Open: daily except Sunday and
Monday, 9am-12noon, 2-6pm.

Châteaubriant
Rue du Château
☎ 40 81 04 53
Open: daily except Sunday, 9am-
12noon, 2-6pm.

Château-Gontier
Mairie

☎ 43 07 07 10
Open: daily except Sunday, 10am-
12noon, 2-6pm.

Châteauneuf-sur-Sarthe
Quai de la Sarthe
☎ 41 69 82 89
Open: daily except Sunday and
Monday morning, 9.30am-
12.30pm, 2.30-6.30pm.

Clisson
Place Minage
☎ 40 54 02 95
Open: 9am-12noon, 2-6pm during
July and August only.

La Flèche
Place de Marché-au-Blé
☎ 43 94 02 53
Open: daily except weekends
9am-12noon, 1.30-5pm.

Fontenay-le-Comte
Quai Poey d'Avant
☎ 51 69 44 99
Open: daily except Sunday 9am-
12noon, 1.30-7pm.

Fontevraud
Hôtel de Ville
☎ 41 51 71 41
Open: daily 9.30am-12.30pm, 2-
6pm.

Guérande
Tour St Michel
☎ 40 24 96 71
Open: daily June-September, 9am-
12noon, 2-6pm.

Laval
Place de 11 novembre
☎ 43 53 09 39
Open: daily except Sunday, 9am-
12noon, 2-6.30pm.

Luçon
Place du Général Leclerc
☎ 51 56 36 52
Open: daily except Sunday, 9am-12noon, 2-6pm.

Le Mans
Place de la République
☎ 43 28 17 22
Open: daily 9am-12noon, 1.30-6pm.

Montreuil-Bellay
Mairie
☎ 41 52 33 86
Open: daily except weekends, 9am-12noon, 2-6pm.

Nantes
Place Commerce
☎ 40 47 04 51
Open: daily except Sundays, 9am-7pm.

Noirmoutier
Route du Pont
☎ 51 39 80 71
Open: daily except Sunday, 9.30am-12.30pm, 2-6pm.
Access either via the Gois causeway (see notices at Beauvoir), or via the toll bridge.

Pornic
Place Môle
☎ 40 82 04 40
Open: daily, 9am-12.30pm, 2-6pm.

Pouzauges
Mairie
☎ 51 57 01 37
Open: daily except weekends 9am-12noon, 2-6pm.

La Roche-sur-Yon
Rue Clemenceau
☎ 51 36 09 63
Open: daily except Sundays 9am-12noon, 2-6pm.

Les Sables d'Olonne
Rue du Maréchal Leclerc
☎ 51 32 03 28
Open: daily except Sunday 9.30am-12noon, 2-6.30pm.

Sablé-sur-Sarthe
Place Elize
☎ 43 95 00 60
Open: daily except Sunday 9am-12noon, 2-6pm.

Saumur
Rue Beaurepaire
☎ 41 51 03 06
Open: daily except Sunday 9.15am-12.30pm, 4-6pm.

La Tranche-sur-Mer
Place de la Liberté
☎ 51 30 33 96
Open: daily except Sunday 9am-12noon, 2-6pm.

5 • Poitou-Charentes

As the A10 is the 'beaten track' which so many use, it is perhaps appropriate to use this as the starting point. The motorway drops down from Tours towards Poitiers following the Santiago de Compostela pilgrimage route. Leave the motorway at Châtellerault, a typical Loire Valley town, and start to work back in time. Take the N10 through and out of the town, and then turn left onto the D1 across the River Clain, turning right onto the small road that runs beside the river. A short drive brings you to some interesting Roman remains at **Vieux Poitiers**, with ruins of a theatre and kilns. Close by is the site of the eighth-century Battle of Poitiers, where the invading Moors were finally defeated; a defeat all the more psychologically crucial when one realises that Poitiers itself was the first major Christian centre in France.

A pleasant route towards Poitiers is to follow the River Vienne from Châtellerault as far as **Chauvigny** which boasts four *châteaux*, thus indicating its strategic position. There is no reason why you shouldn't continue along this very pretty river towards **Civaux**. There are a number of early churches at Civaux and St Pierre-les Eglises, where there are some interesting early wall paintings dating from the ninth or tenth century.

Of more interest, though perhaps the route to reach it is not quite as picturesque, is the small village of **St Savin**. Take the N151 from Chauvigny. The village is not really the object of this visit, rather the abbey church. Founded in the ninth century, the original abbey was ransacked by the Normans, and rebuilding didn't start until the late eleventh century. The abbey was subsequently fought over in the Hundred Years War and during the Wars of Religion, with the result that by the seventeenth century the place was almost in ruins. It is all the more surprising then, that the church contains the finest group of wall paintings from the eleventh century in the whole of France.

The church building itself is large if somewhat stark, with a long nave. There is some carving on the capitals, but the glory is the paint-

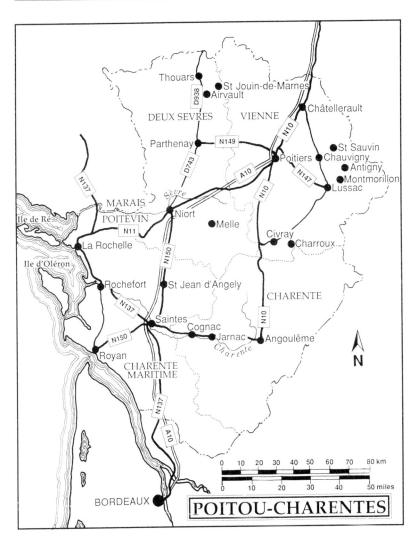

ings. Some, inevitably, have disappeared or suffered the ravages of time, but the porch, and especially the nave and crypt have outstanding frescoes. In the porch are scenes from the Apocalypse, the lighter tones in the paintings compensating for the lack of light. The nave paintings depict the early part of the Old Testament, beginning at the Creation (left-hand side), then the Flood, the Exodus, and Moses. The right-hand side tells the stories of Abraham and of Joseph. The crypt paintings are more sombre, depicting primarily scenes from the lives of the church's patron saints — Savin and Cyprien.

St Savin lies on the River Gartempe, and now follow the river southwards taking the D11 through **Antigny** to **Jouhet**. Both of these villages have churches with further wall paintings. Antigny's are of the Passion, Jouhet's (dating from the fifteenth century) of the Old Testament, the Nativity, and the Final Judgement. From Jouhet continue along the D5 to **Montmorillon**, which again has wall paintings in the Ste Catherine crypt of the church (Notre Dame), depicting scenes from Ste Catherine's life. From here, take the D727 to Lussac, where it is possible to pick up the GR48 long distance footpath, and then the N147 to Poitiers.

Poitiers is well worth a visit to see its quite remarkable selection of historical monuments. It is a good touring base, with an excellent selection of hotels. Its importance as an historical centre of learning is not to be overlooked. In the Middle Ages control of the city passed from English to French and back again, notably after one of the fiercest battles of the Hundred Years War, won by the Black Prince. Poitiers' least known, but perhaps most important, claim to fame is that the road from the north, heading south-west through the gap between the higher ground, marked the change from the *langue d'oil* and the *langue d'oc*, the northern and southern versions of spoken French in earlier times.

At Poitiers the motorway, and the pilgrimage route, head south-west towards Saintes. It is possible to keep to one of the other pilgrimage routes heading due south to Angoulême, roughly following the N10, or much more preferable, the River Clain to Vivonne. This passes through some fine rolling countryside, and almost any side turning will take you into unspoilt villages.

A detour off this road takes you through the pleasant town of **Civray**, albeit restored, with a fine, twelfth-century church (St Nicholas) with an interesting façade of traditional theme. This road then leads to **Charroux** and the Abbey of St Sauveur. To look at the ruins today, partly hidden beneath present building, one could not imagine the importance of the abbey, whose holdings at its peak included land in England. The source of this importance were the relics that it possessed — parts of the True Cross, as well as flesh and blood of Christ. The abbey's luck ran out in the Wars of Religion in the eighteenth century, and much was demolished. Restoration and archaeological work has continued during this century, and the abbey makes an interesting visit, especially to see some of its treasure which includes some fine ivory. The abbey tower gives an inspiring impression of what the original building must have been like. The ground plan runs below many of the surrounding buildings.

Heading south-west again towards **Angoulême**, one has no

Façade of the church at Angoulême

doubt of the importance that this town must have had in earlier times. The fortified centre rises up above the rest of the town and the surrounding countryside. The old quarter of the town presents a good feel of tiny streets and small, busy shops; and the long walk around the town walls is made more than worthwhile by the superb views across the Charente countryside. There is a reasonable amount of hotel accommodation. Much of Angoulême's wealth was built on paper mills (because of the quality of the water), but only a couple of mills are working now.

From Angoulême one of the prettiest trips in the whole area is to follow the valley of the Charente River downstream. In doing this one can travel a pleasant cross section from the hills that are now appearing in the south and east across to the Atlantic. The Charente, too, passes through important agricultural and wine-growing areas, before winding through the coastal plain and marshes, offering opportunities at the coast to see oyster beds.

It is possible to hire boats and cruisers on the Charente from a couple of locations, and this makes for an excellent way to explore this part of the countryside at a very slow speed. The river is slow moving, and the flatness of the land is borne out by just twenty-one locks along the hundred-mile length between Angoulême and Rochefort. The local or regional tourist offices can provide details, or the major boat companies in Britain usually book craft.

The River Charente (from which the *départements*, like so many, take their name) was described by Henri IV as the most beautiful river in his kingdom. Much of the surrounding landscape is dedicated to vineyards growing grapes for the production of Cognac. And whether you travel by car or boat (or, indeed, foot) Cognac is the town which acts as a focus for this area. The road follows the river along almost the whole of its length, with the more attractive lanes hugging the opposite banks, and the length of the valley can be explored by switching from one side to the other.

Almost all the villages are unspoilt and often quite charming, and many of the bridges, especially at St Simeux with its watermill, have superb views. There are regular appearances of *châteaux* or their remains either in the riverside towns, or close by. One of the prettiest is just inland from **Châteauneuf-sur-Charente** at Bouteville, where there are nice views both of the *château* and of the countryside. Returning through Châteauneuf, take the road back onto the north side of the river towards Jarnac. **St Simon** is a pleasant village, the houses overlooking the quiet quayside with shady trees. A little further is Bassac Abbey.

Originally founded in the eleventh century, the Benedictines built the abbey church, which has been added to, fortified, and restored across the years. The stark bell tower looks incongruous against the rest of the church, with four stories, each smaller than the previous, and topped by a spire. The interior of the church was completely altered at the start of the eighteenth century, with some wonderfully carved stalls, an eagle lectern, and the high altar, all the work of the monks and local artisans. Monks returned to the monastery after World War II.

The importance of Cognac (the brandy, not the town) is now well in evidence, with small producers offering their own wares, or most likely, Pineau; an interesting combination of brandy and wine. **Jarnac** is the next most important town to Cognac for production of brandy, and visits to many distilleries are available. It is easy to ignore the smaller producers in favour of the well-known, but the

Half-timbered buildings, Rennes, Brittany

Rochefort-en-Terre, Brittany

Flower-bedecked house in Rouffach, Alsace et Lorraine

smaller ones are often the most interesting in terms of both the distillation process and the drink itself.

After Jarnac the river widens out, and the roads tend to keep just a little away from it. Keep to the north side, so you can visit the impressive dolmen at Garde-Epée, and then into **Cognac**. Brandy, of course, dominates this town, with most of the producers being close to the river, as this was the main method of transporting the brandy. There is also a Cognac museum. The town retains some of its old quarter, but the walls have gone, although the Porte St-Jacques overlooks the river. Many of the houses in the old quarter are blackened by the fungus which grows, encouraged by the evaporating alcohol. However, other than for the dedicated alcoholic, Cognac offers little else of interest.

After Cognac the river begins to meander down to Saintes. It is possible to hug the river, take a more direct route to Saintes, or head northwards a bit towards Burie and St Jean d'Angély to visit the ruined *château* of Richemont, in the quiet valley of the Antenne, and then the ruined Fontdouce Abbey, just off the D131 towards Saintes. Some buildings still stand, and the other ruins give an idea of the size and prosperity of the abbey.

The countryside remains quite calm and flat until one reaches the large and busy city of **Saintes**; large and busy since before the Romans invaded Gaul. Consequently the town retains bits and pieces of its history through the ages, including some impressive Roman ones. Saintes was also an important point on another of the Compostela pilgrimage routes, and has some impressive religious buildings. The motorway passes close to the city, but to escape one can follow the River Charente towards the sea. Saintes' importance as the regional capital and its position on the Compostela route, means that all around in the villages there are exquisite examples of Romanesque churches, often in the pale local stone. The simplicity of the design is often made up for by outstanding carving on the façades or other stonework.

Before heading north-west with the river, it is possible to make a loop down towards the Gironde, dipping (just) into the start of the Bordeaux wine region. A little way south-east of Saintes is **Pons**, situated on a hill, and once a most commanding fortress. The Lords of Pons were hugely influential in their corner of France, ruling over some sixty towns and over six hundred parishes. The *château* gives an impression of the power of the lords, being a solid stone keep, dating from the twelfth century, some 27m (90ft) high with three separate stories. The fanciful battlements were added at the turn of this century. There is a lovely view from the top of the keep.

Being on the Compostela route the church (St Vivien) is quite typical of the local style; and on the outskirts of the town is part of one of the hospices, where pilgrims could rest. The importance of this area during the twelfth century, and then later, during the Renaissance, means that there is a surfeit of churches and *châteaux*. Depending on one's interest it is possible to see one or two, or a dozen.

The Château d'Usson is a good example of a Renaissance *château*, but visiting is very limited, and only the exterior. Likewise, Plassac, further south. Between Usson and Plassac are some four churches worth looking at, Fléac (Renaissance), Avy, Marignac, and Chadenac (all twelfth century) which boasts a quite lavish façade with superb carving representing the struggle between Good and Evil.

Swing westwards, and head towards Royan, but call in at **Talmont**, which is a very pleasant seaside town with a lovely Romanesque church (Ste Radegonde) which sits on a rocky cliff overlooking the Gironde. After Royan, the countryside slips into sandy undulations, and the route heads northwards again towards Saintes.

From Saintes one can head up the coastal strip, or through the hinterland. The coastal strip is well trodden, with the two towns of Rochefort and La Rochelle acting as key points. Both are well covered elsewhere, and, unless you are visiting well out of season, are definitely on the beaten track. Even in the height of summer, the interior is remarkably quiet and uncrowded, with a pace of life that is far more heartening and relaxing.

Heading north-eastwards, towards Niort, one is tracing the main pilgrimage route to Santiago de Compostela which was followed briefly earlier. This heads through St Jean d'Angély and Aulnay to Poitiers, and the route offers opportunities to meander through the countryside as well as history. Indeed, **Taillebourg**, on the D114 is more famous for a battle which took place in 1242 between forces of Louis IX of France and Henry III of England for control of the bridge over the Charente. A result was only achieved two days later, closer to Saintes, with the routing of the English.

Close by is **Port d'Envaux**, again on the banks of the Charente, with two pleasant *châteaux*. The Château de Panloy, just to the north, is built on the remains of an earlier *château* but has the harmonious style of the Renaissance. The interior of the *château* contains some fine decoration including some tapestries. The Château de Crazannes, about 3km (2 miles) north, is again built on the base of an earlier *château*, has been added to since, and still retains some of the original fortifications.

If *châteaux* are your forté, then you should not miss La Roche-Courbon a few miles to the west. In launching his campaign to save the *château*, the writer Pierre Loti immortalised it as Sleeping Beauty's *château*, lost, as it was, in the heart of a forest. His campaign succeeded and the *château* and its superb gardens were restored during the 1920s. The *château* remains set in the woods, and you pass through the huge Lion Gate to reach it. Originally built in the fifteenth century, the *château* was remodelled in the seventeenth. Its formal gardens and terraces are a joy, and the view of the front, reflected in the little lake with the symmetrical formal gardens, is how you expect a French *château* to be.

From La Roche-Courbon one can cut back across country, over the Charente, to **Fenioux**, another stopping point on our now familiar pilgrimage route. Despite its twelfth-century façade, most of the church dates from the ninth century. The arches depict the seasons, the signs of the Zodiac, and the struggle between Good and Evil, all familiar to us from other churches in the region, and popular Saintonge themes. An interesting feature here is the graveyard *lanterne des morts*, a grouping of columns, and especially tall.

It is only a short run from Fenioux to **St Jean d'Angély**, set on a hill around which the River Boutonne curls. The centre of the town is a myriad of narrow streets and squares (known as '*cantons*') with several timber frame houses from the fifteenth and sixteenth centuries and some fine town houses of the seventeenth and eighteenth centuries. Ironically this town, once a major stopping point on the Compostela route, was a key centre during the religious reform of the sixteenth century.

The original abbey, of which some ruins remain, was destroyed by the Huguenots in the sixteenth century, but rebuilding was started in the eighteenth century. It was interrupted by the Revolution (when part of the new building was used as a prison), so that the abbey is unfinished. The façade however is impressive. Close by in the Canton du Pilori is a pretty well with an elaborate Renaissance cover which comes originally from a nearby *château*.

Heading northwards again on the historical route from Saintes to Angers the road arrives at **Aulnay**. Here the route moves from the Saintonge (the area influenced by Saintes) into Poitou and so the church reflects something of a change in style. The twelfth-century church of St Pierre stands alone, but its fine stonework and colour produces a rare harmony of style. There is some fine stone carving with traditional images, reflecting the traditional style of the building. Nearby churches also reflect the styles, and, moving further northwards, one notes a slight change. Not far from Aulnay is a pleasant *château* at **Dampierre-sur-Boutonne**. A Renaissance *château* built on an island in the middle of the River Boutonne, the main part remains, defended by two towers, and is divided into two galleries. The upper gallery has delicate carvings on the ceiling of emblems and proverbs, as well as the personal monograms of various worthies.

From Aulnay head straight for Niort, or back towards Poitiers. This latter route is worth holding to as far as Melle. En route pass the Forest of Chizé, some 5,000ha (12,500 acres), part of the Val de Sèvre Regional Park. There are lots of opportunities for walking and riding and it is possible to hire horse-drawn caravans from Aulnay. **Melle** is the last stop on the main Compostela pilgrimage route which comes from Poitiers, as afterwards the route heads northwards. It is best seen for the first time from the south, to appreciate its position in the narrow valley of the River Béronne, and owes its existence to the lead mines, and subsequently a mint. Its importance as a pilgrimage staging post is borne out by the number of churches in such a small area. St Hilaire's church is twelfth century, but in a pure Romanesque style, with a sober façade. Above the north doorway is carved a horseman, found on churches in this area, and the cause of great scholarly argument. A man sits on a horse which is trampling a sitting figure. This is supposed to represent Charlemagne or Christ overcoming the old ways, or Constantine defeating paganism. The interior has some lovely carvings, especially on the capitals. Two other churches in the town are worth visiting. Both are twelfth century, and both are in a simple Romanesque style, with decoration. These are St Pierre (on the northern side of the town) and St Savinien (just off the Avenue Bernier). St Savinien was used as a prison from the early nineteenth century, and is different in that the east door reflects the Limousin style rather than Poitou.

From Melle it is only a short hop to **Celles-sur-Belle**, which is dominated by the bell tower of the old abbey. The abbey is perhaps less famous than some of its abbots, which included Geoffrey d'Estissac, who is closely linked with Maillezais Abbey to the north-west of Niort in the Marais Poitevin; and Talleyrand, a famous French diplomat and politician of the late eighteenth century. It is possible to visit the refectory, the kitchens, and a part of the cloisters. The town church of Notre-Dame attracts a local pilgrimage on the first Sunday of September. The church was destroyed by the Huguenots in the sixteenth century and rebuilt in a fifteenth-century style. Part of the old church remains in the form of the large doorway — it is interesting in that its design reflects the oriental influences that returned up the Compostela route from Spain.

The countryside has changed during the drive inland into the higher ground, but the route turns back towards the sea, and the sea's influence, heading towards **Niort**. This is a good touring base, within reach of much of the southern part of this area of France. The change in the countryside towards the sea is reflected very much in that Niort has long been tied to the sea, as an important port for the area. As a result the place has a quiet bourgeois feeling to it. The town grew up on the banks of the Sèvre (known as the Sèvre Niortaise to distinguish it from the Sèvre Nantaise which flows further north to Nantes and the Loire) in Roman times, and of which nothing remains. In the Middle Ages great wealth came to the town, under the protection of Eleanor of Aquitaine. Jean de Berry, Count of Poitou, created the port, which quickly grew to export salt, cereals and wool throughout the Western European seaboard. In return, animal skins were imported and used in the extensive local leather industry, which still plays an important role today.

Niort retains several Middle Ages buildings, notably the castle, built on the edge of the river, and the sixteenth-century town hall (now a museum). The castle, started by Henry II (of England) and finished by Richard the Lionheart, was regularly fought over through the ages, ultimately ending up as a prison, and now an interesting regional museum. This contains traditional costumes and head-dresses, and the interior of a peasant home in the early nineteenth century — an excellent introduction to the local area.

The former town hall was built in a triangular shape in the sixteenth century and now houses the Musée du Pilori, a diverse series of collections, most with local interest. A short walk away is another museum — Beaux-Arts (fine arts) — with some interesting tapestries, and the church of Notre-Dame with a fine tower and steeple. The town offers a limited amount of accommodation, as well as train connections to Paris.

Before leaving the town, though, visit one area which, although it is partly in the Vendée and so in the Pays de la Loire, is best explored from Niort. This is the marshland area between Niort and the sea, lying either side of the Sèvre Niortaise and known as the Marais Poitevin (Poitevin Marshes). This strange and beautiful countryside has a character very much of its own.

In ancient times the coastline was much further inland and a huge bay extended from Jard-sur-Mer past Luçon, Maillezais, and Coulon, curving back round to Esnandes. In this bay were a number of islands. The action of the sea and of the various rivers led to the deposition of sands and alluvials, and the silting up of the whole bay, thus giving marshes.

From early on man sought to exploit this as the soil was extremely fertile, and the way was led in the eleventh century by monks from the abbeys in the marshes. They built fishponds, mills, and water control systems. These were elaborated in the thirteenth century when five abbeys cut a canal to drain the northern marshes. Bit by bit work continued, with more drainage canals until today, where the coastline is several miles away from where it once was. Today the marshes— which extend across some 60,000ha (150,000 acres) — divide into two parts. The 'wet' marsh lies inland, roughly between Niort and Damvix, and also goes under the name of the 'Venise Verte' or Green Venice. The 'dry' marsh, between Damvix and the sea is the largest area, primarily drained land turned over to pasture.

The 'Venise Verte' is the more attractive of the two, as the narrow canals criss-cross the area like a spider's web, beneath a canopy of trees. While one needs a car to explore, the best way to appreciate the area is to take to the water. A number of towns and villages offer boat trips around the year, notably Arçais, Damvix, Maillezais, Coulon and St Hilaire-la-Palud. Costs vary, but you need to allow about 1-2 hours for a trip, depending on your start point. Despite what you might see on postcards, you are unlikely to come across cattle being transported in the small punts. However, only by taking to the water can you appreciate the unspoilt nature of this corner of France.

From Niort then, head for Coulon, once a village of sailors, as the houses either side of the canalised river testify. Coulon is the main departure point for boat trips, but it is best to wait until you reach the Abbey of Maillezais. From Coulon follow the river to Arçais, then Damvix, both villages typical of the area. At Damvix take the D25 towards Vix, but turn off to the Abbey of Maillezais. The abbey is just a little further on than the village.

When the abbey was founded in the tenth century, it stood facing the sea, and has faced battles ever since. The beautiful buildings were sacked in the thirteenth century, and devastated during the Wars of Religion in the sixteenth century, when the bishop's seat was transferred to La Rochelle. Some substantial ruins remain — enough to give an idea of the size of the original abbey, and much of the ground plan is marked out. Building began in the eleventh century, with additions and alterations in the thirteenth, fifteenth and sixteenth. The monastery was largely completed in the fourteenth century, and one wing still stands, and can be visited. A little further down from the abbey you can take a trip on a punt through the canals for about 45 minutes. From Maillezais one can continue into the 'dry' marsh, or return to Niort.

From Niort the route now moves northwards again towards Parthenay. A little north of Niort, at **Echiré**, is the Château de Coudray-Salbart, a fine thirteenth-century fortress overlooking the Sèvre Niortaise, and dominating the countryside. The walls have six towers, and a passage for the defenders inside the walls has arrow slits facing inside and outwards so the castle could defend itself even if attackers reached the courtyard inside the walls.

A little further northwards, just before Champdeniers, a detour is called for to explore the pretty river valley of the Egray as far as St Ovenne. Here it is possible to take to byroads back towards Niort, otherwise, continue to **Parthenay**. Parthenay's location on a meander of the River Thouet and on a hillside meant it had great military value, as its fortress testifies. This is best appreciated from Pont-Neuf (on the N149 taking the main road north). You can see some of the ramparts and the old main entry gate of Porte St Jacques, with its narrow bridge, as well as the geographical location of the town. The town gate leads to Rue de la Vaux-St Jacques, once the main road, and lined with half-timbered houses. The fortress ramparts can again be seen in the small square at the top of the road, and the main entry to the fort is round the corner, through the Porte de l'Horloge (the Bell Gate) named after its bell and the fact that it was a belfry. The old quarter has a fascinating selection of shops, but there is limited hotel accommodation in the town, mostly in the newer parts.

At Parthenay the visit to Poitou-Charentes is nearly complete, but there is still quite a lot to see. From Parthenay head northwards, but bear westwards on the D19 towards La Chapelle St Laurent. This road runs through some very pretty countryside, especially between Clessé and La Chapelle. At La Chapelle, continue on the D19 to Moncoutant, and pick up the D38 north to Bressuire. Again, this is a very pretty road, going into the heart of the *bocage* countryside.

Bressuire is the first indication that this is further north, for the architecture is beginning to show other influences. In its church (Notre-Dame) the influence of the Loire Valley, or rather of the English can be seen! Although there are Romanesque aspects there are also Gothic and Renaissance features. Bressuire is important though, not for its church, but for the fact that it played an important role during the Vendée wars in the 1790s.

From Bressuire, head eastwards again, back down the N149, but then across country (and back into the hills) on the D725 to Airvault. **Airvault**, now a peaceful village, was an important centre of learning under the protection of the *château* of the Vicomtes of Thouars. The church (St Pierre), is an important regional monument, and again, as at Bressuire, there is a mixing of Romanesque and early Gothic styles. The fine porch leads into a delightful interior, with fine sculpture and carving. A little remains of the abbey itself — part of the cloister, and chapterhouse. A small museum of local folklore is also close by.

Not far from Airvault is **St Jouin-de-Marnes**, which has another abbey, of which only the church really remains. However, it is interesting to compare St Pierre at Airvault with St Jouin. Some elements are similar, such as the vaulting, but others have been affected by fortification and restoration. There is a fine façade outside, with another horseman, and traditional themes. The choir has some fine work.

From St Jouin head northwards again, taking a short diversion from the D37 to **Oiron**, whose *château* does strike memories (or foresights) of the Loire Valley. A fine building of sixteenth and seventeenth centuries, with a super gallery on one wing. The interior is beautifully decorated, with some superb ceilings, and a long gallery with fourteen frescoes based on the *Illiad* and the *Aeneid*.

Oiron is the last stop before reaching **Thouars**. The old part of Thouars juts out on a promontory, and its position is consequently well defended on three sides. The town's museum is a good introduction, as indeed, is a wander along the main road from the *château* to the church of St Médard. The *château* is of the seventeenth century whereas St Médard is twelfth century, and a fine example of the now familiar Poitou style. The façade has the familiar themes, and there is even a trace of Moorish influence, which no doubt came up the Compostela routes. Elements of the northern France influences can be seen in the town, as indeed can those of English rule at the Tour du Prince de Galles (Prince of Wales Tower). Thouars is a good place to end the tour, for from it you can head in any direction to find many more places of interest.

Further Information
— Poitou-Charentes —

Museums and Other Places of Interest

Angoulême
Town Museum
Open: daily except Tuesday, 10am-12noon, 2-6pm.

Archaeological Museum
Open: daily except Tuesday, 2-5pm.

Charroux
St Sauveur Abbey

Open: daily 10am-12noon, 2-6pm, except Tuesdays and holidays.

Châtellerault
Local History Museum
Open: afternoons daily except Sunday.

Science and Car Museum
Open: daily, 9am-12noon, 2-6pm.

Vieux Poitiers Roman remains south of town. Open: afternoons at weekends.

Cognac
Cognac Museum
Open: afternoons 2.30-6pm except Tuesdays and holidays.

Cognac Distilleries
Most offer visits between 9-11am and 2-5pm except weekends and, with very few exceptions, in July and August.

Coudray-Salbart
Château
Open: daily 10am-12noon, 2-5pm, except Tuesdays and holidays.

Crazannes
Château
Open: afternoons, 2.30-6.30pm, during French school holidays, and weekends.

Dampierre-sur-Boutonne
Château
Open: 10am-12noon, 2.30-5pm June to September, otherwise Sundays only.

Fontdouce Abbey
Open: daily except Friday, 10am-12noon, 2.30-5.30pm.

Maillezais Abbey
Open: daily 9am-12.30pm, 2-6pm. Boat trips available beside abbey — same times.

Niort
Castle Keep, Old Town Hall, Fine Arts Museum
Open: daily except Tuesday, 9am-12noon, 2-6pm, one ticket admits to all.

Oiron
Château
Open: daily except Tuesdays and Wednesdays, 10am-12noon, 2-4pm.

Panloy
Château
Open: Sundays and public holidays, 2.30-6pm.

Poitiers
Palace of Justice
Open: daily 9am-7pm.

Ste Croix Museum
Open: daily except Tuesday, 10am-12noon, 2-6pm.

La Roche-Courbon
Château
Open: daily except Wednesday, 10am-12noon, 2.30-5.30pm.

Saintes
Fine Arts Museum
Open: daily except Tuesday, 10am-12noon, 2-5pm.

Talmont
Interior of Ste Radegonde only open during July and August.

Tourist Information Offices

Angoulême
Place St Pierre
☎ 45 95 16 84
Open: daily (not Sunday) 9am-12.30pm, 1.30-6.30pm.

Bressuire
Place de l'Hôtel de Ville
☎ 49 65 10 27
Open: Tuesday to Saturday, 10am-12noon, 2-6pm.

Châtellerault
Boulevard Blossac
☎ 49 21 05 47
Open: daily (not Sunday), 8.45am-12.15pm, 2.15-6.30pm.

Chauvigny
Hôtel de Ville
☎ 49 46 30 21
Open: daily (not Sunday), 9am-12.30pm, 2-6pm.

Cognac
Place Monnet
☎ 45 82 10 71
Open: daily except Sunday, 8.30am-7pm.

Coulon
Place de l'Eglise
☎ 49 35 99 29
Open: June-September, 10am-12.30pm, 2-6.30pm.

Jarnac
Place du Château
☎ 45 81 09 30
Open: daily (not Sunday), 9am-12noon, 2-6pm.

Montmorillon
Avenue Tribot
☎ 49 91 11 96
Open: daily (not Sunday) 10am-12noon, 2-7pm.

Niort
Place de la Poste
☎ 49 24 18 79
Open: daily (not Sunday) 9.15am-12noon, 1.30-6pm.

Parthenay
Palais des Congrès
☎ 49 64 24 24
Open: Tuesday-Saturday, 9.15am-12noon, 1.30-6pm.

Poitiers
Rue Victor Hugo
☎ 49 41 58 22
Open: daily (not weekends) 9am-12noon, 2-5.30pm.

Pons
Castle Keep
☎ 46 96 13 31
Open: June to September 10am-12noon, 3-7pm.

St Jean d'Angély
Square de la Libération
☎ 46 32 04 72
Open: Tuesday-Saturday, 2-5.30pm.

Saintes
Esplanade Malraux
☎ 46 74 23 82
Open: daily (not Sunday or Monday) 9am-12noon,1.30-7pm.

Thouars
Place St Medard
☎ 49 66 17 65
Open: daily (not Sunday), 9am-12noon, 2-6pm.

6 • Aquitaine

Variety, they say, is the spice of life — a cliché which makes Aquitaine one of the most highly-seasoned areas in France. Nor does it do anything by halves. To the west, the Bay of Biscay hurls long Atlantic rollers against the most impressive sand dunes in Europe, the high Pyrénées with their summer flowers and winter snows provide a frontier with Spain while, to the north, the Parc Régional des Landes de Gascogne maintains that its forest is more extensive than any other on the Continent. Added to this are lakes and rivers filled with fish, pastures and vineyards, ancient towns, isolated villages and coastal resorts busy planning their way into the twenty-first century.

Historically the contrasts are just as obvious. The earliest residents, who hunted mammoths in the area anything up to 20,000 years ago, have left plenty of evidence of the kind of life they lived. The Romans moved in considerably later and under the Emperor Augustus extended the northern boundary from the River Garonne to the Loire. In the twelfth century the English, united with Normandy for the time being under one ruler, added it to their other possessions on the Continent. They lost it again, together with the Hundred Years' War, at the battle at Castillon, near Bordeaux, in 1453. The kingdom of Navarre did not survive much longer. The southern part went to Spain in 1516 and the northern section became part of France in 1589. After some three centuries the British moved back without firing a shot, simply by adding Biarritz to their list of popular holiday resorts after Napoleon III and the Empress Eugénie decided that the little fishing village would make an acceptable summer residence. Biarritz is still sophisticated inspite of modern additions like camping sites but the British have largely switched their affections to the Perigord where they have settled in force and give every impression of making their invasion a permanent one.

Aquitaine, south of the River Garonne, is largely off the beaten track with few places of international repute apart, of course, from

Bordeaux itself, Biarritz and Lourdes. The bigger towns are scattered thinly over the region, interspersed with villages and hamlets which, between them, have a considerable amount to offer the visitor. Most have at least one *auberge* with comfortable beds complete with bolsters and, usually, extra pillows tucked away in the cupboards for anyone who needs them. The cooking tends to be traditional and based on local produce. Oysters are particularly good round Arcachon, the famous Bayonne hams are made in Orthez and buntings are a speciality in the Landes along with mushrooms and asparagus. Fish comes in all flavours from salmon to carp stuffed with *foie gras*, steaks are served with truffle or red wine sauces and venison, wild boar, woodcock and partridge all appear on local menus. Many of the wines are justly famous, particularly Bordeaux and Graves, but each region has its own local favourites. Madiran concentrates on red, the Béarn mostly on *rosé* and the Landes on white. Sweet wines appear as *apéritifs*, with fruit and with *foie gras* while Armagnac, the famous and ancient brandy of the country, takes pride of place with coffee. Fruit soaked in Armagnac is delicious as are the various cheeses that the shepherds have been making from ewe's milk for many generations.

Sports are very much part of life in Aquitaine. Tennis courts can be found nearly everywhere along with swimming pools, some of which are heated. Riding stables cater for anything from an hour out in the countryside to a full-blown pony trek while some experts insist that it is the best place to go in France for a golfing holiday. Fishermen can choose between salmon, trout and shad in the rivers or pike, bream and roach in the lakes and ponds and there are routes designed for long-distance hiking as well as short rambles lasting only an hour or two. The Pyrénées offer plenty of opportunities for mountain climbing and, of course, all the usual winter sports during the season. The seaside resorts are equipped for activities of every description, the small ones having a fairly modest range but the larger ones add things like deep-sea diving and fishing and boats for water-skiing to their other attractions. Over and above all this the surfing, especially in the Biarritz area, is said to be the best in Europe. The majority of villages in the Basque country have their own pelota courts, pool tables appear in the most unlikely places, rugby is becoming increasingly popular and there are casinos in the larger centres, especially on the coast. Bullfights pull in the crowds as do the many *fêtes* and festivals that take place during the summer.

Apart from hotels and *auberges* there are villas and apartments, *gîtes* that can be anything from a country cottage to part of a private

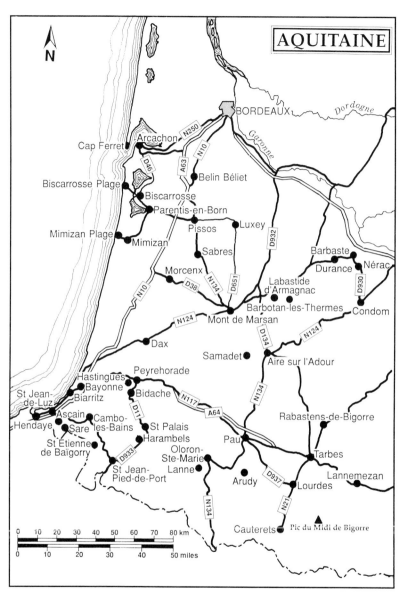

house, holiday villages, sites for tents and caravans and, in keeping with the times, half a dozen centres where visitors need a toothbrush but no clothes to feel perfectly at home. Fortunately the weather lends itself to naturism with hot sun during the summer season although the spring can be chilly and winter in the mountains is decidedly cold.

It can be a trifle disconcerting to discover that all those French lessons, even when augmented by a dictionary and a book of useful phrases, fall short of requirements in some of the more outlying areas. This is because the traditional language is 'Oc', the word for 'yes' in southern France as opposed to 'Oïl' which was confined to the country north of the Loire. Even the *langue d'oc* varies to a certain extent from one region to another, especially where the accent and intonation are concerned. However *langue d'oïl* has become the official version for the whole country and even elderly people who have not caught up with it yet can get the general drift. If not, the gaps are filled with polite attention, plenty of gestures and warm, friendly and encouraging smiles.

Getting to Aquitaine presents no problems at all. Paris is an hour away by air with daily flights to and from Bordeaux, Biarritz, Pau and Agen. There are also direct flights to several European capitals and to more than a dozen French cities, among them Nice, Lille, Grenoble and Clermont-Ferrand. The train services are equally accommodating, providing daily opportunities for travel from Paris to Agen, Dax, Hendaye and Pau and back again as well as facilities for taking the car by rail if the destination is Tarbes, Bordeaux or Biarritz. Motorists who prefer to find their own way to Aquitaine have a choice of three motorways that run north to Paris, east to the Mediterranean and south to Spain. Other main roads fan out in all directions and there is an extensive network of secondary roads linking hundreds of small towns and villages. Generally speaking the surfaces are good but where road works are in progress the deviations can be bumpy to say the least of it. Some little lanes call for even lower speeds and more constant attention, particularly where there is only room for one car and a distinct possibility that another vehicle or a flock of sheep will be coming in the opposite direction.

Many people with a tour of Aquitaine in mind will probably start from **Bordeaux**. Not only is it the capital with all the advantages of an airport, a busy harbour and a goodly number of very comfortable hotels, coupled with a wide choice in the less-expensive bracket, but it also abounds in places to see and things to do. Having once set foot there, any traveller worth the name would be curious to see exactly what the city has to offer before setting out for parts other visitors often ignore. Its many churches include a cathedral, the basilica of St Michel which almost, but not quite, overlooks the river and the more centrally-situated church of Notre-Dame. Nearby is the Grand Théâtre, solid and frequently traffic-bound, where opera lovers congregate for the Bordeaux Festival. It is all of a piece with the shopping area where large windows tempt passers-by of every income and persuasion. The city is rich in museums, the two main ones being the Musée des Beaux-Arts with paintings covering every school from Rubens to the twentieth century, and the Museum of Decorative Arts where the emphasis is on the eighteenth century, exactly matching the building in which it is housed. Among the smaller ones the Musée d'Aquitaine delves back into prehistory before bringing local matters up to date; the more unusual Musée des Douanes tells the story of smuggling and the customs men who tried to stamp it out; the Centre Jean Moulin concerns itself with World War II and the large public gardens have a natural history museum of their own. Visitors with only a passing interest in matters such as these can head for the racecourse, play tennis or golf, set off along the Canal-du-Midi which comes out in the Mediterranean, or opt for any of a number of water sports.

The nearest place to find both sea and sand is **Arcachon**. It is a biggish town that shares its name with a large sea-water bay-cum-lagoon where oysters take second place to tourists, but only just. The shores are a mass of small villages and camping sites, all spending their time keeping holidaymakers entertained and happy. There is a yacht harbour with boats for hire, deep-sea diving and fishing, surfing, wind-surfing and waterskiing with a choice of casinos and a museum of the sea. Apart from displaying leftovers from the Iron Age and other relics that have turned up in the area from time to time, it has an aquarium with more than five hundred different species, making it difficult to see them all at once.

There are plenty of shops, a wide range of hotels, little trains that chunter backwards and forwards to the sea and boat trips round the Bassin d'Arcachon as far as the lighthouse at Cap Ferret, stopping just short of the Bay of Biscay itself.

Behind the enormous sand dunes, **Pyla-sur-Mer** has the highest of all, a line of lagoons runs parallel with the shore, getting smaller and smaller all the time until they peter out completely a little north of Bayonne. The Etang de Biscarrosse et de Parentis, one of the larger, more northerly ones, has some difficulty in deciding whether it should be a holiday playground or concentrate on oil. As a result it has a small land-locked marina and a sprinkling of pumps that are hard at work all the time. The water can be unexpectedly rough in windy conditions and although there are places to park better spots can be found for bathing or having a picnic. **Biscarrosse Plage** takes its role as a seaside resort quite seriously and keeps a watchful eye on bathers who wander off on their own when the sun umbrellas and beach beds get too numerous for comfort. The town itself breaks new ground with a seaplane museum while **Parentis-en-Born** invites motoring enthusiasts to inspect its petroleum museum.

A large military zone, peppered with shellholes and other tell-tale traces of modern warfare, marches south with the dunes, successfully cutting off all access to the sea between Biscarrosse Plage and **Mimizan**. This is a rather self-important little town which had an abbey church back in the thirteenth century but now draws attention to local history, including traditional arts and crafts, by means of a small but carefully planned museum. It also has its own *plage* (beach) very much in keeping with all the other similar places further along the coast. As they are not linked together, special short detours are needed to inspect each one, to be greeted by silver sands, camping sites, functional shops, an occasional tennis court and, sometimes, pedalos for hire. Eventually, perhaps, they will all link hands, with hotels and high-rise buildings, villas and promenades presenting the same united front that one sees on the Riviera, but for the moment the dunes facing the Atlantic are relatively undisturbed. Everywhere the breakers look perfect for surfing but it is as well to remember that there are strong currents which make it a dangerous pastime for anyone, with or without a board. It is more sensible to keep an eye open for warning notices and stay within sight of the lifeguards than to test the water alone.

Holidaymakers whose horizons extend beyond a mixture of sun, sea and sand will find that there are any number of attractions well away from the coast. The forests of the Landes, vast as they are, only form part of the Regional Park that begins at the Bassin d'Arcachon. At one time the area consisted largely of marshes and moorland with sand blown in by winds from the west gradually taking it over and turning it into a wilderness. The first attempts to control nature began at the end of the eighteenth century and within a remarkably short time pine forests had sprung up and large sections were drained, ready for cultivation. Today there are cornfields, strawberry patches and asparagus beds flourishing alongside the trees which, in turn, provide both wood and resin. The River Leyre runs through the park, bordered by oaks, alders and chestnut trees. However these are by no means newcomers to the region. The alder was, and still is, used almost exclusively for making *sabots* (clogs) acorns were fed to pigs and sheep and the chestnut, in company with beans, was the only source of starch before the Spaniards brought back potatoes from Peru in the early sixteenth century.

Apart from being a viable commercial proposition the area is

Stilts were once used extensively when keeping watch over sheep

ideal for research into the environment and for open-air holidays. Visitors are encouraged to explore on foot, by canoe, on horseback or on bicycles. To make life easier for them the authorities have provided two holiday centres and extra accommodation in half a dozen other villages round about. Anyone who could not find something to interest them in the area would be extremely hard to please. The forests are full of ferns and gorse; foxes, squirrels, deer and wild boar have their homes there and more than two hundred different kinds of birds are to be seen in residence or just passing through. Typical wattle-and-daub type houses can be discovered hidden away in isolated clearings and a request for a glass of water may lead to an invitation to share a fish soup or a pigeon pie. By way of entertainment the villagers enrich their summer festivals with calf races, their own version of bowling competitions, music and dancing and racing on stilts. These used to be everyday wear for shepherds keeping watch over their flocks and both men and women could spend hour after hour perched upon them quite comfortably. For all practical purposes this art is now a thing of the past although some young men say that they can stay up there all day, possibly leaning on a long pole or a convenient tree while they have their lunch.

Another thing that comes as a mild surprise in the Landes is the sound of bagpipes, an accomplishment which has been handed down through the ages and often accompanies traditional songs. The place to find out all about them is the Lapios Centre in **Belin-Béliet**, just off the *autoroute* from Bordeaux. It is a little place that can rustle up a tennis court, a bedroom with a private bath and some delightful home cooking. It is only one of several small hamlets in the area with something out of the ordinary to offer. **Pissos**, further south, falls into the same category although its offerings include an artisan's house, the remains of an ancient glassworks and a twelfth-century church. It holds two fairs every year, one at Easter and the other towards the end of August, and makes a practice of selling handicrafts during the summer. **Luxey**, on the other hand, focuses its attention on ecology with a most informative resin museum. This traces the story from the moment the pine is tapped and the resin collected in small clay pots, although these have been replaced by plastic bags in some cases, and follows the process through to the boilers which hive off the turpentine. The remaining mixture, once used for candles, is stored in special barrels made on the premises, and the demonstration ends with a display of the final products. They are many and extremely varied, causing one visitor to remark, 'My family are always buying lipstick and chewing gum and covering themselves with paint. I never knew I had pine trees to thank for it.'

Sabres diversifies to a much greater extent. It is the site of one of the special holiday villages, has facilities for riding and pony trekking, is equipped for tennis and does much of its shopping at the open-air market on Thursdays. A tiny Napoleon III museum, standing alone except for a small church in the forest on the road to Solferino, is open all the year round provided someone is at home to answer the door or the telephone. However, Sabres is known first and foremost for the Ecomusée, an authentic village which has been completely restored and goes under the name **Marquèze**. There are no roads up to it and visitors have to take a small train from Sabres which is all that remains of a line that used to carry passengers and timber to Mimizan a hundred years ago. It runs at weekends and on holidays from March to November, operates on weekdays as well between June and September but grinds to a halt for the rest of the year.

Not unnaturally there is a certain commercial side to Marquèze, mainly confined to the reception area, where everything from aspirin to postcards is on sale, to the children's playground and the picnic area close by. These aside it is partly a research centre and partly a nineteenth-century hamlet operating more or less as it did in the olden days. Before setting off to explore what turns out to be quite a sizable area it is an advantage to see the model of the museum to get

The Ecomusée of Marquèze can only be reached by train — there are no roads

an idea of where things are and the part they play in the general scheme. The master's house, the biggest of course, has been restored and furnished with everything necessary to make it habitable; the miller's home, dating from 1834, is a trifle smaller and conveniently close to the old mill, while the cottage is typical of those provided for farm workers and other people employed on the land. There is a communal bread oven which doubled as a drying cupboard for hemp and flax, an 1857 sheepfold that is still in use and beehives with Tauzan oaks nearby, specially pruned so that the swarms can settle on them easily. The fields are sown with original crops and culti-vated by traditional methods in order to compare them with modern ones and there are chicken coops and pig pens, vegetable gardens, fruit trees and vines. Specialists are on hand to explain the finer points of the enterprise, such as the reason for so many different types of grain, the importance of sheep and bees in the natural cycle and the advantages of planting root vegetables in the later phases of the moon. Two regulations are rigidly enforced — 'no smoking' and 'dogs must be kept on a lead'.

Apart from a sprinkling of *auberges* in this rather sparsely popu-lated area there are some *gîtes*, quite a few farms identified by the sign *'Chambres d'Hôtes'* or *'Fermes d'Hôtes'* which are good for bed and breakfast and the usual variety of camping sites. In addition places like **Morcenx** qualify for a mention in the official list of country holiday resorts and have cafés and shops that are perfectly adequate for everyday needs. **Mont-de-Marsan**, further south, is quite large by local standards, possessing half a dozen hotels, a golf club with a 9-hole course and a municipal museum specialising in sculptures created between the wars. Some are dotted about the garden of the old building, which has survived from the Middle Ages and is open every morning and afternoon except on Tuesdays. A small natural history museum is housed in what was once a chapel.

Dax, on the banks of the Adour, is another matter altogether. To begin with it is an important spa with literally dozens of hotels, at least four of which are highly rated, furnished villas and apartments and sites for tents and caravans. The town with its hot water springs has been known since Roman times and it has the remains of an ancient wall to prove it. The Borda Museum goes into past history very thoroughly, collecting coins and items of archaeological interest, highlighting popular traditions and providing libraries of books and photographs. However it is not simply a choice between taking the waters or browsing about in the archives. Bullfights are staged in the middle of August, there are theatres and cinemas, concerts and festivals and a very popular casino. Sports on offer include tennis and swimming, riding and shooting with surfing a short drive away at Hossegor.

The inveterate viewer of ancient buildings would find an equally short drive to the south every bit as rewarding. Across the river from Peyrehorade is the little fortified town of **Hastingues**, founded by an Englishman, John Hastings, in 1289 on the orders of Edward I, who also ruled Aquitaine. Its fortunes were bound up with those of the Abbaye d'Arthous, founded in the twelfth century and up-dated at intervals during the next five hundred years. Part of the building is half-timbered and the rest, including the church, is stone. Its present function is to give house-room to the Musée Archéologique Départemental and display a comprehensive collection, the most modern part of which goes back to ancient Rome. It is open both morning and afternoon and anyone who is anxious to look round is invited to ring the bell.

The Romans, who thoughtfully left behind so much for the museum, also built the baths at Sorde l'Abbaye further to the east. Although they were used as the foundations for part of a monastery established there in the Middle Ages, sections of the system and some mosaics can still be seen, along with a highly decorative mosaic in the eleventh-century church. It would also be a pity to miss the ruins of the Château de Gramont on a hill overlooking Bidache. The somewhat grim little fortress came into being in the fourteenth century with an extension two hundred years later for Duke Antoine III, Marshal of France and a force to be reckoned with at court.

Bayonne, as well as being a busy port, with obvious Roman connections, is worth a visit for two quite different reasons. In the first place it provides easy access to the magnificent beaches further south and in the second, it has a handful of memorable attractions of its own. The old quarter is virtually surrounded by huge stone walls protecting, amongst other things, the impressive cathedral not unlike the one at Reims. Along with a fourteenth-century cloister and sixteenth-century stained glass windows there is a distinctly twentieth-century plaque in one of the little chapels. It recalls with gratitude the Miracle of Bayonne in 1451 when the surrender of the English garrison was attributed to timely intervention from on high. No such phenomenon appears to have taken place when Wellington marched in from Spain after winning the Peninsular War but there is a monument which calls the occasion to mind and commands a spectacular view at the same time. Bayonne's Museum of Fine Arts is one that should not be missed. It includes a collection presented to the town by the artist Léon Bonnat, who was born there. In sharp contrast the Musée Basque, a couple of blocks away, is mainly concerned with the way of life, fashions, crafts and sports peculiar to the region, with special emphasis on pelota.

Getting around is really quite simple because, like a number of other towns in the south, it appears to have evolved a one-way traffic system that actually works. Parking areas are available, making it easy to leave the car and wander about inside the walls. However there has been so much expansion outside that the visitor, and probably many of the inhabitants, would be hard put to decide where Bayonne ends and Biarritz begins. There are some attractive little gardens, plenty of trees and the Rue du Pont-Neuf, linking the cathedral with the lively Place de la Liberté, provides ample opportunities to sample the local chocolate. This has been a speciality ever since cacao nuts were brought back from the New World in the seventeenth century. Incidentally, it would be difficult to find a restaurant that does not serve those very thinly-cut slices of raw smoked ham that take their name from the town. Bayonne's Grandes Fêtes at the beginning of August attract large crowds who spend the entire day, and most of the night, celebrating in traditional style.

Biarritz has a more international flavour, although it also puts on some extremely colourful Basque festivals during the season. The resort has been an exclusive holiday playground for more than a hundred years. In spite of the fact that, in some ways, it is past its glittering prime, the town has managed to update its attractions without entirely losing the original atmosphere. Empress Eugénie's summer residence is now a palatial hotel, there are thoroughfares named after Edward VII and the Prince of Wales and a *château* on the Lac de Brindos is beautifully decorated and serves delectable food. There is no good reason for including it amongst places which are off the beaten track save for its curiosity value and the facilities it provides for all maner of sporting activities. The absence of historic buildings and quaint, medieval streets is offset by five golf courses within easy reach, swimming pools and tennis courts, a skating rink, riding stables and, above all, superb beaches for surfing, splashing about or simply lying in the sun. There are some impressive views, especially from the Rocher de la Vierge, connected to the mainland by a footbridge not far from the Musée de la Mer. Strangely enough, it is the only museum to be found. However it makes up for this by displaying all the different scientific aspects of marine life alongside an enormous aquarium, a pool for sea lions and a section devoted to birds.

On the far side of Biarritz a road runs along the cliffs above sandy beaches and some not particularly noteworthy resorts. **Bidart** has its fair share of hotels and places to pitch a tent while **Guéthary**, an ancient fishing port on its own little inlet, is popular with people who know the area well. It has a small church of some interest, opportunities for swimming, tennis, deep-sea diving and walking and a few hotels, one with a menu that attracts gourmets from miles around. It is also the last stopping place before **St Jean-de-Luz**.

Whaling used to be the main occupation for local fishermen but these days the emphasis has switched to tuna fish and anchovies which keep the port very much on its toes. St Jean-de-Luz is a fascinating town, full of life and colour, owing as much of its atmosphere to Spain as it does to France. It is full of picturesque seventeenth-century houses, the biggest and most decorative being the Maison Louis XIV where the royal apartments are open during the summer months. The church of St Jean-Baptiste may not look very inviting from the outside, but the interior is both ornate and unusual when compared with churches further north. Tiers of galleries with wooden balustrades and long oak benches line the walls, giving it the appearance of a rather strange theatre with massive religious overtones. A ship under full sail looks perfectly at home, as do the statues of popular local saints, several angels, the decorative arches and a retable resplendent with gold. Coupled with all these treasures from the past are the many attributes so essential to a modern holiday resort. There are two golf courses, both of which call for a certain amount of skill, although if you do take your eye off the ball at the Nivelle Golf Club you can always blame the view. Apart from tennis courts there is a yacht harbour with a sailing school, deep-sea diving and a long sandy beach overlooked by the casino and by hotels of various sizes, each with a restaurant attached. The Festival of St John is held in June with a Tuna Festival a month later and a whole range of entertainments during the summer in which pelota and bullfighting play a prominent part.

Cibourne, on the other side of the river, is practically a suburb of St Jean-de-Luz. The composer Maurice Ravel was born there in a five-storey house in the shadow of the church of St Vincent which is open to view. His parents took him to Paris when he was three months old but in spite of this he was always a southerner at heart. He both spoke and wrote Basque, kept up with all the friends he made during his repeated visits to the area and wrote his *Trio* at 14 Place Ramiro Arrue. A story is told of a friend who called on him one morning when he was staying in St Jean-de-Luz. Ravel was just coming out of his bath but, nothing daunted, he picked out a few notes on the piano with one finger, saying he thought they were 'very insistent'. That is one way of describing his unforgettable *Bolero*.

From Cibourne a busy road runs through Socoa with its old fortress and along the Corniche Basque to **Hendaye**, the last resort before the Spanish frontier. It manages to deal with heavy road and rail traffic and keep holidaymakers happy at the same time. The *plage* has a leisure park, plenty of sand and so many trees and flowers that it ignored the famous Frenchmen who invariably have streets named after them and called its avenues Mimosas and Magnolias instead.

To get the best bird's eye view of the region it is only necessary to drive inland to **Ascain**, a nice little town in its own right, park the car and catch the mountain railway that winds up to La Rhune. This is an exceptional vantage point in good weather, looking across to the ocean, away to the forests and along the Pyrénées, but it is certainly not worth bothering about in mist and rain. There are times when you can stand up there and not see the mountain in front of your nose.

An alternative to La Rhune for anyone with an aversion to climbing Pyrénéan peaks would be to follow the winding road to **Sare**. It boasts a typical Basque church, shady streets, a small hotel with an excellent restaurant and some not-too-demanding grottos a short distance away. **Aïnhoa** has just as good views, slightly more up-market hotels, a restaurant to rival the one at Sare and is on the direct route to **Cambo-les-Bains** in the valley of the Nive. As the name implies, Cambo has its own thermal establishment but the main place of interest is a small museum in the Villa Arnaga, on the road to Biarritz, filled with souvenirs of the poet and author Edmond Rostand.

Cambo is one of those places which mark the parting of the ways, unless of course enough time is available to follow a zig-zag course. As always the long way round provides the most variety. To begin with, a series of minor roads thread their way through undulating country where the pastures are dotted with patches of dense woodland and filled to bursting point with sheep. A sign which does not seem to be pointing anywhere in particular announces the Grottes d'Isturits et d'Oxocelhaya, down a narrow lane which would otherwise have little to recommend it. On closer inspection Isturits turns out to have been a popular residential area in prehistoric times while Oxocelhaya is full of stalactites and stalagmites enhanced by a waterfall which sparkles even though it is petrified. They are open each morning and afternoon and do not even bother to close for lunch during the high season.

St Palais, the next town of consequence along the route, makes no attempt to delve so far back into the past. Instead it is content with being the capital of the Navarre and a stopping place on the ancient pilgrims' road to Compostela. The main square, filled with trees and surrounded by old houses, has changed very little over the years. A picture in one of the hotels bears this out, the only difference being that it now has 'no entry' signs and parking space for cars. There is a sports complex with volley-ball, tennis and swimming, a camping site along the banks of the river, footpaths of varying descriptions and a tea room with upholstered seats, something of a rarity in this part of the world. Horses, fishing and pelota all appear on the list of holiday activities, there are some quite reasonable shops as well as a market every Friday and a typical Basque festival on the first Sunday after 15 August. During the summer Christmas-type decorations are festooned across the streets, everything from flowers to stars and guitars, all picked out with white lights. Tucked away in the woods to the south is **Harambels**, a little hamlet with an ancient chapel that was also on the pilgrims' way.

A pleasant small road with off-shoots that wander aimlessly about, only to end quite suddenly, leads to **St Etienne-de-Baïgorry**. On the way it passes Iholdy where the church is worth a glance because of the wooden gallery attached to the outside. St Etienne is

The square at St Palais

built along the bank of the river and is a good place for exploring the Vallée des Aldudes and clearing customs before heading across the Pyrénées and into Spain. The main hotel, with river frontage, has been in the same family for generations and has an excellent restaurant which specialises, among other things, in a fish mousse which is delicious.

A scenic road links the village with **St Jean-Pied-de-Port**, the ancient capital of the Basse-Navarre. The town has expanded considerably since the days when it was necessary to fortify in order to survive and the fifteenth-century ramparts are now surrounded by quite modern houses, garages, a railway station and a leisure park. Inside the walls the atmosphere is totally different with narrow streets, buildings that have been there since the sixteenth century, a squat stone church and an ancient hospital containing a library and a small local museum. Unfortunately the citadel is not open to the public but any time is visiting time for the Roman bridge of Eyharalerry which may well have proved useful to Charlemagne when he arrived in the vicinity with his army towards the end of the eighth century. There are a number of hotels, and provision is made for tents and caravans but it is as well to uncouple the latter if you intend to spend a lot of time exploring in the mountains.

The area to the south is a maze of steep little roads in not particularly good condition which keep doubling back on themselves in a most neurotic fashion. There is a dearth of villages, but plenty of streams and woods with places to stop for a picnic or a gentle stroll. Exceptional views are hard to find and most of those that do exist are on the road from St Jean-Pied-de-Port, through the Col Bagargui, to Larrau which has two small inns but nothing that could really be called attractions. In order to become better acquainted with the Pyrénées it would be necessary to deviate still further through Lanne, Aramits and Arette before heading south again towards Arette-la-Pierre-St Martin, known for its cross-country skiing. The church at **Lanne** was originally a chapel attached to the Château de Isaac de Porthau who gained immortality as Porthos in *The Three Musketeers*. Dumas also drew on Trois-Villes and Aramits for his masterpiece but it is difficult to visualise those swashbuckling heroes against the background of twentieth-century white houses with red or brown shutters and gardens filled with flowers. **Arette**, which has the same air of apparent affluence, had to be largely rebuilt after an earthquake in 1967 so it is no good looking there for any literary clues.

Oloron-Ste-Marie is every bit as delightful as it sounds. Built on a hilltop site once occupied by a small Roman settlement, it manages to combine the best of two totally different worlds. The main road through to the south, along the River Aspe, is full of little shops including some quite acceptable boutiques. Behind them a promenade marks the line of the ramparts which originally protected the domain of the Vicomtes de Béarn. Gaston IV was an enthusiastic participant in the Crusades, a fact which is illustrated to good effect on the splendid entrance to the thirteenth-century cathedral church. There are prisoners brought back in chains from the Holy Land, a statue of Gaston on horseback, wildlife both real and imaginary and a telling interpretation of St John's vision of the Apocalypse. The old quarter of Ste Croix, in a kind of wishbone-shaped area between two rivers, takes only a short time to explore even including a visit to the local church and a few minutes spent admiring the view.

The only reason for stopping off in **Arudy** would be to visit the Maison d'Ossau, a museum that complements the Parc National des Pyrénées. It takes a look at the past history of the area as well as all the flora and fauna to be seen there today. The park, which adjoins the Spanish National Park of Ordesa, is one mass of lakes and waterfalls, mountain peaks reached on foot or by cable car, deep valleys threaded through with little streams, forests where you could come face to face with a bear and open spaces resplendent with rhododendrons, iris and edelweiss. The only trouble is that the more places you want to see the more you have to keep doubling back on your tracks. There are comparatively few roads, and some of them have stretches which can be anything from difficult to dangerous. However, with a little ingenuity it is possible to discover delightful hamlets consisting of a few houses and a small basic inn where the owner will be only too pleased to draw attention to anything of interest, be it scenic or historical. In the absence of any informed advice the temptation to branch off along a likely looking shortcut ought to be resisted whenever possible. The chances are that you will run out of road before you get where you are going, which means leaving the car, probably under a tree, and completing the journey on foot. Unless this sort of thing appeals to you it is far better to stick to the larger roads or decide to walk or go by bicycle, taking advantage of paths and cart tracks which lead to otherwise inaccessible places. There are opportunities for shooting, fishing, climbing and potholing and the local information offices will provide all the necessary details such as where to go, what to take and whether or not a licence is necessary.

Even without venturing into the wilder sections of the National Park there are just as many different activities available and as great a variety of things to see. For instance, the underground caves at **Betharram**, discovered nearly two hundred years ago, are well equipped to receive visitors. They are open both morning and afternoon during the season with boat trips along the subterranean river, a little train that cuts down walking time and a selection of fascinating grottoes to explore. The nearby sanctuaries of Betharram include a seventeenth-century church while St Pé-de-Bigorre, about the same distance away in the opposite direction, was the site of an abbey dedicated to St Peter whose name, for some reason or other, has been abbreviated to St Pé. The Wars of Religion took their toll but a fourteenth-century statue of Notre-Dame-des-Miracles has survived and can be seen in the sanctuary. Further afield there are enough forests and streams to satisfy even the most demanding open-air enthusiast in addition to several hills that are worth climbing for the view. Le Béout makes things easy with a cable car to the summit where the panorama takes in a couple of valleys, as well as many other peaks and more than a casual glimpse of **Lourdes**.

If, as the publicity brochures insist, 'all the world goes to Lourdes' one would expect to find a sprawling metropolis filled with high-rise hotels and apartment blocks, supermarkets, boutiques and souvenir shops. Naturally they do exist, but in spite of this the description is wide of the mark. By no stretch of imagination could this beguiling town with its reputation for miracle cures be described as 'off the beaten track' but it is unlikely that any traveller, however allergic to crowds, would pass by without a second glance. Lourdes was originally a stronghold belonging to the Counts of Bigorre but in 1858 young Bernadette Soubirous told her family and friends that she had seen and talked to the Virgin Mary in a grotto on the far side of the river. After the same thing had happened several times even the clergy were inclined to believe her. She went into a convent run by the Sisters of Charity and in 1933, a little more than 50 years after her death, she was canonised. In the meantime the grotto and the fields about it had changed considerably. A statue of the Virgin was placed in a niche in the rock, a rather severe altar was added, invariably surrounded by bowls of fresh flowers and lit by dozens of candles, and building work began in earnest. Three superimposed churches appeared between 1871 and 1889, followed in 1958 by a huge underground basilica which can hold 20,000 people. The miraculous water that figured largely in the visions of Ste Bernadette was directed into fountains and from there to pools designed especially for invalids. As the number of pilgrims increased so did the museums devoted to religious matters and soon a variety of places associated with her began to attract large crowds. They include her birthplace at Cachot, the parish church where she was baptised and the old hospital with all its pictures and souvenirs. During the season there are ceremonies every day ending with a torchlight procession in the evening. Pilgrimages are organised at intervals from Easter to the middle of October, starting with a Festival of Music and Sacred Art.

Although the town is somewhat preoccupied with the spiritual side of life there is no reason why the out and out pagan should not enjoy a visit just as much. The fortified castle, reached by a lift, a long ramp used by the one-time owners or a formidable number of steps, dominates the scene, rising out of a tree-covered hill overlooking the river. It is open throughout the year and contains an old chapel and an extremely interesting Pyrénéan museum. When history palls there are areas set aside for football, rugby, tennis, pelota and clay pigeon shooting, not to mention judo, karate and athletics. Swimmers have a choice of two municipal pools, one of which is covered and heated, or the lake which is shared by fishermen, boat owners and water-skiers. Riding stables can be found at Benac and St Pé-de-Bigorre, the streams are stocked with trout and the mountains are ideal for climbing and walking. Some half dozen ski resorts operate well into the spring and a funicular railway up to the Pic du Jer runs at regular intervals all through the year. Excursions are available to any number of places in the vicinity including spectacular mountain passes, attractive lakes and waterfalls and spas like Cauterets that have quite a few attractions of their own.

Lourdes shares a large airport with **Tarbes**, 19km (12 miles) away. It is a much bigger town concerned mainly with commerce and industry and is decidedly short on buildings of historic or architectural interest. However it has some very comfortable hotels and anyone of a military turn of mind would probably spend a few days there most profitably. The first place to see is the Jardin Massey, partly because it is a delightful park and partly on account of the Musée International des Hussards. This covers some five hundred years of army history, with particular emphasis on the cavalry, and is full of lifelike figures decked out in the appropriate uniforms, fully equipped and armed to the teeth. Apart from Mondays and Tuesdays, it is open every day with a 2-hour break for lunch. A short walk away is the house where Marshal Foch was born. As one would expect it traces his career in considerable detail from his enlistment in 1870, through his outstanding achievements on the Western Front during World War I to his death in 1929 when he was buried with due ceremony at Les Invalides in Paris. A little further down the appropriately-named Avenue du Régiment-de-Bigorre, more or less opposite the barracks, is a large stud which has been training and providing horses for the French cavalry during the past hundred years or so. There are guided tours each afternoon except on Sundays from July until early in February.

Less than half an hour's drive to the south-west is **Capvern-les-Bains**, a spa town that not only ministers to the sick but takes an interest in keep-fit fanatics. There are several hotels and *auberges*, any number of furnished apartments and a couple of caravan sites. Visitors can play tennis or golf, use the gymnasium and the sauna, go for long walks and gamble at the casino. The Château Mauvezin, which like the castle at Lourdes once belonged to the Counts of Bigorre, is an added attraction. It is open daily from May to October and has, among other things, a folklore museum and a good view of the ancient Abbaye de l'Escaladieu which is also open to the public, except during January and February.

Somewhat less inviting is the ruined fortress at Montaner, much closer to Tarbes in the opposite direction. It is described as an ancient *château* but in fact looks much more like an arena with a tower attached. It might or might not be open on Sunday afternoons but there is nothing to prevent sightseers wandering round outside the walls at any time. It is reached by way of a series of little roads through countryside which is pleasant enough although not particularly scenic. Tiny hamlets pop up now and then and the traffic is much lighter than the volume that sometimes has to be contended with on the main route from Tarbes to Pau, the capital of the Béarn.

Anyone who knows **Pau** and is asked to describe it usually starts off with the word elegant, which is precisely what it is. Of course this does not apply to the suburbs which have a tendency to sprawl and are much the same as the outskirts of any other town. However, they have not been allowed to encroach on the historic centre with its beautiful parks and gardens and the famous Boulevard des Pyrénées looking out over the river towards the mountains. At one end is the Château de Gaston Fébus, designed as a fortress but transformed into a castle in the early sixteenth century by Marguerite d'Angoulême, sister of François I, who married the King of Navarre. Several other heads of state, including a brace of Louis and as many Napoleons, looked in now and again, each one adding a touch or two of his own. The result is a fascinating mixture of styles surrounding a large courtyard with a triple arch at one end and a tower at each corner. The royal apartments on the first floor have been incorporated into the National Museum with decorations and furniture that would make Henry IV feel perfectly at home. His tortoise shell crib stands in the room where he was born, there are some regal tapestries on the walls, not much in the way of carpets and several chairs are drawn up to a table beside his bed as if a few friends were about to join him for a game of Cardinal Puff. The third floor of the *château* is given over to the Musée Béarnais which includes a little bit of everything from folklore and furniture, through local architecture and traditional costumes to birds and bears.

The Musée des Beaux Arts has a building all to itself and has got together a varied collection spanning some four hundred years, augmented by medals and coins. Finally there is the Musée Bernadotte, the birthplace of Jean-Baptiste who rose to the rank of marshal in Napoleon's armies before being crowned King Charles XIV of Sweden in 1818.

It was shortly after this that the British began to set their seal on Pau. A certain Doctor Taylor encouraged his more well heeled patients to winter in the Béarn and they, in turn, introduced steeplechasing, with a course reputed to be second only to Aintree, fox hunting and golf. The 18-hole course, laid out beside the river in 1856, is the oldest on the Continent and has recently been joined by the Royal Golf Club du Domaine-St-Michel where members can swim and play tennis and squash as well. Apart from other tennis courts and swimming pools Pau has a motor racing circuit for Grand Prix events and a sailing school, provides routes for hikers and caves for potholing as well as an attractive casino in the tree-filled Parc Beaumont at the eastern end of the Boulevard des Pyrénées. There is no shortage of hotels of any size or of restaurants offering international cuisine alongside good home cooking. Shops can be anything from small, sophisticated and expensive to covered markets which are essentially cheap and cheerful. They are particularly useful for anyone renting an apartment or parking a caravan on one of the sites outside the town.

Several museums in the region display what they describe as 'Pièces de Samadet', one of the largest collections being in the *château* at Lourdes. It is a distinctive type of earthenware, decorated with fairly basic flowers, butterflies and so on, which was all the rage at court in the eighteenth century until the Revolution put a temporary stop to such frivolities. One of the best places to inspect it is in **Samadet** itself where a most informative museum has been opened in a house that once belonged to the Abbé de Roquépine. It traces the whole process with life-size figures demonstrating the various stages of their art. A potter, seated on a bench, appears to be turning a large wheel with his feet in order to rotate the smaller one on which the clay is worked. Next door a painter, using a design pricked out on transparent paper, creates various patterns with something that looks rather like a quill. The job completed, the plates are stacked in a rack, half a dozen or more at a time, and put into the old kiln in the corner to be fired. Examples of the finished articles are displayed in glass cases in an adjoining room.

The museum also provides an accurate picture of the way people lived in those days. The labourer has an all-purpose room with a fireplace, a bed covered by what could easily be taken for a modern duvet and two oxen with their heads protruding through an opening in the wall. Apparently this was the way cattle were fed during the winter, which is a trifle confusing as there does not seem to be anywhere for fodder to be stored. A bourgeois family with a much higher income possesses some excellent furniture including a superb grandfather clock, has carpets on the floor and a bed warmer which consists of a pot of live coals suspended inside a metal contraption which, hopefully, prevents the bedclothes from catching fire. In the well stocked kitchen something exactly like a ladder is suspended high up in front of the fire. It would have been ideal for airing the laundry but in fact was used for storing bread and hams. Elsewhere there are all the tools necessary for making rope-soled shoes and *sabots*, spinning hemp and flax, operating a forge, cutting up logs and running the farm.

Roughly half way along the road to Aire-sur-l'Adour there is a branch off northwards to **Eugénie-les-Bains**, famous mainly on account of a hotel run by Michel Guérard whose name is painted in large letters on the surrounding wall. Quite a few people consider it to be one of the best hotels with undoubtedly one of the most superb restaurants in the whole of France. It has all the decorative refinements of the nineteenth century allied to every modern comfort, is set in delightful gardens full of trees, ponds and flowering shrubs and provides tennis and swimming but, sadly, all this luxury does not come at bargain prices. The village is a pleasant little place with thermal baths and half a dozen other hotels, some of which also offer their guests tennis and swimming and refuse to accept dogs, however small.

Aire-sur-l'Adour is known as the *foie gras* capital, and you cannot get more up-market than that! Along the roadsides in every direction are signs inviting passers-by to call in for truffles, *foie gras* and, occasionally, Armagnac. Provided the visitor has had the foresight to buy some delicious fresh bread, a little butter and a bottle of Tursan wine before working out the quickest way to a shady river bank, this must surely be one of the most satisfying places to have an impromptu picnic. The town itself is small and moderately industrial with a church whose history goes back to Roman times. It contains the body of the martyred Ste Quitterie encased in marble in the crypt. There is also a fairly run-of-the-mill cathedral, a racecourse, an arena, a swimming pool and a handful of modest hotels with menus to match.

Still heading north, a spiderweb of reliable little roads tempt the traveller into the heart of the brandy country where every second village has 'd'Armagnac' tagged on after its name. The area is fairly wooded between the vineyards and is criss-crossed by small streams that run in and out of tiny lakes and ponds. Anyone who is planning to take home a bottle of Armagnac, but whose motto is 'try before you buy', would be well advised to make for **Labastide d'Armagnac**. It is a very small town indeed, hardly more than a square surrounded by arcades attached to elderly houses with a church in one corner, but it is the nearest place to the seventeenth-century Château Garreau. A road that could certainly do with some expert attention leads to the *château* which specialises in brandy of various ages, half a dozen different liqueurs, trains young people and runs a miniscule museum. It is open all year round with a tour of the cellars and distillery

Le Mans cathedral, Pays de la Loire

Malicorne, Pays de la Loire

Angers - the château, Pays de la Loire

thrown in on Tuesdays and Thursdays. Machinery, some of it well over a hundred years old and showing its age, stands around the walls, leaving space for a counter where samples are offered for tasting and bottles are sold. Among the list of suggestions put forward by the management are iced Armagnac served 'on the rocks' and Floc de Gascogne, described as a liqueur but intended as an *apéritif*, well chilled and accompanied by *foie gras* or *confits*, a national delicacy made from pork or duck. These are also sold on the premises along with various fruits preserved in the appropriate manner.

Visitors feeling a bit peckish and in need of something more substantial for lunch are directed to any of three *auberges* a few minutes' drive away. Tourists on bicycles might well decide to set out fractionally early in order to visit the chapel of Notre-Dame-des-Cyclists, just off the road to **Barbotan-les-Thermes**. This is a small spa with beautiful gardens, an attractive main street lined with shops and lovely wooded country all round. It is also rather overblessed with hotels which means that it can be crowded. On the medical side it concentrates on rheumatism and its allied complaints but also provides tennis, riding and naturism for people who have no need to take the waters in search of a cure. A direct route, due east, passes through Casteinau with its little lake, Montréal complete with a ruined church and the remains of a Roman villa at Séviac about two kilometres (a mile) away and Larressingle, an ancient fortified village that has been completely restored.

Condom, more fortunate in its history than in its name, is worth a visit, partly to see the Gothic Cathédrale St Pierre. It was built in the early sixteenth century and is filled with statues, the one in St Peter's chapel looking exactly like Joan of Arc. It has been embellished quite recently and is unexpectedly light inside. Next door is the ancient Chapelle des Evêques and behind them both, a block away, are streets of old houses presenting more or less the same united front as they did some two hundred years ago. The Musée de l'Armagnac has taken over part of the original Palais des Evêques and is open daily but closes on Mondays and on most official holidays. The Abbaye de Flaran, to the south, was founded in 1151 with a cloister added a couple of centuries later but it is no longer inhabited by monks. Instead it has been transformed into a cultural centre which is always shut on Mondays.

La Romieu, east of Condom, owes its existence to Arnaud d'Aux, a relative of Clement V, the first pope to hold sway in Avignon. It has not fared particularly well over the past seven hundred years but there is a good deal to see, including the tombs of the cardinal and

Henry IV mill at Barbaste

members of his family and the remnants of a palace that was once his home. By completing three-quarters of a circle round Condom, more for the drive than anything else because there is little to recommend it apart from an odd view and a means of avoiding the main roads to the north, it is an idea to stop briefly at **Fources**. Brief is the operative word because it is an incredibly small and completely circular fortified hamlet founded by the English in the thirteenth century, and does not appear to have changed much since. The houses are built on arches overlooking an open space in the middle with their backs to the walls and that is all there is to it, but the atmosphere is worth the extra mileage. The same could be said of **Durance**, although it is decidedly angular and looks rather the worse for wear. An extremely solid tower-archway promises great things but produces nothing except two dilapidated old houses and several comparatively new ones. It is necessary to search round for the ruins of a *château* that belonged to Henry IV and the ancient Grange Priory on the edge of the forest. It is much easier to find the twelfth-century *château* at Xaintrailles which was modernised three hundred years later by Jean Poton who fought alongside Joan of Arc.

Barbaste is infinitely more rewarding for anyone who wants to come to terms with Henry IV or simply needs a shady spot to park a caravan. The king had an impressive mill on the banks of the river, reached by a fascinating bridge, built of stone and wide enough for a single horseman, with small triangles jutting out at intervals on either side. They are just big enough to hold an armed soldier or give refuge to anyone unfortunate enough to be caught in transit when the royal party arrived home from hunting or fighting a minor war. The mill, which in spite of its name looks more like a smallish palace, was well fortified and must have been a thoroughly desirable country residence in its time. However there seems to have been a fire or some other disaster quite recently and the walls are plastered with notices warning of 'danger unto death' on entry. As a result there is, sadly, no chance of looking round until it is either restored or someone clears away all the rubbish piled up inside. The town on the other side of the river is small and friendly and the caravan park seems to be quite well equipped. However, travellers in search of a bed for the night would be wise to press on to Lavardac with its little *auberge* or head south to Nérac where there would probably be less difficulty in finding a room.

Whichever way you look at it **Nérac** is an enchanting town. The old quarter is a tangle of twisted alleys with houses that have not changed very much since the castle was built back in the Middle Ages. The church of Notre-Dame is tucked away towards the far corner, almost opposite a sixteenth-century bridge and no distance from the Palais du Tribunal and a seventeenth-century town hall. Further up river is the large Garenne Parc with a profusion of trees and several fountains including the aptly-named Fountain of Daisies and the Castle of Nazareth that once belonged to the Templars. The whole area is overlooked by the castle of Henry IV, named after him in spite of the fact that it was actually built before he was born. It is a typical blending of half-timbered apartments protected at strategic intervals by high stone walls and it is not difficult to visualise Marguerite d'Angoulême, Catherine de Medici and members of the Valois family drifting through the various rooms. The museum which has taken their place brings history to life through collections of prehistoric and Roman relics and illustrates the subsequent life and times of ancient Nérac with many personal touches and some rather nice old paintings. The somewhat dour church of St Nicholas is right beside it and the little streets beyond are full of attractive houses but very few hotels.

The country round about is not especially interesting although Nérac is one of Aquitaine's designated holiday resorts. It puts itself out to entertain visitors, even to the extent of building two new golf courses and keeping the castle museum open all through the year. In addition it is only 30km (18$^1/_2$ miles) from Agen and the River

Henry IV castle at Nérac

Garonne , or a trifle more if the drive is planned so as to include the *château* at Estillac and the small village of Aubiac where there is an old church. **Agen** itself is fairly large and lively with arcaded streets, river frontage and an attractive bridge spanning the canal. The cathedral of St Caprais dates from the twelfth century but it is less absorbing than the Musée des Beaux Arts. The tapestries, furniture, medieval jewellery, ceramics and paintings all attract their own particular crowds and there is a natural history section to round off the visit. A few small gardens can be found quite close to the centre of the town and there are plenty of hotels and restaurants which are quite adequate without being in any way spectacular and some of them stay open twelve months of the year.

The only thing one has to decide when leaving Agen is which route to take on the journey home. There is a fairly direct road up to Paris through Limoges and Orléans, a whole host of alternatives for anyone with enough time left to sample the delights of the Perigord, while the average driver who chooses the Autoroute des Deux Mers should take no more than two hours to reach Bordeaux where the trip began.

Further Information
— Aquitaine —

Museums and Other Places of Interest

Agen
Museum of Fine Arts
Open: daily 10am-12noon and 2-6pm.
Closed Tuesdays.

Arcachon
Museum of the Sea
Open: 10am-12 noon and 2-7pm. Palm
Sunday to end October. All day during
July and August.

Arudy
Museum of Flora and Fauna
☎59-05-80-44 for details.

Barbaste
Henry IV Mill
Not open at time of going to press.

Bayonne
Basque Museum
Open: 9.30am-12.30pm and 2.30-
6.30pm (10am-12noon and 2.30-5.30pm
in winter). Closed Sundays and public
holidays.

Béliet-Belin
Lapios Centre
Traditional music and bagpipes.

Betharram
Caves and Sanctuaries of Betharram
Open morning and afternoon during
the season. Enquire at the tourist office
in Lourdes.

Biarritz
Museum of the Sea
Open: 9am-7pm daily in summer.
Otherwise 9am-12noon and 2-6pm.

Bidache
Castle Gramont
Open: no specific times, enquire from
caretaker.

Biscarrosse
Sea Plane Museum
Open all day during summer, no
specific times.

Bonnat
Museum of Fine Arts
Open: 10am-12noon and 4-8pm in the
season. Varies in winter. Closed
Tuesdays.

Bordeaux
Casa de Goya
Open: 2-6.30pm. Closed Saturday and
Sunday.

Centre Jean-Moulin Resistance
Museum
Open: 2-6pm. Closed Saturdays,
Sundays and public holidays.

Contemporary Arts Museum
Open: 9am-12noon and 1-6pm. Closed
Sundays.

Customs Museum
Open: 10am-12noon and 1.30-5.30pm.
Closed Mondays.

Decorative Arts Museum
Open: 2-6pm. Closed Tuesdays.

Fine Arts Museum
Open: 10am-12noon and 2-5pm.
Closed Tuesdays.

Musée d'Aquitaine
Open: 2-6pm. Closed Tuesdays and
Sundays.

Natural History Museum
Open: 2-5.30pm. Closed Tuesdays and
mid-September to mid-June.

Cachot
Birthplace of Bernadette
Open: daily 2.30-5.30pm.

Cambo-les-Bains
Musée Rostand
Open: May-September 10am-12noon

and 2.30-6.30pm; October 2.30-6.30pm only.

Between Cambo-les-Bains and St Palais
Grottes d'Isturits et d'Oxocelhaya
Near Cambo-les-Bains
Open: mid-March to mid-November 9am-12noon and 2-6.30pm.

Capvern-les-Bains
Château de Mauvezin
Open: May 10am-12noon and 2-7pm; June to mid-October 9am-12noon and 2-7pm; Sundays and holidays to 7.30pm; mid-October to April, Sundays and holidays 2-6pm.

Condom
Armagnac Museum
Open: June-mid-September 10am-12noon and 2-6pm. Otherwise closed at 5pm. Also closed Mondays, Sundays in winter, 1 January, Ascension Day, 14 July, 15 August, 1 November and 25 December.

Dax
Musée Borda
Open: 2-6pm. Closed Saturday and Sunday, November to May.

Hastingues
Abbaye d'Arthous nearby
Open: April to October, 9am-12noon and 2-6pm; November to March 9.30am-12noon and 2-5pm. Closed Tuesdays.

Labastide-d'Armagnac
Museum and brandy tasting
Open: daily 9am-12noon and 3-7pm.

Lourdes
Château and Pyrénéan Museum
Open: 9-11am and 2-6pm. Closed at 5pm September to June.

Pavillon Notre-Dame
Open: 9-11.45am and 2.30-6pm. Closed at 5.30pm on Mondays and from mid-October to Easter.

Luxey
Resin Museum
Open: June-mid-September daily with tours at 10 and 11 am and 2, 3, 4, 5 and 6pm. Otherwise 10am-12noon and 2-7pm. March-November Saturday afternoons, Sundays and holidays only.

Mimizan
Museum
Open: mid-June to mid-September 10.30am-12.30pm and 2.30-6.30pm. Sundays 2.30-6.30pm. Closed Tuesday.

Mont-de-Marsan
Musée Despiau-Wlérick
Open: 9.30am-12noon and 2-6pm. Closed Tuesdays.

Musée Dubalen
Open: 9.30am-12noon and 2-6pm. Closed Tuesdays.

Open-Air Museum
Open: 9.30am-12noon and 2-6pm. Closed Tuesdays.

Nérac
Henry IV Castle Museum
Open: 9-11am and 2-5pm. Closed Mondays and 1 January, 1 May, 1 November and 25 December.

Pau
Béarnais Museum (in *château*)
Open: 9.30am-12.30pm and 2.30-5.30pm

Bernadotte Museum
Open: 10am-6pm. Closed Mondays.

Musée des Beaux Arts
Open: 10am-12noon and 2-6pm. Closed Tuesdays.

National Museum (in *château*)
Open: 10am-12noon and 2-5.30pm in summer. Closes at 4.45pm in winter.

Parentis-en-Born
Petroleum Museum
Open: Easter to end October 9am-12noon and 2-6pm. Closed Tuesdays.

Sabres
Ecomusée Village
Trains daily at frequent intervals when the village is open.
Open: mid-June to mid-September daily; March to November Saturday, Sunday and holidays, pm only.

St Jean-de-Luz
Maison Louis XIV
Open: 10.30am-12.30pm and 3.30-6.30pm July and August. 10am-12noon and 3-6pm June and September. Closed Sunday mornings.

St Jean-Pied-de-Port
Basque Museum
No specified opening times. Enquire at the Information Office.

Samadet
Musée des Faïences de Samadet
Open: daily 10am-12noon and 2-6pm. Closed Monday and Tuesday.

Tarbes
The Harras
Open: July to mid-February. Guided tours 2.30-5pm. Closed Sundays.

Maréchal Foch Museum
Open: July to mid-September 8am-12noon and 2.30-5.45pm. Otherwise 2-5pm only. Closed Tuesdays and Wednesday, 1 January, 1 May, 1 and 11 November and 25 December.

Musée Internationale des Hussards
Open: daily 10am-12noon and 2-6pm. Closed Mondays and Tuesdays.

Tourist Information Offices

Arcachon
Place Franklin Roosevelt
☎56-83-01-69

Bayonne
Place de la Liberté
☎59-59-31-31

Biarritz
Square d'Ixelles
☎59-24-20-24

Bordeaux
12 Cours 30-Juillet
☎56-44-28-41

Capvern-les-Bains
Rue Thermes
☎62-39-00-46
Open: May to mid-October.

Dax
Place Thiers
☎58-74-82-33

Lourdes
Place du Champ-Commun
☎62-94-15-64

Mont-de-Marsan
22 Rue Victor-Hugo
☎58-75-38-67

Nérac
At the Mairie
☎53-65-03-89

Oloron Ste Marie
Place de la Résistance
☎59-39-98-00

Pau
Place Royale
☎59-27-27-08

St Jean-de-Luz
Place Maréchal Foch
☎59-26-03-16

St Jean-Pied-de-Port
Place Charles de Gaulle
☎59-37-03-57

7 • Beaujolais

This region is perhaps best known for its wine and a series of novels about a village called 'Clochemerle' by Gabriel Chevallier. However, the region is more than celebrated red wine and novels, for it is part of the Massif Central — a complex upland of old rocks, deep gorges and rugged landscapes.

The Pays de Beaujolais is contained in the department of Rhône. Its northern boundary is Mâconnais, and it extends southwards 60km (37 miles) to the River Turdine, and the lower Azergues north-west of Lyon. Eastwards it borders the River Saône, and westwards the Monts de Beaujolais merge into the Loire Valley. It is an extremely picturesque region of hill and vale, cut by the long valley of the Azergues running diagonally into the heart of granite uplands. These hills rise to over 1,000m (3,280ft) in the north (Mont St Rigaud 1,012m, 3,319ft), and are covered with rough grass, gorse, chestnut groves and pine forests.

In contrast the Jurassic limestone slopes that sweep eastwards to the Saône are mainly covered with vines, but there are also orchards, verdant meadows and small cornfields. The vineyards suffered the ravages of phylloxera in the nineteenth century, and for a long time they never quite recovered their former glory. Now with the emphasis upon lighter wines rather than years in the cellar, they have come into their own whether drunk young or *château* bottled.

There are broadly three wine areas, and the same grape, Gamay Noir, is used in the 22,000ha (54,340 acres) of vineyards. In the north, on poor granitic soil is the district of the nine *Grands Crus*: Juliénas, Moulin-à-Vent, Morgon St-Amour, Chénas, Fleurie, Chiroubles, Brouilly, and Côte de Brouilly. In the north-centre are the thirty-five communes that make up the *appellation* 'Beaujolais Villages', and in the south, on the limey soil that colours the stone of the villages of the region known as 'Pierres Dorées' ('Golden Stone'), they produce simply 'Beaujolais' or 'Beaujolais Supérieur'.

The main valleys are well populated with large farms, and vil-

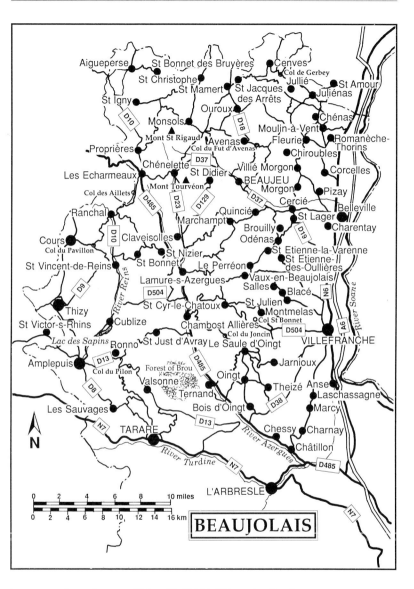

lages are found up to 800m (2,624ft). Historically there was a cottage textile industry of, originally, wool, later silk and finally cotton. Thus there are many isolated manors, scattered hamlets, village clusters and in the western valleys several small textile towns.

The regional capital is Villefranche on the N6 Paris-Lyon road, and close to the *autoroute* A6. It is the centre of the wine trade, and in spite of being busy, its older architecture is worth investigating. In the Turdine Valley is Tarare, a textile town famous for its muslins, and on the 'Route de Sapins'(firs) in the western hills are the small textile towns of Amplepuis, Thizy and Cours. In the north is the old capital (until 1592), and attractive town of Beaujeu, in a narrow valley surrounded by vines and forests. Finally, near the N6 from Mâcon is Belleville, a wine centre convenient for seeing the northern vineyards.

The attractions of the region — apart from the wine and food — lie in the landscape contrasts as between the southern vineyard villages of golden stone, often perched on hills, and those of the *Grands Crus* in the north. Higher up, above 500m (1,640ft), in the hills where the vines give way to field and forest, walking in the pure air gives a supreme pleasure, along with horseriding, fishing and *ski de fond* in Haut Beaujolais. As for exploring, although the region is not vast, it is possible to believe oneself lost in the narrow valleys, steep winding hill roads and the green ocean of vines. A splendid landscape to wander in without a fixed route, the nuances of the scenery are many with discoveries round each corner in the remoter parts of the region.

The climate is seasonal, with variations due to aspect and altitude. The summers are sunny, often hot (21°C/70°F) with frequent hailstorms. Winters are cold (2-3°C/36-7°F) and sometimes misty. Springs are bright and often rainy, with occasional disastrous frosts. Autumns by contrast can be truly golden, and are a good time to see the landscape colours. Rainfall is moderate with 800-1,000mm (31-40in) on the slopes, and heavier 1,000-1,500mm (40-60in) in the granite uplands.

The region is very accessible, as the eastern borders are parallel with two main roads (N6 and A6), and a rail route from Paris to Lyon.

Road: From Paris (Orly or Charles de Gaulle airports) A6 *autoroute* (463km, 287 miles). From Lyon (Satolas airport), *autoroute* A43, then A6 to Villefranche (55km, 34 miles). From Marseilles (Marignane airport) A7 *autoroute* to Lyon (315km, 195 miles).

Rail: TGV (high speed) Paris (Gare de Lyon) direct to Lyon (Part Dieu) 2hr Marseilles (St Charles) to Lyon (Perrache) TGV ($2^1/_2$hr); then change trains to Belleville or Villefranche.

A route exists from Paris to Lyon via Nevers, Moulins, Paray-le-Monial and down the Azergues Valley through spiral tunnels, but there is only one train a day in each direction.

Haut Beaujolais

This northern hilly district is centred on the historic capital of an

Beaujeu, with its Syndicat d'Initiative, 'Temple of Bacchus' and museum

ancient barony which gave its name to the region, and guarded an important route via the narrow defile of the Ardières Valley.

The long, narrow main street (Rue de la République) of **Beaujeu** seems to hide its best buildings, but once abreast of the fine Romanesque twelfth-century church, and within the Place de la Liberté, the town shows itself. Opposite the church is the well preserved Rennaissance Maison du Pays, which, with its tower and its neighbours at differing heights, presents a remarkably harmonious group. Moving on to the Place de l'Hôtel-de-Ville with its drinking fountain and trees, there is a building which houses a very efficient Syndicat d'Initiative (tourist office). Upstairs is a museum containing sections devoted to dolls, wine and geology. Underneath is a *caveau* (cellar), called 'Temple of Bacchus', where one can sample and buy by glass, bottle or box, 'Beaujolais Villages', for Beaujeu is a centre for this *Appellation Contrôlée*. Return to the main street with its many good restaurants: Anne-de-Beaujeu for example, in a fine old house (No 28), named after the daughter of Louis XI, is excellent for cuisine, décor and service.

Eastern Haut Beaujolais

From Beaujeu a route which explores eastern Haut Beaujolais leaves
the main street by the D136 past the ancient Hospice de Beaujeu and
climbs steeply with hairpin bends past vineyards, and then quite
wild scenery of heather, bushes and stone blocks to the Col du Fut
d'Avenas (762m, 2,499ft). Here is an immense panorama embracing
the plain of Bresse and, in clear weather, the Alps and Mont Blanc —
the area surrounding the col is well named La Terrasse. Nearby is the
caveau/restaurant Vignerons de Chiroubles (*Grand Cru*). Turning
left onto the D18, soon the village of **Avenas** is reached with its
delightfully small restored old stone church (1180). This has a superb
limestone altar, and fine modern stained glass. From here one can
explore a variety of routes to St Mamert: via D18 to Ouroux (Grosne
Oriental Valley), or along D18e and off on the right (D32) or continue
via D18e to the Col de Crie, where there is an information point
(panel). Then the D23 goes through the Forêt de l'Hospice de Beaujeu
and intensely green fields to **St Mamert** which seems full of turkeys.
In the fields roundabout are goats grazing like cattle, and overlooking it all is a huge red-tiled Romanesque church with a central tower
and presbytery attached.

On to **St Jacques-des-Arrêts** which has a beautiful church with
classical windows. It maybe noticed that this area has a great variety
of trees: ash, oak, chestnut and acacia, along with ferns, briars and
hedged fields. Keeping on the D23 through high country the attractive village of Cenves, with its large farmhouses, is reached. A typical
farm hereabouts is 15ha (37 acres), with goats, cattle and sheep. The
road (D23) now descends sharply and rises to the D68 and the Col de
Gerbe (610m, 2,000ft) with goats everywhere in high fields. Then to
the Col de Siberie — it must be cold here during winter — and a sharp
winding descent to the pleasant village of Jullié, past the seventeenth-century *château* of La Roche, with its swing bridge (unique in
the world) pivoting on a pillar in the middle of the moat.

Jullié is surrounded by mountain slopes and trees. It has a *caveau*
(Juliénas wine, *Grand Cru*), with a fine avenue of plane trees to the
church, and in the village square is a plan of local walks. The restaurant, La Vigne Gourmand, can be thoroughly recommended with its
sorbet vigneron (*cassis* and *marc*). From Jullié the narrow D68e is taken,
threading through the dispersed vineyard village of Emeringes to
the D26, which is followed via the Col de Durbize (550m, 1,804ft with
information point) and the Col du Truges (445m, 1,460ft) with good
views above the vines to St Joseph. Here the church has twin towers,
and the Stations of the Cross are through a vineyard. Then the road

descends to arrive back at Beaujeu.

Western Haut Beaujolais

To explore western Haut Beaujolais, leave Beaujeu by the main road (D37), up past Les Dépôts to **Les Ardillats**, a high, pretty wine village; then right to a narrow road (V4) along the Ardières Valley past fish farming ponds. Here is superb scenery of hills, high vineyards, hedges and stone farmhouses, changing to a leafy lane with ferns, Douglas firs, spruce and pine. The road joins the D23 to the Col de Crie, where an ascent can be made of Mont Rigaud (1,012m, 3,319ft) by a paved forest track. It is heavily wooded with many paths to explore, but the views are limited by trees.

Continue from the col by the D43 to the large village of Monsols, a disappointing place with too much obtrusive new building. Then the route goes via the D22 and the Grosne Occidental Valley to **St Christophe-la-Montagn**e, with its simple tenth-century church high up with good views. Then by D52 to the hamlet of Vaujon, turning right on to a side road via Mussery and a landscape of rural France at its best, to **St Bonnet-des-Bruyères**. The church here is large with an interesting combination of granite plus sandstone quoins and pillars. From here, by the D5, we pick up the headwaters of the Sornin, and reach the main N487 and the pleasant village of **Aigueperse**, which has a totally different type of church with a central tower. A short way westwards along the main road, the route turns left on to the D66 through green and wooded granite country with oak, beech and ash.

Go on to the D43 and the village of St Igny-de-Vers (information point), where *ski de fond* can be practised in season, and along to the Col du Champ Juin (742m, 7,434ft). The route here turns right (D52), into much rougher country with conifers and meadows. To the east are the slopes of Mont St Rigaud, and after the hamlet of Ajoux is a viewpoint. Next, the road passes near the impressive *château* of La Farge — white with red tiles — half hidden amid the trees. Soon **Propières** appears, a large village (information point) on the D10; from here the western outposts of Haut Beaujolais can be explored — Azolette and St Clément-de-Vers. Then the route continues southwards on the D10 to **Les Echarmeaux** (information point), an important road junction, and viewpoint, from where the D37 can be taken direct to Beaujeu, Belleville or Villefranche.

From Beaujeu there is an interesting walk of 8km (5 miles), leaving the main street and crossing the Ardières by a small bridge, then under the main road, and climbing up steeply to the hamlet of

Château St Jean. Thence by the farm of Ruettes, past the remains of the *château*, through forest to the Les Laforêts farm, and descending on a paved road to the hamlet of Longefay, then turn left to reach Beaujeu (GR76). These farms sell wine and cheese.

La Vallée d'Azergues

The long valley of the Azergues marks the frontier between southern Beaujolais and the forests to the north and west. It offers many chances to explore steep winding side roads, lanes, forests and high cols.

Haute Azergues

The first route begins at **Chénelette**, a high village (661m, 2,168ft) almost at the head of a tributary valley, surrounded by forests, including chestnuts, and overlooked by Mont Tourvéon (953m, 3,126ft) on the D23 (D37 Haut Beaujolais). The road is followed down to Claveisolles, and in the nearby Forest of Corcelles are the twenty oldest Douglas firs in Europe (1872). From here, turning left on to the D129, the road climbs to the Col de Casse Froide (741m, 2,430ft). Here is a good view of Mont Soubrant (878m, 2,880ft), and at the col, maize and wheatfields with a large lime tree under which it is very peaceful to sit on a summer's day.

Continuing on the D129, there is a long, winding, wooded descent to the pleasant village of **St Didier-s-Beaujeu**. Here is an unusual church tower with a broached spire, but the village is better known for bottling wine for export. Sometimes children can be seen on bicycles, driving goats with huge wooden crosses around their necks. From St Didier the route goes up the narrow, steep D129e and D139 past the southern slopes of Mont Tourvéon to Chénelette.

The second route starts at **Les Echarmeaux** (D37 Haut Beaujolais). Turning sharp right on to the D110 at La Scierie, the route follows the river, and the railway after Poule, to Le Prunier (D485). Then it descends along the main road, a steep-sided valley with much woodworking, past the entrance to the spiral tunnels, and arrives at **Lamure-s-Azergues**. This small town has the fifteenth-century Château de Pramenoux in a wood off on a steep road to the right, but the route is to the left on the D44, a very picturesque road to the Col de Croix Montmain (737m, 2,417ft). Then take the D88e, narrow and wooded, to the Col de la Croix-Rosier — the visitor might be surprised to find a night-club (Le Pressoir) in this remote spot. There are also good views over the vineyards. Continue on the D72 to the

Girl with goats at St Didier-sur-Beaujeu

village of **Marchampt,** nestling in the fold of two valleys surrounded by vineyards, orchards and forests. From here much may be explored, but an excursion along the D9 to see the Château de Varennes with turrets on the walls and towers amid the trees is well worthwhile. Returning from here on the D9 via the Col de la Croix de Marchampt (685m, 2,247ft) the route continues through to Pont Gaillard, near the other side of the spiral tunnel, and so to **Le Gravier** on D485, where in the Café Gravier some interesting walks are advertised, ranging from semi-Marathon du Beaujolais (22km, 13½ miles) in April to Corrida de Beaujolais Villages Nouveau in November. Then continue to Lamure.

St Cyr and Corniche du Val d'Azergues
From Lamure the D485 descends to Chambost-Allières, a small industrial outpost (metals and plastics). Here the D504 is joined, rising steeply to **St Cyr,** where there is an interesting forest walk along a *Sentier Botanique* to the Source Font-Froide in the Cantinière Forest. Then, on the D504 at Le Parasoir, there is a good view of Vaux and the Vauxonne Valley ('Clochemerle', which will be visited later); a short way on and the D44 is taken to the village of **Montmelas**. From here Mont-St-Bonnet (680m, 2,230ft) can be climbed,

from where the Alps may be seen — weather permitting!

Outside the village on the D44 the fortress Château of Montmelas, restored by Viollet le Duc in the nineteenth century, presents a majestic sight. After this the D19 is joined, and taken through Cogny to reach **Le Saule d'Oingt** on the D116 where the Corniche begins. All along this crestline past the Col du Chêne (720m, 2,362ft), and Col du Joncin (735m, 2,411ft) to Chambost is a splendid wooded landscape of oaks and conifers, with panoramas on both sides at Buisson Pouilleux, after La Cantinière. At the village of **Chambost**, just off the road, next to the small honey-coloured stone church (this is the fringe of the 'Pierres Dorées') is a large old lime tree planted in the reign of Henri IV, four centuries ago. The road then descends steeply to Chambost Allières (D485).

The Lower Azergues Valley
and Le Pays de Pierres Dorées

The latter is a relatively new name for an old distinctive region of forty-one communes which have their own Syndicat d'Initiative at Châtillon d'Azergues. The name arose from the setting sun shining on the stone of the villages where the houses, churches and *châteaux* are built of ochre-coloured Jurassic limestone. The typical house is of vaulted construction, and the living room is above the cellar, reached by an outside staircase with a wrought-iron or stone balustrade — the more beautiful houses are protected by a porch with stone or wooden columns. It is impossible to do justice to this area quickly, and exploration has to be on foot or slowly by car. It is, of course, a wine area.

An 8km (5 mile) walk in and around **Theizé** begins at this well sited and most picturesque village (D96). Starting from the centre of Theizé, by an old column with a cross built in 1567 (La Croix des Enfants de Theizé), take the track called Le Boîtier to the Clos de la Platière. Here is the house of Madame Roland, a famous writer guillotined in the Reign of Terror. It is now a small museum. Then through the vines to the chapel of St Hippolyte (1662). From here a footpath leads to the Frontenas road (D19). At the village, in passing, note the French Revolution inscription on the fifteenth-century church door. The route turns right to Moiré, and up the hill from here, one can see typical Beaujolais countryside. The descent towards Theizé is by a track, past woods and vines and a wayside cross. Below Theizé on the right, is the massive fifteenth-century fortified manor of Rapetour. Returning to Theizé there are two buildings which should be seen: the old fifteenth-century church (deconsecrated),

The chapel of the château
at Theizé

which has a gallery connecting the adjacent Château of Rochebonne (seventeenth century), with its two huge towers and beautiful staircase. Both buildings can be visited and although they have been neglected, they are still superb and are being voluntarily restored.

The medieval village of **Oingt** (D96/D485), perched on its knoll, is a jewel, and full of beautiful buildings. There is the remaining fortified gate of Nizy, a tower providing a fine panorama, a thirteenth-century church with old sculptures in the apse, and a sixteenth-century village hall with exhibitions. In addition to its viticulture, the village has a tile works just outside the village, where a road leads to the Château de Prosny (fourteenth century), for a long time believed to be haunted by 'La Dame Blanche', the unfaithful wife of its seventeenth-century proprietor who put her in a convent for two years. Oingt's strange name is believed to be Graeco-Roman from *Iconium*. Leaving by D96, **St Laurent-d'Oingt** is soon reached with its *cave coopérative*, and then the way descends steeply to the Azergues Valley. The route turns right along the D485 to Les Grandes Planches where, after turning left across the river, is the ancient village of **Ternand** on its conspicuous hill, reached by a winding road (D31e). This was fortified by the Archbishops of Lyon, and its tenth-century church is above a strange, far older fifth-century crypt with ninth-century frescoes, where an exiled eleventh-century Archbishop of Canterbury stayed. In its narrow alleys are some old houses of the fourteenth and fifteenth centuries. From here, a few kilometres away westwards, is the Forest of Brou with many paths.

Returning to the base of the hill, the route remains on the right bank of the Azergues, by turning right on to the narrow V206 by the river. After a few kilometres join the D39 to cross the Azergues, and continue to **Chessy-les-Mines** on the D485. This village has a twelfth-century church connected with the great French financier, Jacques Coeur (fifteenth century), who owned the copper mines here, exploiting the mineral chessylite (copper pyrites). Mining began in Roman times, and only ceased in the last century, but the red spoil heaps can still be seen, away from the old medieval streets and buildings, towards the river.

A short distance further is the village of **Châtillon d'Azergues,** with its remarkable fortified *château* (twelfth century) and keep, now privately restored from ruin, and lived in. The *château* chapel can be visited, but the main feature is not its age, but the beautiful ornate restoration of the nineteenth century with its paintings. In the village is the headquarters of the Syndicat d'Initiative of the Pierres Dorées, housed in a fine building where exhibitions are held and wine tasting takes place. From Châtillon the route takes the D70e on the left from D485, towards **Charnay** on D70. Here is an old feudal *château*, an extremely fine eleventh-century church, and good views.

Continue on the D70 to **Marcy-sur-Anse**, an interesting place not only for its ruined *château* on Montézain summit, but also for a tower overlooking the Saône Valley, restored by the French Post Office. This is the only example left of the Chappe telegraph system using mechanical arms (similar to flags), constructed in 1799, which revolutionised communications in France, and was used until the invention of the electric telegraph and the Morse code. Near the quarry and Lafarge cement works is a 'Geological Path', which shows (with explanatory drawings) a geological fault in a clay/limestone junction after the fault was eroded, and also the local rock succession starting with the Pierres Dorées (Jurassic limestone: the Inferior Oolite of the English Cotswolds). The path is laid with stones to keep visitors' shoes clean.

Now move on to Lachassagne, where, in the church, there is a celebrated crib that took 11 years to make. Then the route turns left on to D39, and climbs to the D38, which is crossed through to Le Boiter (D19), and D96 to **Pouilly-le-Monial**, a village with a fine fifteenth-century church, and a traditional restaurant, La Forge. A side road leads the village of **Jarnioux**, dominated by its *château*, which is one of the most remarkable in the south-east of France. It was thirteenth century originally, but rebuilt in Renaissance times, and has six 'pepper pot' towers, and a majestic entrance. The court-yard can be visited and nearby are some fine old houses. Beyond is Ville-s-Jarnioux, which has a church with Austrian frescoes, relating to their occupation in 1814. From here the route (D116) goes to St Clair, then back down the D120 to Oingt, and on to Bois d'Oingt, a large village with a *cave co-opérative*, and particularly beautiful houses in the famous golden stone.

The Beaujolais Vineyards

Villefranche

Not as old as its neighbours, and of humble origin, Villefranche has long been of commercial importance. The architecture of the houses in the Rue Nationale was curiously determined by a measurement tax, making for narrow façades, but leading to courtyards, galleries and spiral staircases which are gems of the fifteenth to eighteenth centuries. Some of the best preserved, interesting, and beautiful include No 834 (fifteenth century) with superb vaulting and the arms of Anne of Beaujeu; No 790 (eighteenth century), Madame Roland's house with three storeys and wrought-iron balconies; No 528 Auberge Coupe d'Or (oldest inn), with splendid seventeenth-century stone and ironwork.

The town is also the home of a unique and curious *fête*, 'Des Conscrits' in January, which is well over 100 years old. All conscripts aged 20, the new 'class' and those in multiples of 10 years, take part in celebrations both religious and festive over several days, which has its centrepiece on Sunday morning. This is a defile, known as *'la vague'* (wave), when, in evening dress with tricoloured buttonhole and ribbons (green for 20, yellow for 30, orange for 40 etc), white gloves and top hats, each class is arranged in age order and arm in arm, carrying bouquets of mimosas and carnations, they sway in a vast movement behind fanfares and flags, occupying the entire Rue Nationale.

Beaujolais Villages (Appellation Contrôlée)

Leave Villefranche by the D43, and after passing Quilly, turn left on to D35, through fields of maize and sunflowers, and before reaching St Julien, turn right for a short way on the D76 to the Claude Bernard Museum. Situated in a pleasant old country seat, amid a sea of vines, this is a memorial to a pioneer of experimental medicine.

Returning to the D35 the village of **St Julien** soon appears, and on
the left is the thirteenth-century Château de Rigaudière. Go along
the D19 for a short way through vineyards to Blacé where there is a
later classical (eighteenth century) *château* with an enormous flight of
steps. This is already the land of Beaujolais Villages, where it is said
the wine engenders good humour, actions, and leads to paradise.

Back on the D35 again, approaching Salles, there is a panorama
ahead of the Monts de Beaujolais, and far off, the spurs of the
Morvan. **Salles** is a village with some elegant Louis XVI houses, one
of which is connected with the French poet Lamartine, adjacent to the
old Benedictine monastery. The twelfth-century cloisters, and eleventh-century church are worth a visit to see their sculptures.

Climbing out of Salles, join the D49e to reach **Vaux-en-
Beaujolais**. This is probably the best known village in the region —
under its name of 'Clochemerle' — thanks to the novels of Gabriel
Chevallier. It is a very attractive place built on terraces, and in a small
square is a tiny, elegant building known as La Pisotterie — fiction
into fact! There is a good wine-tasting cellar here, La Cave de
Clochemerle, and a less well known building, Les Balmes, where one
can taste the waters of a mineral spring. The twelfth-century church
has a fine door, and a fifteenth-century triptych.

The route leaves here by the D133 for **Le Perréon**, a large village
with a wine co-operative, one of eighteen in the region, which produce about third of all the wine in Beaujolais. There is a small, simple,
but very good restaurant here called La Cloche. Continue on the D62
to the hill village of **St Etienne-la-Varenne** on the right, rather like an
Italian village in Umbria. Near here a large stone house at the top of
a nearby hill, called Champagne, with a vineyard of 7.25ha (18 acres)
could well represent the typical 'Villages' *vigneron* (vine grower)
who does not own, but leases and cultivates the vineyard, sharing
the proceeds with the landowner who provides all the equipment,
under a very old form of contract. Fifty per cent of Beaujolais is
worked by *vignerons* in this way

The D62 is followed to **Odenas**, where some way off amid the
vines is the fine Château de la Chaise (1675), which was built by the
nephew of Père La Chaise, the confessor of Louis XIV, who gave his
name to the cemetery in Paris. The *château* has a vaulted wine cellar
104m (341ft) long but this cannot be visited.

After Odenas (D43), the Col de Poyebade is mounted, and a steep
little road on the right leads to the summit of Mont Brouilly (483m,
1,584ft), with superb views, and a small chapel (1857). This was
dedicated to the Virgin by *vignerons*, after the disease of oïdium had

Vaux-en-Beaujolais
('Clochemerle')

been cured by sulphur treatment and every year on 8 September there is a rather vinous pilgrimage by *vignerons*. These slopes lower down form the Côte de Brouilly, typified by the small Château Thivin, once the home of a famous *viticulteur*, Claude Geoffray, and with the hamlet of Brouilly below on the D43e, 'Côte de Brouilly' and 'Brouilly' are two of the Beaujolais *Grands Crus*, rich fruity wines.

Return to the D43, and follow it until just before the junction with the D37, where the route turns sharp left, onto a side road following a stream, and goes up to **Quincié**, a pleasant village with the rather dilapidated fifteenth-century Château de la Palud, which has great charm. From here take the D9 to the hamlet of St Vincent, and cross the Beaujeu road (D37), to reach on the left a narrow road leading to **Lantignié** (D78). Just north of this small village is Château de Tholon, which seems to have suffered through the ages, but has two fine courtyards, a vaulted kitchen, and beautiful staircases. On by D135 to **Regnié**, where there is large farm, La Grange Charton, belonging to the Hospices de Beaujeu. The buildings form a quadrilateral around a courtyard of 3,000sq m (32,275sq ft). It is remarkable for its fermentation vats, cellars and housing for *vignerons*, was built at the beginning of the tenth century, and can be visited.

Keep on the D135, which soon meets on the right, the D68, and reach the village of **Cercié** where the chapel of St Ennemond (D68e) and the Château de la Terrière (fourteenth century) can be visited. The *château* still has the great door and machicolation (openings in the parapet) in front of the ancient moat. The wine from this commune is known as Pisse-Vieille, after an old legend.

After this visit St Lager (D68), where one can taste Brouilly at Le

Château de Varennes, Quincié

Cuvage des Brouilly, and then on to the village of **Charentay**, where there are interesting and curious buildings. First, on the right, is the eighteenth-century Château de Sermézy, and then in the village itself are the houses of the *tonneliers* (coopers), with their glass roofs. After this, in the Domaine des Combes, is the Tour de la Belle-Mère (mother-in-law), built in the last century by a very possessive woman, who wished to watch the activities of her son-in-law. Built of brick, it is no less than 35m (115ft) high! Finally, continuing on D68, the once huge fortress of the Knights Templars, the incredible Château d'Arginy, is reached. Built and fortified in the twelfth and thirteenth centuries, all that remains of the original twenty-two brick towers is a single one called 'Sept Béatitudes', where new knights were initiated. When the Templars fell, the *château* was abandoned, then rebuilt in the sixteenth century, only to become a victim of the Revolution. The present owner maintains that the 'Treasure of the Templars' (many tons of gold bars and money in amphoras), is buried beneath the *château* in caves within a bed of salt, guarded by traps.

After this the route joins, on the right, the D19 to **St Etienne-des-Oullières**, where there is a *cave co-opérative* and two *châteaux* which are worth a look: Milly, rebuilt in 1840, and Lacarelle with parts dating from the sixteenth century. Then the D43 can be taken back to Villefranche.

Northern Beaujolais and the Grands Crus

A tour of northern Beaujolais and the *Grands Crus* begins at **Belleville**, a very ancient place of Roman origin (*Lunna*), which was eventually burnt by the Saracens in 732, and rose from the ashes in the eleventh century under the name of Bellavilla, hence Belleville. It became a wine centre, and was noted for cooperage (barrel making), but the trade has recently died out. The Romanesque church (1158) is a very fine building, particularly the tower, apse, door and the nave with nine bays. The other interesting building is the pharmacy of the Hôtel-Dieu (Sisters of St Martha, Order of Beaune), where there is a remarkable collection of old pharmaceutical pottery, glass and instruments which can be visited.

Leave Belleville by the D37, and after crossing the N6, turn right on to the D18, over the Ardières River to **Pizay**. Here there is the Aero Club de Beaujolais (established in 1931 from Belleville), and a fourteenth-century *château* with an ornate square keep (fourteenth century) and a garden by Le Nôtre. This can be visited as it is a restaurant and hotel.

From here the D69 is taken to **Morgon**, then D68 to **Villié-Morgon**, a village that was on the old Roman road from Lyon to Autun, and it is around here that geology contributes, not for the first time, to the taste of wine. For the *cru* of Morgon has the nuance of kirsch, due to the ancient schists that make up the 707ha (1,746 acres) of its *vignoble*, termed *roche pourrie* by the local people.

The route now winds up by the D86 to **Chiroubles**, where its 320ha (790 acres) of vines grow on a natural terrace to 750m (2,460ft) and the *caveau* for tasting is appropriately named La Terrasse. It is a silky, light wine, and is drunk younger than any of the other *crus*. Victor Pulliat, one of the saviours of the European *vignoble*, was born here and following the epidemic of phylloxera in 1860, he grafted on native American vine-stocks. A curiosity of Chiroubles is its turnips, dug after the first frosts, which, if cooked in a certain way, are reputed to be delicious.

The route descends next to the D68, and **Fleurie**, which lives up to its name both in the pleasantness of its site, with superb views, and also in its wine, which is scented, flowery and light. Strange that the acid granitic soil of its 800ha (1,976 acres) should produce a wine of which it is said: 'One glass pleasure, two joy, three good luck, and beyond — the dream.' Fleurie has a *cave co-opérative*, as well as a *caveau* — both for tasting. Before the Revolution Fleurie used to be a frontier town between Beaujolais and Mâconnais.

The route continues to **Chénas**, a curious *appellation*, because its

220ha (543 acres) of *vignoble* covers only the west and north of the commune, the smallest of the *Grands Crus*. The name comes from its ancient oaks (*chênes*), from the time of the Druids, but the oak one sees in Chénas now is not from the district for it forms the medieval arches of the *château* which is the *cave co-opérative*, as well as the barrels in it.

For the eastern and southern parts of the commune, move down the slope of oak trees to near the hamlet of Les Thorins on the D266 to the only remaining windmill in Beaujolais, but what a mill! For not only is it a classified monument, but it also gives its name to the most prestigious *cru* in the region: **Moulin-à-Vent**. Once again geology seems to be significant for the 560ha (1,383 acres) of its *vignoble* are planted in friable pink granite soil rich in manganese, which gives a deep, rich iris-scented wine that has a longevity exceptional for Beaujolais. It can be tasted in the *caveau* at the base of the famous mill itself.

Returning to the D68 the route continues via the D95 to **Juliénas**, whose 520ha (1,284 acres) of *vignoble* are spread through this and two other communes, Jullié and Emeringes (see Eastern Haut Beaujolais). There is an ancient *château* here with huge cellars, that once belonged to the Lords of Beaujeu, most of which was rebuilt at the beginning of the eighteenth century. But the building to see is the Maison de la Dîme (1647), with its two storeys of arcades. Here the tithes were collected, half to the Chapter of St Vincent de Mâcon, and half to the parish priest. There is a *caveau* for tasting this rich, fruity, full-bodied wine at Le Cellier de la Vieille Eglise here, and a local proverb says: 'Beware of those who drink their glass of Juliénas in one gulp'.

From here take the D169 to **St Amour**, and cross from the Rhône department into the department of Saône et Loire, where its 240ha (593 acres) of *vignobles* is around the picturesque flanks of the Mont de Berrey between Beaujolais and Mâconnais. Viticulture here has been known from times immemorial, and was under the patrimony of the Canons of Mâcon, so perhaps it is surprising that the commune did not get its *appellation* until 1946, due to a former mayor and *vigneron*. The name, St Amour, would appear to have originated from the amorous propensities of the visiting canons from Mâcon. The wine is soft, delicate and fine, and can be tasted at the *caveau* in the village.

From this northerly village follow the D31 until it meets the D186 on the right. Take this to the D166, then turn left to the N6. Follow the N6 to the Maison Blanche, and take the D95 to **Romanèche-Thorins**.

*Moulin-à-Vent, now sailless and the only remaining windmill in Beaujolais,
which gives its name to the most prestigious* cru *in the region*

Here a typical Beaujolais house has been transformed into a museum, which shows the work of Benoît Raclet on the protection of vines early in the nineteenth century.

From here the route south is by the D486, and the D9e to **Corcelles**. The *château* here is one of the best in the region, a Renaissance jewel, altered in the nineteenth century, and restored a few years ago with intelligence and taste. Particularly worth seeing are the wells in the courtyard, the armoury and the fifteenth-century chapel. From Corcelles the D119 is taken to the N6, and via this road either Belleville or Villefranche can be reached.

The Monts du Beaujolais

This is the high land west of the Azergues Valley, between the Rhône and the Loire, a landscape of forests and steep valleys with plenty of opportunities to explore the wild and isolated uplands.

The Route de Sapins (The Road of Firs)

This route begins from Lamure-s-Azergues on the D485, which is followed northwards to the D9 on the left above Le Gravier. This road winds up steeply to **St Nizier**, a pleasant little village perched on hillside bends.

From here the road climbs through forests with occasional views to La Croix Nicelle (786m, 2,578ft) with a distant view northwards of the conical Mont-St-Rigaud which appears like a coniferous volcano. Then on to St Bonnet-le-Troncy, and a winding descent (D9) to **St Vincent-de-Reins**, which, although an industrial village with several outlying hamlets, is really quite beautifully sited in the valley of the Reins. There is a 17km ($10^1/_2$ mile) walk starting from the church, which gives good views of the valley, and then goes via the Col Burdel (680m, 2,230ft), climbs to a high point above La Chapelle de Mardore (748m, 2,453ft), continues through forests to above Les Filatures, and returns to St Vincent above its valley.

From here the route follows the D108 along a very wooded up-and-down way with a great variety of trees: Douglas firs, Norway spruce, beech, oak, chestnut and ash to the Col du Pavillon (695m, 2,280ft). Then follow the D64, and climb to the small textile town of **Cours-la-Ville**, in an area which is quite scenic, with several local walks of varying lengths (10, 20 and 35km, 6, 12 and 21 miles) marked yellow and white. From here the Trambouze Valley (D8) is followed, and the fir forests tend to be above the villages on the crests, which are good walking areas.

The route reaches the outskirts of Thizy, which, with Bourg-de-Thizy, is a rather confused sort of place, but old and picturesque with the interesting eleventh-century Chapelle St Georges. However, the town can be skirted by turning left on the main D504d for a short way, then turning right on to D9e, thence D9a to the pleasant village of **St Victor-s-Rhins** dominated by a huge and rather fine railway viaduct. (Reins changes to Rhins because it is in the department of Loire.) The church (eleventh century) is from the priory of Cluny, and the route continues along D9/D13 (same road) to the important textile town of **Amplepuis**, which has a museum (Place de l'Hôtel-de-Ville) named after the inventor of the sewing machine, Barthélémy Monnier. There is a walk here of 18km (11 miles) from the Place Belfort, taking in woods and the Château de Rochefort; path marked yellow.

From Amplepuis there is a very pleasant wooded route (D8) climbing steeply up to Les Sauvages (723m, 2,371ft) Here was an historic meeting between François I and James IV of Scotland to which a monument can be seen. From here, on the left, is a narrow wild high winding route with conifers and deciduous trees to the Col de Cassettes (622m, 2,040ft). Then the D56 is joined and followed with forests of beech and firs, and high open meadows with isolated plots of beans and cabbages — a landscape similar to the Swiss Plateau or Mittelland. Later there are tremendous views on either side, before the D13 is reached and traversed. The D56 is again joined to **Ronno**, a picturesque village, where all services (electricity, water etc), are put underground. From here the D56 goes through woods to Bancillon in the Reins Valley (D504), which widens out into the large artificial, but very scenic Lac de Sapins, which can be walked round.

And so to the pleasant town of **Cublize** with three walks (marked yellow), and a long walk of 31km (19 miles) (blue and white, part GR7) high and wooded. From Cublize take the D504 to the junction with D10. Follow this road up the very picturesque valley of the Reins via the village of Magny to St Vincent. Then, the road continues northward past Les Filatures (textile village) to the upper Reins, now very wooded and rural, to Ranchal. From here the road (D10), climbs steeply to a viewpoint off the road on the right: Notre Dame la Rochette (where there is a shrine). Still going upwards the route reaches the high Col des Escorbans (853m, 2,798ft), and then plunges down through forests, and up again to the Col des Aillets (716m, 2,348ft). From here one can see eastwards over to Mont Tourvéon (953m, 3,126ft) wooded to its summit and reflect upon these dense forests of Haut Beaujolais, and how, in the 1950s, a British aircraft mysteriously disappeared and was only found by chance in November 1960. From the col the road descends, and mounts again to Les Echarmeaux, where one can go direct to Beaujeu (D37) or by D485 to Lamure-s-Azergues.

Alternative Routes into the Monts du Beaujolais (Route de Sapins)

The visitor could go from Chambost-Allières on the D485 to the D98 on the right, then to St Just d'Avray. Before the village there is the fairy-tale *château* of La Valsonnière with fine trees in the grounds: glaucus, magnolias and limes. At the village there are splendid opportunities for walking with two of 11 and 14km (7 and $8^1/_2$ miles Pierre Plantée and Roches Fayettes walks), the route then goes on to either Ronno or Amplepuis.

Alternatively, go from Les Ponts-Tarrets on the D485 by D13 to St Clément-s-Valsonne, and Valsonne, both amid forests and meadows. Then climb to the Col du Pilon (727m, 2,385ft) and from there it meets the route from St Just d'Avray.

Further Information
— Beaujolais —

Museums and Other Places of Interest

Amplepuis
Sewing Machine Museum
Open: Saturday and Sunday 2.30-
6.30pm all year.

Beaujeu
Museum
Open: April-June, October and November daily except Tuesday, 2.30-
6pm, also 10am-12 noon Saturdays
and Sundays; July -September 10am-12
noon, 2.30-6pm.

Châtillon d'Azergues
Château Chapel
Mme Givel
Esplanade du Vingtain
69380 Lozanne (key)

St Julien
Bernard Museum
Open: November-February 10am-12
noon, 2.30-5pm; April-October 10am-
12 noon, 2.30-6pm, daily except
Mondays. Closed Christmas week,
New Year, all of March and 15 August.

For vineyard *châteaux* (except *caveaux*)
enquire Mairie (town hall) of commune.

Tasting Cellars of Places not Men-
tioned in Text
St Jean d'Ardières; Pommiers; Chasse-
las; Leyres.
Also *cave co-opératives* Bully and
Létra.

Tourist Information Offices

Belleville
105 Rue de la République
☎ (74) 66 17 10

Beaujeu
Sq de Grandhau
☎ (74) 69 22 88
Mle Lauterbach: information on
châteaux.
Open: mid-March to mid-December.

Bois d'Oingt
Mairie (town hall)
☎ (74) 71 60 51
For *châteaux* enquire at Mairie of
commune (Jarnioux, Montmelas,
Charney)

Châtillon d'Azergues
Place de la Mairie
☎ (74) 65 27 58
Open: early May-early November,
Saturday and Sunday 10am-12 noon,
2-6pm.
Mme Faure (Présidente)

Monsols
☎ (74) 65 43 51
Open: Saturday morning all year;
afternoons also in summer.

Theizé
Office (old church)
For visit to church and *château* contact
M. Guillot
☎ (74) 71 64 27

Villefranche
290 Rue de Thizy
☎ (74) 68 05 18
Open: April-September 9.15am-
12.15pm, 2.30-7pm; October-March
9.15am-12.15pm, 2.30-6pm. (Houses in
Rue Nationale include Nos 816, 761,
706, 673, 594, 588, 494, 476, 465, 407,
375.)

Wine
210 Boulevard Vermorel
☎ (74) 65 45 55
Headquarters of wine co-coperatives,
many wine associations and Les Com-
pagnons du Beaujolais.

8 • The Cévennes

The mountain chain of the Cévennes has been known since ancient times, for Strabo speaks of 'Kemménnon Oros', Pliny of 'Gebenna' and Caesar of 'Cevenna'. They all referred to the south-eastern edge of the Massif Central, which stretches from the mid-Rhône valley to the Montagne Noire.

In the seventeenth century, the Lieutenance Général of the area consisted of the Gévaudan, Vivarais and Velay, but after the revolt of the Camisards (Cévennes Protestants) in 1702, this was replaced by the Pays de Cévennes, which was the land between Mont Aigoual and the southern slopes of Mont Lozère with Florac (then in Bas Gévaudan) as its chief town. In 1790 the Pays was divided between the departments of Gard and Lozère.

However, even in the late nineteenth century, outside of the Cévennes proper, the word referred to a much larger region. Then the name became familiar to English-speaking readers through the journey of Robert Louis Stevenson as described in his book *Travels with a Donkey*.

Today, the official geographical region of the Cévennes proper (1947), is the northern slopes of Lozère, Montagne du Bougès, the region of the Gardons (rivers) and the southern slopes of Aigoual. This region is bordered to the west and south by the limestone Causses; eastwards lies the Alès coalfield, and to the north are the Margaride and the Vivarais. This with minor changes, is the region described here.

In 1970 most of the Cévennes, and parts of the adjoining Causses became the Cévennes National Park to safeguard the landscape already deteriorating due to rural depopulation, and to and try and improve the life of the remaining Cévenols. There is a central protected zone of 84,200ha (207,480 acres) surrounded by a larger peripheral zone. The central zone is subject to certain regulations, such as camping and caravan parking, but although the park seems to have been an environmental success, there exists some dissatisfaction — indicated by unwelcome anti-park slogans daubed on walls etc, in western areas of the park. This may be due to hunting restrictions, reafforestation and banning of unsightly buildings, voiced by people who have been away from the region for a long time, and have returned to live there. Thus, it appears the term Cévennes means all things to all men.

The physical landscape of the south-eastern edge of the Massif, and hence the Cévennes, is sharply defined by a huge fault line scarp — a fracture of the earth's crust exposed as a steep face — which runs from north-east to south-west. Eastwards another great fault meets it running southwards from Villefort, and along this fault line are several Cévenol small towns and villages from Ste Cécile d'Andorge to La Bastide Puylaurent.

East and north of these fault lines are the mountains of the Cévennes, which are a rolling tableland of crystalline rocks — granites and schists — at about 1,300m (4,264ft), with gently flowing streams on the western side like the Tarn and Lot. Northwards the granite mass of Mont Lozère reaches 1,700m (5,576ft), its bare slopes scattered here and there with great piles of granite blocks; whilst southwards is another *massif*, Mont Aigoual, reaching 1,565m (5,133ft), where the granite overlaps schists, and the summit has a meteorological observatory which gives magnificent views.

The eastern or Mediterranean slopes of the Cévennes are in complete contrast to the west or Atlantic side, as they are steep and abrupt with deep ravines called *valats*, separated by narrow rocky ridges known as *serres*. Down these deep valleys rush torrential streams called Gardons, which flow to the Rivers Cèze, Hérault and Gard. They are fed by a high rainfall, over 2,000mm (80in), which comes in great bursts and sometimes destructive downpours.

For centuries, this landscape contrast reflected the way of life but there was always a struggle between pasture and woodland (*cebenno* in patois meant a wooded slope). For the people gradually cut into their once thick forest of beech, Scots pine and ash, and their sheep and goats finished off the destruction. By the 1870s the landscape was almost bare, deforested and suffering from soil erosion, but in 1875, George Fabre, a state forester, began a long-term scheme on Mont Aigoual of reafforestation. It was not without, at times, savage opposition.

On the Mediterranean slopes with a more benign climate it was a different story. There on the lower terraced slopes were mulberries — grown for a once prosperous silk industry — olives, vines, and, in stone-walled orchards, apricots and peaches. Higher up were apples and little irrigated market gardens. Still higher, up to 950m (3,116ft),

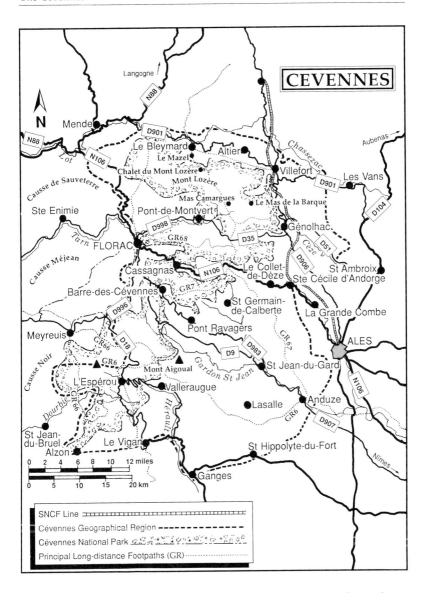

were carefully cultivated chestnut groves; some actually flourishing on bare outcrops of schist, and even today the still remaining trees are the glory of the Cévennes.

The chestnut was a veritable breadfruit tree — for the people ate them raw, roasted or boiled in harvest time, but most were dried in special small stone buildings called *clèdes* which smoked for months. When dry and peeled, porridge was made from the flour, used at all meals or for fattening pigs. Livestock grazed on the ungathered nuts, sheep and goats ate the leaves, which were also used for litter; branches were made into baskets, and the wood for rafters and furniture — it was almost a chestnut 'civilisation'!

The undergrowth and suckers were always cleared before the harvest, but unfortunately nowadays many trees are untended, dead branches pile up, and diseases spread. However, many trees have been replaced by grafting the smaller Japanese chestnut, and the swiftness with which the chestnut regenerates suggests that it will be there for a long time.

Another former industry was mining; silver, lead and zinc from the granite mass of Mont Lozère at Le Bleymard and Vialas; and lead at Villefort and Cubières. Now uranium has been discovered at several places on Mont Lozère, but the National Park has opposed the exploitation.

There has been an inevitable rural exodus on both sides of the Cévennes, and the way of life has obviously changed with the spread of cars and holiday homes, but there is still much to see, and many opportunities to explore. These Cévennes landscapes are of great variety depending upon the geology, vegetation, aspect and human history. They range from granite moorland with peat bogs, the beech forests of windy Aigoual, the superb gorges on the border of the Causses to the sierras and deep valleys of the schist regions, where to discover them you must get off the road and follow the rivers or lanes from valley to valley. However, wherever one goes in the Cévennes there is a reminder of one historical event which remains in men's minds — the War of the Camisards — and the spark which ignited it took place at Pont-de-Montvert.

The background to this event was the revocation of the Edict of Nantes in 1685 by Louis XIV in a misguided attempt to unify his kingdom by forbidding the cult of the Protestant religion. This meant destruction of their churches and the exile of their pastors. But in the Cévennes, the Protestants, in spite of great danger, practised their faith secretly, often deep in the mountains — known as the Desert — both literally and figuratively. The revolt was also a mystical one, for the leaders were often prophets, known as the 'Fous de Dieu' ('God's Fanatics').

In 1702 the Abbé Chayla, 'Inspector of the Missions in the Cévennes', arrested a small group of fugitives and had them imprisoned in the presbytery at Pont-de-Montvert. They were rescued by a group of armed rebels; and in the ensuing mêlée, the Abbé was killed. This was the signal for a general revolt of the mountain people, henceforth

Little Venice, Colmar, Alsace et Lorraine

Solesmes Abbey, Pays de la Loire

Kaysersberg, Alsace et Lorraine

to be known as the Camisards (from the patois *camiso*, a shirt), for many were poor. The war was ferocious and lasted 2 years with 3-5,000 Camisards fighting never less than 30,000 troops under three marshals. They had two celebrated leaders: Roland and Cavalier, but one was betrayed and the other submitted, later taking service with England. Finally, after some years of persecution, in 1787 Louis XVI signed the Edict of Tolerance.

The wild life of the Cévennes has been greatly reduced by man in the course of history, most of the larger mammals having disappeared. In the twentieth century the wolf, hazel partridge and the griffon vulture were eliminated, although wild boar still exist and birds of prey like the golden eagle remain. The National Park has been active in re-introducing the beaver and griffon vulture, and protecting many others. As for the flora — a third of all French species flourish in the region — but some are under threat like the Carline thistle, St Bruno lily and orchids.

Undoubtedly the main attractions of the region are scenic and outdoor, although there are some very interesting buildings and museums worth visiting. For the long distance walker the region contains fourteen Grandes Randonnées, and several *gîtes d'étape*. Opportunities are plentiful for riding, kayak-canoeing, fishing, swimming, tennis and skiing. The climate varies according to altitude, but generally during the summer months everywhere is dry and hot with occasional storms. The contrast between the two slopes — Oceanic and Mediterranean — is shown in the seasons of late autumn and early spring when there is an abundance of rain in heavy brief outbursts on the eastern side, and more steady rain in the west. The winters can be severe with frost, high winds and snow on the high Lozère plateau with heavy rain on the Mediterranean slopes (especially Mont Aigoual with 2,250mm (90in) on the summits plus winds, snow and ice). But it is often sunny; although the European climate has changed, as 1987 showed, so the seasons are less regular.

Access to the Cévennes is quite good, both by road, and rail for so remote a region:

Road: N9 (Paris)-Clermont Ferrand-Béziers to Marvejols thence N108 to Barjac, N88 to Balsiège, N106 to Florac (633km, 392 miles), *autoroute* A7 (Paris) to Bollène, Pont d'Esprit, Alès exit then N86 to Bagnols, D6 to Alès then N106 to Florac (767km, 475 miles).

Rail: Paris (Gare de Lyon) via Clermont Ferrand to Villefort, Génolhac and Alès June to September. Fast train 'Le Cévenol'. Paris (Austerlitz)-Béziers line to Marvejols (connection to Mende and La Bastide Puylaurent). Paris (Lyon) by TGV to Avignon($3^1/_2$4hrs) then road to Alès by N100, D981 or TGV to Nîmes (4+hrs), then train to Alès.

Nearest Airports: Nîmes (Garons): then D42, N106 to Alès ($2^1/_2$ hrs) then to Florac. Montpellier (Fréjorgues): D66 to A9, then Vendargues exit, N110 to Sommières, D35 to Anduze ($2^1/_2$hrs), and then St Jean-du-Gard (D907).

In the Steps of Stevenson

The publication of Robert Louis Stevenson's *Travels with a Donkey* not only fascinated English speakers on both sides of the Atlantic, but later great interest was shown in France itself. For Stevenson was a pioneer in more senses than one — he virtually invented the sleeping bag — and probably outdoor camping as we know it. In modern times the publication of the complete diary of the trip (*The Cévennes Journal*) in 1979 has stimulated further interest in his journey, especially the last part through the Cévennes proper.

Here, it is proposed to follow his route from the Trappist monastery of Notre Dame des Neiges (Our Lady of the Snows) on the border of the old regions of Gévaudan and Vivarais (now Ardèche) to its end at St Jean-du-Gard in the Cévennes. To reach the monastery by road from northwards (Le Puy) take the N88/N102/N106 to Langogne, the D906 to La Bastide, then the D4a to the monastery. Southwards (Alès) take the N106/D906 to La Bastide. But a far more interesting and exciting journey is to arrive by train ('Le Cévenol') as it follows Stevenson's route closely at times and can be picked up *en route* either southwards or northwards. Alternatively one can arrive by branch line from Mende to La Bastide. Besides using D roads the route often follows 'Sentiers de Grandes Randonnées' (GRs), the long distance footpaths waymarked by white and red bars.

The monastery of Notre Dame de Neiges has changed somewhat since Stevenson's day. The original buildings were burnt down in 1912, and Stevenson's small guest-wing for travellers and those in retreat (including, nowadays, the monks' relatives) has been replaced by a modern building and a souvenir shop. There is a large group of buildings devoted to the sale of local products like cheese, chestnuts and wine. Not only sacramental wine, but there are cellars for the ageing of wine brought up from the Midi (Gard), and the making of table and sparkling wine and liqueurs. It seems that keeping wine at this altitude (1,081m, 3,545ft) produces a remarkable ageing and all these products can be tasted!

From the front of the monastery, where there is an enormous

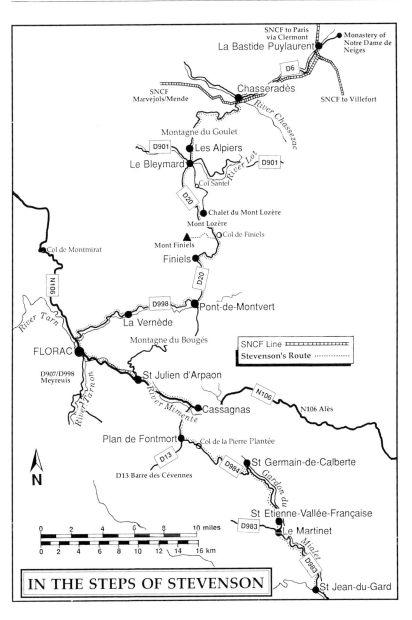

IN THE STEPS OF STEVENSON

vegetable garden, the footpath GR7/72 leads past some Douglas firs to a narrow paved road, later a track which in July is bordered by a mass of flowers like small gentians, harebells, heartsease and willowherb. After 3¹/₂km (2 miles) La Bastide is reached, a rather dour town, which possesses one unusual feature — a stained glass teaching centre. Stevenson left it by following the River Allier to **Chas-seradès** along what is now the D6 road ($9^1/_2$km, 6 miles). An alternative rural route is from near the church by GRs 72 then 7A to Chasseradès station on the line to **Mende**, and an appropriate place to reflect that Stevenson spent the night here (11 km, 7 miles).

From here Stevenson set out for Le Bleymard across the Goulet mountain, by its summit with no marked road, but the GR7A leads through Mirandol, then crosses the Chassezac — here a brook — and runs near the railway to reach L'Estampe with its *gîte d'étape* (3km, 2 miles). Then there is a very pleasant forest road over the mountain by a col (1,413m, 4,634ft), and descends to the hamlet of Les Alpiers. From here the GR7A goes by an old bridleway and emerges near a bridge over the infant River Lot on the main D901 (Mende to Villefort). Along the D901 and by the D20 to **Le Bleymard**, and this is almost the Cévennes proper. Stevenson left here, taking the ancient *draille* or drover's road up the northern slopes of Mont Lozère.

These ancient droving routes are prehistoric, and were made originally by wild animals long before they became the great transhumance routes for sheep in later centuries. This route begins on the left side of the cemetery in Le Bleymard, and climbs upwards, sometimes beside low walls and rejoins the GR7, which goes to the Col Santel (1,200m, 3,936ft), where it crosses the GR68 (Tour de Lozère). Then the GR7 climbs gently through the forest to the Chalet du Mont Lozère at 1,412m (4,631ft) with its chalet-hotel and *gîte*. From here the route takes the *draille* again which becomes the D20 and climbs up to the Col de Finiels (1,511m, 4,956ft) Here is granite country indeed, and an alternate route to the col is by the GR7 and up the Montjoie Heights — heaps of granite marking the way. From the col, the summit of **Mont Lozère** can be reached, the highest point in the Massif Central outside the volcanoes of Le Puy and Mézenc. It was here that Stevenson, coming up in the clear morning air, saw the blue hills of the Cévennes at his feet and remarked 'only this confused and shaggy country ... has any title to the name ... these are the Cévennes of the Cévennes'.

One will have noticed that the grassland which covers this high plateau and its crests is of the mat variety — the result of a thousand years of pastoral pressure and transhumance, but the latter has declined, and already bilberries, heather and shrubs are beginning to establish natural forest cover. Returning to the col the road southwards is now the D20, and on the left as the descent is made can be seen great piles of granite blocks and boulders called *chaos* in French. In English they are known as tors.

Pont-de-Montvert, with the old toll house on the bridge over the River Tarn

The road now winds round the plateau to reach the village of **Finiels**. Then it follows the Rieumalet stream to the confluence of the River Tarn and the Martinet, to **Pont-de-Montvert** (32km, 20 miles from Chasseradès).

The first thing Stevenson saw, as he came down the path to the village (which can be seen today as it leads to the Mont Lozère Eco-Museum) was the Protestant church. On going further: 'The place, with its houses...wore an indescribable air of the South'. The village is undeniably attractive with its seventeenth-century humped-back bridge upon which is a old toll tower, now the information office of the Cévennes National Park which was entered after Le Bleymard. Here, of course was the event which started the War of the Camisards — the Abbé Chayla's house is still there, but rebuilt, although it is now a souvenir/grocer's shop, but the cellar and kitchen-garden remain.

The way from Pont-de-Montvert to Florac is by Stevenson's 'smooth sandy ledge', now the paved D998 for 21km (13miles) (there is an infrequent bus service). It follows the valley of the Tarn, and is a very pretty route. Later Stevenson had breakfast in the hamlet of **La Vernède** with its Protestant chapel perched on a knoll. Soon on a rocky point the fourteenth-century *château* of Miral is seen, and about here the rock changes from granite to schist, and two villages appear, **Cocurés**, and further down on the opposite bank, **Bedoués**, with its collegiate church and behind it the beech oakwoods and conifers of Mont Bougés. Beyond here is the confluence of Tarn and Tarnon, and soon the picturesque old town of Florac is reached, just below the confluence in the Tarnon valley.

Florac is most impressively sited at the foot of the huge dolomitic cliffs of the Rocher de Rochefort. The town is near the entrance to the gorges of the Tarn, close to the Causse Méjean and not far from Mont Lozère and the southern Cévennes. It is therefore a good central point for exploring the region on foot, horseback or car. It was sited here on account of its water supply, like other villages, at the rock junction of limestone or dolomitic and impermeable schists. In consequence a stream called the Source de Pêcher, a principal resurgence from the Causse Méjean, flows gaily through the centre of the town with little waterfalls giving it an unusual character. This small river is much used for fishing, its real name being Pesquié (fishpond).

The original population of Florac was 'English', ie, Anglo-French from the English-held provinces of Aquitaine and Anjou, but the town's history has been a stormy one with the religous wars of the sixteenth century followed by the War of the Camisards, when the seventeenth-century *château* was fortified by palisades, *'cheval de frise'* (iron spikes set in wood to stop cavalry) and cellars. Before leaving, note the large severely classical Protestant church in the Place de Souvenir, which in spite of its puritanical appearance holds many cultural activities including concerts with musicians from Canada and the USA.

The town is left by the D907 (Avenue Jean Monestier), and the Tarnon crossed by a stone bridge (Pont de Barre), and the valley of the River Mimente entered by the N106. This can be followed via the village of Salle-Prunet or a path on the left bank overlooking the village and going via the hamlets of La Borie and Ventajols; and then **St Julien d'Arpaon** with its ruined castle on a rocky peak is reached. The road following the river now goes through a landscape of craggy schist, but from the church at St Julien the old railway line (if not too tangled with scrub) can be followed to the village of **Cassagnas** (off the main road). This gives good views of the river, and soon the cluster of Cassagnas' roofs are sighted perched on the slopes of Mont Bougès and surrounded by chestnut trees. Nearby, in the caves of the mountain was one of the five arsenals of the Camisard legions, where they stored arms, food and forged their weapons, and also where their sick and wounded were visited secretly by surgeons. A more pleasant reminder of history is an inn called the Relais de Stevenson. Here Stevenson crossed the Mimente, and realised he was on the

The château *at Florac*

divide of two vast watersheds; behind him all the streams flowed into the Atlantic, before him they led to the Mediterranean. Our route crosses the river by the D62, and then shortly by the D162 up a very steep little road to the Plan de Fontmort (896m, 2,938ft) where there is a monument to the Camisard's revolt erected in 1887. From here the old road to St Germain de Calberte is taken, which is the GR7/67 to a junction (3km, 2 miles), where the right-hand fork (GR67A) is followed to the Col de la Pierre Plantée (891m, 2,922ft) where as its name suggests, there is a menhir. Descend quickly to **St Germain de Calberte** (14km, 8¹/₂miles from Cassagnas).

This small town is surrounded by terraced gardens in a Mediterranean-like vale with ilex, maritime pine and chestnuts. It has an old twelfth-century church with a fine doorway — a historical monument — and the Abbé Chayla whose murder started the Camisard's War is buried here. He had been an early missionary in China (seventeenth century), suffered martyrdom, then became a Christian persecutor. He lived here with his missionaries, and the town became a little Catholic metropolis enclosed by Camisard legions.

Stevenson left here for **St Etienne-Vallée-Française** besides the Gardon de Mialet along the modern D984, then at **Le Martinet** the D983 is joined. After here there is a long climb to the hill of St Pierre. Then comes a long and wooded descent to **St Jean-du-Gard**, and the journey is ended. The town is a very pleasant one in the heart of the 'Mediterranean' Cévennes, and the Camisard country, but the Gardon — here called St Jean — is subject to floods (*cardonnades*) due to heavy rains caused by clouds coming from the Mediterranean in contact with the Cévennes mountains. There is a very interesting museum here inside a seventeenth-century *auberge*, called Musée des Vallées Cévenoles, dealing with all aspects of life in the region including chestnut culture and the old silk industry.

Finally, Stevenson left here for **Alès** by diligence and we can continue by taking the tourist steam train to Anduze. It is an extremely picturesque route alongside the Gardons de St Jean and Anduze, and passes by the Bambouseraie de Prafrance (Bamboo Forest). Here a stop can be made to visit 34ha (84 acres) of exotic parkland, a giant bamboo forest including trees imported from Japan, China and USA, an Asiatic village and gardens. It was created by Eugène Mazel in 1855 after a voyage to the Far East to study mulberry trees for the silk industry. The line continues by a long tunnel to Anduze. From here (if wished) one can go to Alès by bus (13km, 8miles).

Mont Lozère and Bougès Mountain Region

Eastern Lozère

Begin at the small village of **Ste Cécile d'Andorge**, just off the main N106 (Alès to Florac), and along the narrow winding wooded D276 above the railway from Alès to Villefort (on the line of the Villefort fault) to the Col de Bégude (510m, 1,672ft) at the head of the Andorge valley. Turning right at the col on the D52, equally wooded and sinuous it meets a very ancient highway, the Régordane, which linked Nîmes to the Ile de France. This road (D906) leads to the pleasant little resort town of Chamborigaud, in the valley of the Luech, where by turning on to the Pont-de-Montvert road (D998) this valley is climbed under the flank of Mont Lozère, which here is tree-clad almost to the summit of Bouzèdes (1,235m, 4,050ft).

Some way along and below a rocky ridge, known as the Rocher de Trenze, where Lozère granite meets the schists of the southern Cévennes is the village of **Vialas** with its narrow streets on two levels, and apples and vines on the slopes above. This is a splendid little unspoilt place, with its old low granite Protestant church (1612) on the outskirts, very peaceful with hollyhocks, lavender and petunias, belying its stormy history of religious strife. From here alleyways join the different levels, and in the upper street is a small traditional restaurant, Les Sources, which serves tiny ungrafted pears ($1^1/_2$in) from its garden. From the village, a footpath (3hrs) leads to

The Protestant church at Vialas, with the Rocher de Trenze behind

Bourdouze, joining the GR68 (Tour of Lozère). On to **Les Bastides** where honey, cheese and beeswax can be bought, and soon the infant Tarn is crossed and **Pont-de-Montvert** reached with its tall old grey houses. The village is usually busy in summertime, especially if it is a Wednesday (market day) when leather goods are on sale.

From the village the D20 is taken, but immediately afterwards turn right towards Villeneuve (*gîte d'étape*), and continue to **L'Hôpital**, a ruined and abandoned hamlet (1975). Its granite buildings were also the religious home of the House of St John of Jerusalem (Knights of Malta) who managed much land on Lozère; later the buildings were burnt and pillaged during the Wars of Religion (1615) and the Camisards revolt (1702). On to Mas Camargues, a vast farm building (used up to 1922), restored by the Mont Lozère Eco-Museum (information centre). From here is a walk (GR72) following one of the great sheep trails crossing the Tarn, and over pastures and peat bogs farmed co-operatively by tenants of the National Park. There is a special flora here of mosses, sedges and flowers like sundew and bogbean; also birds like the lapwing and the sandpiper. Returning via GR7 and 68 to L'Hôpital, the route goes by the road (without tarmac) to **Salarials** (one of the highest hamlets in the Massif Central at 1,412m, 4,631ft), and through wild scenery, to rejoin the D20 striking northwards over the Col du Finiels (see Stevenson's walk).

The D20 now descends to **Le Mazel** (information centre, *gîte* *d'étape*) where there are old silver and lead mines; then on to **Le Bleymard** with its thirteenth-century Benedictine priory and the D901 road is joined. The valley of the Lot is left, and the route passes through wild country to the watershed of the Lot and the Altier at the Col de Tribes (1,131m, 3,701ft). Then take the road left for Cubières (old lead mine), by the Altier River, and climb again into the higher valleys of Mont Lozère with hamlets, meadows and beechwoods to the Col de Bourbon, and down to **Pomaret**, where houses are built of three Cévennes rocks: limestone, granite and schist. Then the valley of the Altier is rejoined (D901), wooded and with apple orchards (Canadian 'reinettes'), then past the medieval Château du Champ to **Altier**, an old fortified village. Soon the granite towers of the Renaissance (1578) Château de Castanet appear, which can be visited during July and August (all day). It seems incredible that this beautiful building was only just saved from demolition in 1964, when water was being put in the hydro-electric power lake of Villefort, upon which it now stands (watersports).

On to **Villefort** itself (information centre); this little town is on the Régordane fault line which was crossed earlier, and lies in a ravine. It has many old houses (Rue de l'Eglise), and fifteenth-century town hall. From here the D66 is taken via the villages of Palhère and Costeilades in a glacial valley with terraced gardens, and houses covered with roofing stones called *lauzes*, actually mica-schists (Lozère is derived from this word). The views are good, with the Alps sometimes on the horizon. As the road rises, the landscape becomes covered with great blocks of granite, then passes through a relict wood of beech and firs, and soon, a turn on the right appears, leading to **Le Mas de la Barque**, a ski station with a *gîte d'étape* (horse-riding as well and GR72). Back to the road, now D362, and it climbs to the Belvédère de Bouzèdes (above at Vialas), which at 1,235m (4,050ft) presents a fine panorama. Then comes a tremendous winding descent, plunging 800m (2,632ft) to **Génolhac** far below. With its red tiled roofs, the view is distinctly that of the Midi. The town (information centre) is on the Régordane Way, and is interesting architecturally: façades of old houses, and shady promenades by the River Gardonette. Its history is linked with the locally born Camisard leader, Nicolas Jouany, who often 'occupied' the town during the rebellion.

From Génolhac the route now goes southwards on the D906, and crosses the D998, where the tour began earlier. Continue southwards to Chamborigaud, and the junction with the D52, and you can either return to Ste Cécile d'Andorge or continue direct to Alès.

The Cèzarenque (Upper Cèze Valley)

This short diversion shows the contrast between the high plateaux of Mont Lozère and the Cèzarenque with its sub-Mediterranean climate. It is a foray into rather unknown country.

From Génolhac the steep and winding D134 is taken south-westwards, and followed until it crosses the Cèze, a valley full of orchards and sunflowers. The route then rises steeply to the village of **Aujac** (D51), on a kind of sandy ledge above the river (caused by a fault). There is a backdrop of sunny wooded rocky slopes of the 'Cham' (plateau) of Bonnevaux. From Aujac go eastwards for half a kilometre, and perched on a hill among stumpy ilex trees above the valley is the fine Château du Chaylard. Already one can sense the Mediterranean-like atmosphere.

Returning to Aujac, the route continues along the D51, and glancing westwards, the massive bulk of Lozère dominates the skyline. The landscape gradually becomes more and more rocky with the trees a mixture of conifers and holm oaks, until the ruined Château de Bresis is reached at a road junction, and near the bridge over the Cèze. It is right on the fault here, and this extraordinary twelfth-century building is perched on a pile of shattered schists, its old square tower intact, and the rest ruined, although part seems to be used for a farm and lived in. It is possible to walk round, but one side falls steeply to the river. The high bridge is crossed and the road followed to **Vielvic**, with its sixteenth-century houses; then the D451 is taken to the main D906, and after a short way along, the red roofed village of **Concoules** is reached by turning right on to the D315.

Here on the eastern flank of Lozère was a little Catholic community, which along with others, organised themselves into armed bands, called 'Florentins' to combat the Camisards. The church has a twelfth-century bell tower from the Auvergne, and there is an agreeable restaurant here. Further south past the hamlet of Aiguebelle was the tile works of Nicolas Jouany, the Camisard leader, and one can see ruined tile-ovens along the road to Villefort. After this return to Génolhac, and so the contrast is complete.

The Bougès Mountain

This *massif* lying between Lozère and Aigoual, has its northern granite face separated from Lozère only by the Tarn valley, but the southern slope of schists is Midi in character. A further contrast on that side is the watershed between the Mimente (Atlantic) and the Gardon d'Alès (Mediterranean).

The route starts at Pont-de-Montvert, and the D20 is followed southwards as the road mounts the forested slopes of Scots pine. About 3km (1.8 miles) on the left is a forest track leading to the Col du Bougès (1,362m, 4,407ft, 4hrs) and GR72 (Barre-des-Cévennes). The road goes on through the Bois de Altefages (beech and conifers: the name means 'high beech'). In this wood the capercailzie (grouse) is being reintroduced. We have now crossed from granite to schist, and just before the Col de Sapet is a panorama which contrasts the two faces. At the col the GR68 leads to the highest point of Bougès (1,421m, 4,660ft). The road, now narrow, winds down to St Julien d'Arpaon on the N106, and then the route goes eastwards. After passing the Col de Jalcreste the route follows the Gardon d'Alès (Vallée Longue), and continues for 16km (10 miles) until on the left is a narrow lane winding upwards (unnumbered) 1km (half a mile) before Collet-de-Dèze.

This is indeed 'off the beaten track', and rather hazardous, but will show the Midi side of Bougès with its chestnut groves, ilex trees, herds of goats, two hamlets (Loubreyroux and Pénens) and a way of life, apart from cars, which is little changed. An alternative route is by the D29, 6km (4 miles) past the Col de Jalcreste via St Frézal-de-Ventalon.

The two routes converge some way below the summit where the D35 is taken to the left to the Col de la Baraquette with good views, then to the Col de Berthel, where the GR7 goes to the summit of Ventalon (1,350, 4,428ft) not far along an old sheep trail. After this take the D998 to Pont-de-Montvert.

Between the Causses and the Cévennes

This route shows the great contrasts in the landscapes of the area. Coming from the north, ie Mende, the Cévennes are entered via the N106, the Florac road. On entering the Bramon valley the first glimpse is seen of the spurs of Mont Lozère, then the Truc de Balduc (1,100m, 3,608ft). This is an isolated small limestone *causse*, wooded with abrupt slopes. At the hamlet of Molines turn left on the D125 to the village of **St Etienne-du-Valdonnez**, interesting for its unusual shop fronts, and an old farm. At the southern end of the village a forestry road along the upper Bramon Valley is used to reach the junction of the GR44, where after a walk of half a kilometre the hamlet of **La Fage** is approached.

Here is a surviving traditional Lozère granite bell tower, formerly very much apart of life in the community. Not only tolling noon and angelus, but summoning schoolchildren and recalling harvesters, and also guiding lost travellers, shepherds, pedlars and pilgrims in fog or snowstorms. By its side are some restored objects: a village oven, fountain and a *trave* (for holding oxen while being shod).

From here the forest road is regained, until the D35 is met. Turning left, and taking a lane after 2km (1.2 miles) on the right and going down it, some menhirs will be passed, and then **Les Bondons** reached. This is a hamlet, and a group of strange limestone hillocks, where uranium has been found recently. In the hamlet itself, the architecture is interesting as houses are built of sandstone, limestone, dolomite and granite — the geology of the region in one building!

Returning to the D35, and turning left, the route is continued to the Col de Montmirat (1,046m, 3,430ft). From here, between Mont Lozère and the Causse de Sauveterre, is a superb panorama. Ahead is the Tarn valley, and beyond, the great scarps of the Causse Méjean, whilst on the left are the sharp crests of the Cévennes, and if it is clear — Mont Aigoual.

After this there is a fine descent along a corniche above the Tarn in its valley carved out of schist. Enter **Florac** on the right over the Tarn bridge on to the D907 (see Stevenson's walk for Florac). Continue on the D907 southwards out of Florac along the valley of the Tarnon (where beavers have been reintroduced), and under the lee of the Causse Méjean, and past old bridges built of schist to the village of **Salgas** where there is an eighteenth-century *château*. But it's not the original, as that was demolished by order of Louis XIV, and its owner, the Baron, sent to the galleys for collusion with the Camisards.

The route continues past a series of villages sited along a spring line on the slope where the limestone rests on non-porous rocks like marl or schist giving a water supply. At Les Vanels the road becomes the D996 and climbs through **Frassinet de Fourques** with its Romanesque church, and winds up to the Col de Perjuret (1,028m, 3,370ft). Here is the meeting point between the limestone Causses and Mont Aigoual schists, with fine views of the Méjean escarpment, towards Florac and Mont Lozère. Here also the GR60 (Draille d'Aubrac — sheep trail) crosses on to the D18, both going to Mont Aigoual. The way now descends along the upper Jonte valley and reaches the pleasantly sited town of **Meyrueis**, within the National Park, but outside the Cévennes proper. It was famous for its weavers and serge cloth, and pioneered tourism, as its hotels catered for people visiting the gorges in the nineteenth century. It has some superb sixteenth- and seventeenth-century houses with carved mullioned windows (*gîte d'étape*, GR66 Tour of Aigoual).

Mont Aigoual and Lingas Mountain Region

The granite and schistose *massif* of Mont Aigoual is the highest point
of the southern Cévennes (1,567m, 5,141ft). It is in effect a huge water
tower, being the meeting point of damp Atlantic and Mediterranean
winds; hence its name — derived from the Latin *aqualis* (watery). On
the Mediterranean slope precipitous valleys alternate with sharp
crests, and on the Atlantic side gentle slopes merge into the limestone
Causses.

It was always heavily forested with beech and Scots pines until
the nineteenth century, when there was a vast increase in the transhumance of sheep on its slopes, and shepherds and farmers increased pasture at the expense of the forest. After some diastrous
floods in the lower Mediterranean areas due to heavy rainfall and
soil erosion in the 1850-60s the forest was virtually recreated by the
State, and the efforts of George Fabre. His idea was to leave the good
farming land, and have a mixed forest of beech and pine. So he
thinned the meagre beech copses to grow thick tall trees, and planted
hardy conifers like mountain pine on the higher degraded land, Scots
and Austrian pine on the limestone soils westwards, and used
Norway spruce and larch. This was achieved in spite of hostile
communes, and shepherds who sometimes burnt the young plants.
But he not only reafforested, but created footpaths, arboretums to
study the different species, restored forestry houses and instituted
an observatory.

The Atlantic Side of Mont Aigoual

The route begins at the small town of **Meyrueis**, at the confluence of
the Rivers Bétuzon, Brèze and Jonte whose upper valleys are covered
by the great Aigoual forest (National Park information centre).

Taking the D986 road, a short diversion on the left leads to the
fifteenth-century Château de Roquedols (National Park information
centre), built of pink sandstone flecked with ochre, situated in verdant surroundings. The D986 now climbs through forest by the River
Bétuzon to the Col de Montjardin, then passes into a larch forest,
whilst on the right is the old arboretum of La Foux. This has a walk
among species such as a huge Chile pine. It is worth going into
because birds like the small-toed eagle, honey buzzard and black
woodpecker might be seen.

Soon there is a change of rock from the schists, and the curious
spectacle of an abyss on the side of a huge limestone cliff, from which
cascades the Bonheur stream. This is also called the 'Bramabiau'

(Bellowing Ox), because of the noise of its waters from the subterranean caverns in the small Causse de Camprieu (may be visited). Then on the left is the hamlet of **Camprieu** (*gîte d'étape*, ski station). The GR62/66A meet, and if the GR62 is followed up the Bonheur valley an eleventh-century ruined priory is reached. After this take the D986/D269 to the Col de la Sereyrède (1,300m, 4,264ft and a watershed), where the huge gash of the Hérault valley falls away. Here also was where the great Draille du Languedoc (transhumance sheep trail) crossed from the arid *garrigues* to the pastures of Aubrac, Lozère and the Margaride.

From the col the road with superb views then plunges into magnificent beechwoods, and $1^1/_2$km (1 mile) from the summit there is a botanist's walk in the arboretum of L'Hort de Dieu (God's Garden), made by the botanist Charles Flahaut helped by G. Fabre. Not only are there exotic species to see, but the walk gives a wonderful series of views. Then the summit is reached with the 1887 meteorological station, which has important functions, notably giving warning of torrential rains. The views from here are exceptional, with an immense panorama. It is however, always windy, and in summertime often hazy, and early mornings in September are best. In the winter Mont Blanc and Maladetta (Pyrénées) have been seen simultaneously — a distance of 625km or 400 miles! There is an orientation table on the tower (views to the Alps, Cantal, Mediterranean etc).

From the summit the D18 is followed down to Cabrillac, with its forested slopes, sheep pastures and houses with porches for protection against snow. From here the narrow D119 is taken across rock strewn ground and dip down into the granite gorges of the Tapoul valley to the village of **Massevagues** (*gîte d'étape*) perched on the valley side. Here Henry Castanet, forester, wool-carder and Camisard leader, who established his *'quartier-général'* on Mont Aigoual, was born. Continue on through the gorges to Rousses, where the D907 can be taken to Florac.

The Southern Face of Aigoual and the Lingas Mountain

This route starts from the Col de la Sereyrède southwards on the D55, where on the left one can glimpse the cascade of the infant Hérault before reaching **L'Espérou** (ski centre and GR7). Here the D986 is followed as it descends in an incredible series of long loops to the valley floor. The contrast between the south facing slopes of chestnuts and ilex, and the northern ones forested with beech is well marked. The drop here from the summit is 1,200m or 4,000ft in only $6^1/_2$km or 4 miles. Near the bottom is a very pleasant restaurant/

camp site (two-star) called Le Mouretou. Next visit the very Midi-like charming old town of **Valleraugue** with very tall houses, some six or seven storeys high, and the River Hérault opening out to form a waterfront as it passes through. There is a huge Protestant church here. It was a much bigger town once with 4,000 people, now 1,050. From here there is a tough walk to the summit of Aigoual, called '4,000 steps' (in name only), very scenic, though wild with heather and broom, taking a day up and down. On to **Le Mazel** where there are an impressive spinning mill, and on the road very tall houses with a sheepfold, living space and silkworm rearing houses in successive storeys.

Eventually the route leads to Pont d'Hérault, turning left on the busy D999, and 6km (4miles) later reaches **Le Vigan**. Here is really a lively and interesting Midi town, in a picturesque setting, with a beautiful promenade of huge old chestnut trees, an old Gothic bridge, and a museum in an eighteenth-century silk mill; devoted to all aspects of Cévennes life (park information centre).

The route leaves the town on the D999, and turns right on to the D48 up the Coudoulous valley — very Mediterranean in aspect with vines, olives, mulberry trees, cypresses and scattered houses — then begins to climb the chestnut-covered slopes. Somewhere amid these hills is a small herd of mouflons (Corsican wild sheep) introduced in the 1950s. Soon on an enormous hairpin bend at La Cravate, there is a viewpoint of wooded ridges, Languedoc and the Arre valley. On climbing higher into beechwoods, certain butterflies like the rosalie alpine (blue-black, long antenna) might be glimpsed. Then the Col du Minier (1,264m, 4,145ft) is reached, and the route left on to a forest road. At first through beeches, and then there is complete change of landscape as the road passes on to an open grassy plateau encircled by distant trees. It is bright with flowers: yellow gentian, clover, daisies, toadflax, tiny buttercups, yarrow and scabious. This is the granite *massif* of Lingas, not well known, for as one goes on further the terrain becomes difficult with unpaved forest roads, but the route goes on to Pont du Lingas, across the Lingas stream. Then beyond, the road goes through woods of mountain pine and spruce to the open Col de Homme Mort (1,300m, 4,264ft) with eroded granite scenery of boulders and patches of sand, where the paved surface ends. There is a great deal of country to explore in this region, either by forest tracks or the GR66 (Tour of L'Aigoual) and GR71 or simply walking where you choose.

Return to the Col du Minier, and continue on the D48 through forest, where there are some very tall beeches, and into open land again where herds of fine Aubrac cattle graze. Below westwards can be seen the meanders of the River Dourbie. At a road junction, the D151 is taken to follow the valley of this river with Lingas rising to the south. Then the village of **Dourbies** is reached (accessible from Lingas by forest road), and the gorges begin, cut into schist, but the high cliffs of the Cade rock are made of that most resistant rock quartzite (metamorphosed or altered sandstone). At the Col de Pierre Plantée, the route turns north to the village of **Trèves** via D157, famous for its February carnival of the 'Pétassou', who walks the streets clad in coloured rags carrying a pig's bladder, which the villagers try to burst, while he wards them off with his broom. Then comes the narrow defile of the Trévézel Valley with massive limestone cliffs — at one point only 30m (98ft) apart. Then on the left the D252 takes one up a steep little road past the old silver mines of Villemagne to the D986, where left goes to the Meyrueis, and right goes to Mont Aigoual.

The South-Eastern Cévennes Valleys

This is the region of ridge and vale, '*serres et valats*', where erosion has cut countless crests and ravines in a mass of schists (with occasionally other rocks), but it is one of the most rugged landscapes in all France.

The Can de Hospitalet and the Corniche des Cévennes

The route leaves Florac south by the D907, then D983 to St Laurent de Trèves, on a limestone spur, where the footprint of a dinosaur was discovered, dating from 190 million years ago (protected site; may be visited). At the Col de Rey, continue down the D983 for a diversion to **Barre-des-Cévennes** (3km, 1.8miles). This small town has a high street with tall dark houses, that seems unchanged since the sixteenth century. Behind is a small limestone hill, the Castellas, on which was a fort; lower down is the twelfth-century church, Notre-Dame de l'Assomption; the Protestant church is at the entrance from Florac. Barre had a garrison during the War of the Camisards, which stayed for many years. It has a scenic site, and access to all the roads along the Gardons (*gîte d'étape*: GR7, 72, 67, Tour of Gardons, information centre).

Returning to the Col de Rey (992m, 3,253ft), take the D9, and here the Corniche begins across the windswept limestone plateau of the Can de Hospitalet. Reaching the Col de Farsses (1,026m, 3,365ft) a panorama of the Gardon St Croix in the upper Vallée Française can be seen. On to **L'Hospitalet,** where there is an old farm (*gîte d'étape,* GR67), behind which, among beech trees and rough blocks of dolomite, was a famous Camisard secret assembly point. Continuing along the plateau with views southwards of Aigoual, the road descends to the village of **Le Pompidou** amid chestnuts and schist, with its two churches not far apart. The road now runs along a ridge through chestnut woods and meadows, which in spring are bright with narcissii.

As one looks across eastwards over the Vallée Française there is a great line of crests, at much the same height, which are sometimes termed 'an accordance of summit levels'. This means here, many millions of years past it was almost a plain, then it was covered by a sea (Jurassic), and later slowly eroded to its present state.

Then the pleasant village of **St Roman-de-Tousque** appears with its equally pleasant L'Auberge de la Patache. The route changes so that it overlooks the Borgne valley, and at the Col d'Exil (705m, 2,312ft), it again alters with superb views of Mont Lozère and the Cévennes crests. And thus, on to the Col de St Pierre (597m, 1,958ft). Here is a marked rocky path (blue/white) to a viewpoint and an orientation table, where one can see Aigoual, towards Nîmes and the distant Mediterranean.

Now the road begins a picturesque winding descent to St Jean-du-Gard, and as the Gardon is reached, the schists are left behind, and the river is seen as a beautiful meander enclosed in a steep valley of very hard ancient rock (gneiss). Soon the town with its old humped-back bridge comes into view, and the journey ends.

St Jean-du-Gard to Anduze via Mialet

This route is an alternative to the D907 along the Gardon St Jean, and the steam railway. Incidentally, for the enthusiast, No C27, a large freight locomotive (2-8-0), built in 1917 at Glasgow (French design), works the line well in spite of its 70 years service. Leave St Jean-du-Gard by D983, and soon on the right is a track (GR61, 4km, 2.4 miles) direct to Mialet, but by road continue until on the right is a narrow steep lane D50, that leads to Pont des Abarines on the Gardon de Mialet, and Mialet itself (*gîte d'étape,* GR61/67). Further along, and on the left is a road leading to the hamlet of **Mas Soubeyran.** Here amid rather severe scenery of the surrounding mountains is the house where Roland, the Camisard leader was born (although of humble origin, he was always referred to as 'Count Roland', by the English Queen Anne, who resolved to help the Camisards). In this house, now the Museum of the Desert, is the history of the Protestant struggle, and particularly in the Cévennes. Each year, at the beginning of September, under the nearby trees is held a huge 'assembly' of up to 20,000 Protestants.

Continuing up the road for 3km (1.8 miles) now in limestone scenery, is the Grotto of Trabuc — the largest in the Cévennes. It has a long history of occupance from Neolithic times through brigands and refugee Camisards. But its deep exploration is quite recent, and now 12km (7.4 miles) of huge galleries are known, along with lakes, and curious calcite underground landscape. There is a mysterious group of stalagmites, known as the '100,000 soldiers', giving the illusion of a besieging army (may be visited). Returning to the D50 (GR61) the road goes by the Gardon with good views past the confluence of the Gardon St Jean, and a railway bridge until the village of Générargues and D129 is reached. Turning right the route passes close to the Bambouseraie de Prafrance, and then through a narrow defile of towering limestone cliffs ('Porte de Cévennes') to **Anduze**.

This charming small town — very busy during summer — is a good centre for exploring the southern Cévennes, but with its narrow streets, alleys and fourteenth-century clock tower, near the old *château* is worth exploring in its own right. In the seventeenth century it was known as the 'Geneva' of the Cévennes, being fortified by the great Protestant leader, the Duc de Rohan, who also built an embankment to protect the town against flooding. Later it became the great supply town for the Camisards; afterwards achieving much prosperity through the silk industry, fruit, vines, distilling and potteries. Around it are some very good marked walks (yellow and white):

1. To viewpoint of St Julien, from the old *château*, 1 hr.

2. To Peyremale, cliffs above the Gardons, from the bridge (Alès Road), 2hrs.

3. To dolmens of Pallières, from 'Vitrine Cévenol' $1^1/_2$km (a mile) from Anduze D907. (Smoking is forbidden on these walks!)

The Vallée Longue (Gardon d'Alès)

Ste Cécile d'Andorge

Ste Cécile, although near the N106, is little visited, but there is plenty to explore in the remote valleys of its hinterland. This village, high up, is reached off the D276 (2km, 1.2 miles), Catholic and nowadays rather sleepy, but has an interesting church, and had 104 houses burnt by the Camisards in 1702. (Hardly that number exist now!) Later, the villagers became (as others did) *mineurs-paysans*, working

Ste Cécile d'Andorge

their land and going to the mines, either coal at Alès or lead-silver
locally, usually by train, for years until the mines closed (1950-75).
From the village the route on the left is followed (possible by car, but
better to walk) along an intensely wooded track above a valley,
which is eventually reached, Valussière, with terraced vines, fruit
plus acacia, ilex, chestnuts and pine. This can be then taken far to its
head past remote farms, or on the left is a track which climbs steeply
to a crest giving fine views of the HEP lake far below in the Gardon.
This area in summer is full of butterflies: Apollo, clouded yellow,
marbled white and orange fritillary — species long gone from other
areas.

Returning to the village, descend to the level crossing, then on
turning immediately right a track is taken down to the floor of the
stony Andorge valley, and continue up past the massive railway
embankment. Here the line of the great Villefort fault is clearly
visible, and going on further under a remarkably fine disused railway viaduct, the valley can be explored passing the odd large old
farmhouse with not so old red roof tiles — a feature to be explained
later. For the adventurous the disused narrow gauge line to Florac
can be followed from the viaduct via a tunnel, until tangled vegetation stops all progress. One can return to Ste Cécile via the road that
leads from the hamlet of St Julien des Points.

From Le Collet-de-Dèze to St Germain de Calberte

From Ste Cécile follow the N106 for 6km to **Le Collet-de-Dèze** a village with an interesting Protestant church below the road level, where most of the old village lies. It escaped demolition during the War of the Camisards by the villagers giving it to the Marquise de Portes; today it is a light, airy building with clean lines, and obviously used. Here one can reflect on these Cévenols — austere, hard-working craftsmen, literate — and realise that even until the 1960s Protestants rarely inter-married with Catholics, in most villages they lived harmoniously — but separately.

From here just beyond Le Collet, the D13 is taken, a narrow winding, but picturesque steep lane, with, off on the right, another 'hidden' hamlet of **St Michel-de-Dèze** that has an excellent bar-restaurant, La Rivière. Continuing, the D13 climbs steeply to the Col de Pendédis (666m, 2,184ft) a kind of mountain crossroads, with steep schistose valleys on all sides. From here there is a good view of surviving traditional cultivation terraces, (*bancels* or *faïsses*), laboriously enriched with baskets of earth. Nearby is a hamlet (*gîte d'étape*, GR67), and an old farm with red roof tiles, and the reason for these is that during the last war, Lozère prospered, and afterwards the heavy roof slabs (*lozes*) were replaced by tiles, as roofs were often damaged. Turning left for a short way (D54), there is an abandoned '*clède*', adjacent house, and untended chestnut groves, mute evidence of rural exodus.

The D54 can be taken in the opposite direction to the hamlet of **Les Ayres** amid its orchards and sheep, where curious rural fairs were held for labourers to get work in silkworm rearing, harvesting chestnuts, threshing wheat or the *vendanges* (ripening of vines). Returning to the col and the D13, the road continues upwards through remote country to the Col de Pradel (785m, 2,574ft) (GR67), where there is a splendid vista of serried ridges and valleys to the far horizon.

The road now descends in a series of tight hairpins to the Gardon de St Germain, past the restored ancient *château* of St Pierre perched on a knife edge ridge. Here in Gardons like these the beaver has been re-introduced, but he is a nocturnal, and only a silhouette of this majestic animal in the gloaming is all that is often glimpsed. Likewise the slough of the couleuvre de Montpellier, the region's largest reptile (2.5m, 8ft long) is all one would normally see of this snake on exposed slopes.

Soon the village of **St Germain de Calberte** is reached in the heart of the Mediterranean Cévennes (see Stevenson's journey) (park information centre).

Further Information
— The Cévennes —

Museums and Other Places of Interest

Anduze
Bambouseraie de Prafrance (Générargues)
Open: March-October 9.30am-12noon, 2-7pm. Steam railway station.

Meyrueis
Château Roquedois
☎ M. Bonnet (66) 45 62 81
Open: July-August daily.
At other times contact M. Bonnet.

Mialet
Desert Museum
Open: July/August 9.30am-6.30pm; March-October 9.30am-12noon, 2.30-6pm.

Trabuc Grotto
☎(66) 85 33 28
Open: June-September, guided visits lasting 1 hour.

Mont Aigoual
Brambiau
☎(67) 82 60 83
Open: all day April-September, restricted October-November.
Closed mid-November-March. For ski station Prat-Peyrot
☎(67) 82 60 17; Camprieu ☎(67) 82 60 26.

Pont-de-Montvert
Eco-Museum
Open: June-September and school holidays daily. Rest of the year Thursday, Saturday and Sunday.

St Jean-du-Gard
Steam railway station
☎(66) 85 13 17
Trains: May-September in steam Thursday, Friday and Sunday and public holidays.

Cévenol Valleys Museum
☎ M. Vriet (66) 85 10 48 Tuesday and Thursday
Open: June-September daily except Monday and Sunday morning.

Le Vigan
Cévenol Museum
Open: April-October inclusive except Tuesday.

Tourist Information Offices
(Syndicat d'Initative)

Anduze
Plan de Brie
☎(66) 61 98 17
Open: June-September all day.

Florac
National Park HQ
BP 15 Le Château 48400.
☎(66) 45 01 75
Information centre for all activities within the park.
Open all day July/August; September-June every day except weekends.

Syndicat d'Initiative
Ave Jean Monestier
☎(66) 45 01 14

Génolhac
Mairie
☎ (66) 61 10 55
Open: 9am-12noon and 2-6pm.

Meyrueis
Mairie
Rue Apies
☎(66) 45 62 64

St Jean-du-Gard
Place Rabot
☎(66) 85 32 11

Valleraugue
Mairie
☎(67) 82 22 78

Le Vigan
Syndicat d'Initiative (National Park Information)
Place du Marché
☎(67) 81 01 72
Open: daily except Sunday afternoon and Monday morning.

Villefort
Mairie
Rue Eglise
☎(66) 46 80 26

9 • Ardèche

The publicity issued by the Comité du Tourisme de l'Ardèche describes six regions of Ardèche which are summarised here. The department is the ancient province of Vivarais, hence some of the terms used:

The Rhône Valley
The Rhône flows south from Lyon to the Mediterranean and forms the eastern boundary of the department. This is a fertile, alluvial plain, with vineyards, orchards and small industries. Old cities were established to repel invaders. This area has the highest population.

Haut Vivarais
This is the area of high plateaux at 500m (1,600ft) plus. Cattle breeding and cereal growing are predominant — do look at the farms, both large and small. Annonay, the former *préfecture*, is the main town; it was a centre of printing and parchment due to the purity of water from the River Cance. Today it is involved with the textile and car industries.

La Montagne (The Mountains — the Massif Central)
On the high plateau, Mont Mézenc 1,754m (5,753ft) is the highest mountain at the north-western point. The River Loire rises at Le Gerbier de Jonc, but had it risen a few miles further south it would have flowed into the Mediterranean. The watershed between Atlantic and Mediterranean is nearby, and clearly marked on most main roads (*Routes Nationales*). In this area, there are many extinct volcanoes, lakes, rock formations and man-made barrages or dams.

Le Moyen Vivarais
This area extends from the middle of the Ardèche Valley to the Rhône and includes the valleys of the Eyrieux and Doux and the plateau of the Coiron. Many geological variations may be seen, mostly limestone and sandstone.

Les Cévennes
This area shows where the stalwart people of the Ardèche managed

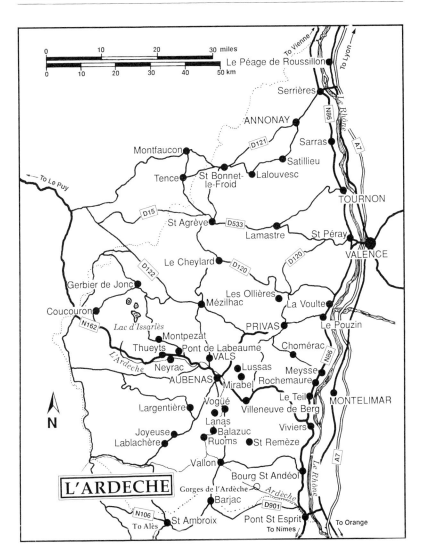

to farm on the terraces without the use of modern implements. They survived on chestnuts and vines, and olives on the southern slopes. Largentière had a silver mine until 1985, but this was the only real 'industry'. Most people work on the land or as entrepreneurs in building and domestic services.

Le Bas Vivarais

This is where the 'Midi' begins, therefore approaching the climate of the Mediterranean. There are olive groves in profusion; spectacular rock formations through the Gorges of the Ardèche (with caves to visit); the Bois de Païolive (a limestone 'forest'); the valley of the Chassezac; dolmens and old ruins from prehistoric times.

The climate of the Ardèche is mild to the north, warmer as it passes southward into the 'Midi' and not as hot as Provence but warmer than further north. In July and August it is hot and dry, excepting thunderstorms in the mountains which are intermittent and short-lived. The seasons of spring and autumn are generally very mild although temperatures drop a lot after sunset; even then eating out-of-doors can be a real pleasure.

Watch out for 'Le Mistral', particularly in the Rhône Valley. It emanates from the cold air over the Massif Central and affects mostly the eastern part of the department. It can last 3, 6 or 9 days according to local information. If you are stuck with it, seek sheltered valleys. The consolation is that when it does blow, the sky will be clear. 'Le Midi' is the south-west wind which tends to bring heavy rain. In winter (December to February) the temperature drops dramatically the higher you get, snow being most prevalent in January/February.

The developed areas are mainly the Rhône, the Ardèche and the valley of the Eyrieux. In spring, the blossoms of peaches, apricots, cherries, pears and apples are a spectacular sight and apples and pears are frequently grown in cordons. Buy fruit in season from roadside stalls or fruit co-operatives — cheap by the *plateau* or box. Grapes are cultivated mostly on small plots. In the period of harvest (*le vendange*) it is most interesting to see the local farmers taking their grapes on their tractors to the local *cave co-opérative*. (It is quite an experience to see how this operates — if you ask nicely, most *caves co-opératives* will let you stand by and watch.)

On the hills there is a mixture of deciduous and coniferous woods — oak, beech and chestnuts. In autumn you are likely to run over the fruit of the latter on the road. Don't gather them near a village or farm, as this is part of their livelihood. There is wild cherry blossom in spring and wild flowers are abundant including daffodils, pansies, violets, cowslips and orchids; hillsides are covered with many varieties of wildflowers in summer including broom and heather. There are also numerous varieties of wild mushrooms, but be warned: do not offend local people by gathering at random near villages; and if you find them, check with *pharmacies* who are very knowledgeable and usually display charts of those which are safe and those which are not. There are three particularly good varieties — *ceps, bolets* and *chanterelles*, all of which are quite safe, and delicious. They are often available in markets.

If you like dried flower arranging, the thistles are pretty (and prickly). Several variations: one much sought by the Ardèchois (therefore difficult to find) is one which grows close to the ground. It is called *porte bonheur* (bring-good-luck) and may be seen pegged to doors of houses in the countryside.

This is an area rich in wildlife. There are buzzards in the mountains, occasionally kites and eagles and also kestrels and magpies. Flocks of goldfinches are quite common, as are wheatears and stonechats in higher areas. Jays have colonies in some valleys. Blackbirds and thrushes have been hunted in the past and are less common (though hunting is now more restricted); black redstarts and bluetits, great-tits and robins are fond of leftovers. There are rabbits, hare and some deer in the forest though these are not easily seen. Local hunters also seek pigeon and wild boar, though the wild boar are rare and their haunts are only known to the locals, so don't expect to come face to face with one!

Several varieties of grasshopper can be seen; praying mantis, which are beautiful and harmless; large black flying beetles and small green ones, and large 'ladybird' types, fascinating for the observer. Cicadas 'sing' loudly in hot weather, and frogs may give you a chorus near streams and under bridges.

With a lot of water around, there are inevitably some mosquitoes, but these are not generally troublesome; flying ants may get attracted to outdoor lights at night. Lizards scamper everywhere over stone walls, mostly tiny, but there are some large green ones which are very beautiful and very shy. If you walk on hillsides and on scree, wear sensible shoes — there may be adders, but usually they are more afraid of you!

Most beautiful are the butterflies in summer. There are many varieties — they feed on the wild flowers and they are always attracted to washing lines. It is worth finding an identification book from a library if you are interested in the subject. Beautiful moths are also attracted by the lights at night, and there are many varieties which are not seen further north.

The history of the Ardèche goes back to the Neolithic age, evidence of which can be found in the valleys leading to the Rhône (the Ardèche and Chassezac in particular), and Neolithic cave paintings and dolmens can be found. The Gaulois, the Helvians and the Romans followed: the old city of Alba and the town of Les Vans are important archaeologically.

The Middle Ages provided many fortified sites, towns and

châteaux, though many of the *châteaux* are now, regrettably, only ruins, having been destroyed in the Wars of Religion between 1562 and 1629. (It is common to find both Catholic and Protestant churches in some towns and villages.)

The department of Ardèche is bounded by the Rhône Valley in the east, the Massif Central in the west, the Cévennes in the south-west and Languedoc in the south. It is an area of great contrasts, and is a paradise for anyone interested in geology.

The Rhône Valley is an alluvial plain, most land being devoted to fruit and vegetables, and vines, though maize and sunflowers are also important. Climbing to rockier areas, lavender fields and small market gardens can be seen, on land carefully terraced to extract the maximum from inhospitable ground.

In the north — Haut Ardèche/Haut Vivarais — there is pasture-land for cattle and sheep. This is a granite area, reflected in the construction of buildings with 'fish-scale' roofs (of split stone). This feature is in contrast to the split pots (clay) roofs of the more southerly parts of the Ardèche. It is indeed a green and pleasant land, being a mixture of pasture and mixed woodland. Here, timber is the most important source of heating in winter and it is interesting to see the neat piles of logs alongside the farms and in the villages. Snow is all-pervasive in winter and villagers must be very self-sufficient. However, the snow brings some benefits because there is now an increasing interest in cross-country skiing.

Further south volcanic areas are encountered — still high pasturelands interspersed with volcanic peaks and sources of rivers from this immense watershed between Mediterranean and Atlantic. In spring the meadows are carpeted with wild daffodils, narcissi, orchids and pansies, which seem to appear overnight when the snow disappears. Once seen they are never forgotten. In autumn, the colours are spectacular because of the mixed varieties of woodland, and in summer, wildflowers abound.

The Ardèche in its early stages flows through some really wonderful basaltic formations, as do some of its tributaries. Visitors who are adventurous enough to follow some of these will be rewarded with some fantastic sights. South of the volcanic area 'Le Tanargue' is a mountain range composed of a mixture of granite and crystalline rock and has many interesting rockfalls. It forms the southern boundary of the river, and is transformed when broom is in flower in early summer.

To the east and south of Privas is limestone country — the Plateau du Coiron is fascinating in this respect, and there are unusual strata

to be seen. It is a harsh area for agriculture, though there are sheep
and goats, with maybe the surprise of a field of lavender or small
farms in unexpected places. Travelling southwards to reach the
Gorges of the Ardèche, observe what water does to limestone! Further south and west is a very dry limestone area with spectacular
rock formations, caves, dolmens and prehistoric sites.

The Ardèche is not as well known gastronomically, or for its wine,
as are many other regions of France. However, the local produce is
worth sampling.

Charcuteries (delicatessens) are a feast for the eyes and the palate.
Try *saucisson de montagne* — rather dry in texture but full of flavour
and not too strong; *boudin* — a sausage, red or white (the red akin to
black pudding), delicious boiled or sautéed, served with local
vegetables; *sanglier* (wild boar) — sometimes possible to buy cuts in
wine sauce which are tender and delicious. Also *pâté de sanglier*, pigs'
trotters and *jambon cru* (raw ham) — deliciously prepared and
presented; *pâtés* — local *pâté de campagne* (*not* heavily laced with
garlic) and many local specialities also to seek out.

Cheeses are available from all regions of France, but for local
specialities try: Tome, a hard mountain cheese; Fromage de Chèvre
(goat cheese) from farms, markets or supermarkets; Cantal, Bleu
d'Auvergne and Roquefort from neighbouring departments.

It is a statutory requirement to state the source of vegetables with
prices, so look for '*Pays*' for local produce on price tickets. In season,
asparagus is quite cheap, and very good. Look out for huge cauli-
flowers for economical meals; also leeks, onions, carrots and white
turnips. *Bettes* (or *blettes*) — more commonly known as Swiss chard
— can be found in shops and markets. Tomatoes grown locally are
usually better flavoured than those from other regions. There are
also lots of courgettes and aubergines. Occasionally you may find
something strange which looks like giant celery called *cardons*, traditionally used in the region at Christmas braised like celery.

Local chickens are fed mostly on maize and the skin is yellow —
don't be put off — the flavour is very good. Guinea fowl (*pintade* or
pintadeau) are delicious and an extremely good buy in both markets
and supermarkets — quite a small one easily serves four people.
Turkey (*dinde*) and pheasant (*faisan*) are readily available; rabbit
(*lapin*) and hare (*lièvre*) can be found in markets. Quail (*caille*) are
available in *charcuteries*. (*Caillettes* are something different — almost
a French version of haggis!) Sometimes you will see '*grives*' or '*pâté
de grives*'. This is wild thrush so don't buy if you don't like the
shooting of these lovely birds.

The *boucheries* are excellent and offer cuts of beef, lamb and pork with no waste. Offal is good and, if you like the stronger taste, ox liver (*foie de génisse*) is excellent value. Those partial to hamburgers may choose their piece of meat and have it ground specially — ask for *hachée* — perfect for barbecues. If you are so inclined, there are horse-meat butchers (*chevalines*) in many towns.

Markets usually have stalls run by those whose source of fish is the Mediterranean. There are many varieties which are not usually found outside France — do try them even if the name is unfamiliar. Fresh tuna (*thon*) and mixtures for *bouillabaisse* can be found at these stalls. Try smallfry (*fritures*) and cook like whitebait, sautéed in a little butter. Oysters are available in profusion in season — they are regarded as a special dish for New Year (Réveillon).

Eggs from small shops and supermarkets are very good but those from markets are even better. Butter from farms may be found in markets, either unsalted or lightly salted.

The first purchase most people make at *boulangeries* is bread. Small local shops are better than those in towns. In the Rhône Valley area try *pognes* which are slightly sweet. Elsewhere *pain de campagne* or *campagnard*, or *pain de siègle* (rye bread, a tough texture but delicious when eaten fresh). For local *pâtisserie*, try *tarte au châtaignes* (chestnuts), Ardèchois biscuits with almonds, or *beignets* (miniature doughnuts — a Christmas speciality).

The Ardèche is not specially known for vintage wines, but the term 'Côtes du Rhône' encompasses the eastern limit of the department. However, St Péray and Cruas produce good sparkling wine and St Joseph is reasonably well known. If you wish to try the wines from local vineyards, select from: Côtes du Vivarais (from the Gorges de l'Ardèche); Vins de Pays de l'Ardèche; and Vin d'Orgnac, or otherwise visit local *caves co-opératives* and take advantage of any *dégustation gratuit* offered before you buy — they are mostly cheap and very pleasant. If you are so inclined, you can buy in quantity, 5 or 10l (about 1 or 2gal) of the lowest alcohol content at incredibly low prices. Look for signs saying *vins en vrac* — take your own container or buy one there, tasting first! A *vrac* is a 5 or 10l container, usually plastic, but a water bottle would suffice.

In season, eat all you can of peaches, cherries, pears, greengages, redcurrants and melons (*Charentais* type). *Pêches blanches* (white peaches) are particularly good, and the cherries are dark and sweet. *Fruit co-opératives* will sell by the box (*plateau*) and there are roadside stalls — the latter are better and cheaper off major roads.

Privas is the centre for *marrons glacées*, try them in various forms:

crème de marrons; — tins or tubes; boxed and sweets (quite expensive); fruit bottled in brandy or *eau de vie* are specialities — not cheap but a delicious luxury; honey is a 'must' — preferably buy from farms or where you see signs for *miel de pays* (also available from *alimentations* and supermarkets). Flavours vary from one flower to another including acacia, heather, thyme, lavender or *'mille fleurs'*; *fromage de chèvre* (the goat's cheese mentioned above) is frequently signposted at farms. It is very good, rather dry in some forms, but sometimes you may find a very soft one (this is delicious eaten with a spoon with a sprinkling of sugar).

The Mountains and the North (Haut Vivarais)

Starting from Privas, take N104 to Aubenas/Le Puy. After about 10km (6 miles) just before Col de l'Escrinet, turn right on D122 towards Mézilhac. This is a very winding road with splendid views into steep valleys and masses of broom in summer. At Col de la Fayolle there is a sign indicating that snow tyres are required in winter. Follow the road to Col de Quatre Vios at 1,149m (3,768ft), so you will be climbing all the way. This part of the road gets very icy in winter due to snow drifting onto the road. The *crêperie* here is a must, for pancakes and local produce and there is also walking in the woods, and a walk to a ruined *château* (signposted). In late summer bilberries may be gathered in the woods and near the roadside, but parking places are limited. Continue to **Mézilhac**, where there is a *teleski* (ski-lift) and walking tracks, and to Lachamp Raphaël — both have road junctions to Aubenas and Vals-les-Bains. Continue on N104 to the junction to Le Gerbier de Jonc, 5km (3 miles). This is a volcanic peak which can be climbed on a marked footpath. There are several pleasant places to eat local specialities, and the source of the Loire — in an old farmhouse — can be visited (you may taste the water). Follow D378 to Mont Mézenc — the highest point is at 1,753m (5,750ft). There is a marked route — Les Pieds de Mont Mézenc — which can be followed for good views and Mont Mézenc itself can be climbed on footpaths by walkers.

A diversion can be made on D631 to **Les Estables** (the road to Le Monastier), a village which is expanding to accommodate those interested in skiing. There are also walking tracks (*Grandes Randonnées*) well marked in this area.

Next take the road to Fay sur Lignon (D410/D262). Here the route goes briefly out of the Ardèche, but not for long. Continue along the valley of the Lignon to join the road to **St Agrève** (D15) and turn right. After Mars you are back in Ardèche. The area around St Agrève is wonderful to explore: there are many woodland trails for walking and in winter it is described as a *Zone Nordique* with good cross-country skiing. Take time to look at the villages *en route* and note the change in buildings, from split pot roofs and stone in the south, to granite and 'fish-scale' (split stone) roofs in the north.

From St Agrève follow the D9 towards St Bonnet-le-Froid. At **Devesset**, there is a reservoir with sailing, wind-surfing, swimming and picnic areas. At St Bonnet-le-Froid 20km (12 miles) from St Agrève join N105 and turn right to Annonay, following the River Cance. **Annonay** was the original *préfecture* of the Ardèche, and it is a fascinating old town to explore. It boasts three heroes — Marc Séguin (1786-1883) who was a notable engineer (see Tournon), and the Montgolfier brothers (Joseph and Etienne) who were the first people to ascend in a hot air balloon. There are statues to these remarkable inventors in Annonay, and also a museum of local history which commemorates their work.

From Annonay go to Peaugres on N82 (towards Serrières) to visit a large safari park. It is not cheap as the entrance fee is per person, not per car, so it is worth allocating most of a day for the visit. There are picnic areas and restaurant and toilet facilities. From here, return to the Rhône Valley and N86 at Serrières, or find some minor roads which drop down into the valley.

The Ardèche: From Source to the Rhône

The Ardèche rises north of the road N102 from Aubenas to Le Puy near Le Col de la Chavade. The source is in the middle of scrub and on private property. However, it crosses N102 very soon and drops into the southern valley on the way to Aubenas. To see it in its infancy, take a small side road to **Astet**— a road not usually used by tourists — following the valley and then coming back to **Thueyts**. This is the best place to see the river. In the middle of an avenue of plane trees and opposite a *co-opérative des fruits* — follow, on foot, a sign to L'Echelle de la Reine. A footpath passes behind some houses and apartments and leads to a broad stone staircase (easy walking) dropping down to a Roman bridge (Pont du Vernade) where there is a deep pool for swimming and rocks for scrambling. Also a track (devious but fun) which goes over the hill on the south side. The basalt rocks here are very fine.

In Thueyts, park in a shady square and take advantage of the small shops and restaurants and pretty backstreets. As you leave, look for the *belvédère* at the eastern end, and park for an excellent view. There is also a marked footpath to L'Echelle du Roi, Le Pont du

Segré, Pays de la Loire

Valleraugue, with River Hérault, Cévennes

Open-air market in Aubenas, Ardèche

A simple Ardèche village church

Diable (Roman bridge) and La Chaussée des Géants. It is not too difficult, but the ascent of L'Echelle du Roi is not for the overweight as you have to climb up through a small fissure in the rock — have good strong shoes and enjoy the effort! Towards Aubenas, it is possible to get to the river by taking a right turn, on a sharp bend, to **Mercier**. There is a pleasant camping site at the bridge and access to the river. A small road is signposted to Le Pont du Diable and La Chaussée des Géants — note that parking is limited, but worth trying for a scramble down to the river where there is a sandy beach for paddling and deep pools. There are fine views of basalt formations here too.

From N102 a small diversion can be taken to **Neyrac-les-Bains**, a mini-spa specialising in the treatment of skin diseases. There is a good hotel/restaurant, camping, and pretty views. From this point, the visitor can continue to Aubenas through small towns, some with old textile mills, and with campsites on the river. However, if you wish to follow the river, there is an alternative: after the sign to Meyras (a small village possibly meriting a detour), when the road crosses the Ardèche, do not do so; go straight on (N536) to Montpézat and Burzet and the Château de Ventadour. At a corner, where the road bears left, there is a small parking area. Walk back a few yards to a gap in the wall and descend some steps to a sandy beach at the junction of the Ardèche and the Fontolière for a sandy shore, shallow swimming and a deeper pool. (This area can also be reached from the bend of N102 near to Pont de Labeaume, but you have to watch out carefully for it.) This is on the fringe of **Pont de Labeaume**, and in the village, off N102 is a Roman bridge and old church, dominated by the Château de Ventadour, which was important in the history of the area; it is being restored and likely to be open to visitors in the near future.

To follow the river from here, turn sharp right over the bridge and sharp right again to Vals-les-Bains via Arlix. There are several places to bathe and picnic, but you have to seek out parking spots. A small railway carrying local freight winds to and fro. It is possible to climb up through Chirols to Vals — tortuous but with splendid views — or carry on through Arlix. **Vals-les-Bains** is a health spa and is quite sophisticated. Visitors don't need to take the waters — they may try them in kiosks in the main street. It is a good centre for touring, with numerous hotels, restaurants, two cinemas, a theatre, a casino, skating rink and gymnasium. It is the most important centre in France for the treatment of diabetes. In addition to all these facilities there are beautiful gardens to enjoy and shady cafés in which to while away your time, as well as good local shops and there is a *source intermittent*, a spring which appears every 6 hours. The therapeutic value of the waters was discovered in the seventeenth century and many famous people have been visitors. The climate is mild and dry.

Go now to **Aubenas**, a charming market town with a lot of history. From its hilltop site there are wonderful views over the valley of the Ardèche and there is a panoramic point/orientation table. The town is dominated by its *château*, the oldest part dating from the twelfth

The château *and Hôtel de Ville at Aubenas*

century; there is also the Dôme St Benoit (formerly a Benedictine monastery, dispersed at the time of the Revolution), a 25m-high (82ft) *donjon* (keep) with two large towers, a Renaissance courtyard and an eighteenth-century staircase. There is an excellent market in the square by the *château* (now the Hôtel de Ville) on Saturdays, with people coming from a wide area. Go early to find a parking place or be prepared to walk a little — it is worth the effort. The most interesting stalls will be out of stock by noon. The market spills over now into the pedestrian areas of the old town, but on other days these are pleasant to explore for shops with basic requirements, local specialities and good quality souvenirs. There are two good cinemas, one with four screens, the other with two. Programme times are, however, a little difficult to understand and are usually at 9pm but vary. One of them, Le Navire, also has a pleasant restaurant/bar. The Syndicat d'Initiative (Information Office) is at Centre le Bournot, an old school building, which also has a small theatre and exhibition space — check for details at time of visit. There are several pleasant restaurants which are reasonably priced and an excellent pizzeria for more casual food. (Here you will also find one of the few 'washeterias', ie launderettes.) Most French banks are represented as well as a large post office; a modern hospital; a bus station; and a whole street with agents of most European cars for service and advice. The cathedral is very fine and has occasional organ recitals and international concerts. There are several hotels and restaurants, and pleasant camping sites nearby (particularly on the hills south-west of the town).

This first section of the route will take some time if the diversions are followed, so if time is limited, the next section could be explored separately.

L'Ardèche-Aubenas to Rhône

To visit the Gorges de l'Ardèche, take N104 from Aubenas to Alès. At St Etienne de Fontbellon you may care to stop to visit the church where there is a splendid organ and sometimes recitals. Then, turn left on D579 to Vogüé, Ruoms, and Vallon Pont d'Arc. **Vogüé** is dominated by a *château* incorporating a seigneurial mill of 1458. There are medieval streets to explore, bathing, fishing, campsites and *gîtes rurales*. Do *not* cross the river here, but turn right on D114 to Ruoms. Halfway there take a diversion, turning right to **Balazuc**. This site was inhabited in prehistoric times; in the year AD1 it was discovered when the Roman road from Poitiers to Nîmes passed through. See the ruins of a Roman church, covered passages, ramparts and a *donjon*. The streets are narrow, therefore parking is limited, but by the river there is excellent swimming from a sandy shore.

Continue to Ruoms and see a beautiful example of limestone cliffs. The town itself is also very pleasant, with old ramparts and a Roman church. There are good beaches (and canoeing) between Vogüé and Ruoms as well as riverside camping and hire of *vélos* (two-stroke cycles). Nearby at **St Alban-Auriolles** is the Museé Alphonse Daudet at Mas de la Vignasse (Alphonse Daudet wrote *Lettres de mon Moulin* and other novels). It was his family home and contains many interesting documents as well as collections of old tools for milling grain, and shows the history of the silk industry and domestic life in the nineteenth century. Also nearby, the River Chassezac joins the Ardèche. To find the 'join' is a test for the map reader. It is quite complicated, but if you get there, well worth the trouble. The visitor can bathe on a shingle river bed with some deeper pools when the water is high.

From Ruoms proceed to **Vallon Pont d'Arc**. In July and August this is the busiest place in the Ardèche; enthusiasts for canoeing and naturism come from all over Europe and the population increases tenfold! However, the town itself has pleasant old streets and good restaurants; the campsites are numerous and excellent, and offer entertainment during summer. It is recommended to those who want to be involved in activity holidays and meeting other campers, but it is possible to bypass the town if you are touring and want to get to the Gorges. It is clearly signposted, near a factory processing grape skins for use as fertiliser! This is the 'Route Touristique des Gorges' (D579) with the ruins of 'Vieux Vallon' on the left merging into the hillside. Soon the Pont d'Arc 60m-high (197ft) is reached — formed through many centuries of erosion of the limestone. The river is normally very calm and camping sites in this area offer swimming, fishing, trips in canoes-kayaks and barges.

After the Pont d'Arc, the road winds for about 30km ($18\,^1/_2$ miles); there are numerous places to stop to admire the view which are well signposted. (This road did not exist until the late 1960s, but it is now an accepted tourist route to those who know the area.) There are some interesting limestone caves to be visited around here and many places to visit, some of which will be briefly described.

The Château de la Bastide du Virac is a fourteenth and fifteenth-century *château*, partly furnished, which also contains a display of the life cycle of the silkworm, and historical documents and implements. A small shop sells lovely silk items — scarves, lampshades, pictures, etc — which are not cheap but are authentic. Aven Orgnac, an excellent cave, has easy access and good facilities. A museum of prehistory in course of preparation is due to open in 1988; near to Vallon, the Grotte des Huguenots, covers spelaeology, archaeology and prehistory. There is also a private museum covering the history of the silk industry. Also along the Gorges road is the Grotte de la Madeleine and, by turning off, towards St Remèze, is the Aven de Marzal (the latter now has an underground prehistoric zoo with life-size models). Also nearby is the Grotte de la Forestière which is signposted. If you wish to picnic, there are numerous tracks off into the bush, where you can be quiet, but there are no snackbars except for the occasional ice-cream van or *crêperie* in parking areas.

After all these distractions, continue to **St Martin d'Ardèche** where the river opens out into the Rhône Valley. Here there is a fine sandy beach which you can drive onto via a concrete ramp. This is the border of the department, but there is one thing left to try — the confluence of the Ardèche and the Rhône, though this is, in fact, just outside the limit of the department. Continue to the junction with N86 at St Just, then turn left towards Bourg St Andéol. After about 2km ($6\,^1/_2$ miles), just before a level crossing and opposite a garage, turn right along a small road. Follow it to the end and then bear left. On the right is a stone gateway to a house called Les Mouettes. Park nearby and look for a little track to the right to a small bridge where there are some quite steep steps down to the river. Be warned, however, that it is not easy to find.

Privas to Aubenas and the Plateau du Coiron

This is not strictly a tour, because it dots around, but it does suggest points of interest.

At Le Pouzin, take N104 towards Privas, following the valley of the Ouvèze — an interesting introduction to the Ardèche and its limestone hills. The visitor will pass through a number of small villages on this route. As the road climbs, divert to **Coux**, a very interesting medieval village — it is necessary to park and then walk to reach it.

Privas is now the *préfecture* of the Ardèche. It has been the centre of production of *marrons glacées* since the reign of Louis XIV, the industry having been developed by Olivier de Serres in the nineteenth century. The history of Privas is closely connected with the Religious Wars. It was a fortified town for the Protestants after the Edict of Nantes in 1598 and was razed by Richelieu's troops. Diane de Poitiers inherited the sovereignty of Privas in the sixteenth century, although she never actually lived there. Most existing buildings are eighteenth century, classical in style and there are many sidestreets to explore and a beautiful eighteenth-century bridge. There are various *fêtes* during spring and summer, and at the beginning of December a *Fête de la Rôtie Géante des Châtaignes,* when chestnuts are grilled and offered to the public with *vin rosé*! There is sometimes a 'cherry auction' in June, but check locally. A cinema (three screens), a municipal theatre, and a good swimming pool can also be found here.

To explore north of Privas take D2/D344 to Les Ollières and St Sauveur. At **Pranles**, visit the Musée du Vivarais Protestant. This old house, birthplace of Pierre and Marie Durand, prominent Huguenots, contains many historic documents concerning the Protestant struggles.

There is much more to see south of Privas, and a choice of routes. The D2 goes to **Chomérac**, towards the Rhône — a pretty village, with an occasional market. The first silk mill in the Ardèche was established here in 1670. At **St Symphorien sous Choméra**c there is a museum showing the history of basketmaking, for domestic and commercial use.

The D7 goes to **Villeneuve de Berg** to visit the Auberge Musée de Verdus. This is a private museum, in an ancient barn, displaying farming implements and domestic utensils from the eighteenth and

Mirabel and the Plateau du Coiron

nineteenth centuries; it is well worth a visit. Food and drink can also be bought there.

Starting again from Privas, to see the Plateau du Coiron join N104 to Col de l'Escrinet (787m, 2,581ft). At the Col there is a two-star hotel and restaurant with splendid views towards the south and southwest. However, regrettably, they do not have a bar for casual drinks at present. For this the visitor should seek bars on the way up or down. There are not many (a bar advertising 'Repas Rurale' is very popular and expanding) but the numbers may increase.

Those who like a good walk and a rough scramble should take D122 towards Mézilhac just before Col de l'Escrinet. Follow the second paved road on the left (after Maison Cantoniale de Cholet) through to a farm then park, and take a footpath to the Roc de Gourdon — it is a rough scramble but on a clear day you can see as far as the Alps and the Massif Central.

From the col, continue on N104 towards Aubenas. In about 6km (4 miles) go right on D536 to St Michel de Boulogne, a splendid ruined *château* with thirteenth-century *donjon* and seventeenth-century gateway. At the corner where the *château* is first seen a small track leads down to the tiny River Boulogne, where you can scramble on to the rocks, picnic and swim in a good pool when there is enough water. At **Vesseaux** there are tennis courts which can be hired (contact the Mairie); the *cave co-opérative* sells local wine; and the church has a simple interior and a beautiful tiled roof.

Carry on to St Privat, amid vineyards and peach orchards, and turn left by a sign for 'Garden Center'(*sic*) on D259 to Lussas. The garden centre itself is worth a visit for seeing local trees, but also for the fact that it is at the confluence of the small River Luol and the Ardèche. Walk to the end and turn left.

The climb to Eyriac and Lussas has many hairpins and stupendous views, and **Lussas** itself, though small, is quite lively. The Mairie is sometimes an art gallery and there is usually a weekend market. There are also local fairs and a film festival in May and September.

There are many things to see on the Plateau du Coiron, and here are some recommendations: at **Darbres** there is good camping; **Freysennet** is a typical village; **Mirabel** has a tower of volcanic rock, privately owned, which is being restored; there are also lavender fields and fossils on tracks. Spend some time meandering , you will be well rewarded.

Villeneuve de Berg (on N102) was very important in the eleventh to fourteenth centuries and there are relics of the Wars of Religion. Olivier de Serres (called the 'father of French agriculture') was born nearby; there is a statue to him in the town and a museum at his birthplace is signposted.

Lavilledieu (N102) has existed in its present form since the sixteenth century. In the eleventh century it had a Benedictine convent which was devastated during the Wars of Religion. In 1944, during the withdrawal of occupying troops, many houses were burned and their inhabitants killed. Nearby, there is Le Petit Musée du Bizarre — it is somewhat bizarre, but exhibits local art and sculpture by young artists.

Alba, just off N102, is a prehistoric and Roman site. Destroyed in the second century, it became important again in the fourteenth under the Bishop of Viviers. The present *château* is sixteenth century, and archaeological sites are being investigated, with some important finds. There are several small camping sites nearby and small hotels and restaurants. The villages around Alba are also well worth exploration.

The Western Ardèche

From Aubenas take N102 and follow it through Thueyts and Col de la Chavade. After another 10km (6 miles) stop at the Auberge de Peyrebeille. This now modern hotel/restaurant has a rather grisly history, for in the nineteenth century the proprietors regularly killed their visitors in order to get their money! The original building is preserved and for a small donation you will be shown the old rooms where this happened. The proprietors were eventually guillotined in the courtyard. The old building contains a shop selling local produce, in what was the kitchen, and the present hotel provides good food.

Just after this, turn right on D16 to Coucouron. A crossroads shows a sign to Lac d'Issarlès, the eventual destination of this tour, but in the village find a small road left to the Lac de Coucouron, a small reservoir, which is a good picnic spot, down a rather bumpy road. From the village, continue to Lac d'Issarlès on D16.

An alternative route from Aubenas would be to take the N102 to Pont de Labeaume, then go right on N536 over the bridge, to **Montpézat**, where there are some find old buildings and a twelfth-century church; also walking tracks, river bathing and a *fête* in mid-August. After Montpézat, in $7^1/_2$km ($4^1/_2$ miles) at Le Roux, take D160 through a tunnel to St Cirgues en Montagne. (The tunnel was originally designed for a railway but the plan was abandoned in World War I and it is now a road.) Follow to **La Palisse** where there is a large reservoir with some water sports. Continue on D116, a winding road, to the village of **Issarlès** and Lac d'Issarlès, which is a lake in a volcanic crater. There is swimming from sandy shores, sailing, a walk around the lake, and good camping shops and restaurants. There are also *fêtes* in June, July and August. This spot is very popular at weekends with the Ardèchois.

The visitor is now near the western limit of the Ardèche. See signs for Le Monastier where Robert Louis Stevenson began his *Travels with a Donkey in the Cévennes* (see chapter 8). Also, just in the Ardèche, near La Bastide-Puylaurent (south of Langogne on D906) is the Cistercian abbey of Notre Dame des Neiges where Stevenson sought refuge. It is now quite a commercial enterprise, with its own sawmill, farm and vineyard. The old buildings are preserved; the shop sells their own honey, wine, jams, and other local specialities. It is a very pleasant visit.

The Valley of the Doux: Tournon, Lamastre and Le Chemin de Fer de Vivarais

There are two ways to take this interesting trip, which follows the valley all the way and enables the visitor to enjoy the steam railway. It is not cheap, and will occupy a whole day, but should appeal to all ages.

The first way is to take the steam train from Tournon early in the morning, spend about 4 hours in the town of Lamastre which is interesting, and walking nearby, and return to Tournon in the afternoon. The alternative is to drive from Sarras, on N86 and follow D221 to Ardoix and St Romain d'Ay, following the small River Ay. There are pretty gorges and places to picnic by the river. Then continue to Satillieu (where the Salle Don Quichotte has interesting tapestries, and where there is an old town to explore). Next to Lalouvesc, where the *basilique* is a centre for pilgrims; there is a nineteenth-century convent and an orientation table describing the Cévennes and the Alps. This is a walking centre, bicycles may be hired, and there is tennis and fishing.

It would be possible to go from here to St Félicien on D532 (10km, 6 miles) where there is good camping, accommodation, a Friday market and a dog fair in July. However, the picturesque way to Lamastre is to go straight on where D532 turns east, on to the D236, where the views are wonderful. After 7km (4 miles), near Col de Buisson at the junction of C6 to Molières, is a miniature Ardèchois village, which is very beautifully executed.

Go then to Lamastre to pick up the steam train. An explanatory leaflet at the ticket office (produced in English) tells you what to look out for. The 33km (20 mile) route takes 2 hours, with a stop for refreshments half-way. This afternoon steam train gives a very short break at Tournon and return on a rail-car to Lamastre.

Le Tanargue

From Aubenas, take N102 towards Le Puy. After Labégude turn left just before Lalevade (D19 to Prades and Jaujac and 'Le Croix de Bauzon'). At Jaujac, take care: there is a conglomeration of roads in the village. For this tour, take D19 left to La Souche (ignoring Pont de Labeaume and Largentière). At La Souche, cross the River Lignon and then start to climb. At the top, after climbing over 800m (2,600ft) there is a small road to the *teleski* and the forest. Here, in summer, are numerous marked walking tracks through the forest; in winter, this is now a popular resort for both downhill and *ski de fond* (cross-country skiing) particularly during school holidays. It is also a wonderful place to walk and picnic, with many quiet places with spectacular views, and there are good restaurant facilities.

Return to the main road and continue west to a fairly major road junction. D239 to the right takes you back to N102 (Le Puy/Aubenas), but instead, turn left on D24 to Col de Meyrand. There are many places to stop for views and picnics on the south side of this mountain range. The villages *en route* show the typical, and hard, rural life.

If you have exhausted your time, either take N104 back to Aubenas or your base or continue to Largentière (covered in another tour) via Valgorge, for walking and seeing the pretty River Beaume which offers swimming, fishing and camping.

The Valley of the Eyrieux

This valley enjoys the reputation of having planted the first peaches in France, in the late nineteenth century. They are delicious, and very cheap in season. From N86, north of La Voulte, at Beauchastel, take N103 towards Le Cheylard. In 3km (2 miles) **St Laurent du Pape** boasts two *châteaux* — du Bosquet (sixteenth century, a classified historic monument) and d'Hauteville. There are also two notable potteries, fishing, river, bathing, handball, tennis and *boules*, hotels/ restaurants and camping. There is also Grande Randonnée 42 (GR42) for walking and horse-riding. Follow to **Les Ollières** at a bend of the river, a quiet village with pleasant hotels/restaurants and good walking. Here, either turn south towards Privas via Pranles, or follow this lovely valley to St Sauveur de Montagut. The road (and track of old railway) closely follow the river and views are excellent, but it is frustrating that access to the river is very difficult. If there is somewhere to park it may be possible to scramble down in places, so check in the villages with local people.

Nearer **Le Cheylard** the valley widens and there are camping sites near the river. This town is described as midway between the snow and the olive trees, and the climate is very moderate. It is an excellent centre for excursions on foot or on bicycle; there is fishing, bathing, tennis and a *boulodrôme*; municipal camping and small hotels and restaurants. There is a fair in mid-July, and regular organ concerts in the eleventh-century church.

Here, either turn north towards Lamastre on N578 or make your own way back to base.

Le Cascade du Ray Pic

From the northern end of Vals, take N578 towards Antraigues/ Mézilhac. After about $1^1/_2$km (almost a mile), turn left at a rather hidden turning onto the D243 to Labastide. This is the Route de Besourges. Cross the river and look for a place to bathe and picnic (there is limited parking and a scramble down to rocks, with a tiny waterfall and deep pool). Continue climbing to **Lachamp Raphaël**, stopping where you can to enjoy the views. On joining N535 to Le Puy, turn left, and almost immediately left again on D215 to Burzet, Vals-les-Bains and Aubenas towards the Cascade (signposted $7^1/_2$ km, $4^1/_2$ miles). Enjoy the sight of broom and heather in season.

Approaching the Cascade, there is a small café/snack bar which is open in summer, and there is a marked parking area. This is a 20-minute walk along a good but sometimes rough track (so have sensible footwear). In spring, after melting snow or periods of heavy rain, the double waterfall falling over basalt rocks is really spectacular and is a paradise for photographers!

Continue on D215 to **Burzet** ($7^1/_2$km, $4^1/_2$ miles) which has a fifteenth-century church, a thirteenth-century *calvaire* (calvary) (with a procession on Good Friday) and a local fair at the end of August. There is also walking and fishing nearby. Continue to N536 and to N102 to get back to Vals or Aubenas.

The South — Bas Vivarais

This area is particularly interesting geologically and archaeologically, but has charm for all visitors.

From Aubenas, take N104 towards Alès. Visit **Largentière** by taking a right turn, N103, via Vinezac (a pretty village with a *château*), and pass the silvermines (now closed) which gave the town its name. (It is also possible to get to Largentière from N104 via D5, after Uzer.) Do take the opportunity on the descent to the town to stop and look over the wall at the rooftops. There is good parking outside the entrance to the town, so do not attempt to drive around the narrow streets. Walk through the archway to find many interesting buildings as well as small shops and restaurants. There is a market in the square on Tuesdays. The *château* is twelfth century — check locally for visiting it — while the church is thirteenth century and well worth a visit. Much restoration of old houses, built of beautiful local stone, has been done recently and is still in progress.

Continuing south on N104, turn right on N104A at Lablachère to Les Vans, or after about 8km (5 miles) at Maisonneuve, take D252 signposted to Casteljau and Bois de Païolive. The latter is a 'limestone forest' with limestone rock formations which are named as resembling animals. It is possible to scramble here, but parking places are limited. The villages on this route are very pretty, particularly Banne and Casteljau.

Les Vans has many old streets and arcades and a *place* with plenty of parking. Shopping for necessities and souvenirs is good. The municipal museum is extremely interesting, covering archaeology, geology and local crafts as well as milling and farming machinery. A map in the museum shows the history of the area. On the main road, visit Grospierres — a very old village. Those interested can check at the local *mairie* where to see ancient dolmens.

As you reach the southern limit of Ardèche, on N104, visit Les Grottes de la Cocalière, south of St Paul-le-Jeune. These beautiful limestone caves may be seen on a conducted tour lasting just over an hour of easy walking. At the end of the tour the visitor returns to the start on a small train, and there is a good shop with excellent souvenirs of semi-precious stones (not cheap, but from the region), as well as a good restaurant and toilet facilities (including those for the disabled).

The Rhône Valley

Follow N86 from Vienne, west of the Rhône and enter the department at Le Péage de Roussillon. At **Charnas** there is a viewpoint across five departments on a clear day. There is also a beautiful church, *fêtes* in July, and clay-pigeon shooting (ball-trap) in August. **Limony** has two historic monuments: one to a slave adopted by his master; the second a remarkable silver cross.

Serrières is an old fishing village. Le Musée des Mariniers et de la Batellerie du Rhône, in the church of mariners shows some history of this area. Explore old parts of the town. Around Whitsun (*Pentecôte*) look out for *joutes* or jousting on canal barges, which is great fun. Four kilometres (2¹/₂ miles) further on at **Peyraud**, walk either from the church to Verlieux (2km, just over a mile), or from the old bridge, following the stream to a small waterfall. Nearby at **St Désirat** is an ancient cross behind the church and another superb view. The wine in this area is *appellation contrôlée*; St Joseph is excellent and not expensive. Look out for *dégustation gratuit* signs and try before you buy.

Ozon has a river walk and children's playground; a local *fête* in late August, ball-trap in May; and water skiing areas are being developed near the barrage. **Tournon** is dominated by the feudal *château* of the Counts of Tournon, perched on an enormous rock. This contains Le Musée de la Ville with many things of regional interest. Explore the town on foot — the old streets are pedestrianised: see the collegiate church with seventeenth- and eighteenth-century paintings; the Lycée Gabriel Faure with wonderful tapestries, and a Jesuit chapel. The original suspension bridge across the Rhône to Tain was the first iron suspension bridge in the world, designed by Marc Séguin of Annonay. It has been replaced by a more modern one, regrettably, but is still very fine. This is an excellent touring centre for both the valley and the mountains.

At **Châteaubourg** a medieval castle dominates the Rhône, and houses a pleasant and not too expensive restaurant. **St Romain de**

Lerps has an orientation table, a *château*/hotel, camping and horse-riding. **Cornas** is grouped around its bell-tower, and there is a wine fair here on the first Sunday of December.

St Péray is famed for white sparkling wines. There are fairs in summer and autumn, and there are always *dégustation gratuit* signs on the roadside to tempt you to taste (and probably buy!) the local product. There are also riverside walks here, a heated swimming pool and many hotels and restaurants. Nearby, the ruined Château de Crussol is attainable by a marked footpath.

La Voulte sur Rhône is a commercial centre. Its fifteenth- and sixteenth-century *château* was badly damaged in 1944 and is in process of restoration. Park near the river and walk: there are many narrow streets and old houses. The church has a sixteenth-century bas-relief and the suspension bridge is said to be the longest in France. This is a sporting town and rugby, soccer, volleyball, basketball, motocross and *boules/petanques* are all enjoyed. There are also many hotels and restaurants, making it another good touring centre.

Le Pouzin was a Protestant stronghold during the Wars of Religion, and was burned and pillaged in 1628. In 1944 it was damaged again by American bombardment and burned by retreating German troops. The new Hôtel de Ville has an exceptional 'Salon de Mariages' decorated by a regional artist, and the church, though modern, has preserved the regional character. Nearby, sporting activities include water sports in a *bassin nautique* and there is tennis and a gymnasium. There are local *fêtes* in June and September and a torchlight procession on 14 July with folklore groups and fireworks. Many excellent camping sites and small hotels can also be found.

Baix has ruins of a feudal *château* razed by Richelieu's troops; a seventeenth-century chapel; fifteenth- and sixteenth-century houses with frescoes; a Louis XIV fountain and a clocktower. Local *fêtes* are held during July and August.

Cruas has remains of eleventh-century buildings in the foundations of the church. (The abbey here was involved in the Huguenot struggles and suppressed by the Bishop of Viviers in the eighteenth century.) There is a nuclear power station development nearby (strongly opposed by local people). In summer there is a programme of guided tours, including walking to an old *château* at St Vincent de Barres (bearing the arms of Diane de Poitiers), camping, a swimming pool and *boulodrôme* and a *fête* at the end of July.

At **Meysse**, turn left to pass the old station to get to the Rhône. The track alongside is a very good place to picnic and watch the river.

Rochemaure should definitely be visited. It is a medieval town

Viviers cathedral

with a colourful history and a majestic *château* which is well-signposted. Pass under the Roman wall which runs down to the valley, park where indicated and do the last bit on foot. Also visit the Chapelle de St Laurent and Pic du Chenevari (507m, 1,663ft). These are pleasant and easy walks. This was an important centre for the silk industry for two centuries up to World War II, but now most people work in wool and synthetic mills, and at local crafts such as basketmaking.

Le Teil was classified as a *bourg* (a small market town) in letters patent of Henry IV. There is a baptistry and old streets and the nearby church at Melas is ninth century. There are many hotels and restaurants, a municipal swimming pool, tennis and fishing, as well as camping, a *salle des fêtes*, cinema and dancing. Near Le Teil is the giant Lafarge cement plant, on both sides of the road, but it does not spoil the town and provides much local employment.

Viviers has existed since Roman times. The first cathedral and convent of Notre Dame de Rhône was constructed in the sixth century and the present cathedral is twelfth century. The Bishops of Viviers ruled a huge domain (hence Vivarais) and controlled all of the abbeys in the province. The old town must be visited on foot. From N86, turn on to the N86A towards Montelimar and then left to the parking area in the *place*. See the 'Maison des Chevaliers', with its beautiful stone carved façade of coats of arms. Off Grande Rue, climb the steps to the cathedral — the porch, choir and nave walls are all original. The altar and other parts are of marble. There are two splendid Gobelin tapestries, two huge chandeliers and fine stained glass windows. A very tranquil place.

Outside, walk to see the fine spire and take a path to the Vieux Château — its remaining tower looks over old rooftops and the Rhône Valley. It is sad that the town has become depopulated in recent years, but the remaining shops supply the essentials. The church of St Laurent has an interesting belltower; there are several hotels/restaurants; also facilities for tennis, *boules*, a swimming pool and canoeing/water skiing areas in course of development. Local *fêtes* are held in July and August.

After 7km (4 miles) turn west to **St Montan**. This very beautiful village is being lovingly restored by local conservationists. Park in the square and walk through the cobbled streets to see archways and buildings of beautiful golden stone. There is an eleventh-century *château* and two twelfth-century *chapelles* — all designated as historic monuments. Small shops sell locally produced articles.

Back to the main road, go to **Bourg St Andéol** — another Roman town. The body of St Andéol is interred in a sarcophagus in the twelfth-century church; a bas-relief of the god Mithra, a convent, a monastery and an ancient palace of the Bishops of Viviers can also be seen. There are markets on the quays of the Rhône on Wednesdays and Saturdays and a *marché aux puces* (flea market) on the first Saturday of each month. There are also wine fairs in July and September.

St Marcel d'Ardèche is described as 'still Vivarais but already Provence', as the valley and rugged country give way to olives, asparagus, citrus fruits, herbs. It is a charming and unspoilt village with good hotels, restaurants and camping sites nearby. Just before Pont St Esprit, the visitor leaves Ardèche and enters Gard. (See tour of the Gorges for confluence of Ardèche and Rhône.)

Further Information
— Ardèche —

Museums and Other Places of Interest

The Comité Départmentale du Tourism, Cours de Palais, Privas, 07002, can provide an excellent booklet entitled 'Musées d'Ardèche', published by the Conseil Départemental de la Culture.

Annonay
Musée César Filhol
Regional exhibits, featuring Montgolfier brothers and Marc Séguin.
Open: All year, Wednesday, Saturday, Sunday 2-6pm; August, every day. Allow 1 hour for visit.

Aubenas
Château and Dôme St Benoit
Open: Easter-July and September-October, Saturday 3-6pm, Sunday 10am to 12noon; July-end August: every day 10am-12noon and 3-6pm.

Grospierres
Archaeological Museum
Open: July/August every day 3-7pm.

La Bastide de Virac (near Vallon)
Medieval *château*, partly furnished, showing life cycle of the silkworm.
Open: June-September every weekday, 10am-12noon and 2-7pm. Also Easter and Whitsun weekends.

Lavilledieu
Le Petit Musée du Bizarre
Modern art and sculpture.
Open: 10am-12noon and 3-6pm every day in summer.

Marzal
Aven Grottes de Marzal
St Remèze
Underground museum of pre-history and spelaeology, limestone cave.
Open: March-November, weekends and public holidays; April-September every day 9am-12noon and 2-6pm.
Wear warm clothing.

Aven Orgnac
Limestone cave and museum of pre-history
Open: check locally for museum; caves 9am-12noon and 2-6pm in season. Wear warm clothing.

Pranles
Protestant Museum
Open: April-mid-June and mid-September-November, Saturday and Sunday, 2.30-6.30pm; mid-June-mid-September every day, 10am-12noon and 2.30-6.30pm except Sunday morning.

Privas
Musée du Verdus
Agricultural and Rural Museum

Open: out of main season, Saturday and Sunday 2-11pm; mid-July-
mid-September, every day, 2-
11pm.

La Chapelle de l'Ancien Collège
Religious Museum (municipal)
Open: all year, Wednesday-Satur-
day, 3-5pm.

Municipal Museum
Geology and archaeology
Opening times not specified, check
locally.

St Alban-Auriolles (near Ruoms)
Musée Alphonse Daudet
Mas de las Vignasse
Family and local history.
Open: all day May-October (may
be closed 12noon-2pm for lunch).

St Symphorien sous Chomérac
Art and history of basketmaking.
Open: April-October, every day
except Tuesday, 10am-12noon and
2-7pm. Other times, weekends, or
by arrangement 2-5pm.

Serrières
Maritime Museum
Open: Saturday, Sunday and
public holidays-1st Sunday April-
last Sunday October 3-6pm. (Visit
lasts $1^1/_2$ hours).

Tournon
Museum of Regional History at
the *château*
Open: April-end May, 2-6pm; Sep-
tember-end October, 2-5pm; June-
end August, 10-12noon and 2-6pm.

Vallon Pont d'Arc
Grotte des Huguenots
Spelaeology
Open: June-September, every day
10am-7pm. One evening a week,

there are slide shows and meet-
ings, and occasional concerts.

Magnanerie
Silk museum, with guided tour.
Open: May-September 10am-
12noon and 2-6pm.

Agricultural Museum
Historical tools and displays.
Open: Easter-end August, every
day, 9am-12noon and 2-6pm.

Les Vans
Museum of Archaeology, Geology
    and Local History (Municipal
    Museum)
Open: July/August, Tuesday-Fri-
day 10am-12noon and 1.30-5pm,
Saturday 2-5pm. Other times,
Thursday 2-5pm.

Vogüé Château
Old documents and archives of
Ardèche
Open: Easter-July and September-
October, Sundays 3-6pm; July-end
August, every day 3-6pm.

Maps

Michelin: 969 Grandes Routes (for
planning); 76 Aurillac-St Etienne;
80 Rodez-Nîmes both 1cm-2km;
Green Guide-Le Vallée du Rhône
gives very detailed information.

IGN — Institut National Géogra-
phique: 59 Privas/Alès 1cm-1km;
see also Carte Topographique
4cm-1km — numbers 2836 to 3038.

Editions Didier et Richard: 21
L'Ardèche Méridionale: 2cm-1km
(showing footpaths, etc).

Carte Département Orientation 07
— Editions Ponchet: This is a good
overall map of L'Ardèche.

10 • Le Queyras

This isolated region lies in the extreme south-east of the High Alps bordering Italy on three sides, forming part of the Cottian Alps and within the old province of Dauphiné, which has been French since 1349. Today it is in the department of Hautes Alpes, and since 1977 the Queyras has been a regional nature park.

The heart of the region is the basin of the River Guil, the source and upper course of which is a splendid cirque dominated by the graceful Italian pyramid of Monte Viso (3,841m, 12,598ft). The middle course of the river forms the meeting point of several high open valleys, their slopes covered with very fine larch woods. Lower down the river steepens and narrows its course into the Combe du Queyras and then flows through a high and precipitous limestone gorge to join the River Durance near the old fortified town of Mont Dauphin.

The Alpine landscape of the Queyras is dry, wild and rocky — though not austere — with bare crags and screes, especially in the east where the rocks are glossy schists glistening with flakes of mica, but there are high lakes, waterfalls and snow-capped peaks. The lower slopes and valley floors are green with woods and irrigated meadows mown for hay, but cultivation is scanty. Nevertheless, there are still some picturesque vestiges left of a much older mountain civilisation based upon the rhythm of the seasons, and there is also some transhumance practised, but the grand sight of long columns of sheep has long gone to be replaced by trucks. Above the valleys there are high grazing meadows often with a group of chalets set round an ancient chapel.

However, the jewel of the Queyras is its magnificent climate, an important consideration now that so much of Europe is in the throes of a climatic downturn. Here it hardly ever rains during the summer, the hazard of fog is unknown, and it is no exaggeration to say that 300 days of the year are sunny. Moreover the brightness of the southern sky added to the freshness of the high mountain air makes for a delightful feeling of well-being.

The alpine phenomenon of the south-facing sunny slope or *adret*, which is usually cleared for settlement or cultivation as opposed to the *ubac* or shady side — empty of man — and usually thickly forested is particularly emphasised in the Queyras where many valleys run west-east. This has been a factor in the development of skiing and tourism seized upon by the few remaining native residents who have supplemented their incomes from a land that yields only a moderate reward. But this pleasant combination of Mediterranean and alpine climates has had another effect, for the flora of the region is rich in variety as there are some 2,000 species found in stages, the Mediterranean plants grow at the foot of the slopes and gradually change upwards into alpine varieties towards the high summits. The flora of the Queyras as a result is of great interest to botanists the world over.

So, one may see typical Mediterranean flowers like blue or silvery-white thistles on a dry sunny valley pasture. Then higher up on thin hill grass you might come across the violet alpine pansy, and in the high alpine meadows see the bright yellow globeflower, and amongst the arid rocky summits the pink flowers of a variety of stonecrop called Jupiter's beard. Near the end of June is best when almost the whole of the Queyras is one mass of flowers. The attractive larch is the dominant tree, its bright green leaves throwing but a thin shadow, so that grass grows between the boles, and if you are walking amongst the larch woods on the shady or *ubac* side there is a pleasing brightness about the undergrowth, and often growing amid the grass are the flowers of the alpine pink family — typical of the Queyras.

The Queyras has its alpine animals too; high on the remote cols there is often a chance of seeing chamois, and on the slopes and mountain meadows the marmot is common, whistling like a kettle when they think danger threatens. With the coming of autumn the variable hare appears, so called because in summer he is brown and hardly visible, and then with a hint of snow in the air he is able to camouflage himself and becomes white to fool his enemies. There are typical birds as well, the small alpine grouse flits amongst the larch woods and myrtle bushes; and higher up the ptarmigan is seen near the lakes and rocky pools.

There are no towns in the Queyras as such, only the small one of Guillestre at the 'gate' or south-western entrance to the region. In spite of its size — less than 2,000 people — it is an interesting and lively place with plenty of shops, restaurants and hotels. It is a stage

on the 'Grande Route des Alpes' from Evian on Lake Geneva to Nice down on the Mediterranean, which passes through the region along the D902 from the Col d' Izoard to the Col de Vars. The nearest large town is the old fortress city of Briançon some 35km (21 miles) north of Guillestre on the N94 in the Durance valley. Nevertheless, villages are spread throughout the region, and some such as Abriès, Aiguilles, Ceillac, Molines and the best known — St Véran — have been expanded due to increased skiing facilities, regrettably neither improving on the vernacular architecture nor the environment.

Undoubtedly the greatest attraction of the Queyras is the way its superb climate makes outdoor pursuits such a pleasure, especially all forms of walking from gentle valley promenades to tough mountain hikes during late spring, high summer and early autumn. For long-distance walkers the Grande Randonnée GR5 (Amsterdam to Nice!) passes through by way of Brunissard, Château Queyras, Col de Fromage, Ceillac, Lac Ste Anne and the Col Girardin. Within the region is the GR58 Tour de Queyras circling the entire area with variations. These are waymarked and there are rest places along these routes in the form of high mountain refuges, *gîtes d'étape* (lodgings) and isolated unmanned simple camp sites and the use of alpine huts belonging to the local inhabitants. Thus a whole infrastructure is provided for walkers for whom the region is ideally suited.

A certain amount of riding is possible using the long valley tracks; and there is a climbing centre at Abriès, but most of the high peaks are on the frontier fringes such as the Pain de Sucre (3,208m, 10,522ft) with access from a refuge at Col Agnel. During the long winter season skiing is a great attraction with the sunlit slopes and brilliant light, but almost as popular and far less expensive, and suitable for all ages is *ski de fond* (using long narrow skis and low shoes) which is a speciality of the Queyras, Ceillac being the chief centre. However, a whole series of recognised skiing itineraries exist at some very high altitudes.

Most places are accessible by car except the extreme ends of some valleys where the road usually deteriorates to pot holes and then becomes a very rough track. Some of the roads are narrow, steep and sharply curved like the entrances to glacial hanging valleys such as the valley of the Cristillan (Ceillac), and now that the locals all have cars they seem to think that everyone knows the road so be cautious and don't drive at night unless forced.

All this plus the guaranteed sunshine and clear skies makes the Queyras the ideal region for exploration. There are many small side valleys and wooded combes with high paths that are rarely trodden, and one can penetrate into Italy on foot with the assurance that there is some sort of shelter if needed.

The Queyras is a little difficult to get to. There are four routes by road, but three are high mountain passes:

Col'd Izoard (2,361m, 7,744ft) from the north via Briançon (D902), closed by snow October to June; Col de Vars (2,116m, 6,940ft) closed by snow December to April. South from Nice via Italy or Barcelonette (Ubaye); Col Agnel (2,744m, 9,000ft) from Italy, but although a new route definitely not recommended, unless using 4-wheel drive, as road is in a bad state; Via Guillestre (1,000m, 3,280ft). Normal point of entry from Durance valley either Briançon or Gap (N94).

The easiest route by car is from Grenoble by the Route Napoléon (N85) to Gap, thence Embrun to Guillestre: 240km, 146 miles.

The shortest route from the nearest airport is from Turin (Italy) then via Susa and Col de Montgenèvre (1,850m, 6,068ft) open all the year round; thence Briançon to Guillestre: 144km, 88 miles.

Other airports are Marseilles (Marignane) — 244km, 149 miles; Lyon (Satolas) — 266km, 162 miles; Nice (Côte d'Azur) — 293km, 178 miles.

There are direct trains to Guillestre from Paris, Grenoble and Marseilles which stop at the Gare de Montdauphin-Guillestre, 4km (2.4 miles) from the town, and buses run from the station to Guillestre and main places in the Queyras.

Approach via Col d'Izoard to Château Queyras

By far the most interesting and spectacular route into the Queyras is from Briançon over the Col d'Izoard. From the town the D902 runs along a corniche above the gorge of the River Cerveyrette and past the village of Cervières, and then winds up to the col through a landscape that gradually becomes more arid.

Some little way below the summit on the left is a refuge built in 1858 by Napoleon III. But he is not the Napoleon it commemorates, for this is one of six refuges built on particularly exposed cols with money left by Napoleon I to the department of Hautes Alpes — in recognition of the enthusiastic welcome he received in Gap on his escape from Elba. At the summit (2,361m, 7,744ft) on the right is another monument to the French Alpine Army which built many of the roads and passes in the region.

The views from here are superb, and southwards is the first glimpse of the mountains of the Queyras. Away on the left of the road is a steep and rocky path leading to the **Col Perdu** and a dun-coloured mountain called Arpelin (2,601m, 8,531ft) which is really a fine arrêt flanked by massive screes. From the col is a full face view of the Grand Pic de Rochebrune (3,325m, 10,906ft), a huge brown rocky pyramid that will not be seen again until far into the Queyras. Back on the road, the route passes along another corniche through a remarkable area called the **Casse Déserte**. This is a series of enormous screes descending from the crags above with needle-like pinnacles projecting through them like rows of obelisks. The whole region here is a classic example of erosion, the rocks being limestones and dolomites. This desolate scene in almost perpetual sunshine receives occasional publicity through press photos of many cyclists struggling up to the Col in the Tour de France.

The road now descends in steep narrow bends surrounded by trees and soon there is a magnificent view of the valley of Arvieux with its wide, flat, inclined floor and steep wooded slopes. Then, on the right is the hamlet of **Brunissard**, developed for skiing and where the Grandes Randonnées GR5 and GR58 cross. A new paved road leads north-westwards — the route of GR5 — and a few kilometres further on the right is an unfenced attractive camp site, manned only during summer months. The road ends in a track amidst the trees, but continue on the GR5 below it and reach the Chalets de Clapeyto (2,230m, 7,314ft). On the way is the huge square alpine meadow of Pra Premier with the massive peak of Haut Mouriare (2,810m, 9,216ft) behind it. All of which is a reminder of the old way of life here. Back on the D902, now very straight, the small hamlet of **La Chalp** appears on the left. Here another recent road turns off, very steep and curved at first, leading to a high wooded plateau 4km (2.4 miles) on, and the Lac de Rouet (1,854m, 6,000ft). From here are two remarkable views, eastwards to Château Queyras, and south-westwards over the Combe du Queyras (valley of the River Guil).

The straight D902 now descends gently to the very pleasant village of **Arvieux** grouped around the fine tall building of its sixteenth-century church. This is a good place to stop, for here is a small friendly hotel-restaurant,'La Borne Ensoleillée', set in an old courtyard. Arvieux has a reputation for its cheese. A route to explore is behind the tiny hamlet of Le Coin off on the right as you enter Arvieux, where the Combe Bonne leads to a number of rarely trodden paths.

From Arvieux, the D902 joins the D947 on the left, running through the Combe du Queyras, and soon a quite remarkable building comes to view. This is the fortress of Château Queyras dating from the thirteenth century, when the region was part of a mountain republic including neighbouring Italy. The castle was later restored by Vauban, but the dungeon remains to remind one of those times. The site — the most impressive in the Queyras — is because it is a superb example of a *verrou* or remnant of the Ice Ages. This blocks the valley so completely that the river has to saw through it, and the road can only just squeeze past at the side of the rock through an old village.

Château Queyras to St Véran

From Château Queyras two hamlets, **Les Meyries** and **Rouet** (5km, 3 miles), can be reached by a side road (D444), which winds up on the left to what is the balcony of the River Guil, giving a beautiful view of the valley. Continuing on foot from the end of the road at Rouet, an old asbestos mine road leads to the Bergerie de Péas (sheep-fold) at 2,024m (6,638ft) by the Péas stream with a good view of the high valley of the Péas. The more energetic can continue by leaving the mine road, and going up to the Col de Péas (2,629m, 8,623ft), to be rewarded by an impressive view to the west by the pyramid of the Pic de Rochebrune (3,325m, 10,906ft).

On returning to the valley road (D947), it leads straight up the broad trench of the Guil past L'Iscle camp site, with splendid larch forests on the *ubac* slopes until the village of **Ville-Vieille** is reached. This forms one commune with Château Queyras known as Château Ville-Vieille. Here the road to St Véran (D5) turns right, and starts to twist up into the steep valley of the L'Aigue Blanche. On the first bend to the left, there is a forest route to the Bois Foran (1,804m, 5,917ft), which is a reasonable 2-hour walk. Continuing up the D5, the valley now becomes the Ravine de Prats, and on the right is a remarkable geological feature. This is a *demoiselle coiffé* (girl with a hat), a tall earth pillar topped by a large stone boulder.

Soon the view opens out, with the valley being dominated by the mountain of the Tête de Longet (3,151m, 10,335ft), and beyond lies the hamlet of **La Rua**, a very narrow street of some typical Queyras houses of half wood and half stone construction in seventeenth- to eighteenth-century style. Then follows the larger old village of **Molines**, which includes several outlying hamlets, where the road divides. A hundred and fifty years ago it was much larger with over a thousand people, when the Queyras reached its peak figure of 7,700, but the rigours of peasant life, and two World Wars led to a decline. However, in the last two decades, the almost inevitable development of skiing has stabilised the population, and even increased it — 243 in 1968, and 288 in 1975.

But the hamlet of **Gaudissard**, above the village, had another kind of emigration earlier — religious intolerance — and over 100 left Molines, amongst them the people of Gaudissard, who went afar. So that today in the Hesse province of Germany, there exists the village of Godihardessen (German for Gaudissard), believed to be founded by French Protestants. From here there is a walk leading to Prat Haut above the ravine, and one can continue along the forest road of Chanteloube, where there are picnic sites, and eventually right through to Aiguilles.

Our route leads through the narrow streets of **Molines** with its picturesque houses, then comes the long valley of the Aigue Agnel, with the most interesting hamlet of **Pierre Grosse** appearing. Here is a genuine survival of the typical Alpine house with its enormous *grenier* (loft), where the harvests of hay and forage are stored, but nowadays less and less. On the slopes above Pierre Grosse is the outlier hamlet of Le Coin — grossly, and incongruously expanded by chalets, apartment buildings, and a hotel.

But just below Pierre Grosse is a delightful small tranquil un-
guarded camp site by the river, in a charming setting, a leafy oasis in
a rather stark valley. The valley road, however, is an ancient route to
Italy, which is thought to be Hannibal's route, and above the hamlet
of Fontgillarde is a massive boulder called 'Hannibal's stone'. The
road has recently been revived as a through route, but it is not in a
good condition. Although as a forest road it makes a good walk to the
Col Agnel on the Italian frontier from Fontgillarde, where there is a
mountain refuge, from which many high walks can be made. On the
way there, you will pass the ruins of another refuge, one which is
similar to that on the Col d'Izoard built with Napoleon's bequest.
From the road above Fontgillarde, two mountain walks may be
attempted: one to the Pas de Chai (2,790m, 9,150ft) in $2^1/_2$ hours, and
the other to climb the mountain of Grand Queyras (3,114m, 10,217ft),
which takes 4 hours.

Returning to Molines the D5 continues through forested meadows past the hamlet of La Chalp to **Le Raux**. Here is a very pretty
walk, part of the GR58, by going down to the bridge over the Aigue
Blanche, and following the path up by the wood of Bois du Moulin.
Then comes a mountain stream, the Torrent de Lamaron, which is
followed as far as a ravine, afterwards climbing up a steep zigzag
path by a copse and a crest (2,380m, 7,806ft). Then, the stream is
rejoined, and by its long upper valley the Col Estranques (2,651m,
8,695ft) is reached, with very good views, and a panorama which
takes in Font Sancte (3,387m, 11,109ft). On the way down look out on
the left for a fine distant view of the Pic de Rochebrune (3,325m,
10,906ft).

Back on the road (D5), at length the curious terraced village of **St
Véran** is reached, and at 2,040m (6,700ft) is the highest in Europe. The
houses with their vast *greniers* — mostly of wood — are arranged *en-
echelon* to avoid being in each other's shade, and of course the risk of
fire. The parish church is very interesting, with heavily gilded ornamental saints' statues, and an upper gallery for the choir and the old
people of the village.

Outside is a marble porch with crouching lions, showing Italian
influence, and rather similar to Guillestre and Embrun. A little further below on the edge of the village is the Protestant church, with its
tall sombre steeple. The village has been largely developed for skiing
in conjunction with Molines, which means expansion — so far it is
not too spoilt — but the danger, and temptation is ever present.

From St Véran the D5 goes on a further 6km (3.7 miles), passing
old copper mines and a marble quarry, to the Chapel of Clausis, a

St Véran (2,040m, 6,690ft), the highest village in Europe

shrine to which there is an annual Franco-Italian pilgrimage on 16 July. This road is only open in the summer months before 9.30am, and after 5.30pm, for it connects with important high alpine pastures, and is much used by cattle and sheep.

From St Véran, east of the village, an interesting and alternative route up the valley can be made. The route follows the D5 until the first ravine is reached, that of the St Luce stream, then it forks right going down to cross the Aigue Blanche. After crossing this river, it goes upstream on the left bank, which on a hot day can give some shade. At length past the old copper mines, another bridge is reached, which is the Pont sur l'Aigue Blanche (2,340m, 7,675ft), under the Chapel of Clausis.

Then the route continues to the confluence of the streams, and the junction of the footpaths. Here a choice can be made to the Col de Chamoussière (2,884m, 9,459ft). Either the direct route can be taken, or which is perhaps preferable, though a little longer, via the Col de St Véran, and passing through alpine meadows. When the Col (2,853m, 9,357ft) is reached, there is a surprise waiting, for the Italian side is steep and abrupt, opening on to the Chianale valley, with its large blue hydro-electric power lake far below, and the peak of Monte Viso in all its glory. In this area are many marmots, for it seems to be quite a colony. Here it is interesting to reflect, that in October

1742 a Spanish army of 40,000 men crossed the Col de St Véran, but being surprised by the onset of sudden cold weather, abandoned their treasure chests to the south on Col Blanchet (2,897m, 9,502ft), and on the mountain known as Tête Noire (3,176m, 10,417ft); in spite of intense searching they have never been found. The way continues to the Col de Chamoussière, then down to the Col Agnel (2,580m, 8,462ft) and the Refuge Agnel, and a sizeable section of the GR58 (Tour of the Queyras) has been covered.

Ville-Vieille to the Belvédère de Monte Viso

Returning to the Guil valley, this route continues upstream in a fine open section forested with larch and pine, the Bois Foran. Then comes the village of **Aiguilles** set in a splendid site, and a most convenient centre for the High Queyras. The old village is most attractive, and seems full of fountains and balconies, while the character of the larger more recent houses is in harmony as well. It is a ski centre, and some of the outskirts lack the same taste, but all in all it is a very pleasant place.

From Aiguilles there are some good forest walks like the one to the hamlet of Peynin, which starts from the bypass road on the right of the village, and goes up through alpine meadows. A longer walk is to the Bergerie de Lombard (an ancient sheep-fold), some $3^1/_2$km (2.2 miles), and one can go on to the lakes of Malrif (described later).

Leaving Aiguilles by the valley road (D947), another 400m (1,312ft) further on, and over a bridge on the right is the municipal camp site of Le Gouret. Although, only rated two stars, it is one of the best sites in the region, with its situation in the Forest of Marassan, with acres of space, and myriads of alpine flowers all around.

On to **Abriès**, at the confluence of the Rivers Guil and Bouchet. This is an agreeable little place, rather more modern, having been rebuilt since 1945, and also, an important skiing centre. It has some excellent restaurants, one, also a hotel, La Mouffe, can be particularly recommended for its cooking, covering many French regions, especially Alsace, for there are no regional dishes in the Queyras, although the food is always fresh and good. Abriès offers a variety of routes to explore, with an easy way to have a fine view by taking the *telesiège* (chair-lift), open in the summer (July and August) to the intermediate station at 2,020m (6,625ft) and then an hour's walk brings one to the Colette de Jilly (2,366m, 7,760ft), where a perspective of the Guil valley, and Monte Viso can be seen.

A long walk, part of the GR58, starts by the picturesque and very

Monte Viso (3,841m, 12,598ft) from one of the ski pistes near Abriès

steep Stations of the Cross, and then for nearly 5km (3 miles) is the most exhilarating in the Queyras, eventually to an old chapel above Abriès. It then continues along a mountain shoulder, and round into the deep valley of Malrif. After some time the abandoned village of **Malrif** (1,841m, 6,038ft), appears with its curiously separated church dating from about 1830, and campanile perched apart on the sides of a deep ravine. Beyond are splendid flowery meadows, until two rushing streams meet at the Bergerie de Bertins (2,040m, 6,690ft). Here marmots are heard with a whistle similar to birds of prey, whilst falcons circle overhead. From here on the walk to the lakes is difficult but worth the effort, for the lakes themselves, as they seem continually to change colour, and also the panorama of the sea of peaks, inevitably dominated by the summit of Monte Viso. Here a curious phenomenon is sometimes seen, that of a distant curtain of smog behind Monte Viso, coming up from Italy — the industrial city of Turin is only 70km (43 miles) distant. Fortunately, the prevailing westerlies keep it from the Queyras, and it disperses at night.

Back at Abriès, take the D441 on the left to the hamlet of Le Roux, and here, turning sharp right, continue along the road until the chalets of Valpreveyre are reached, with good views of the pyramid of Bric Bouchet (3,261m, 10,696ft), and the Tête du Pelvas (2,929m,

Tête du Pelvas (2,929m, 9,607ft), Col d'Urine, Valpreveyre

9,607ft). There are two splendid walks here. The first through a larch-filled valley upstream of the Bouchet valley to the Col Malaure (2,740m, 8,987ft), and the second to the Col d'Urine (2,525m, 8,282ft). This last walk could well represent the alpine flora of the Queyras. For the path passes by a stream, then through larches, and a large meadow full of buttercups, globeflowers, violets, pansies, white anemones, and Star of Bethlehem (starry flowers, glistening white tepals), then a ridge, and an open windy knoll with treacle mustard (small clusters of yellow flowers), as one approaches the col. Going down there is a path variation, that passes a bank massed with white St Bruno's lilies (a threatened species in some parts of France) and finally through a meadow full of globeflowers just before reaching Valpreveyre.

Returning to Abriès the road continues on upstream, the high valley now a little severe, to the village of **Ristolas**, badly damaged during the war, and now rebuilt. Along this stretch of road many high walks begin, from Ristolas up the valley of the Ségure to the Pic de Ségure (2,990m, 9,807ft) in 4³/₄hrs. Further along is the hamlet of **La Monta**, another war victim, from where one can climb to the Col de la Croix (2,229m, 7,311ft) in 2³/₄hrs. At length L'Echalp is reached, now the terminus of wheeled traffic. The road continues right up to the Belvédère du Cirque (9km, 5.6 miles), but is now cut (summer

1987) on account of many accidents. So all excursions to the various belvederes have to be on foot.

Starting with the forest route to the Chalets de la Médille, on the right, $1^1/_2$hrs from L'Echalp, which is an ancient alpine meadow full of flowers, and a good view of Viso, one can continue on to the Col Vieux (2,806m, 9,203ft) by way of two lakes, Lac Egorgéou first, and then Lac Foréant (2,618m, 8,587ft). Between them it is possible to see numerous chamois, and at Col Vieux, where Hannibal may have crossed into Italy, one can go on, and climb the Pain de Sucre (3,208m, 10,522ft) right on the Italian frontier. It is not difficult, taking but $1^1/_2$hrs, and the view takes in Savoy, the Italian Alps and even Switzerland — a vast panorama, which is accessible to non-climbers.

If the original road (D947) is taken, first after 3km (1.8 miles) comes the Petit Belvédère, and further along the Grand Belvédère, by a mountain hut, with already a magnificent view of Viso, and the high Guil valley. If the last 2km (1.2 miles) can be managed to the Bergerie-sous-Roche, the cirque and the majestic full face of Monte Viso is seen. It is possible to make a three stage tour of Monte Viso using refuges via the Col de Traversette (Refuge Sella), Passo San Chiaffredo (2,764m, 9,065ft) and at Castello, a hotel (1,660m, 5,444ft).

The Combe du Queyras — Château Queyras to Guillestre

From Château Queyras it is possible to go up to the Sommet Bucher (2,257m, 7,402ft) by road (11km, 6.8 miles), which starts on either side of the fortress. It was built by the Chasseurs Alpins of the French Army in 1934. The road is wide enough, but here and there are potholes, ruts and odd obstacles, which call for cautious driving. The views are superb of the Château Queyras, and the Guil valley as it winds up and up through pine, and larch woods carpeted with flowers. At the summit amid alpine meadows is a radar station, and an orientation table, as the view takes in a vast panorama of high peaks: Monte Viso, Font-Sancte (3,387m, 11,109ft), Rochebrune (3,325m, 10,906ft), and the Massif of Pelvoux westwards. On returning one takes the left fork at the bottom to rejoin the main road, thus avoiding the narrowness of Château Queyras. From here, the GR5 also climbs up cutting across the bends of the Sommet Bucher road to the Col de Fromage (2,301m, 7,547ft), a very long walk (4hrs), but the views are extremely good.

The valley road continues westwards to the junction of the route to Arvieux and the Col d'Izoard, becoming the D902, then begins the gorge of the Guil marked by the Rock of the Guardian Angel, and a war memorial to the men of the Queyras.

At the hamlet of **Chapelure** the gorge widens out, and in this area are three hamlets perched high above the valley: **Montbardon** on the left, further along is **Bramousse**, and right opposite, the ancient hamlet of **Escoyères** reached by a path. From these the GR58 offers high walking, but as can be imagined, climbing up from such a deep gorge, these routes are very steep!

The road now goes past pine-covered slopes to the Maison du Roy, and on the left the steep road (D440) leads up through the precipitous valley of the Cristillan, with many hairpin bends encased in trees.

On reaching the summit of the valley shoulder, for this is a classic glacial hanging valley, one sees **Ceillac** situated on a broad alp, enclosed by immense bare slopes, forming a Y-shaped valley feature. On the right is the larch-covered valley of the Mélezet, shut off by a huge cirque, and on the left the steep and bare valley of the Cristillan, with a long paved road, ending in a forest track and path to Col de Cristillan 2,961m (9,715ft). Ceillac has been heavily developed for skiing, and apartment blocks rather overshadow the pleasant old village, where the Mairie is dated 1558. The present parish church is a rather unusual building, whilst the former church is a tall elegant structure, now the chapel of Ste Cécile, set amid the meadows of the alp in splendid isolation.

From the village the road up the Mélezet valley goes to the Cime de Mélezet past the hamlet of Pied de Mélezet close to a very fine waterfall — the Cascade de Pisse! From here the GR5 path winds up in a larch forest, near the chair-lift (open in the summer months), and crosses a ridge to a very blue cirque or corrie lake — Lac Ste Anne at a height of 2,415m (7,921ft) below some large screes. The nearby chapel (Ste Anne) has a pilgrimage each 26 July from Ceillac, and Maurin over the Col Girardin (2,699m, 8,852ft) in neighbouring Ubaye.

Another walk is to cross the river from Pied du Mélezet, and go up the left bank of the stream, there joining a path up the alluvial fan north of the waterfall, and rejoin the stream which feeds it, and you arrive at a delightful little lake, well named Miroir. The path from the lake goes down through a wood, and joins the route of the chair-lift.

If the Mélezet valley road is taken to its limit at La Raille, a walk from there through a larch wood, and among half-ruined hamlets with a curious chapel, brings a good view of Font Sancte (3,387m, 11,109ft).

Molines, bridge over the River Aigue-Agnel, Le Queyras

Agay, near St Raphaël, Côte d'Azur

Aigues-Mortes, Languedoc-Roussillon

Carcassonne, Languedoc-Roussillon

Limestone screes, Casse Déserte, Col d'Izoard (2,361m, 7,744ft)

Ceillac is the crossing point of the GR5, and GR58, offering many high walks to the Col de Fromage (2,301m, 7,547ft), Col des Estronques (2,651m, 8,695ft), and a forest walk along the Cristillan valley to the Bergerie de Bois Noir. It may be noted here that these routes can be used by good skiers between December and March — Ceillac being the chief centre for *ski de fond*.

Returning to the Maison de Roy, the gorge proper is entered, with its towering sides of Triassic limestone and dolomite, along a corniche with many tunnels until the Pied la Viste is reached. Here is an orientation table on a high rock giving good views of the upper Durance valley, and the far-off majestic peaks of the Massif of Pelvoux.

Just before entering Guillestre, there is a very agreeable tranquil camp site, within an old farm, off a bend in the road. From here there is an extremely pleasant walk up the valley of the Escreins — a splendid mountain stream — leading through orchards and meadows, giving fine distant views of the Ecrins, and then passing through woods and screes.

Guillestre is really a crossroads town between three regions: Embrunais, Queyras and the Ubaye, but it is an ideal starting point for the Queyras because of its facilities. It has an interesting sixteenth-century church, inspired by the ancient twelfth-century cathedral of Embrun. The porch has four columns of rose marble, having at the base two crouching lions in the style of Lombardy. This rose marble, quarried locally, which was used to make all the pavements in the town, unfortunately much has been replaced by rather soulless cement. However, good specimens still exist, an example being the steps outside an ironmonger's shop (Ets Favier) in a small square off the main street.

One place worth visiting, 6km (3.7 miles) from Guillestre, is the old fortified city of Montdauphin on top of a scarp, which dominates the confluence of the Guil and Durance. Its construction was ordered by Louis XIV in 1693 following the campaign against Savoy, and duly built by Vauban, who fortified Château Queyras, and Briançon at the same time.

Further Information

—— Le Queyras ——

Useful Information for Visitors

Seasons: Summer June to September. Winter late December to mid-April. Most hotels are shut outside these periods. Those open all the year are sometimes closed in November.
Office Hours: for SIs (Tourist Bureaux): normally 9.30am-12noon and 2.30-5pm.
Shops and restaurants are often shut out of season.
GTA = Grand Traversée desAlpes.

Abriès (05460)
Hotel: La Mouffe
Gîte d'étape: Di Marco (50pl) GR5 GTA, open all year ☎ (92) 45 71 14
Tourist Office: ☎ (92) 45 72 26 morning/afternoon
Sport: Tennis Courts ☎ (92) 45 72 26
Ski School ☎ (92) 45 71 47
Taxis: Soissons ☎ (92) 45 75 66 and winter , Frendo ☎ (92) 45 71 16
Market: Friday

Aiguilles (05470)
Hotels: Combe Rousset**
☎ (92) 45 77 15
La Chenaie ☎ (92) 45 72 59
Gîte d'étape: Mme Simon (20pl)
GTA ☎ (92) 45 70 40, open all year
Tourist Office: Mairie ☎ (92) 45 70 34
Office of Tourist Promotion in Queyras: ☎ (92) 45 76 18
Sport: Tennis Courts ☎ (92) 45 76 38
Ski School (92) 45 73 73/77 19
Skating Rink ☎ (92) 45 76 68
Market: Thursday

Arvieux (05350) (Château Ville-Vieille)
Gîte d'étape: (Brunissard 3km, 1.86 miles north) (24pl) M. Faure
☎ (92) 45 73 85 GTA all year
Tourist Office: On main D902, open 9.30am-12noon and 2-5pm
☎ (92) 45 75 76
Sports: 2 Tennis Courts at Brunissard; Minigolf; Volleyball; Kayak-Canoe ☎ (92) 45 72 73 , Ski School
☎ (92) 45 71 69

Ceillac (05600)
Gîte d'étape: M. Fournier GTA
(80pl) ☎ (92) 45 00 23
Tourist Office: ☎ (92) 45 04 74
Sport: 2 Tennis Courts
☎ (92) 45 04 74
Ski School ☎ (92) 45 10 58
Market: Wednesday (summer)
Taxi:: Favier ☎ (92) 45 01 91

Château Ville-Vieille (05350)
Hotels: Le Guilazur**
☎ (92) 45 74 09
Relais de Charpenal
☎ (92) 45 71 70
Tourist Office: ☎ (92) 45 70 70
Taxi: Audier ☎ (92) 45 70 61
Sports: 2 Tennis Courts, Volleyball
☎ (92) 45 70 70

Guillestre (05600)
Hotels: Les Barnières**
☎ (92) 45 04 87/45 05 07,
Le Catinat Fleuri** ☎ (92) 45 07 62
Tourist Office :Pl. Salva, open 9am-
12noon and 2.30-7pm (6pm non-
season) ☎ (92) 45 04 37
Sports: Swimming pool (heated), 4
Tennis Courts, Mini-golf,
Horseriding, *Ski de Fond* and Ice
Rink

Molines (05390)
Tourist Office: ☎ (92) 45 83 22
Sports: 2 Tennis Courts
☎ (92) 45 83 80/29
Ski School ☎ (92) 45 81 51
Taxis: E. Garcin ☎ (92) 45 83 01;
Taupin ☎ (92) 45 83 70

Pierre Grosse
Hotel: Les Mélezes** ☎ (92) 45 83 64
Gîte d'étape: At Fontgillarde M.
Bonnet winter/summer
☎ (92) 45 83 17

Ristolas (05460)
Hotel: Les Eterlous du Lestio** all
year (exc. November)
☎ (92) 45 76 07
Gîte d'étape: La Monta M. Frendo
☎ (92) 45 71 35 (60pl)
Sports: 2 Tennis Courts, Volleyball
☎ (92) 45 71 54
Tourist Office: ☎ (92) 45 72 76

St Véran (05490)
Hotels: Châteaurenard**
☎ (92) 45 81 70
Le Lievre Blanc** ☎ (92) 45 82 57
Gîte d'étape: M. Brunet (30pl) GTA
☎ (92) 45 82 19
Tourist Office: ☎ (92) 45 82 21
Sport: Ski School ☎ (92) 45 81 20
Taxi: Frendo ☎ (92) 45 71 35

11 • Provence and the Côte d'Azur

Provence is the sun-drenched part of France that runs east from the Rhône estuary to the Italian border. It is most famous for the Riviera, the playground of the rich and those who want to lap up the sun on crowded beaches. Places like Cannes, Nice, St Tropez are renowned but there are many other towns and villages inland with much to offer the visitor and without the teeming crowds.

The coastline is divided into the Riviera and the Côte d'Azur. Originally the Riviera was the name given to the coastline around Nice, and the name Côte d'Azur was introduced in 1888 to distinguish the French Alpes-Maritimes coastline from the Riviera dei Fiori in Italy. Inland there is a glittering array of things to see and do, and after a day spent exploring you can still have time to drive down to the beaches and enjoy a swim when most of the crowds have left. It takes only 2 hours to travel from the Mediterranean to the alpine peaks. Along the 112km (70 mile) stretch of beaches there are twenty-six major resorts and every conceivable kind of sport on offer from fishing and scuba diving, to flying and pot holing. There is golf, horse riding, pelota, archery and even fencing.

This region was colonised by the Greeks in about 600BC. It is typical Mediterranean countryside. The rocky soil affords scrub vegetation and olive trees but little else, except in those small patches where vines can be grown. As one climbs into the hills, however, the vegetation becomes sub-tropical and there are orange trees, oleanders, cacti and eucalyptus. The best time for plants is in the late spring, when the rains have passed and the flowers, especially the bougainvillaea and mimosa, are out. It is really the only time of the year when the countryside can be said to look pretty, although the resorts maintain some magnificent gardens throughout the year. As the sun rises higher in the sky during the summer, the plants die away, the grass turns to hay and the earth is baked hard. In the summer, temperatures on the rocky coastal plain can rise to unbear-

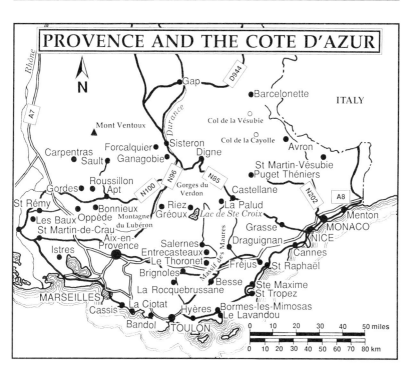

able levels, but there is usually a welcome breeze to be found on the beaches and in the pine-coloured hills if you venture further inland. The region boasts up to 2,800 hours of sunshine a year and fewer than 75 rainy days. Nice has about 3 days of frost a year and Menton claims to have a foggy day once every 10 years. While the summer days are hot, the evenings are warm and balmy. One can see why they are known as 'velvet nights'.

Although the Greeks established Marseilles as a trading settlement little remains of their presence today except the vineyards. It was the Greeks who introduced the first vines and while the wines of Provence are still not widely known outside France, great efforts are being made by the producers to promote sales in Britain and North America.

There is a wine tour which you can follow which passes close to Toulon, France's largest naval base, and follows a large circle, through most of the wine producing areas of Côtes de Provence. Even in the summer, this wine trail is not overcrowded, except in the more famous production areas like Bandol and Cassis.

It is much better to follow your nose and to visit those producers off the official route. Their wines are every bit as good and they will welcome you with open arms. A wide variety of wines are produced and there is no difficulty finding the right one to go with the cuisine of the region, almost a reason in itself for visiting Provence. Marseilles has given the world the famous fish soup *bouillabaisse*, which is usually a meal in itself. Fish figures prominently on the menus of restaurants while the farther east you travel, the greater the influence of Italian cooking becomes, with pasta dishes and a French version of the pizza.

If you are interested in getting off the main tourist routes you can explore some of the beautiful, picturesque villages inland, go walking or horse riding in the hills or caving. There is much of antiquity to be discovered as well. Although the Greeks were the first foreigners to colonise the area, it was the Romans who have left their mark. It was they who built the great towns which now dominate the east of the region but Provence is still basically a place to relax in, for leisurely explorations, for bathing, basking in the sun, eating some fine food and drinking some very agreeable wines — what more could anyone want?

Provence consists of six *départements*, three along the coast — Bouches-du-Rhône, Var and Alpes-Maritimes, and three inland — Vaucluse, Alpes-de-Haute-Provence and Hautes-Alpes. The areas of the French Alps that fall in Provence include some marvellous walking, at both low and high altitudes. The Alps really plunge into the sea at Menton, close to the Italian border. From here they climb gradually throughout Provence with their highest peaks being about 2,000m (6,560ft), in the Hautes-Alpes. The Alps also boast many excellent national parks where you can walk all day long without seeing another soul. National parks include those of Barre des Ecrins, Queyras and Mercantour. For higher altitude walking some experience is necessary and a degree of fitness, but there are wonderful routes for the hiker and backpacker. Travel throughout the region could not be easier. There are fast toll *autoroutes* to speed the tourists to the beaches, but a good network of secondary routes to take you inland for exploring.

There are daily flights into Marseilless, Nice, and Nîmes from Paris and international flights to Marseilles and Nice. Nice-Côte d'Azur is France's second largest airport. It takes $10^1/_2$ hours to fly from New York to Nice and just over $1^1/_2$ hours from London. The rail link between Paris and Avignon, Marseilles, Toulon and Nice is also excellent. You can sleep the night away as you travel down from Paris with your car safely aboard the daily motorail service. It takes $10^1/_2$ hours by train from Paris and 20 hours from London. There is also the famous Blue Train plying between Calais and the Côte d'Azur, with sleepers and couchettes. There is a direct Paris-Nice motorway, and frequent coach services from Paris and other leading towns in France and Europe to the Côte d'Azur.

Car hire is available at all airports, near most main railway stations and in all large towns and cities. For the energetic bicycles can be hired, and for those not so keen, mopeds or motorbikes.

There is a large network of bus services to different parts of the region, but most provide only a daily service to villages.

In Provence you can enjoy the journey aboard the Chemin de Fer de la Provence, which runs from Nice to Digne. The train stops frequently and is an excellent way of exploring the countryside, especially the mountains. At many of the stops you can catch a connecting bus service to take you even further afield.

If you want to take in a little of the coastline, the following two tours will enable you to see something of the tourist spots while allowing you to enjoy the countryside inland, and let you stretch your legs with some walking.

Tour of Hyères and Surrounding Area

Start the tour at Hyères to the east of Toulon, just north of the airport into which you can fly from Paris. Drivers may take the N7 or the toll Autoroute de Provence. Trains run from Marseilles or Toulon where car hire is available. Local transport in this area is available, but not to be relied on for getting to, and more important, getting back from the outlying districts.

Hyères is the oldest resort on the Riviera which is why it deserves a visit. Cathérine de Medici planned to build a summer palace there in the sixteenth century, but the plan came to nothing. Queen Victoria visited it regularly, and novelist Robert Louis Stevenson lived there for a time. The town is a few miles inland from the coast, and there are palm tree-lined avenues and well irrigated flower gardens. There are the ruins of a castle on the hill overlooking the town, and a municipal museum which is worth visiting because it houses many remains found locally from the Greek and Roman occupations.

The townspeople are rightly proud of their parks and gardens and you should visit them, especially the Jardins Olbius Riquier and Parc St Bernard. Other things to see are the Place St Paul and the Chapel of Notre-Dame de Consolation. There are many good hotels and restaurants both in and around the town, and it is a pleasant place to make a base, close to the sea and giving easy access for exploring inland.

The beaches are found about 7km (4.3 miles) to the south at the end of the peninsula. The drive down the Route du Sel goes past the salt pans at Les Pesquiers to La Tour-Fondue. From here, the islands of Ile de Porquerolles, Ile de Port Cros and Ile du Levant are just offshore. Together the islands are known as the Iles d'Hyères and can be reached by a 15-minute boat crossing from La Tour-Fondue. The peninsula on which the beaches are situated used to be another island in this chain, but it became landlocked many centuries ago. Severe storms still occasionally sweep the area in winter, and in 1811 a fierce storm actually forced a channel through the peninsula, separating it again from the mainland briefly, but the sands quickly returned. Even today, if the weather is bad, this road can be closed. There are vineyards on Ile de Porquerolles, and many charming walks on all three islands, although the Ile du Levant is in part occupied by the French Navy and access to some of their land is restricted.

From Hyères, take the N98 to **Le Lavandou**, which gets its name from the lavender fields cultivated along the banks of the River Batailler; it is a charming little fishing port. There are good beaches along the coastline here, and inland the Massif des Maures dominates the landscape and does so until Fréjus is reached. The coastline here is known as the Côte des Maures, which is named after the hills, which in turn were named after the dark-coloured pine trees on their slopes. The densely-wooded hill slopes have some marvellous walks, and the villagers from the many hamlets of the Massif still earn their income in part from gathering the sweet chestnuts that thrive here, and collecting the bark from the cork trees.

Just north of Le Lavandou is the hilltop village of **Bormes-lès-Mimosas**, which is worth a visit. There is a sixteenth-century chapel to St Francis, and in front of it there is a statue to Francesco di Paola, who is said to have saved the village from the plague in 1481. The village, with its large tree-lined square and old houses, has been little changed by the tourists who now visit in growing numbers.

Circular Tour from St Tropez to Toulon

This tour starts in Bormes and the next stop is St Tropez which can be reached by either taking the coastal road through some marvellous little resorts with splendid beaches, or the higher road a little way inland, through Cogolin. On the lower route, are the beaches where the Allies landed in 1944; and if the higher road is chosen you can do a little wine tasting along the way. There are cellars and tasting centres at Bormes, La Môle, La Croix-Valmer and Cogolin.

The rocky coast of the Esterel corniche near St Raphaël

St Tropez is, of course, a legend. It is one of the most famous resorts in the world, bursting with fine hotels, restaurants and night-life. It has always attracted artists because of the near-perfect light, and many of their works are now housed in the town's museum of modern art. There is also a maritime museum in the citadel with many exhibits from the old town. It was only 80 years ago that St Tropez got its first proper road into the town; before then people used the narrow-gauge railway, or the ferry from St Raphaël.

The harbour at St Tropez still houses the traditional fishing boats, but they are now dwarfed by the luxury yachts of the rich, while the quays are packed with artists dashing out oil paintings to sell to the tourists. The main sights to see are the sixteenth-century chapel of Ste Anne, just outside town; and also the statue of the French Admiral Bailli de Suffren, who, with a tiny fleet of five ships, managed to harass the Royal Navy around the globe in the mid-eighteenth century. His home was Château Suffren, in the old town, near the town hall.

St Tropez is surrounded by huge beaches, and the new marina-holiday complex of Port Grimaud. Cars are not allowed, and it is a little like a mini-Venice, to be visited only on foot or by boat, with conducted tours available through the maze of canals.

Continuing along the N98, the family resort of **Ste Maxime** is popular throughout the year with lively evening entertainment, and many sporting facilities. It also has many good restaurants, and a fine reputation for its food. Detours are also possible from here into the hills, to sample more of the local wine around Plan-de-la-Tour and La Garde-Freinet.

Fréjus, once a Roman harbour, is now a couple of kilometres inland, and there are some fine ruins to explore. They include the remains of a fifth-century baptistry. There is an incomplete Roman theatre to the north of the town, now used for French bullfights, and there are guided tours of the thirteenth-century cathedral and cloisters of Notre-Dame-de-Victoire in the town centre. There is a museum containing antiquities found in the area. **St Raphaël**, Fréjus' neighbour, has a twelfth-century church of the Knights Templars and a fine archaeological museum.

From Fréjus and St Raphaël the route turns inland, away from the beaches and into the hills and the vineyards. **Draguignan**, a small town with a reputation for good food, both in its restaurants and its shops, is the first main town. It has many fine old buildings and fountains, and the centre is dominated by the seventeenth-century Tour d'Horloge. There is a medieval gateway and the façade of a thirteenth-century synagogue in the Rue de la Juiverie. A museum is housed in the eighteenth-century former summer palace of the Bishops of Fréjus.

Nearby is the spectacular area of gorges and plunging waterfalls known as the Verdon Gorges. There are wine tasting cellars in Draguignan and in many of the villages on the road to Brignoles, especially Les Arcs, Vidauban and Le Luc.

Brignoles is another market town and agricultural centre, famous for its museum, which houses amongst other things, the oldest Gaulish Christian sarcophagus, dating from the third century. Just south of Brignoles is **Besse**, the home of Gaspard de Besse, a sort of eighteenth-century French Robin Hood. He was finally captured and executed at Aix-en-Provence. There is also a beautiful Cistercian abbey at **Le Thoronet**, and many of the original twelfth-century buildings have been restored to their austere splendour. Other places to visit in the area are **Salernes** with its thirteenth-century castle ruins; **Entrecasteaux**, a medieval village with *château* and fortified Gothic church; and **Tourtour**.

From Brignoles, drive in a sweeping curve back down to the coast using the N560 and taking in **La Roquebrussanne**, and a small detour off to La Ste Baume, where legend has it that Mary Magdalene lived in retreat in a cave for the last 30 years of her life. The cave,

The spectacular chasm of the Verdon Gorges

Grotte de St Pilon, can be reached on foot from the D80.

Continue on the D80 down to **Glémenos** with its eighteenth-century *château* and nearby chapel of St Jean de Garguier, with its collection of religious paintings dating back for the last 500 years, and then on to **La Ciotat**, on the coast, a former Greek settlement. The Musée Tauroentum, built on the site of a Roman villa, and housing many of the Roman finds discovered nearby should be visited. Then it is just a short drive to Bandol.

Bandol is the home of one of the region's most famous wines, and you can sit out at one of the many beach cafés and sample it at leisure. Just off the coast is the Ile Bendor, now a tourist trap with art gallery, museum, zoo and the World Museum of Wines and Spirits.

The final point of call before returning to Hyères should be to **Toulon**, a bustling, crowded city, with few attractions having survived the heavy bombardments during the last war. There are some good restaurants, however, and the fish and vegetable markets are worth visiting, as are the maritime and archaeological museums.

Walking in Provence

No other area in France affords the walker so much choice of countryside to travel through. If you want to get away from the crowds there are high mountains to walk in the summer, shaded woody hills to get out of the heat of the sun, vineyards to explore and the wine to taste, and it is still possible to walk along the coastline so you can plunge into the sea if it gets too hot. There are walks and climbs to suit all levels of fitness and skill, in almost every part of Provence.

It is best to divide the walking into two groups, the lowland and the highland sections. Gradually as you move both east and north the altitude rises and you switch from rugged hills into towering mountains. The lowland walking starts as soon as you cross the Rhône. As you travel east from the river there is the large plain known as the Crau, dealt with in more detail later, but an excellent place both to walk and birdwatch. It is the home of the little bustard and the majestic red kite. To the north of the Crau the land rises as you approach Les Baux. There is excellent walking here and especially north of Carpentras where the countryside is dominated by Mont Ventoux, which rises to 1,909m (6,260ft) above sea level. This area, known as the Baronies, is rugged but great walking and backpacking country.

If you proceed east you reach Aix-en-Provence, another great base for walking trips. To the north is the National Park of Lubéron through which runs the River Verdon. The Gorges of the Verdon, especially between the eastern boundaries of the national park and Castellane are spectacular with many walks, although some are only for the more experienced hikers. The locals refer to the gorges as the

Grande Canyon, and while it is not as large as its American name-sake, it is still impressive. There is also good walking in the Alpes-de-Haute-Provence, and Alpes-Maritimes, and both walking and mountaineering opportunities in the Hautes-Alpes.

North of Le Lavandou is the range of the Massif des Maures, a ridge of hills rising up to 600m (1,968ft). The ridge runs in a north-eastern line between Toulon and Fréjus and from most points there are views of the Mediterranean. Around Grasse, world famous for its perfumes, the hills of the Alpes-Maritimes start to rise. The rolling hills are between 1,000 and 1,200m (3,280 and 3,936ft) and there are marvellous panoramas. North-east of Grasse is the Gorges de la Vésubie, also worth exploring, and then it is on and up into the mountains near the Italian border, where the air gets thinner and the walking tougher.

There are remote villages like St Etienne, St Martin-Vésubie and Auron, and more gorges to walk, such as the Gorges de Daluis and the Gorges du Cians. The mountains along the border rise to almost 3,000m (9,840ft), the highest being Mont du Grand Capelet at 2,935m (9,626ft) and Mont Neillier at 2,785m (9,134ft). There are many quiet alpine villages to stay in if you want a base from which to walk.

Apart from some tricky sections in the Gorges du Verdon and in the higher regions close to the Italian border there is nothing to daunt the serious, reasonably fit walker. Heat can be a major problem in the summer with temperatures regularly in the 'nineties' (30°C) and often going higher. The mistral normally blows in the spring and during the winter, but can occasionally occur in the summer, and a few fierce thunderstorms sometimes roll around the hills. The main rule for the summer walker is to be careful of the heat. It can get blisteringly hot as the sun pounds down on bare rock, so wear a cap and carry some liquid refreshment. Apart from the Gorges du Ver-don, where you will find other tourists, most of the walking areas of Provence are still pretty deserted, and you can enjoy your solitude.

Carpentras and Sault make great bases from which to walk around Mont Ventoux to the north, and the Lubéron National Park to the south. The Lubéron is fast becoming one of the best wine-producing areas of the south of France, so you can combine your walking with a little tasting along the way. If you just want to concentrate on the Lubéron area, Apt makes a good base. The Lubéron National Park is an area of pine-covered hills. For centuries the area was used for grazing sheep and they would then be driven across country to the markets. There are still scores of old drove trails criss-crossing the park, usually following the highest land, and beside them you will spot derelict inns and old shepherds' huts. La Garde Frénet is a good base for walking in the Var if you don't want to stray too far away from the coast. From here you can make a number of excursions into the Massif des Maures, and because you are so close to the coastal towns, there is a reasonably good local bus service to get you to and from your starting and finishing points. If you want to be more intrepid and tackle the Gorges du Verdon over three or four days — why rush it if you are on holiday — there are a number of places to base youself, such as Moustiers-Ste Marie, Gréoux or Castellane.

Walkers are welcome in Provence and almost all the local Syndicats can supply details of interesting routes which they have waymarked well. The tourist office in Aix has produced a very good handbook of local walks, many of them around Mont Ste Victoire. There are a score or more of waymarked routes around Menton ranging from a 2-hour stroll to a good day's hike.

Long-distance Grande Randonnée routes include the GR6 Alpes-Océan, which runs from Sisteron through Vaucluse to Beaucaire, the GR Tour du Lubéron, a walk covering a number of trails totalling about 160km (100 miles), the GR9 and 98 Var and Bouches-du-Rhône, a walk taking you round the coastline, and the GR91 Vercors-Ventoux, a walk of just over 160km (100 miles) through the Drôme, Hautes-Alpes to Mont Ventoux. The GR4 Méditerranée-Océan takes you from near Grasse in a 160km (100 mile) trip to Lubéron before leaving the region, while the hardest walk is the GR5-52 Hollande-Méditerranée, which runs from Larche to Menton through the Parc Naturel du Mercantour, in the highest parts of the Alpes-Maritimes.

The Mercantour park is really in the highland walking section which covers the Hautes-Alpes and Alpes-de-Haute-Provence, where many peaks are 2,000m (6,560ft) or more. Snow can be expected from October on and lies on the highest peaks well into June, and sometimes July. There are many glaciers in the area.

This is real rugged, backpacking country where you should be really fit and have a reasonable knowledge of mountain craft, map and compass reading and basic survival, just in case you are caught out by the weather. Sudden storms, low cloud and mist can all be problems.

In the Hautes-Alpes there are two nature parks, the Ecrins, famous for its alpine plants and flowers, generally between 2,000m (6,560ft) and 3,000m (9,840ft), although rising to 4,102m (13,454ft) on the summit of the Barre des Ecrins; and Queyras, which straddles the Italian border. There are many routes both in and around these parks. There are camp sites on the edges or near the parks.

You should also spot quite a lot of wildlife as there are chamois, marmot, golden eagles and many other species of mountain birds.The Alpes-de-Haute-Provence stretches from the hills around the Gorges du Verdon in the south to peaks 2,500m (8,200ft) and more in the north. It is a great place for backwoods camping and backpacking. A small railway line, the Chemin de Fer de Haute Provence climbs its way into the hills and you can choose any one of its many stopping places to start your walk.

The newest park is the Parc National du Mercantour which opened in 1979. It lies close to the Italian border and varies in altitude between 1,000m (3,280ft) and 3,000m (9,840ft). The whole park is worth exploring and there are very many waymarked trails.

The whole of the Alps are criss-crossed by a large number of long-distance footpaths, and many of them pass through the mountains of Provence. Most demand a high state of fitness and are rated as hard or difficult walks.

But, don't let that put you off. As the crowds squeeze on to the beaches, why not enjoy the peace and quiet of the mountains and hills.

Exploring the Crau

The Crau is a stone desert, a vast flatland to the east of the Rhône, rich in wildlife, yet hardly visited by tourists to the south of France. It is well known to ornithologists but most head for the Camargue, so this little corner of Provence is well worth exploring. The area is bordered in the west by the river, in the north by the Alpilles, in the east by the Etang de Berre and in the south by the sea.

St Martin-de-Crau just to the north, or Istres on the eastern shores of the Etang, make good bases for exploring the area, although it is only a short drive from Arles, Salon or Aix-en-Provence. The N568 runs diagonally across the Crau to Fos on the sea and from this road there are many lanes to follow to give you access to most of the area. There is a French air base just outside Salon and the jets do come screaming overhead, but the birds seem to have got used to it.

The Crau is all that remains of the alluvial flood plain of the Durance, a river which flows down from the Massif des Hautes-Alpes. Thousands of years ago, it forced a deep channel through the Alpilles, a valley known now as the Pertuis de Lamanon, and flowed straight into the Mediterranean. Today the Durance is a tributary of the Rhône, and the Crau is what remains of the mountain debris once deposited by the river as it rushed into the sea.

In some places the stones are 15m (50ft) deep but much of the Crau, which covers more than 50,000ha (123,550 acres), has been converted into agricultural land.

A complicated series of canals in the north and east of the Crau has enabled vineyards and olive groves to be planted. The grazing here is much lusher than in the rest of the Crau where the sheep roam the flat, drab landscape looking for something to eat among the sparse vegetation. What makes the Crau so interesting is the wide range of birds that gather there, especially many rare breeding species. There are many reptiles to be seen if you are careful, including five species of snake, none of them dangerous to man. Alas, snakes are no match for motor vehicles and you will see many crushed on the road. If out exploring you may also see scorpions and tarantula spiders — two creatures which seem to strike fear into many people quite unnecessarily. The tarantula belongs to the wolf spider family. In Italy it was thought that a bite from a tarantula turned you insane unless you performed a feverish twirling dance to shake out the poison — the origin of the tarantella dance. Tarantulas will bite if attacked, and while painful it is not in the least bit dangerous. While tarantulas generally hunt by night, they do like to spend the day sunning themselves outside their homes, usually a camouflaged hole in the ground. Scorpions are quite common in the Crau. They like to shelter under stones or wedges in behind the bark of a tree during the day because they too, are nocturnal hunters. It is possible to find them by gingerly turning over stones with your boot or a stick.

There are two sorts of scorpion found in the Crau. The first species grows to about 10cm (4in) in length and the sting in the tail is no more irritating than that of a bee or wasp. The second species is larger, usually coloured a yellowish-brown, and its sting is much more painful, but still not fatal.

On a stifling hot summer's day it is quite possible to see a posse of different birds of prey soaring majestically over the Crau, using the thermals that rise over the hot stones. The Montagu's harrier swoops close to the ground in the hope of driving small birds up into the air where it can catch them. Several pairs breed on the Crau, laying their eggs on a carpet of trampled down grass which serves as a nest. Other birds of prey to be seen include Egyptian vultures, which nest in the Alpilles, the northern edge of the Crau; golden and Bonelli's eagle, sparrow hawk, goshawk, black kite, all the harriers, short-toed eagle, osprey, peregrine, hobby, kestrel and lesser kestrel. One part of the Crau has been used as a rubbish tip to dispose of the garbage from neighbouring towns, and it attracts thousands of birds, both birds of prey and many species of gull looking for easy pickings. Another rare breeding bird that is ideally suited to the Crau is the stone-curlew. It is quite a large bird, up to 40cm (16in) long, with large eyes. If it is disturbed during the day it will run to escape or will flatten itself against the ground, and its colouring allows it to merge into the stony background. Even its eggs are camouflaged to look like stones, and are laid in a stony nest on the ground. Some of the other rare species that can be spotted are the little bustard, the great spotted cuckoo, Calandra lark, lesser grey shrike, short-toed lark, subalpine warbler, black-eared wheatear, pratincole, and pin-tailed sandgrouse. All the other colourful birds of the Camargue can also be seen here such as the roller, bee eater and hoopoe.

The most magnificent of the five species of snakes, none of which is dangerous, is the Montpellier snake which can grow to almost 2.2m (7ft) in length. The Montpellier is found all along the Mediterranean but its numbers are falling. The southern smooth snake grows to about half a metre (about 2ft) long, and while it can give you a nasty bite if cornered, it tends to slither away out of trouble rather than seek a fight. The viperine water snake can grow to more than a metre (3ft) in length and while its markings resemble those of the common adder, it does not bite (the adder is not found this far south). If surprised, however, it might release the stink glands at the base of its tail.

The other snakes that can be seen are the harmless grass snake and the ladder snake which likes to lie out on an exposed piece of rock lapping up the sun. It grows to about 1.5m (5ft) long and constricts its prey.

If you are lucky, you may spot pond tortoises and terrapins, mud frogs and natterjack toads. You should certainly see the magnificently coloured green tree frog, and there are edible frogs and laughing frogs about.

The Crau is certainly not a beautiful landscape, except perhaps where it starts to climb into the limestone hills of the Alpilles. Even here it is spectacular rather than pretty, with its densely wooded valleys and lower hill slopes. Despite this, however, it has an enormous amount to offer whether you just want to go walking or want to observe the wildlife. There may be thousands of birds to be seen, but you won't see many other people.

Exploring Upper Provence

The Verdon Gorges are France's answer to America's Grand Canyon but on a smaller scale. In places the cliffs tower more than 620m (2,000ft) above the narrow river floor and the green waters of the river after which it was named. The walking possibilities in this area have already been mentioned, but if you are less energetic but still want to explore this spectacular countryside, there are many routes which you can drive.

Castellane, is a small but bustling health resort at the eastern end of the gorges. It nestles in a natural river basin surrounded by mountains and makes an ideal base for touring the area by car. There are a number of hotels in Castellane and some pleasant cafés and restaurants, but few other points of interest. There is the Chapel of Notre-Dame du Roc, the Romanesque church of St Victor, and a pentagonal tower, but the main sights are beyond the town.

There are a number of routes to follow through the mountains. Many of the mountain roads are narrow, most are twisty and in some places there are near heart-stopping sheer drops just a few feet from your wheels, but the careful driver has nothing to worry about.

All the tours start in Castellane, and a map of the area is essential.

Tour 1   The Gorges du Verdon (about 128km, 80 miles)
Take the road out of Castellane leading to Draguignan, this follows the north or right bank of the gorges and gets you used to looking down on the river. Travel through the small village of Porte de St Jean and then follow the curve of the river round to Pont de Soleils. For the first part of this trip the road runs parallel to the GR4 long-distance footpath, so you can get out and stretch your legs provided you can find somewhere safe to park. Just before Pont de Soleils you will pass the Clue de Chasteuil where the gorge narrows and the sides become even more steep.

Stay on the D952 and follow the river round to Point Sublime passing by another constriction, the Clue de Carejuan. The road at this point is almost 930m (3,000ft) above sea level.

Continue on through La Palud, the Col d'Ayen, and up to Moustiers at the head of Lac de Ste Croix. The return journey follows the left bank of the gorges by leaving Moustiers on the D952 then turning off on to the D957 to cross the river over the new road bridge. The road takes you through Aiguines along the route known as the Corniche Sublime. After the Balcons de la Mescala and La Cournuelle, you turn off right on to the D90 through Trigance to rejoin the D955 which takes you back north to Pont de Soleils and then Castellane.

The mountain village of Tourette-sur-Loup, north-west of Nice

The tour is one of the most beautiful and scenic you can take from Castellane and the locals proudly claim it is one of the most spectacular sceneries in the world. The road on both banks overlook the Grand Canyon with cliffs between 279 and 651m (900 and 2,100ft high.

Tour 2   The Northern Bank of the Gorges du Verdon (80km, 50 miles)
It is possible to make a shorter tour of the northern bank of the gorges by following the Route des Crêtes. Take the road leading to Draguignan to Pont de Soleils, then on to La Palud. About 1km (about half a mile) before the village turn left on to the new road to La Palud just after La Maline. This route takes you through some of the highest mountains and there are many fine vantage points and spots to stop and picnic. Many of the picnic spots are in the forests and tables and benches are provided. On the way back just after Point Sublime there is a track down to the bottom of the gorges. The Martel track is just over a mile and strong shoes are essential as well as a torch because you have to walk through several dark tunnels. The walk down is the easy bit!

Tour 3   To Ste Croix Lake (56km, 35 miles)
Follow Tour 1 until you reach the bridge and then take the new road which follows the artificial lake on its left bank to the newly rebuilt

village of Les Salles. Cross the lake by the bridge over the Ste Croix Dam, and drive on the village of Ste Croix. You can then reach Moustiers by the right side of the lake, or go to Riez.

Tour 4   The Upper Verdon Valley (64-72km, 40-5 miles)
This tour takes you up into the Provence Alps. From Castellane take the road to St André-les-Alpes. The road goes over the top of the impressive Castillon Dam, 90m (300ft) high and sheer drops on either side, so not for those who suffer from vertigo, and then along the side of the artificial lake to St André, about 16km (10 miles) on.

Take the road to the Col d'Allos which winds its way through wild scenery to the village of Allos. It is a popular summer centre with walkers but mainly a winter resort affording very good local skiing. If you have the time it is worth making the detour to the Allos lake, which is at an altitude of almost 2,017m (6,700ft). From the village it takes about 45 minutes driving and then 20 minutes on foot to reach the lake.

The road winds its way through large fields which are used as the ski runs during the winter. Barcelonnette is the most northerly point of the tour. It is in the Ubaye valley and from here you have a choice of three routes back to Castellane: La Lauzet and its lake, Serre Ponçon lake, the Clue de Barles, Digne and then the Route Napoléon back to Castellane; the Col de la Cayolle and the Vallée du Var; Jausiers, the Col de Restefond, the Col de la Bonnette with its marvellous views, and the Vallée de la Tinée.

Tour 5   The Gorges du Cians and Gorges du Daluis (about 193km, 120 miles)
From Castellane take the road to St André and at St Julien turn right on the Nice road to Pont de Gueydan. Go to Guillaumes through the famous Gorges du Daluis, carved out of red schist. Take either of the roads to Valberg and Beuil and then drop down the mountain to Puget Théniers through the Gorges du Cians. You can then go back to Castellane either by Entrevaux, Les Scaffarels and St Julien, or, if you have time, via the Clue de St Auban and Le Logis du Pin.

Tour 6   The Lavender Fields (about 180km, 112 miles)
From Castellane take the road going to Draguignan up to the Pont de Soleils and then on to Moustiers, Ste Marie and Riez, following the right bank of the Grand Canyon du Verdon. Go to Valensole, then down to Gréoux-les-Bains, up to Mesel and back to Castellane by the Route Napoléon. This tour takes you through the typical scenery of northern Provence and through many lavender fields which are at their most scented in the summer.

Tour 7   The Gorges du Loup (about 140km, 87 miles)
From Castellane take the Grasse road. At Le Logis du Pin take the
road to Thorenc and Gréolières. The Gorges du Loup are situated
between Gréolières and Gourdon. You can see them from either bank
and can return to Castellane by St Vallier or Andon. These gorges are
cut vertically into the mountains of Grasse. Gourdon is a delightful
village at the entrance of the Gorges which also overlooks the
Mediterranean.

Tour 8   The Vallée de l'Asse and L'Issole (about 80km, 50 miles)
From Castellane go up to Barrême and take the Nice road. About
2km (1.2 miles) after Barrême turn right on the road to Clumans, and
then on to Tartonne and St André, before returning to Castellane past
the dam.

Tour 9   The Gorges de Robion and Lachens (about 72km, 45 miles)
From Castellane take the road to Le Bourguet then down to Le Logis
du Pin. At the crossroads take the road which leads to the top of
Lachens for the most spectacular views. From here you can return to
Castellane either by the Le Logis du Pin road or by the La Bastide and
Comps road. This is a short trip but well off-the-beaten-track so you
shouldn't meet very much traffic. From the top of the mountain you
have views to the Italian border in the east and the Mediterranean in
the south.

Tour 10   The Lakes of Castillon and Chaudanne (40km, 25 miles)
From Castellane, take the road to Grasse and after about 3km (1.8
miles) turn left on the Demandoix road. Before reaching the village,
turn left again on to the new road which takes you past Lake Chaudanne to Lake Castillon. Just after crossing the Paontas bridge and
before the road starts to descend, you have views of both lakes. When
you reach Lake Castillon, turn right for St Julien and then back to
Castellane by Barrême. If you do not have much time, you can go
back directly by turning left and crossing the Verdon over the dam.
There are also excellent vantage and photographing points of the
lakes and dam from the small villages of La Beaume and Blaron.

Tour 11   The Forests (about 77km, 48 miles)
From Castellane take the Grasse road and after about 3km (1.8 miles)
turn left on the Demandoix road. On the way, you can visit the skiing
centre at Vauplane. Go down to Soleilhas and St Auban, through the
Col de Blaine and then back to Castellane via the Logis du Pin.

Tour 12   The Col des Champs (about 161km, 38 miles)
Take the Allos road (see Tour 4) and when you get to the fortified city

of Colmars take the road up to the Col des Champs through the forest. The Col is just under 1,953m (6,300ft high). You can reach the valley of the Var River at St Martin d'Entraunes, and return to Castellane through the Gorges de Daluis by following the route in Tour 5. This tour is a quickie but it is through marvellous countryside and you can make a day of it by walking in the woods and picnicking.

The Durance Valley

Thousands of years ago the Durance used to flow south straight into the Mediterranean and how it came to be diverted to become a tributary of the Rhône is not certain. What is sure, however, is that this part of Upper Provence and the Durance valley in particular is worth a visit. It does attract tourists but not in huge numbers because most seem to prefer the attractions to the east such as Arles, Orange and Avignon, and to the south — Aix-en-Provence and the coast. The Durance flows south through the mountains of Upper Provence, past Sisteron, and then it starts to sweep westwards in a great curve, as it passes south of the Montagne du Lubéron, on its way to the Rhône.

There are a number of places for a base from which you will be able to explore the whole area. There is the Montagne de Lure to the west of Sisteron, the Plateau du Valensole to the south of the Durance, and the whole of the Lubéron range with its delightful walks and promising vineyards. A road, the Mourre Nègre, runs along the crest of the Lubéron hills, and this follows the traditional path along which sheep were driven to market for centuries. To the north of this road there are many lanes to venture along which will take you to delightful villages such as Ménerbes, Bonnieux, Gordes, Roussillon and Oppède-le-Vieux, a lovely village which has been faithfully restored by the many artists and craftsmen who have moved in.

One of the most noticeable things about this region is the red rock, and in Roussillon, the red stone of the houses blends with the red rocks all around. The village is surrounded by old quarries from which the rock was excavated, and these are worth noticing just to see the remarkable differences in the colours of the stone.

Ménerbes is an ancient village with an old church, citadel and spectacular views. At **Bonnieux** there are many old houses, twisting narrow streets and fountains to see and two famous churches. One dates back only to the last century but houses several fine fifteenth-century paintings of the Old German School, while the other church dates back to the twelfth-century. At **Gordes** there is a Renaissance *château* which has a collection of more than a thousand works of art by Victor Vasarély, a French painter of Hungarian origin born in 1908 and the originator of Op Art in painting and sculpture. Just to the north-west of Gordes is the Abbaye de Sénanque, remarkably well preserved and tranquil. Built by the Cistercians in their simple, almost austere style, the abbey was one of the 'three famous sisters of Provence', the others being at Le Thoronet and Silvacane. Occasionally during the summer, concerts are held there. The abbey also houses an exhibition of the Sahara desert. All over the area you can find the remains of *bories*, simple huts made by the shepherds, and to the south-west of Gordes there is the **Village Noir**, a complete village of these drystone shelters long since deserted. To the south-west of the abbey are the great water-filled caverns which give rise to the Fontaine de Vaucluse, said to be one of the most powerful springs in the world. The underground caverns are filled by the waters of the River Sorgue and it surfaces in a large lake, on whose shores a *son et lumière* is staged during the summer.

The village of the same name nearby, dominated by the ruins of an old castle, was for a time the home of the fourteenth-century Italian poet Petrarch, and there is a small museum in his memory, built, it is thought, on the site of his home. There is also an interesting caving museum in the village

Apt is one of the oldest villages in the area and became a Roman colony during their occupation of Provence. It was known as *Hath* but was renamed *Apta Julia* after Julius Caesar, which over the years contracted to its present name. Its most interesting building is the cathedral of Ste Anne built over two crypts. One crypt lies over the other and the upper one was carved out of the rock in the eleventh-century. It contains an altar which pre-dates the crypt, and six thirteenth-century sarcophagi rest in recesses around the walls. In the lower crypt are the relics of Ste Anne, the mother of the Virgin Mary. The sacred remains are said to have been found in 776 when Charlemagne consecrated the original church on the site.

There has certainly been a church on the site for at least 1,400 years, the first being built on the site of a Roman temple. Archaeological digs around Apt have also discovered a number of sarcophagi dating back to the fourth century AD.

After the discovery of the relics of Ste Anne, Apt became a pilgrimage centre and Anne of Austria came to worship in the crypt in 1623 praying for a child. The valuable gifts she bequeathed to the church are still kept locked in the treasury. Further evidence of the rich history of this area can be gained by visiting the archaeological museum nearby. It contains many items dating back to Roman times which were found locally. Pont Julien is claimed to be the best preserved Roman bridge in France and is found 5 miles west of Apt crossing the River Coulon. The three arched bridge was built in the first century BC.

Cavaillon in the west lies alongside the Durance and is another good base for touring the region. It has a bustling fruit and vegetable market which is worth an early morning trip. The town itself lies in a fertile plain, the Petit Lubéron, and there are field after field of lush melons for which the area is famous. In the town itself there is the Romanesque cathedral of St Véran, an eighteenth-century synagogue and a museum of local Jewish history. The cathedral was built in the thirteenth century and has an octagonal tower, a feature found in many churches in Provence, as well as many fine religious paintings and carvings in wood and stone. In the Grande Rue there is the town museum featuring many Roman exhibits and ancient coins from many civilizations which shows the area must have been on an important route for traders. The Jewish synagogue is in Rue Chabran. There were a number of strong Jewish communities in the region with papal patronage which did not end until the French Revolution. The other communities were in Avignon, Carpentras and Isle-sur-la-Sorgue.

Above the town is **Colline St Jacques**, a flat rocky area which used to be the site of many civilizations. Traces of Neolithic and Ligurian settlements have been found, and these were followed by the Celts, then the Greeks, and finally the Romans who eventually founded *Cabellio* below the rock, later to become Cavaillon.

The **Lubéron Hills** provide excellent walking and there are many roads to drive along which will take you through some of the prettiest parts of this regional park. The Lubéron range extends for about 64km (40 miles) and is divided at Bonnieux into the Grand Lubéron in the east and the Petit Lubéron in the west. The people of the Lubéron are immensely proud of their region and its past. They still live in tight-knit communities in small villages that can trace their ancestry back hundreds of years, back to the bloody persecutions of the sixteenth century. In the fourteenth century, the Lubéron became the centre for the Vaudois sect which had fled Italy to escape persecution. The Avignon popes, presumably because the sect was so close, decided that a lesson had to be taught to the Vaudois. They were declared heretics and papal troops were ordered to destroy all trace of them. Entire villages were destroyed and thousands of people killed. The former capital of the religious sect was Old Mérindol, and it is still preserved as a heap of stones. Today, the Lubéron is a delightful area of rolling hills, many of them densely wooded and the ideal habitat for hare, deer, woodcock and partridge. In the more remote woods there are still wild boar.

The summer heat is intense and the land is baked hard so it seems a strange place to find one of France's most impressive vineyards — the result of a £6 million dollar dream which has now become a reality. The vineyard of Château Val Joanis lies in a valley of the same name on the slopes of the Lubéron mountains. The *château* has had many famous owners and in 1730 was in the possession of Jean Joanis, secretary to King Louis III of Naples, and it still bears his arms today. It can trace its history back to Roman times, and the first vines may have been planted then, more than 2,000 years ago.

Jean Louis Chancel, a self-made millionaire born in the Lubéron, has always had a dream — to make the wines of Lubéron famous throughout the world. In 1978 he bought the *château*, 12 acres of badly run down vineyards, and 650 acres of scrub and woodland because soil analysis had shown the ground was capable of producing quality wine grapes. The hillsides were cleared, the land drained and planted with vines, a new winery built — altogether an expenditure of over £4 million — more than enough to have bought a leading Bordeaux vineyard had he wished. Today the vineyard produces marvellous red, white and rosé wines, and his efforts have encouraged other producers to raise their standards as well, so much so in fact, that in 1987 the Lubéron gained full *Appellation Contrôlée* status for its wines. You must try them.

If you want to base yourself at the other side of this region, **Sisteron** makes a good base. Its massive citadel rises above and dominates the town. There is an imposing cathedral started in the eleventh century, and a delightful colonnade of covered arches down to the river. The town has always held a strategic importance because of its position immediately below the Dauphiné mountains to the north and guarding the way to the plains and coast to the south.

Work is still going on to repair some of the medieval buildings damaged and destroyed during bombing by the Allies in 1944. Many of the buildings have already been carefully restored. Near the town hall are four fifteenth-century towers, part of the old town's fortifications. There is also an archaeological museum nearby. The citadel was started in the eleventh-century but work on the fortifications continued for centuries. It is worth the walk to the citadel for the views it affords.

There are scores of quaint and interesting towns and villages to visit in the Durance valley or immediate vicinity. There is the small spa town of **Digne**, in the heart of the lavender country. In July an international lavender-essence fair is held. It has not much else of interest but many good hotels and restaurants, so could make a base.

The mountains of **Lure** are really an extension of the Mont Ventoux range, an area full of steep hills, caves and springs, and an excellent place for spending a few days walking. There are many paths to follow, and places to explore. The Lure has certainly not yet been discovered by the crowds.

There is a small Romanesque chapel surrounded by lime trees, built on the site of the Lure Hermitage founded in AD500 by St Donat. A road does cross the mountains, but the best way is to get out on foot, although the walk to the summit, at the Signal de Lure at nearly 1,700m (5,500ft) is a tough one. There are beautiful flowers, including several species of orchid to see, as well as a wide range of butterflies, and the views from the top are breathtaking.

Between the Lure mountains and the Plateau de Valensole is **Forcalquier**, another ancient town, known as *Furnus Calcarius* in the Middle Ages because of the local lime furnaces (kilns). There are a number of interesting things to see including the curious cemetery with carved yew trees, the Romanesque church of Our Lady in Provençal and the convent of the Franciscans. The church of Notre Dame was started at the end of the twelfth century and in front of it stands a fifteenth-century fountain bearing a plaque which commemorates the marriage in 1235 of Eleanore of Provence and Henry III of England. The Franciscan convent was founded in 1236 and has been restored well. The cemetery is just north of the town, and is an oddity as far as French cemeteries go. Yew trees have been cut and trimmed to form arches along the terraces on which the *cabanons*, or small dry-stone buildings, were erected.

A little to the north-east is **Ganagobie**, with its marvellous Benedictine monastery founded in 980, but rebuilt on a number of occasions since then. It is famed for its carvings, sculptures and paintings which start as you enter the building. Even the lintel above the imposing gate is decorated.

A final point of call, if you have to tear yourself away, should be to **Riez**, once important as an administrative centre during the Roman occupation. Just outside the town there are the remains of a temple, believed to be to Apollo, with four columns of grey granite remaining. The stone for the temple must have been hauled at least 112km (70 miles) because this is the nearest known quarry with such granite. Another interesting visit is to the baptistry, again on the outskirts of town on the Allemagne-en-Provence road. Nobody knows exactly when it was built, although the experts agree that it was some time between the fourth and seventh centuries. Although square outside and capped with a dome which was added later, it is octagonal inside and divided into four chapels. It contains many sarcophagi, an altar and many columns and carvings.

To the north of Riez is the desolate Plateau de Valensole which is cut in two by the valley of the River Asse. There are some minor roads crossing the plateau but many walks, and it is a rugged but exciting place to backpack.

The whole of the Durance valley is really off the normal tourist route and it has something to offer everyone, whether you want to explore ancient monuments, get out and walk, or hunt out an exciting new wine maker and sample the product.

The Gastronomy of Provence

Olive trees that hug the hillsides and parched plots of land throughout Provence provide the basic cooking ingredient for most of the region's dishes. There are plentiful supplies of fresh vegetables, fresh fish from the Mediterranean, and meat and game from the hills in the north.

The people of Provence have strong fiery tastes which is why garlic, peppers and raw onions all figure strongly in dishes. Marseilles is the home of the fish soup *bouillabaisse*, but soups and stews of fish and meat abound.

Garlic is extensively used. As one moves nearer the Italian border the food changes, and there are many pasta dishes, especially around Nice. There is *canelloni, ravioli* and *gnocchi*, and a French version of pizza called *pissaladière*. There is game, including venison, hare and rabbit, and the beef, which tends to be reared locally needs long, slow cooking in stews, or *daubes*, to be at its best. Garlic soup is offered everywhere. There is *aïgo*, a straightforward garlic soup usually poured over bread in a bowl, and *aïgo bouido*, with olive oil and eggs added together with cubes of fried bread. *Aïgo à la ménagèrie* is garlic soup with onion, leek, tomatoes and poached egg, and *aïgo saou*, or *sou*, is garlic soup with fish and sometimes potatoes. Other regional soups include *soupe d'épautre* made with mutton, vegetables and garlic, and you will often find *méjanels* added; this is a thick pasta made in Provence and added to soups and stews. Accompanying soups of all types you will find *aïoli*, a mayonnaise sauce flavoured with garlic and occasionally breadcrumbs.

Regional speciality fish dishes include anchovies, often served cold with a beetroot salad, sea bream and saddled bream. Look out for *boutargue*, a paste made from dried and salted tuna roe, and *capoum*, the local name for scorpion fish. Eeels are popular, especially when cooked in tomatoes and garlic. Fresh sardines, sea bass, mussels and squid are usually excellent. *Bouillabaisse* is a thick fish stew with conger eel, gurnard and many other species, cooked with saffron, garlic, tomatoes, onions, oil and wine. It is universally popular.

Many meat dishes are served as stews, or *daubes*. Dishes cooked *à la Provençale* means they have been cooked with tomatoes, oil, with herbs and garlic, while *à la Barigoule* indicates they have been cooked with mushrooms, ham, onions, wine and oil. *A la Marseillaise* indicates the dish has been cooked with tomatoes, anchovies, onions, olive and garlic. Snails are popular and there are many local names for them. There are also many vegetable stews featuring artichokes, spinach, cabbage and broad beans, while *porchetta* is a mouth-watering delicacy of suckling pig, stuffed and spit roasted. *Pieds et paquets* is a Provence speciality of sheep's tripe and trotters, cooked with tomatoes in white wine, and there are a host of salads, including *salade Niçoise* made from tomatoes, onions, broad beans, lettuce, olives, tuna, anchovies and hard boiled eggs.

There are sweet fritters, marzipan sweets, raisin cakes and a number of mild local cheeses made from both sheep's and goat's milk, including Banon, usually wrapped in chestnut leaves, and Brousse de la Vesubie, a soft cheese which goes wonderfully with fruit.

Further Information
── Southern Provence ──

Museums and Other Places of Interest

Bandol
Wine Exhibition
Open: 10am-12.30pm and 2-6pm, closed Wednesday.

Sanary — Bandol Zoo
Le Castellet
Open: 8am-12noon, 2-7pm, closed Sunday morning.

Bargème
Romanesque Church
Visiting between 10 and 11.30am
Monday, Thursday and Saturday
after collecting key from town hall.

Bormes-lès-Mimosas
Museum. Open: weekdays.

Brignoles
Museum (with sarcophagi)

Open: March to September 9am-12noon and 2.30-6pm; October-March 10am-12noon and 2.30-5pm.

La Ciotat
Museum
Open: weekdays.

Draguignan
Museum
Open: 10-11.30am and 3-6pm.

Medieval Library
Open: 10-11.30am and 3-6pm.

Fréjus
Archaeology Museum
Open: 9.30am-12noon and 2-6pm, closed Tuesday.

Buddhist Pagoda
Open: June-September 3-7pm.

Fifth-century Baptistry
Rue de Fleury
Guided tours 9.30am-12noon and 2-6pm.

Roman Theatre
Open: April-September 9.30am-12noon and 2-7pm, closed Tuesday.

Thirteenth-century cathedral
Open: 9.30am-12noon and 2-6pm, closed Tuesday.

Zoo
Open: 9am-6pm.

Glémenos
Cistercian Abbey Ruins
Open: April-September 9am-8pm; October-March 10am-6pm.

Hyères
St Paul's Church
Open: 2.30-5pm.

Notre-Dame de Consolason
Chapel
Open: 8.30am-2.30pm.

Museum
Open: 10am-12noon and 3-6pm.

St Raphaël
Archaeological Museum
Open: June-September 10am-12noon and 3-6pm; rest of year 11am-12noon and 2-5pm.

St Tropez
Modern Art Museum
Open: June-September 10am-12noon and 3-7pm; rest of year 10am-12noon and 2-6pm.

Maritime Museum
Open: June-September 10am-6pm; rest of year 10am-5pm, closed Thursday.

Le Thoronet
Cistercian Abbey
Open: May-September 10am-12noon and 2-6pm, closed 5pm February to April and 4pm November-January.

12 • The Midi

Lower Provence, Languedoc-Roussillon and Pyrénées Orientales

The Midi is the name given to this sun-drenched part of southern France which stretches from the Rhône estuary westwards to the Spanish border, and the southern foothills of the Massif Central down to the Mediterranean. Each year it attracts millions of visitors but most head for the coast and the thirty resorts along the 200km (125 miles) of sandy beaches leaving huge areas inland almost deserted. The coastal resorts have everything the tourist could want with casinos, restaurants, cinemas, theatres and discos and a huge range of sporting activities from scuba diving to para-gliding, and tennis to caving. For the traveller who wants to get off-the-beaten-track there are many treasures to explore, some great food to be eaten and good, honest wines to wash it down with. There are canals to cruise, cycle paths to pedal, quiet lanes shaded by plane trees to drive along, and well-signposted paths to hike along. There are mountain trails to walk in the summer and good skiing to be enjoyed in the winter. You can take a canoe high into the Cévennes (see chapter 8) and paddle down through the spectacular Gorges du Tarn, or kayak at a more sedate pace along the many rivers that flow through the area, such as the Hérault, Orb, Aude or Cèze. Travel by boat along the Canal du Midi, Canal du Rhône or Canal de la Robin under the shade of centuries-old plane trees. There are the signposted walking paths, the Sentiers de Grandes Randonnées, and nature discovery paths, several hundred signposted riding trails, riding centres and equipped night stop-overs. Two large nature parks have been established, apart from the Camargue, the National Park of the Cévennes and the Regional Natural Park of the Haut-Languedoc, north of St Pons.

During the winter there is skiing in the Cévennes, the Massif du Mont Lozère, and the Pyrénées. The region has been popular for centuries. The Romans built some of their greatest cities here and

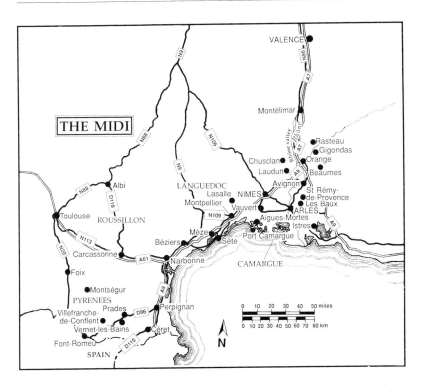

many spectacular monuments still remain. As one stands at the foot of the towering Pont-du-Gard, just west of Villeneuve-lès-Avignon, one can really appreciate the colossal engineering feats of the Roman builders. Stroll around the ancient towns of Arles, Nîmes, Avignon, Perpignan and many others and you can breathe in their past.

You can drive through the Camargue, still one of the wild places of Europe, and watch the white horses and black bulls running through the shallow waters of the salt lakes disturbing the flame red flamingoes. The Camargue is still a mecca for naturalists, especially birdwatchers, but while the horses and bulls still roam on huge ranches, vast tracts have been fenced off to create pseudo cowboy riding ranches, and some of the lakes have been drained for rice production. One advantage of progress, however, is the eradication of the mosquitoes which used to breed there in their millions. Thanks to a government blitz, the nuisance from these irritating pests has been massively reduced.

While the coastline suffers from new developments, marinas and resorts, much of the hinterland of this area has not really changed for hundreds of years. If you really get off-the-beaten-track and travel up into the Pyrénées, there are walking trails where you may not see any one else for hours, and sometimes days at a time. The villages have a sleepy atmosphere and little stirs during the hottest part of the day. The old women dressed in their black clothes sit outside their houses on rickety old wooden chairs in the cool of the evening as the men folk play *boules* on the dusty square. The intense heat in the summer means few crops can survive but olive trees and grape vines abound. This region produces more wine than any other in France and has specialised in making honest, everyday table wines. You can still buy a litre of very drinkable red for a few francs to accompany a picnic feast of french bread, *charcuterie* and olives.

In the foothills of the Pyrénées, one of the hottest and driest regions of France, cherries, oranges and lemons ripen months ahead of anywhere else. One of the interesting ways of getting away from the crowds is to spend a little time visiting some of the vineyards and sampling their wines. As the price of wines from the prestige regions of Bordeaux and Burgundy continue to rocket, regions such as Languedoc-Roussillon are improving their standards by leaps and bounds in order to compete and there are some real bargains to be hunted out. If you are near Sète pop in and visit Listel, by far the largest vineyard owner in France. The winery is surrounded by thousands of acres of vineyards, many of them planted in the sand dunes. And, after a day's exploring away from the tourists what better way to finish off than by dining out at a little restaurant sampling the culinary delights of the region.

You can spend a few days travelling along the Rhône which can offer the tourist almost everything he could wish, from excellent food and drink to spectacular scenery, from majestic castles and antiquities to cathedrals and museums. The constrast from the sleepy villages and historic buildings to futuristic developments like La Grande Motte on the coast makes the area so exciting. No matter what your interests, you will find something to your taste as you explore. The region is rich in culture, not just its history. It is perhaps the warm climate and rich atmosphere that has attracted so many writers and artists. It is the land of the poet Mistral; van Gogh immortalised many scenes around Arles in his paintings; Robert Louis Stevenson and Gauguin spent a lot of time in the area and Kathleen Mansfield lived here for a short time.

Travelling around the region is best done by car if you want to cover a lot of ground, although there are bus and train links between the major towns. Bus services in country areas can be a little hit and miss however. There are daily air services to Avignon, Mende, Perpignan, Nîmes, Montpellier or Béziers from Paris and weekly air

A typical village scene in the Midi

services between London and Montpellier and Perpignan (Dan Air). Or travel down by rail or car. The *autoroutes* are the fastest way of motoring down but most have toll sections and these can add considerably to your costs. Most of the *autoroutes* in Languedoc-Roussillon also have toll sections. If time is not too important, it is always better to stick to the secondary routes. You will not travel so fast but you will see more of the countryside. If you don't want to drive all the way down to the south of France, it is possible to put your vehicle on a train as far as Avignon, or you can pick up a hire car at any of the region's airports or main towns. Even bikes can be hired in some towns, especially those on or near the coast.

Languedoc-Roussillon stretches from the Cévennes in the north to the snow-capped Pyrénées in the south-west, from the bare plateaux in the Causses across the vine-covered plains to the Mediterranean, with its 200km (125 miles) of sandy beaches, dunes, lagoons and resorts. The Camargue, Arles and the towns around the Rhône delta really come under Lower Provence but it is convenient to deal with the whole of this region together.

There is evidence of the presence of early man dating back 300,000 years but most early settlements are now to be found west of the Rhône delta. The Greeks colonised the area around Marseilles 600 years before Christ and spread both east and west, but it was the Romans who had the greatest influence on the region, one that still remains today. The Rhône was the natural transport system into the interior, and settlements were started along its banks which grew into great towns such as Arles and Avignon. As the Romans fanned out, Nîmes became a regional centre, as did Béziers, Carcassone and Narbonne to the west. After the Romans left the area, the coastline in particular was attacked by pirates and then the Saracens, and these raids and incursions lasted for nearly 500 years. The eleventh to the thirteenth century was a period of religious fervour. It was the time of the Crusades and the seventh left the magnificent Aigues-Mortes in 1248. Splendid churches were built throughout the area, including the St Trophime in Arles, which can still be seen with its carved stone façade. The fourteenth century saw the growth of prosperity and culture in the area, as the papal court moved to Avignon; 200 years later though the area was torn as Protestants and Catholics fought the bloody Wars of Religion, followed by religious persecution. As the area settled down and a period of prosperity appeared to be on the way, the plague struck and the population was decimated.

Today, this part of the Midi has everything for the tourist from its sheer natural beauty to historic monuments, from skiing in the winter to sunbathing in the summer. If you want something more active you can play golf, tennis or horse-ride. You can go yachting, river cruising or rambling. There are mountains to scramble up, wine cellars to explore and even thermal cures to take if you have overdone it.

Its great charm, however, is the atmosphere that you cannot avoid. In the summer it is usually too hot to move too quickly so everything settles down into a gentle, relaxing almost sleepy pace. Only the towns really bustle and even these seem to sleep Spanish-style during the afternoons, when it really is too hot to work. It is the time to enjoy a quiet drink in the shade and prepare yourself for the wining, dining and maybe dancing in the evening ahead.

The Pyrénées

The impressive Pyrénées with its towering peaks soaring to more than 3,000m (9,840ft) is the natural barrier between France and Spain. From its highest peaks it falls down to the plains of Gascony in the north and the Mediterranean in the east. It is a walker's, climber's paradise in the summer and offers some excellent skiing in the winter. Despite all this, it still has not really been discovered and therefore it is the ideal place to get away from the crowds. There are climbs that demand a great deal of mountaineering skill, but there are many walks that are well within the range of most hikers. You

The pilgrimage town of Lourdes

could follow the GR10 which traverses the lower levels of the Pyrénées from the Mediterranean to the Atlantic, much of its course taking you through the Pyrenean National Park. Or, you could walk and occasionally scramble your way to the top of Canigou, one of the most impressive peaks in the range rising to just under 3,000m (9,840ft). And, if you like fishing there are scores of well-stocked mountain lakes to try.

Because the Pyrénées has not been developed as a tourist area, prices are still reasonable and basic bed and breakfast accommodation is available at very reasonable rates. Along many of the walking trails there are mountain huts where again you can stay overnight very cheaply. The facilities are basic but more than adequate. And, if you want to camp there are many sites in glorious, unspoiled countryside. Unlike most highland areas of Europe which have been developed to cash in on the skiing trade, there are few signs of this in the Pyrénées. Most of the area has not changed for thousands of years, and there are very few cable cars to take you to higher altitudes. If you want to travel about in the upper ranges of the mountains you will have to do it on foot. Although travel through the mountains is slow it is very enjoyable. There are scores of fertile valleys supporting their own communities to visit, and where you can get get basic accommodation and a hearty meal.

Because of their isolated position, the people have developed their own cultures, folk lore and customs. Many do not speak French at all and this coupled with their special style of food and architecture could lead you to believe you were not in France at all.

Apart from the rather mysterious Andorra which most people have heard of, but few know where it is, the most famous town in the Pyrénées must be Lourdes, which attracts millions of pilgrims every year. It is now world famous because of its miracle cures of the sick. Although Lourdes sprang to fame when a peasant girl saw repeated visions of the Immaculate Conception in the middle of the nineteenth century and the healing spring on the site miraculously appeared, the area has long been famed for its springs and wells with special properties. The Romans used to travel into the Pyrénées to take advantage of the sulphur springs and some are still incorporated into small spa villages where you can breathe the clean air and take a cure.

In the National Park, which runs across the high ground of the Pyrénées and extends into Spain, it is still possible to see a wide range of wildlife, but some of the most famous Pyrenean species are now sadly threatened. You can still see Egyptian vultures, and the occasional soaring eagle together with the Pyrenean chamois, or izard, but the bears have become nocturnal and been driven deep into the forests while the lynx and wolf are becoming rarer. The Pyrénées is, however, very rich in plant-life.

Man has lived in the Pyrénées for centuries and there is evidence of very early cave dwellers. Although the villages are often remote, travellers and pilgrims have been crossing the mountains for centuries on their way to the shrine of St James of Compostela. There are still wonderfully picturesque pilgrimage churches along the route. The Cathars who challenged many of the basic principles of the Roman Church were centred around Toulouse in the twelfth and thirteenth century. In 1209 the Pope, backed by the King of France, sent an army to destroy the heretics. Many of the Cathars (named after the Greek word for 'pure') fled into the Pyrénées to escape the terrible carnage of the Albigensian Crusade. Their long-since abandoned fortresses still stand in seemingly totally inaccessible spots. All the inhabitants of Béziers were slaughtered, the imposing fortress at Carcassonne capitulated after a month-long siege and there were many atrocities ordered by the Crusade's leader, Simon de Montfort. For almost 70 years the Cathars resisted, more than 400 communities were wiped out, and thousands of people killed or executed by the Inquisitors. In 1271 the final resistance was overcome and the lands of the Counts of Toulouse and Languedoc transferred to the Crown.

Because of the ferocity of fighting, few of the Cathar castles remain intact, but many can still be explored, despite their inaccessibility. Most are to be found to the east of Foix and the best examples are to be seen at Montségur, the Cathar capital for a time, Roquefixade, Usson and Puivert, formerly a troubadour court. **Foix** and its surrounding countryside is worth exploring, especially the churches with their Romanesque façades. One of the best vantage points in the whole region is from the Sommet de Portel, reached by driving along the D18 over the Col de la Crouzette and the Col de Péguère. There are a number of largely deforested valleys in the Pays de Foix, once famous for its open cast iron mines. Most of the timber was cut down to provide fuel for the furnaces. There are many caves in the surrounding hills. **Foix** is the principal town of the region, dominated by the castle with its three towers built on the hill above, and a good place from which to set out to explore this part of the Pyrénées.

To the south is the Grottes de Niaux, near the village of Tarascon-sur-Ariège, famous for its cave paintings. Although open to the public it is as well to book your visit in advance to see the magnificent animal and hunting scenes drawn about 15,000 years ago. There are other caves to visit including those at Lombrives, also near Tarascon, where a tour takes up to four hours; and Labouiche, to the north of Foix where you can take a boat trip along the underground river.

As the mountains slope down to the Mediterranean plain one could again be forgiven for thinking that you had taken the wrong turning and were in Spain. This region is even known as French Catalonia, and it has its own dialect, cuisine and customs. As the land drops from the Ceragne plain to the lowlands of Roussillon you travel through one of the most fertile, yet hottest and driest parts of France. At higher levels there are the vineyards hugging the terraces, but as you descend there are acres of fruit orchards. The high mountains here are rugged and forested but provide excellent walking, and are perhaps the most popular tourist spot in the French Pyrénées. Having said that, however, it is still possible to spend hours walking here without seeing anyone else. The resort of Font-Romeu has developed to cater for this tourist trade, walking in the summer and skiing in the winter and it boasts more than 3,000 hours of sunshine a year.

The roads here are good but tortuously bendy and as you drive down to **Villefranche-de-Conflent** from Mont Louis you can appreciate just how steeply the mountain falls away. If driving the mountain roads does not appeal, take the narrow gauge railway from Latour-de-Carol. Villefranche is a medieval fortified town which still guards the entrance to the Têt valley. There is an underground staircase with 750 steps leading through the cliff to the massive fortress which perches 155m (500ft) above the town on the mountain side. To the south is the charming spa town of **Vernet-les-Bains** and the nearby tenth-century Abbaye de St Martin-du-Canigou with its Spanish square. After centuries of dilapidation, the abbey and its cloisters with its magnificent carvings, have been restored and is now used as a retreat. It is possible to take a tour to the abbey but if you are driving go as far as Casteil and then walk up. It is a reasonably stiff walk but the views are your reward, especially if you walk on past and above the abbey. Villefranche was famous for its marble and it was widely used in the construction of the many Romanesque churches in the area under the auspices of the Abbaye de St Michel-de-Cuxa, near Prades, which is worthy of a visit.

As you descend further into the orange and lemon groves and cherry orchards you can see why this area, known as Vallespir, was so popular with artists. Picasso used to frequent the attractive town of **Céret** and there is a modern art museum there as well as a restored fourteenth-century bridge spanning the valley. Between Céret and the coast is the ninth-century abbey church at **Arles-sur-Tech** which was added to for the next four centuries. It contains a fourth-century sarcophagus, revered locally because it is always full of pure water. Near Arles is the Gorges de la Fou which affords some great walks.

Finally you must visit **Perpignan**, capital of Roussillon and the fortress home of the Kings of Majorca who reigned here from 1294 to 1344. Although in Roussillon it is more sensible to visit it as part of a tour of the Pyrénées, because it is still part of French Catalonia. The locals speak Catalan and in the bars they still dance the Spanish *sardana*, Catalonia's national dance. Buildings of interest to see are the palace and fortress of the Kings of Majorca, the town fortifications, the Gothic cathedral, and the Loge de Mer which dates back to the time when Perpignan was a flourishing sea port.

There are literally hundreds of miles of walking in the Pyrénées, especially the eastern area around Céret and Latour-de-France. The valleys of the Têt and Tech are especially beautiful, particularly in the spring when the first of the wild flowers blossom and the fruit trees burst into blossom. Long-distance paths include the GR36 which runs through the Pyrénées Orientales and the GR10, the Sentier des Pyrénées. You can plan walks lasting from a couple of hours to several days depending on how energetic you want to be. Take advantage of the narrow gauge railway from Perpignan to get to Cerdagne, a good place to start a number of walks. You can even

A courtyard in the fortifications at Salses, north of Perpignan

walk across into Spain from here. There are also a lot of good routes for the serious backpacker who wants to get up into the mountains.

Because the frontier is vague in places and you can not always be sure you are still in France, it is a good idea to carry your passport with you.

Nîmes and the Surrounding Area

The whole of Nîmes and the surrounding countryside is worth exploring either on foot, by bike or car. A detour to **St Rémy-de-Provence**, birthplace of astrologer Nostradamus is essential. His life is chronicled at the Museé Alpilles Pierre de Brun. The museum, in a sixteenth-century *château*, also has a collection of local art, and souvenirs of Mistral. His home was at **Maillane**, 4 miles away, where there is another museum to his memory. Also in St Rémy is an archaeological museum housed in the Hôtel de Sade, once owned by the family of the notorious Marquis. If you have time, visit the Roman excavations at *Glanum* about a mile to the south. There is an archway from the second century BC, the oldest surviving in southern France, and an early mausoleum. Digs at *Glanum* have revealed the presence of man as far back as Neolithic times.

Les Baux, some way to the west, attracts visitors in their hundreds of thousands, and the cliff-top fortress carved out of stone, and its unspoilt village (apart from the racks of postcards everywhere), are still very appealing. There are many buildings from the fourteenth century, and the castle dates from the thirteenth. This area is so rich in history that one could spend days exploring. Most of the tourists driving in make straight for the car parks just below the village, but you can park off the road much farther down the hill and walk both to and around the village. By starting your journey on foot lower down the hill, you can get a much better understanding of why the castle was so impregnable. When you climb up the battlements of the fortress itself, it is necessary to exercise care if strong winds are blowing. The authorities have now provided handrails in some areas, but the winds can still prove a hazard. As you drive your way through the hills to Les Baux look out for the massive gun emplacements that were carved out into the slopes by the Germans.

Nîmes is again rich in antiquity, and as in Arles, it is possible to buy a season ticket giving access to all the main sights saving you a lot of money. These attractions include the magnificent amphitheatre, not as large as the one in Arles, but in much better order. It is used for French-style bullfights and throughout the summer mock gladiator fights and chariot races are also staged for the tourists. In the Blvd Hugo is the Maison Carrée, a temple built just before the birth of Christ, in Greek style. It is the finest remaining Roman temple of its type, and has a museum within the sanctum containing antiquities. Also make time to see the ornamental French gardens dating from the eighteenth century in the Quai de la Fontaine. It also contains remains of a Roman bathhouse and the ruined Temple of Diana. Next to the gardens is the Tour Magne, an octagonal watchtower built in the first century BC: it is worth climbing up to the platform at the top with your camera for the views.

In the Rue de la Lampèze there is a Roman collecting basin for water bought in from the Pont-du-Gard. From here it was distributed by ten canals to various parts of the city. The only other structure like it has been found at *Pompeii*. Also see the Porte d'Arles, a Roman gateway in the town walls dating from 16BC. Nîmes has some excellent museums; for instance the Museum of Old Nîmes, with its history of the town, as well as a history of bullfighting, the museum of archaeology, and the museum of fine arts.

Montpellier to Carcassonne

From Nîmes you can journey south-west to Montpellier, which is a thriving town and university centre, but on the way a stop off at **Aigues-Mortes** is essential. It is a perfectly preserved walled town. It is best to park outside between the canal and the Saracen's Tower and to enter the town through the massive archway. Note how thick the walls are. The town is now a tourist trap full of souvenir shops and cafés, but one can still imagine what it was like 800 years ago when the armies started to assemble before setting sail on the Crusades. There are magnificent views from the ramparts and you can walk right round the town along the walls. While travelling from Nîmes, spend some time in the Camargue. It is possible to cut down and use the coastal road which runs between the Etangs but be warned, the surface is extremely bad.

It is still possible to drive down to the sea in the Camargue, and if you are interested in birdwatching, you will be amazed at the variety of wildlife. You can see perching ospreys that seem to have no fear of humans at all. There are bee eaters, rollers, hoopoes, storks, almost all the herons, waders, ducks and a confusing collection of warblers that will have you scrambling for your bird guides. Although parts of the Camargue now constitute a national nature reserve and access is limited, it is still possible to see almost all the species from good vantage points along the road.

Montpellier is an old university town and capital of the Bas (Low) Languedoc region. It is still possible to walk round the roads that ring the old town, and these have been built on the site of the original fortified walls. One must walk down the Promenade du Peyrou, with its seventeenth- and eighteenth-century mansions. The terraced walk also offers views of the Mediterranean. The botanical gardens, founded by Henry 1V in 1593, are the oldest in France. Another essential visit is to the fourteenth-century Gothic cathedral, and the fabulous Fabre museum which houses one of the best collection of paintings in France. The university dates back to the eleventh century, when a school of medicine was founded. The law school dates from 1160, and the university proper was given its charter by Pope Nicholas 1 in 1289. Montpellier is also a good base from which to visit the many vineyards in the area, including Listel, which is just a short distance off the Montpellier to Béziers road.

Béziers is an agricultural and wine town, set in the heart of the vineyards. It produces table wines, especially Muscat, the grape said to have been introduced by the Romans. The town stands on a hill overlooking the River Orb. It was a former Roman town and there are still the remains of the amphitheatre. It was fortified in the twelfth century by the Lords of Carcassonne, but this did not prevent a bloody massacre in 1209, when a force sent by the Pope killed all the inhabitants to stamp out heresy. The Roman-Gothic church of Ste La Madeleine was the scene of some of the bloodiest fighting. In the thirteenth century, the city walls were rebuilt, and at the same time the cathedral church of St Nazaire was constructed on the hill over the town. It is a fortified church and well worth visiting.

Narbonne was founded by the Romans in 118BC, although it then stood on the Mediterranean and became a flourishing port. When the Romans left in the fifth century, it was captured by the Visigoths who made it their capital. Their rule lasted for 300 years, until 719, when the Saracens invaded and took control. Then, the town was controlled by the Counts of Toulouse who ruled one half, and the bishops who ruled the other. It was not until the beginning of the sixteenth century that it was united under the French crown. The thirteenth-century cathedral of St Just was never completed, but the 'choir' and two square towers can still be seen. Additionally, the twelfth-century basilica of St Paul-Serge, and the three square towers of the fortified Palais des Archévêques are worth looking at. The Gothic-style town hall was added to the palace in the nineteenth century. The palace now houses two fine museums, one of art and history, and the other archaeological. It is also worth exploring the narrow, winding streets and alleys of the old town, with its many fine old buildings. Narbonne is another wine town and there many opportunities to taste them both inside and around the town. There is also a wine centre.

Carcassonne, due west of Narbonne, is the capital of the Aude *département*. The River Aude divides the town into three, the town, the lower town and the city (Ville, Ville-Bas and Cité). The Cité contains the finest remains of medieval fortifications in Europe, so is a must for any visitor to this region. The hill that comprises the Cité was certainly occupied in the fifth century BC by the Iberians, then by the Gallo-Romans. The inner ramparts were built in the late fifth century by Euric 1, King of the Visigoths. The fortifications resisted all attempts to breech them for almost 300 years until the Saracens stormed them successfully. Other things to be seen are the Basilique St Nazaire, from the eleventh century; the Château Comtal, incorporated into the fortifications in the twelfth century and now a museum; and the Porte Narbonnaise, surrounded by its twin towers, guarding the entrance to the Cité. When peace was restored to the region in the mid-seventeenth century, the fortifications were no longer needed and fell into disrepair. Work restoring them started in 1844 and continued for 120 years. Today, the city is a living museum to the past. In the Ville-Bas, see the church of St Vincent and the cathedral of St Michel, both from the thirteenth century. Carcassonne is quite magnificent, and it has the additional pleasure of being

Narbonne, where boating is popular

primarily a wine town, so it is possible to sit in one of the shaded street cafés, sip a glass of the local wine, and drink in the history at the same time.

The Camargue

Although the Camargue gets a brief mention in other sections it is so important that it deserves its own passage. Apart from fabulous birdwatching, it offers great walking or cycling, horse riding and even cruising. What better way of unwinding than by gently cruising the waterways of this vast wilderness area, one of the richest wildlife habitats in Europe. It is possible to arrange hire of your boat through British travel agents. The advantage of this sort of holiday is that it really allows you to get off-the-beaten-track. The boats come equipped with bikes, so if you want to explore you simply moor and pedal off. However if you choose to explore the waterways, canals and tributaries of this 800sq km (300sq mile) delta, you will not be disappointed.

The Camargue is the area of the estuary of the Rhône which divides in two just above Arles to form a triangular arm ending at the Mediterranean. The fringes of the Camargue are bordered by rich farmland where corn, vines and now rice grows. As you move into the Camargue, and especially as you move towards the sea the landscape changes dramatically. The reedbeds camouflage what is land and water, and the lakes give no hints as to whether they are fresh or salt water. It is a natural fusion of land, river and sea.

The Camargue is known worldwide for its 'wild' black bulls and white horses but as more land is drained to make way for tourist developments or farms, the area available for these proud animals diminishes. They can still be seen roaming through the salt flats but barbed wire fences mark out their territories. It is the birds alone that now have the freedom to roam unfettered. Horses and bulls, however, have been bred for sport in the Camargue since Roman times although during the Middle Ages most of the land was owned by the monasteries. Most of the farms, or mas, still operating were established between the sixteenth and eighteenth centuries. They grew corn and reared sheep, bulls and horses. Only over the last 130 years have effective dykes been built to stop the devastating floods which occurred regularly.

Today, the wildlife of the Camargue has to compete with the farmers. It is Europe's largest rice producing region, there are large scale salt pans but it still leaves something over 34,400ha (86,000 acres) for the birds and animals. The area enjoys hot, dry summers, and warm, wet winters although it is possible for stagnant water to freeze during particularly cold spells. It is possible to walk or drive down to the sea and enjoy the sand dunes which cover a wide area. There is also an expanse of dune in the heart of the Camargue in the national nature reserve. This area of dunes supports Phoenician junipers growing to a height of 6m (20ft), while in the spring the ground is carpeted with wild narcissi, rock roses, rosemary and gladioli.

The waters are very rich in fish and most private owners lease out the rights to commercial fishermen who use nets and traps. Eels are caught in large numbers, as well as carp. There are opportunities for private anglers to fish from the dykes, if they get permission first. Hunting is more popular than fishing and there is a great wealth of game, from wild boar, hare, rabbit, wild duck, pheasant and partridge. Some species, however, like the flamingoes, egrets and avocets are protected. The bulls of the Camargue are bred for fighting, but usually take part in the French *course à la cocarde*, when young men try to snatch rosettes from the animal's horns. Spanish bullfights, or *corridas*, are held in the Camargue, but the animals as well as the bullfighters normally travel from Spain. Other animals of the Camargue include the wild boar, fox, badger and otter.

If you want to see the flamingoes, the best route is to travel along

St Trophime, Arles, a pilgrimage church built on the route to St James of Compostela, Spain

the *étangs* (lakes) along the coast between Les Stes Maries and Salin-de-Giraud. Here, hopefully, you will not only see flamingoes in their tens of thousands but as many as 330 other different species of birds from Europe and North Africa. Some of the rarer species as far as British and US birdwatchers are concerned, include roller, black-winged stilt, bee-eater hoopoe, purple heron, spectacled and moustached warbler, pratincole, little egret, night and squacco heron, and stone curlew. One of the best spots for birdwatching is along the Digue de la Mer. Although a much less welcoming place in the winter, a trip into the Camargue can be just as rewarding then, with up to a quarter of a million wild duck in temporary residence. The area is equally rich in insects, amphibians, reptiles and wild plants. Whatever time you visit the Camargue a good bird book and powerful pair of binoculars or telescope is a must. And, if you are there in the summer have a good insect repellent as well.

The hot Mistral wind is, of course, famous in this area. It can last a few hours or a few days. When the mistral blows, people are said to do strange things, tempers flare and it was once a defence against a murder charge to blame it on the winds.

Port Camargue is on the western coastal tip of the Camargue, it is a new resort built round a massive marina. Although there is still considerable building going on, the village has been subject to strict planning controls, and unlike developments further along the coast, has not blighted the area. The other town to visit is **Stes Maries-de-la-Mer**. According to local legend the sisters of the Virgin Mary landed here to avoid persecution after the Crucifixion. While pilgrims have come to pray at the tomb of the two Marys since the Middle Ages, gypsies revere Sarah, their Egyptian maid, and every year in May (24 and 25)they assemble from all corners of Europe for their festival. In olden days, when the gypsies travelled by horse and wagon, they would back their vehicles into the sea in an act of ritual purification.

The fortified church is the other main attraction and for a small charge you can climb the steps up to the ramparts for magnificent views over the Camargue and town. In the crypt is the statue of Sarah which is paraded annually at the head of the gypsies' procession. Although the town with its fine beach and bustling marina does get very busy during the summer, it is worth a visit, because isolated as it is by the Camargue and the Rhône delta, it does not seem to have fully caught up yet with the twentieth century. If the idea of a guided boat trip attracts you, you can take one from Stes Maries, and if you want to cruise yourself from the Camargue, the boats normally start at St Gilles, the other gateway to the Camargue. You can even follow the Canal du Rhône west to Aigues-Mortes and moor in the shadow of the city walls.

Arles and Area

If you have driven down from the north via Lyon, **Arles** makes a good base. There are many good hotels to suit all tastes and pockets

One of the many historical sites in Arles

as well as very well equipped camp sites. You could spend several days just exploring Arles itself, especially the quaint narrow cobbled back streets with their curious shops and bars frequented by the locals. You can hire bicycles to get further afield but walking, apart from in and around the town, is not a good idea because of the distances that need covering. There is a good local bus service but it is not too frequent, so you can't afford to miss the last bus back.

Arles was the first major Roman settlement in Gaul and almost everywhere you look there is something of its rich history to be seen. At one stage it was even called 'The Granary of Rome', and later the 'Little Rome of the Gauls'. If you have driven in by car, park it because the only way to explore this town is on foot. There is a Roman obelisk in the Place de la République made from Egyptian stone. It used to stand in the suburb of Trinquetaille in the centre of a chariot-racing arena. The square also houses the famous twelfth-century church of St Trophime with its elaborately carved Romanesque west porch. Researchers have found symbols used in Syrian, Persian, Nordic and ancient Roman art. It is worth stepping inside the church because the narrowness of the nave makes the vaulted ceiling look much higher. There are many fine paintings, carvings, tapestries and sarcophagi. The church is famed both for its antiquity and its carvings, in stone, wood and ivory. It was one of a string of pilgrimage churches built along the route to the shrine of St James of Compostela in Spain. Close by is the Tourist Information Office in what used to be the Archbishop's Palace, and the Hôtel de Ville.

Just an alley away is the Place du Forum with its statue of Frédéric Mistral, perhaps the most famous son of the Camargue. He was not only the region's most outstanding poet, he gave his name to the fierce wind that sweeps the area, and founded a splendid museum, the Museon Arlaten, dedicated to all things Provençale. You can also see, incorporated into the Hôtel Nord-Pinus, two Corinthian columns which, almost 2,000 years ago, formed part of a temple next to the Roman forum.

There are many other historic monuments to visit in Arles, the most important of which is the amphitheatre. All the Roman sites and museums are open to the public and if you are a culture buff, it is worth buying a season ticket which allows you to visit them all at reduced prices. The amphitheatre is still remarkably well preserved, and is supposed to be the twelfth largest of the seventy known from the Roman world. It was built in the first century on the site of an original wooden arena. It could hold up to 15,000 spectators and it is still possible to walk down into the dark depths of the buildings where the cages housed the animals and slaves ready for combat in the arena. During the Middle Ages it was used as a fortress, and two towers remain. It is used now regularly for bullfights, both the Spanish sort and the French. In the Spanish bullfight the animal is killed, while in the French version, young men try to capture rosettes draped over the bull's horns. The latter version is far more exhilarating and enjoyable.

In the Rue du Cloître is the Roman theatre, built in the reign of Augustus. It has many well preserved statues. It could seat 7,500 and it is still an excellent auditorium with wonderful acoustics.

Other things to see are Les Alyscamps, a path lined with sarcophagi with a ruined Romanesque church; the St Trophime cloisters dating from the twelfth century, around an enchanting garden; and the Roman baths of Trouille, said to date from the fourth century and part of Constantine's great palace. The water was carried 15 miles to the baths by aqueduct. There are also many museums, such as the museum of Christian art, in Rue Balze, with the finest collection of sarcophagi outside Rome; the museum of pagan art and the museum of fine arts in the Rue du Grand Prieuré, which includes a collection of old drawings by Picasso. Vincent van Gogh lived in a house in the Place du Forum for about 16 months between 1888 and 1889 and this was the subject of his painting *Café Terrace at Night*. The house is now a shop. He also shared 'the Yellow House' in Place Lamartine with

Gauguin for short time but this was destroyed during bombing in 1944. Other scenes he painted which can still be visited are the cemetery of the Alyscamps and the drawbridge over the Marseilles au Rhône canal just south of the town. The bridge was actually demolished in 1926 but was such a popular tourist attraction that it had to be rebuilt. After a day spent tramping the streets, stroll up the Boulevard des Lices in the early evening and enjoy a drink at one of the scores of bars and cafés, and decide which restaurant you will return to later that night.

About 16km (10 miles) west of Arles is **St Gilles**, definitely worth a visit, and it makes a pleasant cycle trip. It was another pilgrimage stop on the road to Compostela and has a fine abbey church with carvings dating from the twelfth century depicting the life of Christ. In the crypt is the tomb of St Gilles, which dates from the eleventh century. There is a museum to be visited and a spiral staircase with fifty steps to be climbed to the belfry.

Tour of the Rhône Delta

Greek travellers settled at the mouth of this great river in about 600BC. They founded a settlement called *Massalia*, which has continued to flourish and is today one of France's major ports and trading centres, although it is now known as Marseilles. The Greeks established vineyards and these gradually developed inland following the banks of the Rhône. Some of France's greatest red wines are still grown along the Rhône and Hermitage and Côte-Rôtie have been grown for at least 2,000 years. Throughout this time the river has been used as the natural means of transport. As the Greeks influence waned and they were forced to abandon their settlements after attacks from the Gauls, the Romans took over. They named the region *Provincia*, the origin of Provence. They built most of the great towns of the region and most of the bridges and fortifications along the river.

If travelling down from Lyons one should stop off to visit **Vienne**, about 32km (20 miles) south of this great city. There is the Cathédrale St Maurice, the Champ de Mars, the Temple d'Auguste, Roman theatre and many fine churches, buildings and museums, as well as statues everywhere. Across the river is the village of **Ampuis**, famous as the home of one of the world's great wines, Côte-Rôtie. As you travel south you can take in the village of **Condrieu** nestling at the foot of the hills at a bend in the river and thus its name, an abbreviation of Coin du Ruisseau, literally 'corner of the river'. Try the marvellous white wine produced here since Roman times.

Other places to see include Château Grillet, the smallest *Appellation Contrôlée* in France. The 3ha (7$^1/_2$ acres) of vineyards are near the village of **St Michel-sur-Rhône**. The *château* dates back to the reign of Louis XIII when it was a hunting lodge. Since then much has been added. The façade is Renaissance, and some of the walls are 1m (3ft) thick, showing that defence was an important consideration in this trouble-torn region.

The tour proper of the Rhône estuary should start in the spectacular town of **Orange** with its Roman theatre and impressive Arc de Triomphe. It has hotels to suit all pockets and many good restaurants. About 19km (12 miles) north-west on the N575 is **Rasteau** which produces one of France's most unusual and least known wines. It is made in the same way as port and is very popular in all the bars of the region. While in the village have a look at the communal wash-house where the women gather all day it seems, to scrub their family's laundry. To the south is **Beaumes**, another Roman town which became established as a spa resort because of the sulphur springs at Montmirail. There have been many archaeological digs in the area, uncovering Roman swimming pools and plumbing, and above the village a sculpture was discovered depicting winemaking and the treading of the grapes. The village is the now the centre for the production of the fortified, sweet wine, Beaumes-de-Venise, which is becoming increasingly popular with drinkers both in Britain and the United States.

Just to the west of the village is its neighbour **Vacqueyras**, and between the two is the church of Notre-Dame d'Aubune, built on the site where, in the eighth century, the Saracens were defeated by the Gauls. The surrounding hills are filled with caves, and the Saracens are said to have taken refuge in these for months after the battle. Beaumes actually gets its name from an Old Provence word meaning grotto, and every year on 8 September there is a pilgrimage to the church to celebrate the victory. Between Rasteau and Beaumes, close to Mont Ventoux, is **Gigondas**, on the east bank of the river, and like everywhere else along the Rhône a wine centre. The village makes a fine red wine and you can try it in the tasting centre. Most of the houses of the vineyard owners are built on the sites of Roman villas. The area is steeped in Roman history and it is thought that Roman officers chose Gigondas to retire to after seeing service in Orange.

If you return to Orange and cross the river you can travel to Chusclan and Laudun, both wine making villages. **Chusclan** has a tradition dating back to Roman times although Benedictine monks established many of the vineyards that now surround the village.

Their best rosé, the Cuvée de Marcoule is named after the nearby atomic power station. **Laudun** is a beautiful old village although it is blossoming with new housing to accommodate the workers who commute to Orange. Earthen wine jars dating back to the third century BC have been found on the flat hilltop above it, known as the Plateau du Camp de César.

The next port of call is **Châteauneuf-du-Pape**, famous for its wines and its place in religious history. This part of Provence came into its own in 1305 when Bertrand de Got was elected by the College of Cardinals as the new pope — Pope Clément V. His first decision, to end the feuding in Rome, was to move the seat of the papacy to his native France. Avignon became the new seat of power for the Roman Church, and for the next few decades there was feverish activity both in and around the city. New buildings, churches and palaces were built, bridges were constructed and country estates with fine houses surrounded by vineyards sprang up. Because summer in Avignon was, and still can be hot and oppressive, the Pope decided to build a summer palace. He chose a spot about 16km (10 miles) upstream from Avignon on a plateau overlooking the river, and as it was the Pope's new palace it was known as Châteauneuf-du-Pape. The palace was built on the site of a castle destroyed in 1248. It took 15 years to build and was completed in 1333, a year before Pope John's death. Today, little remains of the palace, apart from a tower and some walls, but the village itself is fascinating and a delight to stroll around. It is not known whether it was Pope Clement or his successor John XXII who developed the vineyards, although grapes had certainly been growing there for centuries. While the reign of the Popes in Avignon only lasted for sixty or so years, the vineyards continue to survive and prosper.

In the area it is worth a detour to **Roquemaure**, named after a fort built by the Saracens which has long since vanished. History records that it was here that Hannibal floated his elephants across the Rhône on rafts. The other village to seek out is **Villeneuve-lès-Avignon** which dates back to at least the thirteenth century. Many of the nobles attending the papal court in Avignon chose to build their summer houses here. There are many fine old buildings as well as the imposing fort, the Fort St André, and several excellent eating establishments. Finally, you must spend as much time as possible in and around Avignon itself. As with Arles, it is best to park your car and walk round the town exploring the enormous treasures it has to offer. Its wealth is overwhelming, from the splendour of the Popes' Palace, the impressive city defences, the famous bridge, and the many old buildings. For a small payment you can still walk out on to what is left of the bridge which juts out into the river.

Among the things to be seen are: the Palais des Papes, Pont St Bénézet, the ramparts and fortifications, the palace gardens, the cathedral with its cupola, church of St Pierre, the frescoes in the church of St Didier and the museums of the Petit Palais, Calvet, Lapidaire and Louis Vouland. While travelling through the area, do take the opportunity of tasting the local wines. There are tasting centres in most big villages, and vineyards which have their own tasting facilities advertise this prominently along the roadside.

The Gastronomy of the Midi

The land between the Rhône and the Spanish border plays host to a wide variety of cuisines, many of them reliant on garlic and olive oil which is available in plenty throughout. The sea provides the ingredients for many traditional dishes, while there is lamb from Roussillon, beef from around Albi and Carcassonne, and the magnificent *cassoulet* originated in Toulouse but can now be found, with many variations, throughout Languedoc-Roussillon. *Cassoulet* is perhaps the region's most famous dish, traditionally made from mutton, pork, preserved goose, and any other meats that come to hand, together with haricot beans. Vegetables are plentiful, especially tomatoes and aubergines which figure in many recipes. Because of the poor pasture, much of the meat can be tough unless cooked slowly, but the people realised this long ago and have developed special cooking skills in making casseroles and stews. In the south-west small birds, especially thrushes are roasted and eaten head and all. In the south-west *foie gras*, duck, goose and truffles figure on the menus, and snails everywhere.

There is excellent *charcuterie*, and the Toulouse sausage is especially famous. Offal, including tripe is favoured in the northern districts, while soups of all types can be found. Collioure is noted for its anchovies and sardines. Sète has its famous offshore oyster beds, and Palava has created its own speciality tuna dishes. Rice from the Rhône figures in dishes influenced by Spanish cuisine, while along the coast there are fish soups and stews, and a wide variety of fresh and salted fish.

Desserts include *cruchades*, fritters or pancakes made from maize flour, and *pescajou*, a sweet pancake from Languedoc. *Petit pâtés* are small sweet pastries, and *marrons glacés* are candied chestnuts. It is also worth looking for *pinu*, a small aniseed cake from Languedoc and *touron*, an almond pastry with other nuts, marzipan and chrystallised fruits.

Some of the cheeses of the region include Bleu de Loudes, a blue cheese from the Languedoc, made in the Velay region; it has little smell but quite a strong flavour; Les Orrys, a cow's milk cheese from the hills around Foix, on the River Ariège, to the north of Roussillon, which is strong and tangy. Then there is Passé l'An, really from Quercy, a hard, strong cheese aged usually for at least 2 years, and Pélardon des Cévennes, a Languedoc soft cheese made from goat's milk, which has a nutty flavour. Finally, there is Picodon, goat's milk cheese made in Provence.

Further Information
— The Midi —

Museums and Other Places of Interest

Aigues Mortes
Saracen's Tower
Open: April-September 9am-12noon and 2-6pm; October-March 10am-12noon and 2-4pm.

Alleés des Sarcophages
Open: 9am-12noon and 2-5.30pm (7pm in summer).

Arles
Amphitheatre
Rond Point des Arènes
Open: 9am-12noon and 2-5.30pm (7pm in summer).

Church of St Trophime
Place de la République
Open: daily.

Museum of Christian Art
Rue Balze
Open: 9am-12noon and 2-5.30pm (7pm in summer).

Museum of Pagan Art
Rue de la République
Open: 9am-12noon and 2-5.30pm (7pm in summer).

Museum of Fine Arts
Rue du Grand Prieuré
Open: 9am-12noon and 2-5.30pm (7pm in summer).

Roman Baths of Trouille
Rue D. Maïsto
Open: 9am-12noon and 2-5.30pm (7pm in summer).

Roman Theatre
Rue du Cloître
Open: 9am-12noon and 2-5.30pm (7pm in summer).

Avignon
Palais des Papes
Open: July-September 9am-6pm; October-Easter 9am-11am and 2-4pm; Easter-June 9am-11.30am and 2-5.30pm.

Museum of Medieval Painting and Sculpture
La Place du Palais
Open: April-September 9.30am-11.45am and 2-6.15pm; October-February 9.15-11.45am and 2-6pm.

Bridge of St Bénézet
Open: 9am-12noon and 2-6pm.

Rhône Lapidary Museum
Open: 10am-12noon and 2-6pm,
closed Tuesday.

Calvert Museum
Open: 10am-12noon and 2-6pm,
closed Tuesday.

Les Baux
Museum of Contemporary Art
Open: 9.30am-12noon and 2-
6.30pm, closed Thursdays.

Béziers
Wine Museum
Open: daily 9am-12noon and 2-5pm.

Bollène
Church of St Martin
Open: July-September 9am-12noon
and 3-7pm.

Museum
Open: April-September 9am-
12noon and 2-7pm.

Carcassonne Cité
Château Comtal and Museum
Open: daily 9am-5pm April-Sep-
tember.

Châteauneuf-du-Pape
Père Anselme Wine Museum
Open: Monday-Saturday 8am-
12noon and 1.30-6pm.

Glanum
Prehistoric and Roman Excavations
Open: 9am-12noon and 2-6pm.

Narbonne
Cathedral of St Just
Open: daily except Wednesday.

Fine Arts Museum and History
   Museum
Open: May-September 9am-
12noon and 2-5pm.

Nîmes
Amphitheatre
Blvd Victor Hugo
Open: 9am-12noon and 2-5pm (2-
7pm in summer).

Maison Carrée
Blvd Victor Hugo
Open: 9am-12noon and 2-5pm (2-
7pm in summer).

French Garden
Quai de la Fontaine
Open: daily to 11.30pm in summer.

Tour Magne
Mont Cavalier
Open: 9am-12noon and 2-5pm (2-
7pm in summer).

Museum of Archaeology
Blvd Amiral Courbet
Open: 9am-12noon and 2-6pm.

Museum of Fine Arts
Rue de la Cité-Foulc
Open: 9am-12noon and 2-6pm.

Museum of Old Nîmes
Place aux Herbes
Open: 9am-12noon and 2-6pm.

Orange
Ancient Roman Theatre
Open: April-September 9am-
6.30pm; October-March 9am-
12noon and 2-5pm.

Museum
Open: 9am-12noon and 2-6.30pm.

St Rémy-de-Provence
Musée Alpilles Pierre de Brun
Open: 10am-12noon and 2-6pm,
April-October; 10am-12noon and 2-
7pm July/August. Closed Tuesday.

Serrières
Museum of Batellerie
Open: weekdays.

Sérignan
Museum of National Entomology
Open: weekdays.

Valence
Museum
Open: daily 9am-12noon and 2-6pm.

Valréas
Old Château, Church and Chapel
Open: June-August 10am-12noon
and 3-7pm.

Town Hall
Guided tours 10am-12noon and 3-
7pm.

Index

A

Abbaye de Beauport 63, 68
Aber Wrac'h 42
Abriès 245, 246, 252, 253, 254
Agen 164, 165
L'Aigle 16, 33
Aigoual, Mont 189, 190, 192, 193, 205, 206, 207, 210
Aigue Blanche, Stream 250, 251
Aigueperse 173
Aigues-Mortes 296, 301, 309
Aiguilles 245, 252
Aiguillon-sur-Mer 118
Aïnhoa 151
Aire-sur-l'Adour 160
Airvault 135
Aix-en-Provence 268, 271
Alba 232
Alès 189, 193, 194, 200, 202, 211
Alès, Gardon d' 203, 204, 211
Allos 276
Allouville-Bellefosse 12-13
Alpes de Mancelle 102
Alpes Maritime 262
Alpes-de-Haute-Provence 262
Alpiers, Les 196
Alps, Cottian 243
Alsace et Lorraine 70-100
Altier 202
Altier, River 201, 202
Ammerschwihr 91
Amplepuis 186
Ampuis 305
Ancenis 109, 110, 122
Andorra 291
Anduze 194, 200, 207, 211

Angers 101, 108, 109, 110, 119, 122, 131
Angles 118
Angoulême 126, 127, 136, 138
Anne de Beaujeu 171, 179
Annonay 224, 241
Antigny 126
Antrain-sur-Couesnon 56, 68
Apt 279
Aquitaine 139-67
Aquitaine, Eleanor of 107, 133
Aramits 154
Arcachon 143, 165
Arçais 134
Ardèche 216-42
Ardières, River 173, 183
Les Ardillats 173
Arette 154
Argentan 22, 33
Argentelles Manor 21, 33
Arginy, Château d' 182
Arles 271, 278, 287, 289, 302-4, 309
Arles-sur-Tech 295
Arthur, King 38, 45, 60-1
Arudy 154, 165
Arvieux 248
Arvieux, Valley 247, 255
Ascain 151
Astet 224
Aubenas 226, 241
Aubiac 164
Aujac 203
Aulnay 131
Auray 49
Auron 269
Aven de Marzal 229, 241
Aven Orgnac 229
Avenas 172
Avignon 262, 287, 288, 307, 309
Avranches 32, 33
Azergues, River 178

Azergues, Valley 168, 170, 174, 176, 177, 185
Les Ayres 213

B

Baccarat 79, 96
Bain de Bretagne 60
Baix 238
Balazuc 228
Bandol 268, 284
Barbaste 162-3, 165
Barbotan-les-Thermes 161
Barcelonette 276
Barfleur 26
Bargème 284
Barneville-Carteret 28
Barre des Ecrins 262
Barre-des-Cévennes 209
Le Bas Vivarais 217
Bassac Abbey 128
La Bastide 190, 193, 194, 195
Bastide du Virac, Château de la 229, 241
Les Bastides 201
Baud 52
Baugé 106, 119, 122
La Baule 112, 122
Les Baux 295, 310
Bayonne 149, 165
Beaujeu 171, 173, 174, 184
Beaujeu, Forêt de l'Hospice de 172
Beaujeu, Hospice de 172, 181
Beaujolais 168-88
Beaujolais Supérieur 168
Beaujolais Villages 168, 171, 175, 179, 180
Beaujolais, Monts de 180, 185
Beaumes 306
Bedoués 197
Belin-Béliet 146, 165
Belle-Isle-en-Terre 65

Belleville 170, 170-3, 183
Bellême 17
Bénodet 47
Bergheim 92
Bernay 15-16, 33
Berry, Jean de 133
Besse 266
Betharram 155, 165
Béziers 288, 297, 310
Biarritz 149-50, 165
Bidache 148-9, 165
Binic 63
Bitche 76, 77
Biville 27
Blacé 180
Blain 111
Blavet, River 52
Le Bleymard 192, 196, 197, 201
Bluebeard (Gilles de Rais) 116, 117
Bois d'Oingt 179
Bollène 310
Les Bondons 205
Bonne-Fontaine, Château de 57
Bonnieux 278
Bordeaux 142-3, 165
Bormes-les-Mimosas 264, 284
Bouches-du-Rhône 262
Bouchet, Valley 254
Bouchet, Stream 252
Bougès, Montagne de 189, 198, 203, 204
Le Boupère 117
Bourg St Andéol 240
Le Bourg-St-Léonard 22
Bourgneuf-en-Retz 113, 119
Bouteville 127
Bramabiau 206
Bramousse 256
Brehec 63
Brélés 42
Bresis, Château de 203
Bresolettes 16
Bressuire 135, 138
Brest 40
Briançon 245, 246, 247, 258
Bricquebec 27, 34
La Brière 111, 112
Brignogan-Plage 42, 44
Brignoles 266, 284
Brionne 15
Brissac-Quincé 108, 119, 122
Brittany 27-69
Brou, Forest of 178

Brouilly 168, 181
Brouilly, Côte de 168, 181
Brouilly, Mont 180
Brunissard 247
Bulat-Pestivien 65
Burzet 236

C
Cachot 156, 165
Camargue 287, 299-301
Cambo-les-Bains 152, 165
Camisards 189, 192, 193, 198, 199, 201, 203, 209, 211, 213
Camprieu 198, 206
Cancale 55
Cannes 261
Cap d'Erquy 62
Cap Fréhel 62
Cap Sizun 46
Capvern-les-Bains 157, 166
Carcassonne 289, 298, 310
Carhaix-Plouguer 45
Carnac 38, 49
Carpentras 269
Le Cascade du Ray Pic 235
Cassagnas 198
Casse Déserte 247, 257
Castanet, Château de 202
Castellane 268, 270, 274
Caudebec-en-Caux 10-12, 32
Caulnes 67
Causse Méjean 198, 205
Causses 189, 192, 204, 205, 206
Cauterets 157
Cavaillon 280
Ceillac 245, 246, 256-7
Celles-sur-Belle 132
Celts 38, 40
Cenves 172
Cercié 181
Cernay 86, 96
Cervières 247
Cévennes 189-215, 216, 286
Cévennes National Park 189, 190, 192, 197, 201, 205, 206
Céret 294
Cèzarenque 203
Cèze, River 202, 203
Chabotterie, Château de

la 115, 120
Chaise, Château de la 180
Challans 114, 122
La Chalp 248
Chambois 21
Chamborigaud 200
Chambost-Allières 175, 176, 187
Champ Dolent Standing Stone 56
Chapelure 256
La Chapelle-Montligeon 17
La Chapelle-Souëf 18
Chappe Telegraph system 178
Charentay 182
Charente, River 127, 129
Charnas 237
Charnay 178
Charroux 126, 136
Charton, La Grange 181
Chasseradès 196
Chassezac, River 196
Chauvigny 124, 138
Chayla, Abbé 192, 197, 199
Château-Gontier 104, 122
Châteaubourg 237
Châteaubriant 111, 120, 122
Châteauneuf-du-Pape 307, 310
Châteauneuf-sur-Charente 128
Châteauneuf-sur-Sarthe 109, 122
Châtellerault 124, 137, 138
Châtillon d'Azergues 178
Châtillon d'Azergues, Château de 178
Chauvigny 124, 138
Cheffes 105
Chénas 168, 183, 184
Chênehutte 108
Chénelette 174
Chenillé-Changé 104
Cherbourg 26, 34
Chessy-les-Mines 178
Le Cheylard 235
Chevallier, Gabriel 168, 180
Chianale Valley (Italy) 251
Chiroubles 168, 172, 183
Chizé, Forest of 132

Chomérac 230
La Chouannerie 104, 105, 115
Chusclan 306
Cibourne 151
Cime de Mélezet 256
La Ciotat 260
Civaux 124
Civray 126
Clausis, Chapel of 250, 251
Claveisolles 174
Cleebourg 78
Clemenceau, Georges 117, 119, 120, 121
Clisson 116, 122, 129
Clochemerle (Vaux-en-Beaujolais) 175, 180
Clos de la Platière 176
Coatfrec, Château de 65
Cocurés 197
Cognac 128, 129, 136, 137-8
Cogolin 264, 285
Le Coin (Arvieux) 248
Col Agnel 246, 250, 252
Col Blanchet 252
Col de Cassettes 186
Col de Chamoussières 251, 252
Col de Crie 173
Col de la Croix-Rosier 174
Col de Durbize 172
Col des Escorbans 187
Col de l'Escrinet 231
Col de Finiels 196, 201
Col de Fromage 245, 255, 256
Col de Fut d'Avenas 172
Col de Gerbey 172
Col d'Izoard 245, 246, 2476. 250
Col de Jalcreste 204
Col de Joncin 176
Col de Malaure 245
Col de Montmirat 205
Col du Pavillon 186
Col de Péas 248, 249
Col Perdu 247
Col du Pilon 187
Col de St Véran 251, 252
Col du Truges 172
Col de la Schlucht 86
Col d'Urine 254
Le Collet-de-Dèze 204, 212, 213
Colmar 90-1, 96
Combourg 57-8, 68
Combrit 47, 67

Commana 45
Concarneau 47
Concoules 203
Condom 161, 166
Condrieu 305
Contrexéville 82
Corcelles 185
Corcelles, Forest of 174
Cornas 228
Corniche Angevine 109
Corniche des Cévennes 209
Côte d'Azur 260-85, 263
Côte des Abers 42
Côte des Légendes 42
Côte du Goelo 63
Côte Sauvage 50
Côtes-du-Nord 61-7
Coudray-Salbart, Château de 135, 137
Coulon 134, 138
Cours-la-Ville 170, 186
Court d'Aron 118, 120
Coutainville 29
Coutances 29, 34
Crau 268, 271-4
Crazannes, Château de 130, 137
Cristillan, Valley 246, 256, 257
La Croix-Valmer 264
Cruas 238
Cublize 187
Cunault 108

D
Dampierre-sur-Boutonne, Château 132, 137
Damvix 134
Daoulas 44
Darbres 232
Darney 82
Dax 148. 166
Devesset 224
Diélette 27
Digne 263, 282
Dinan 67
Dinard 54
Dol-de-Bretagne 56
Domrémy-la-Pucelle 82, 96
Dourbie, River 208
Dourbies 209
Draguignan 266, 285
Ducey 32
Durance 162
Durance, River 243, 258, 278
Durance, Valley 246, 278

E
L'Echalp 254, 255
Les Echarmeaux 173, 174, 187
Echiré 135
Ecrins 270
Emerald Coast 62
Emeringes 172, 184
Entrecasteaux 266
Epinal 83-4, 96
Epiniac 56
Er Lannic 50
Escoyères 256
Escreins, Valley 257
L'Espérou 207
Les Essarts 116, 120
Esse 60
Les Estables 223
Estissac, Geoffrey d' 132
Eugénie-les-Bains 160

F
Fabre, George 190, 206, 207
La Fage 204
Falkenstein, Château de 77
Le Faou 44, 46
La Faouët 51
Fauna 193, 206, 208, 212, 213, 244, 251, 253
Fédrun, Ile de 113, 120
Fenioux 131
Finiels 197
Finistère 38, 40-8
La Flèche 106, 120, 122
Fleckenstein, Château de 77
Flers 23, 34
Fleurie 168, 183
Fléville, Château de 79
Flora, Alpine 193, 195, 196, 208, 244, 253, 254
Florac 189, 194, 197, 198, 200, 205, 207, 209, 212
Foix 293
Font Sancte (mountain) 250, 255, 256
Fontdouce, Abbey of 128, 137
Fontenay-le-Comte 117, 119, 120, 122
Fontevraud 107, 122
Fontgillarde 250
Fontmort, Plan de 198
Forcalquier 282
Foréant, Lac 255
Forêt de Brocéliande 53, 60-1
Forêt de Brotonne 14

Forêt de Carnoët 48
Forêt de Pontcallec 51-2
Forêt du Perche 16
Fort-la-Latte 62, 68
Fougères 57
Fources 162
Française, Vallée 209, 210
Franks 38
Frassinet de Fourques 205
Fréjus 265, 285
Freysennet 232

G
La Gacilly 53
Ganagobie 282
Gap 246
Gard, River 190
La Garde Frénet 270
Gardonnette, River 202
Garreau, Château 160-1
Gaudissard 249
Gavrinis, Ile de 50
Gâvre Forest 111
Geoffray, Claude 181
Génolhac 193, 202, 203
Gérardmer 84-5
Gévaudan 189, 194
Girardin, Col 245
Glanum 295, 310
Glémenos 267, 285
Gordes 278
Gorge de Toul-Goulic 65-6
Gorge du Caronc 65
Gorges de l'Ardèche 228
Gorges de la Vésubie 269
Gorges du Daoulas 66
Gorges du Loup 277
Gorges du Verdun 268, 274-8
Goulet, Montagne de 196
Grand 82
La Grande Brière 112, 121
La Grande Motte 288
Granville 29-30, 34
Grasse 269
Le Gravier 175
Gréoux 270
Gréville-Hague 27
Grospierres 241
Grotte de la Forestière 229
Grotte de la Madeleine 229
Grottes des Huguenots 229
Grottes d'Isturits et

d'Oxocelhaya 152, 166
Guebwiller 89
Guéméné-sur-Scorff 51
Guérande 112, 122
La Guerche-de-Bretagne 60
Guéthary 150
Guil, Gorge 256, 257
Guil, River 243, 248, 249, 252
Guil, Valley 248, 249, 252, 254, 255, 256, 258
Guillestre 244, 246, 247, 255-7, 258
Guilvinec 47
Guingamp 66-7
Gunsbach 86, 96

H
Hambye Abbey 31, 34
Harambels 152
Haras du Pin 19-20, 33
Hastingues 148, 166
Haut Azergues 174-9
Haut Beaujolais 170, 172, 173, 184, 185
Haut Mouriare (mountain) 248
Haut-Koenigsbourg 92, 96
Haut Vivarais 216, 223
Hautes-Alpes 262
La Haux 250
La Haye-de-Routot 14-15
La Haye-du-Puits 28
Hendaye 151
Hohenbourg, Château de 77
L'Hôpital 201
Hospitalet, Can de 209, 210
Huelgoat 45
Hunaudaie, Château de la 67, 68
Hunspach 78
Hyères 263, 285

I
Ile de Batz 41
Ile de Bréhat 63
Ile de Fédrun 113, 120
Ile de Groix 51, 68
Ile de Houat 50
Ile de Noirmoutier 114, 122
Ile d'Ouessant 44
Ile de Port-Cros 264
Ile des Pies 53
Ile du Levant 264
Iles d'Hyères 264

Ille-et-Vilaine 40, 53, 54-61
Issarlès 233

J
Jard-sur-Mer 119, 133
Jarnac 128, 138
Jarnioux 179
Josselin 52, 54, 68
Jouany, Nicolas 202, 203
Jouhet 126
Jublains 102
Juigné-sur-Sarthe 106
Juliénas 168, 172, 184
Jullié 172, 184
Jumièges Abbey 13-14, 32

K
Kaysersberg 91, 96
Kercado 50
Kerfons 65
Kergrist, Château de 65
Kerloas Standing Stone 43
Kermanic-an-Iskuit 63
Kernascléden 51
Kientzheim 91, 96
Kintzheim 93

L
Labastide d'Armagnac 160-1, 166
Lachamp Raphaël 235
Lac de Guerlédan 66
Lac de Madine 75
Lachassagne 178
Lamastre 234
Lamballe 67
Lamure-s-Azergues 175-6
Landerneau 44
Landes de Lanvaux 52
Langogne 194
Lanildut 42
Lanne 154
Lannion 65
Lantignié 181
Largentière 236
Largoët Fortress (see Towers of Elven)
Larmor-Baden 50
Lattre de Tassigny, Jean de 117, 120
Laudun 307
Laval 102, 103, 120, 122
Lavilledieu 232, 241
Le Lavandou 264, 269
Lembach 78
Lesconil 47

Lessay 29
Lignol 51
Lingas Mountain 207, 208, 209
Lion d'Angers 104, 109, 120
Loc-Envel 65
Locmariaquer 49
Locronan 46
Loire, River 101ff
Longny-au-Perche 19, 33
Loroux-Bottereau 110
Lot, River 196
Lot, Valley 201
Louppy-sur-Loison 75, 96
Lourdes 155-6, 166, 291
Lozère, Chalet du Mont 196
Lozère, Mont 189, 190, 192, 193, 196, 197, 198, 200, 201, 202, 203, 205
Lubéron 268, 280
Lucerne Abbey 31, 34
Luçon 118, 123, 133
Lunéville 79, 97
Lussac 126
Lussas 232
Luxey 146, 166
Luze 282
Lyon 168, 169, 170, 177, 183, 246

M
Machecoul 114
Mâcon 170, 184
Mâconnais 168, 184
Maillane 295
Maillezais, Abbey of 132, 134, 137
Malestroit 53
Malicorne 106, 107
Malrif 253
Malrif, Lakes of 252, 253
Le Mans 101, 102, 106, 123
Marais Breton-Vendéen 113, 114
Marais Poitevin 113, 117, 118, 133
Marchampt 175
Marckolsheim 89, 97
Marcy-sur-Anse 178
Marlenheim 94
Marquèze 146-7
Marseilles 262
Le Martinet 199
La Martyre 44-5
Marzal 241
Le Mas de la Barque 202

Mas Soubeyran 210
Massevagues 207
Mayenne 102
Mayenne, River 101, 103, 104
Le Mazel (Aigoual) 208
Le Mazel 201
Meisenthal 78
Melle 132
Men Marz Standing Stone 42
Mende 193, 194, 196, 204
Menerbes 278
Menton 262
Mercantour 262, 270
Mercier 225
Merlin 38, 60-1
Mervant-Vouvant, Forest of 117
Metz 75-6, 97
Les Meyries 248
Meyrueis 205, 206
Mélezet Valley 256
Ménez Hom 44
Ménez Kador 45
Meysse 238
Mézilhac 223
Mialet 210
Midi 286-311
Mimente, River 198, 203
Mimizan 144, 166
Mirabel 232
Mirecourt 81, 97
Moiré 176
La Môle 264
Molines-en-Queyras 245, 249
Molsheim 93
Moncontour 67
Monsols 173
La Monta 254
Les Montagnes 216
Mont Bel-Air 67
Mont des Alouettes 116
Mont Dol 56
Mont St Michel 55, 56
Mont Ste Odile 93
Mont Ventoux 269
Mont-de-Marsan 148, 166
Mont-devant-Sassey 75
Mont Mézenc 223
Mont-Ormel 21-2, 33
Montaner 157
Montbardon 256
Montdauphin (fortress) 243, 258
Montdauphin, Gare de 247
Montfort 60, 68

Montmelas 175
Montmelas, Château 176
Montmédy 75
Montmorillon 126, 138
Montpellier 288, 296, 297
Montpézat 233
Montreuil-Bellay 107, 120, 123
Monts d'Arrée 45
Montségur 292
Morbihan 40, 48-54, 55, 60
Morgon 168, 183
Moricq 118
Mortagne-au-Perche 17, 33
Mortagne-sur-Sèvre 116
Le Mougau 45
Mouilleron-en-Pareds 117, 120
Moulin-à-Vent 168, 184
Moustiers-Ste-Marie 270
Mulhouse 87-9, 97
Munster 86
Mur-de-Bretagne 66

N
Nancy 79-80, 97
Nantes 101, 110, 113, 119, 120, 123
Napoleon I 247, 250
Narbonne 289, 298, 310
Neodanus, Roman Fort 102
Nerac 163, 166
Neuf-Brisach 89, 98
Neufchâteau 82
Neyrac-les-Bains 226
Nice 261, 262
Niederbronn-les-Bains 78
Nîmes 262, 287, 288, 295, 296, 310
Niort 118, 130, 132, 133, 134, 135, 138
Noirmoutier, Ile de 114, 123
Normandy 9-36
Notre Dame de Neiges, Monastery of 194, 195

O
O, Château d' 19, 33
Obernai 93, 98
Oberseebach 78
Odenas 180
Oingt 177
Oiron, Château d' 136, 137
Les Ollières 235

Oloron-Ste-Marie 154
Orange 278, 306, 310
Ottrott 93
Ouroux 172
Ozon 237

P
La Palud 275
Paimpol 63
Pain de Sucre, Mountain 246, 255
Palud, Château de la 181
Panloy, Château de 130, 137
Parc de Haye 81, 98
Parentis-en-Born 144
Parthenay 118, 135, 138
Pau 158-9, 166
Pays de la Loire 101-23
Pays de Retz 113
Peaugres 224
Pêcher, Source de (river) 198
Penthièvre Coast 62
Perpignan 287, 288, 295
Le Perréon 180
Perseigné, Forest of 102
Persquen 51
La Petite-Pierre 79
Peyraud 237
Pied de Mélezet 256
Pierre Grosse 249, 250
Pierres Dorées 168, 176
Pissos 146
Pizay 183
Plateau du Coiron 220, 231
Plessis-Bourré, Château de 104, 105, 121
Ploërmel 54
Plogonnec 46, 67
Plombières-les-Bains 84, 98
Plonéour-Lanvern 47
Pointe d'Arradon 50
Pointe de Château 64
Pointe de Dinan 46
Pointe de Kerpenhir 49
Pointe du Chevet 62
Pointe du Grouin 55
Pointe-de-St Mathieu 42, 43-4
Poitiers 124, 126, 130, 131, 138
Poitiers, Battle of 124
Poitou-Charentes 124-38
Pomaret 202
Le Pompidou 210
Pons 129, 138
Pont d'Arc 229

Pont de Labeaume 226
Pont de Soleils 274, 275
Pont-de-Montvert 192, 196, 197, 201, 203
Pont-du-Gard 287
Pont-l'Abbé 47
Pontchâteau 111
Pontigné 107
Pontivy 52
Ponts de Cé 108
Pornic 113, 123
Port Bail 28
Port Camargue 302
Port d'Envaux 130
Port de Juigné 106
Port du Salut, Abbey of 104, 121
Port Grimaud 265
Port Navalo 49, 51
Pouilly-le-Monial 178
Pouzauges 117, 123
Le Pouzin 238
Prades 293
Prafrance, Bambouseraie de 200
Pranles 230, 241
Presqu'île de Crozon 46
Presqu'île de Rhuys 50
Presqu'île de Ste Marguerite 42
Primel-Trégastel 48
Privas 230, 241
Proprières 173
Prosny, Château de 177
Provence 260-85
Puget Théniers 276
Puivert 292
Puy Crapaud 117
Puy-du-Fou, Château du 117, 121
Pyrénées 287, 290-4

Q
Querqueville 26
Queyras 243-59, 262, 270
Queyras, Château 254, 247, 248, 249, 255
Queyras, Combe du 243, 248, 255
Queyras, Le Grand (mountain) 250
Quiberon 50, 51
Quimper 46
Quimperlé 48
Quincié
Quintin 66

R
Rais, Gilles de 116, 117
Ranchal 187

Ranrouët, Château de 111
Rasteau 306
Raux, La 250
Regnié 181
Régordane Way 200, 202
Reins, Valley 186, 187
Remiremont 84
Rennes 58-60
Retz, Pays de 113
Rhône 260
Rhône Delta 305
Rhône Valley 216, 220, 237
Ribeauvillé 92
Richelieu, Cardinal 118
Richemont, Château de 128
Riez 276, 282
Riquewihr 91-2, 98
Ristolas 254
La Rivière 26, 27
La Roche 44
La Roche, Château 172
La Rochère 84, 98
Roche-aux-Fées 59
Roche-Courbon, Château de la 131, 137
La Roche-sur-Yon 115, 116, 119, 121, 123
Rochebonne (Thizy), Château de 177
Rochebrune, Grand Pic de 247, 249, 250, 255
Rochefort-sur-Loire 109
Rochemaure 239
Rochemenier 108
Rohan, Duc de 211
Roland 'Count' (Camisard leader) 193, 210
Roland, Madame 176, 179
Romanèche-Thorins 184, 185
La Romieu 161-2
Ronno 187
La Roque Brussane 266
Roquedols, Château de 206
Roquefixade 292
Roquemaure 307
Roscoff 40
Rosé 113, 121
Rothéneuf 55-6
Rouen 10
Rouet 248
Rouffach 89
Rousseau, Henri 103
Roux, Le 253
Royan 129

La Rua 249
Ruoms 228

S
Les Sables d'Olonne 118, 119, 123
Sablé-sur-Sarthe 105, 123
Sabres 146, 167
Saillé 112, 121
St Agrève 223
St Alban-Aurioles 228, 242
St Amour 168, 184
St André-les-Alpes 276
St Armel 50
St Bonnet-des Bruyères 173
St Brieuc 62
St Cast 62
St Christophe-la Montagne 173
St Christophe-le-Jajolet 19
St Croix, Gardon de 209
St Cyr-le-Chatoux 175
St Désirat 237
St Didier-s-Beaujeu 174, 175
St Dié 92, 98
St Etienne 269
St Etienne du Valdonnez 204
St Etienne-des-Oullières 182
St Etienne-la-Varenne 180
St Etienne-Vallée-Française 199
St Fiacre 51
St Georges-sur-Loire 109
St Germain de Calberte 199, 212, 213
St Germain de Cauberte 213
St Gildas 111
St Gildas-de-Rhuys 50
St Gilles 301, 305
St Gonery 64
St Guénolé 47
St Hilaire-St Florent 108, 121
St Igny 173
St Jacques-des-Arrêts 172
St Jacut-de-la-Mer 62
St Jean d'Angély 128, 131, 138
St Jean Pied-de-Port 153, 167
St Jean, Gardon de 199,

200, 210, 211
St Jean-de-Luz 150-1, 167
St Jean-du-Doigt 48
St Jean-du-Gard 194, 199, 210
St Jean-les-Saverne 79
St Joseph 172
St Jouin-de-Marnes 136
St Julien 180
St Julien d'Arpaon 198, 204
St Just 60
St Just d'Avray 187
St Lager 181
St Laurent-d'Oingt 177
St Laurent du Pape 235
St Léry 53
St Lô 23, 35
St Lyphard 112, 113
St Malo 55, 68
St Mamert 172
St Marcel 52
St Martin d'Ardèche 229
St Martin-de-Crau 271
St Michel, Abbey of 118, 121
St Michel-de-Dèze 213
St Michel-Mont Mercure 117, 121
St Michel-sur-Rhône 306
St Mihiel 75
St Nazaire 101
St Nicolas-de-Port 79
St Nizier 185
St Palais 152
St Pé-de-Bigorre 155
St Péray 238
St Pierre-les-Eglises 124
St Pol-de-Léon 41
St Pons 286
St Raphaël 265, 266, 285
St Rémy-de-Provence 295, 310
St Rigaud, Mont 168, 173, 186
St Romain de Lerps 238
St Roman-de-Tousque 210
St Sauveur, Abbey of 126, 136
St Sauveur, Château de 23
St Sauveur-le-Vicomte 28, 35
St Savin 124
St Simon 128
St Symphorien sous Chomérac 230, 242
St Tropez 261, 264, 285
St Vaast-la-Hougue 25-6

St Véran 245, 248, 250, 251
St Victor-s-Rhins 186
St Vincent-de Reins 186
St Vincent-sur-Jard 119, 121
St Wandrille Abbey 13, 33
Ste Anne, Lac 245
Ste Barbe 51
Ste Cécile d'Andorge 190, 200, 202, 211, 212
Ste Croix 275
Ste Gauburge 18, 33
Ste Marie 276
Ste Marie-aux-Mines 92, 98
Ste Marie-du-Mont 24
Ste Maxime 265
Ste Mère-Eglise 24, 34
Stes Maries-de-la-Mer 302
Saintes 126, 129, 131, 137, 138
Salarials 201
Salernes 266
Salgas 205
Salles 180
Salon 271
Samadet 159, 167
San Chiaffredo, Passo (Italy) 255
Santiago de Compostela 124, 128, 129, 130, 131, 132
Sapins, Lac de 187
Sapins, Route de 170, 185, 187
Sare 151
Sarreguemines 76
Sassy, Château 19, 33
Le Saule d'Oingt 176
Sault 269
Saumur 101, 106, 108, 121, 123
Sauvages, Les 186
Saverne 79, 98
Sées 19, 33
Sélestat 92-3, 98
Les Sept Iles 65
Sérignan 311
Serrant, Château de 109, 121
Serrières 310
Sillé, Forest of 102
Sillé-le-Guillame 102
Sillon de Talbert 63
Simserhof 76
Sion 80-1
Sisteron 281

Solesmes, Abbey of 105, 121
Soligny-la-Trappe 16-17
Sorde l'Abbaye 148
Soultz-Haut-Rhin 89
Stevenson, Robert Louis 189, 194, 196, 197, 198, 199, 200, 201, 213, 233
Strasbourg 94-5, 98
Struthof 93, 99

T
Taillebourg 130
Tallyrand 132
Talmont 130, 137
Talmont St Hilaire 119, 121
Tarare 170
Tarascon-sur-Ariège 293
Tarbes 157, 167
Tarn, River 190, 196, 197, 198
Tarnon, River 197, 198
Le Teil 240
Teildras, Château de 105
Ternand 177, 178
Terrasse La 172
Tête du Pelvas (mountain) 253, 254
Thann 86-7, 99
Theizé 176, 177
Thivin, Château 181
Thizy 170, 186
La Thoronet 266, 285
Thouars 107, 136, 138
Thueyts 224
Tiffauges, Château de 116, 121
Tinténiac 58, 68
Tonquédec, Château de 65
Toul 81
Toulon 263, 268
Toulouse 292
La Tour-Fondue 264
Tourouvre 16
Tournon 237, 242
Tourtour 266

Tourvéon, Mont 174, 187
Towers of Elven 54, 68
La Tranche-sur-Mer 118, 123
La Trappe Abbey 16, 33
Trégarvan 44
Tréguier 63
Trèves 209
Tumulus de Barnenez 48
Turckheim 91
Turdine, River 168
Turdine, Valley 170

U
Ungersheim 89, 99
Usson 292
Usson, Château d' 130
Utah Beach 24

V
Vacqueyras 306
Val Joanis 281
Valence 311
Valleraugue 208
Vallespir 293Arc 242
Vallréas 311
Valognes 24, 35
Valpreveyre, Chalets de 253, 254
Valsonne 187
Vals-les-Bains 226
Vannes 38, 49
Les Vans 236, 242
Var 262
Vars, Col de 245, 246
Vaucluse 262
Vaucouleurs 81-2, 99
Vaux-en Beaujolais 175, 180, 181
La Vendée Militaire 115
La Venise Verte 134
Ventadour, Château de 226
Verdun (Gorge) 268, 274-8
Verdun 74-5, 99
La Vernède 197
Vernet-les-Bains 294

Vesseaux 231
Vialas 200
Vielvic 203
Vienne 305
Vieux-Poitiers 124
Le Vigan 208
Village Noir 279
Villé 93
Ville-Vieille 249, 252
Villedieu-les-Poêles 30-1, 35
Villefort 190, 192, 202
Villefort fault 190, 202, 212
Villefranche 169, 170, 173, 179, 182, 185
Villefranche-de-Conflent 293
Villeneuve de Berg 230, 232
Villeneuve-lès-Avignon 287, 307
Villequier 12, 33
Villié-Morgon 183
Vire 23
Viso, Monte (mountain) 243, 251, 252, 253, 255
Viso, Monte Belvédère du Cirque 252, 255
Viso, Monte Grand Belvédère 255
Viso, Monte Petit Belvédère 255
Vittel 82
Le Vivier 56
Viviers 240
Vogüé 228, 242
La Voulte sur Rhône 238
Vouvant 117
La Vove Manor 17-18, 33

W
Wissembourg 77

X
Xaintrailles 162

EXPLORE THE UNEXPLORED
WITH •

_____ OFF _____
THE BEATEN TRACK

With the **Off the Beaten Track** series you will explore the unexplored and absorb the essential flavour of the countries you visit.

An **Off the Beaten Track** book is the only companion you will need on your travels.

The series includes the following titles which are or will shortly be available:

Off the Beaten Track: ITALY
Off the Beaten Track: FRANCE
Off the Beaten Track: SPAIN
Off the Beaten Track: AUSTRIA
Off the Beaten Track: WEST GERMANY
Off the Beaten Track: SWITZERLAND

Our books are on sale in all good book-shops or can be ordered directly from the publishers.

SIMPLY THE BEST